PR   D0754021   LIFE

"So much grief. So many gone. We need an account—one that is deeply personal and objective. Some way to make sense of what has happened and what is happening to us. *After Life: A Collective History of Loss and Redemption in Pandemic America* is that accounting. Read every page. Absorb its lessons. Feel this book in these challenging times and werfully healing and insightful."

   —Eddie S. Glaude Jr., author of *Begin Again:*
James Baldwin's America and Its Urgent Lesson for Our Own

"Breathtakingly refreshing in scope and content, *After Life* is history the way history should be written. Bringing together an incredibly diverse group of scholars, this book walks us through the worst days of the pandemic but offers us tools to create a better future."

   —**Ibram X. Kendi, coeditor** of *Four Hundred Souls:*
A Community History of African America, 1619–2019

"Sometimes, you don't know what you really need until you read it. In *After Life*, some of America's most searching minds sift through the wreckage of the pandemic to provide us precious shards of light, so that the unfathomable loss of life—more than all the Americans who died in the Civil War or in World War II—will not be in vain."

   —**Nancy MacLean**, author of *Democracy in Chains:*
The Deep History of the Radical Right's Stealth Plan for America

"Do nations have souls? Has America lost its soul? Loss and redemption are two deeply human and American ideas; generally we like the second one better. In this amazing collection of perspectives, loss takes its proper place as genuine tragedy. Largely by tapping historians, Barnes, Merritt, and Williams have found a gold mine of reflection on the moral, medical, racial, and political condition of the American experiment. These pieces show, darkly but beautifully, how thoughtful people have been hurt or destroyed, past and present; but they also inspire paths forward not to a promised land, but to a functional, honest society and a new republic."

—**David W. Blight**, Yale University, author of Pulitzer prize–winning *Frederick Douglass: Prophet of Freedom*

"Rhae Lynn Barnes, Keri Leigh Merritt, and Yohuru Williams have ring-mastered an excellent book of powerful thinkers mourning all the unnecessary losses of the past few years—and pointing, possibly, toward American redemption."

—**Brad DeLong**, author of *Slouching Towards Utopia: An Economic History of the Long 20th Century, 1870–2010*

"How do we make sense of the senseless? This remarkable collection begins to answer that question for the tragedy that was America's politicized response to a lethal pandemic and everything that happened alongside it, including an attempted coup. As daring in scope as it is diverse in voice, *After Life* can help us heal with a fuller understanding of the reach of this formative and often disastrous time. The editors tell us that the early 2020s will define our lives—the sooner we understand that time, the sooner we'll understand ourselves. This book is an indispensable guide."

—**Andrew L. Seidel**, author of *The Founding Myth and American Crusade*

AFTER LIFE

A COLLECTIVE HISTORY OF LOSS AND REDEMPTION IN PANDEMIC AMERICA

Edited by

RHAE LYNN BARNES

KERI LEIGH MERRITT

YOHURU WILLIAMS

Haymarket Books
Chicago, Illinois

Published in 2022 by
Haymarket Books
P.O. Box 180165
Chicago, IL 60618
773-583-7884
www.haymarketbooks.org
info@haymarketbooks.org

ISBN: 978-1-64259-829-2

Distributed to the trade in the US through Consortium Book Sales and
Distribution (www.cbsd.com) and internationally through Ingram Publisher
Services International (www.ingramcontent.com).

This book was published with the generous support of Lannan Foundation
and Wallace Action Fund.

Special discounts are available for bulk purchases by organizations and
institutions. Please call 773-583-7884 or email info@haymarketbooks.org
for more information.

Cover design by Rachel Cohen. Cover art: Still image from digital short
Fractured Light by Larry Barnes, copyright 2021.

Printed in Canada by union labor.

Library of Congress Cataloging-in-Publication data is available.

10 9 8 7 6 5 4 3 2 1

Dedicated to the memory of the millions whose names are unknown

There are years that ask questions and years that answer.

—Zora Neale Hurston, *Their Eyes Were Watching God*

CONTENTS

AMERICAN CULTURE AFTER LIFE

Rhae Lynn Barnes and Keri Leigh Merritt

A*fter Life* is a collective history of pandemic America. Work on this book began with a sense of urgency in January 2021. At that time, 420,000 Americans had died from the first two waves of COVID-19. The number of people who had lost their lives by then was equivalent to the entire population of Oakland or New Orleans, and it surpassed the number of Americans who died in World War II. As the historian Catherine Mas remarked then in astonishment, "The scale of deaths that we're seeing on a daily basis, it's like 9/11 every day. It's like a Pearl Harbor every day." Thinking about such loss through other American tragedies "captures the lethality of this virus," Mas argued. History provided "a kind of reference point that helps us understand as a society what it is we're going through and what we need to do."[1]

Every day, the incomprehensible death count kept ticking up—and up—in grim sidebars on social media, on news shows, and in newspapers announcing both the confirmed death count and the positivity rate by city, county, state, and country. The death toll rose throughout 2021 and 2022 due to a volatile intersection of greed, white supremacy, and governmental failures—the result of much longer histories of inequality—some of which we unravel in these pages. The criminal neglect of the Trump administration (2017–2021) and missteps by the Biden administration (2021–) meant that Americans struggled without coordinated policies for too long. They were left to survive without succor in a do-it-yourself, Hobby Lobby pandemic.

By mid-September 2021, 663,913 people, or one out of every five hundred US residents, had officially died of COVID-19. By October 1, 2021, the city equivalent of the dead had grown: instead of Oakland or New Orleans, it was now as if the population of Boston; Washington, DC; or Seattle had disappeared from the citizenry. By spring 2022, we lost more people than currently live in San Francisco or Austin—an unfathomable scale of grief.[2]

These official numbers likely only account for a fraction of the real numbers of COVID-related deaths. The University of Washington's Institute for Health Metrics and Evaluation examined "excess mortality" during the pandemic, comparing 2020 statistics with nonpandemic years. They found a significant discrepancy in numbers, estimating that by May 2021 the worldwide COVID-19 death toll was almost seven million, more than double the "reported number of 3.24 million." American scientists found a number 57 percent higher than "official figures"—900,000 Americans died in a little over a year.[3]

Americans who went untreated for heart attacks, strokes, cancer, or chronic diseases are missing from the official death totals. When cities could not "flatten the curve" of exponential growth, it was the patients who flatlined due to an overwhelmed healthcare system. In areas hardest hit by the virus, like Latin America, Russia, and India, "the death toll is actually in the millions, rather than the hundreds of thousands," the *Economist* estimated.[4] By the time you read this book, these numbers will have grown, making these numbers outdated. Knowing that is part of what it is to live through this time.

Despite advances in DNA sequencing and viral research, the COVID-19 pandemic is the worst public health crisis in over a century. More people have died of COVID-19 than the so-called Spanish flu (1918–1920), which took 675,000 American lives— one out of every five who contracted it. Before 2020, this earlier pandemic was held up as the paragon of dismay we did not want to approach. The Spanish flu "touched almost every corner of the world," Sandra Opdycke has written; it was "so fast-moving that it circled the globe three times in a single year."[5]

With rapid globalization, epidemics quickly turn to pandemics, as did COVID-19. The Spanish flu struck during World War I, before the average human could board a commercial airplane and arrive anywhere around the world in twenty-four hours. In November 2021, the United States surpassed the Spanish flu's death toll and the highest estimate of deaths in the American Civil War—750,000 people.[6]

The deaths from COVID-19 reflect the vast racial and class inequities in America today; during most of 2020, Black Americans' mortality rate was 2.1 times that of white patients. Civil War deaths reflected these disparities, too, as Black soldiers died nine times more than white soldiers. Systemic racism has widened the gap between the insured and uninsured, as health care is tied to employment, marital status, age, access to transportation, and medical facilities.[7]

Due to an acute understanding of American history, many of us know there is no guarantee that all of us will survive as we document and study the current public crisis and subsequent political, social, and cultural upheaval. Most adult Americans already had to survive approximately a year, from March 2020 to March 2021, to acquire the Pfizer and Moderna mRNA vaccines, beating the World Health Organization's scientific estimate by six months. This was long before most countries had access to this lifesaving technology.

During the first two waves of COVID-19, one consolation was knowing most children would not get sick, become disabled, or die. The first year felt biblical. Our children were spared the sins of their fathers. During the delta surge, though, children fell sick and had to wait until October 2021 for a vaccine approved safe for children between the ages of five and twelve. They were also not immune to heartbreak. An estimated 175,000 children lost a primary caregiver to COVID-19 (a parent or grandparent), and 65 percent of these children "come from racial or ethnic minority groups." California, New York, and Texas experienced the highest of these losses. Put another way, one out of every 515 children lost their caregiver.[8] As a nation, we have not begun to address how to help people—especially children—heal physically, emotionally, and psychologically.[9]

Many Americans in early spring 2022 were still in survival mode, existing from day to day, minute to minute, submerged in paroxysms of grief, and consumed with loss that had little warning as the new omicron variant spread. It sideswiped families with extreme fevers, nauseating headaches, exhaustion, chills, and relentless coughing. One of the authors in this book wrote while bedridden. Americans have lost jobs, careers, and, thus, healthcare—others have lost their savings (if they had any), financial solvency, and homes. Most of us have taken on added care responsibilities—for the sick, the young, and the elderly. Others have more "side gigs."

Americans spent over two years in unsettling isolation—a suspended state of quarantines and intermittent lockdowns, vigilantly waiting for test results (if they were fortunate enough to find a test). Despite the monotony of lockdowns, emotions vacillated from thankful exhilaration to be living another day to floundering loneliness to political rage to helplessness. The scale ranged from fretting over sold-out household necessities to worrying about our nation's moral direction. We have lost parents, grandparents, aunts, uncles, siblings, lovers, friends, colleagues, and neighbors. We are now a ruptured culture entombed in an *after life*, where the unremarkable terrors and everyday joys of being alive meet in the present.

Despite the physical isolation that kept us alive, we chose to come together. We hope that our collective power to document this experience—what captured our imaginations, how we spent our days, and how we made sense of our present through our American past—will ultimately help others. As the acclaimed poet and novelist Amiri Baraka wrote in "Understanding Readiness":

> How do we know who we are
> Except in the world, going through it
> Together.[10]

★ ★ ★

After Life is a bold experiment inspired by the writers who documented American life during the Great Depression and World War II for the Works Progress Administration (WPA). We asked twenty-first-century writers to try and understand America in a moment that seemed, at once, to be both rapidly descending into something long feared and, simultaneously, to be rebirthing into something wondrous at all costs. We asked them to create a collective history about the start of this epoch as it unfolds. We envisioned a book that gave historians and legal experts a chance to write about their present—as long as they meditated on the long 2020 through the prism of American history. What the authors chose to write about grew out of their own experiences and how the unprecedented disruptions ushered in by a global pandemic, massive demonstrations for racial justice, and a near presidential coup in 2021 following the 2020 election led them to reflect on the importance of history and the lessons in perseverance it can impart. Many turned back to the most human connections: their family, their family's history, and their links to America's past. From the intensely personal to the strictly historical, their choices of topics reflect what captured their historical imaginations and expertise during these dark American days.

Although this book initially focused on the historic year of 2020 in prevaccination America, it quickly became the story of the beginning of a decade. A single author or authoritative voice cannot clarify this historical era, and it would be unethical to pretend it could. An accurate accounting of the early 2020s in the United States in historical context must reflect the lives of Americans from all backgrounds and attempt to understand the multidimensional power structures in this country that allowed 2020 to fester and explode into a more protracted catastrophe. The pandemic impacted different racial groups and regions disproportionately, inflaming racial, cultural, and socioeconomic tensions that have deep historical roots in the violence and inequalities of mid-nineteenth-century America during the American Civil War. Our writers, hailing from a dynamic cross section of backgrounds and intersecting identities, including race, religion, ethnicity, gender, sexuality, class, and geographic location, represent a broad swath of the American public and reveal the commonality of collective national consciousness and culture.

The authors are historians and legal experts who study and analyze human culture. Despite stereotypical representations, historians and legal scholars are not repositories of information about the past and precedent. Historians are thoughtful interpreters of documents, ideologies, cultures, and myths. We notice subtle shifts and emerging patterns that have consequences. Historians never stop thinking about America, so we think about America differently.

As Franklin Delano Roosevelt observed about the people who lived through the Great Depression, "This generation of Americans has a rendezvous with destiny." The truth is, given the historical events of the past several years, we now do, too.[11] Activists understood this and seized upon history and the quest for historical truth in the summer of 2020. Brandishing the historical record to undergird their calls for immediate change as they tore down Confederate monuments and demanded new forms of legal and social justice, activists asked Americans to imagine what the abolition of the police would look like. Americans called for navigators to help them understand the complexities of our nation's past.

Historians and legal scholars *are* in a position to anticipate, from a distinctive vantage point, which of the recent events are likely departures from the standard narratives we tell about America's past, because we—by our training and teaching—are the people most familiar with those narratives and their intricate structures. The struggles documented in this book are timely and timeless. The pandemic exposed America's ills, many of them legacies of white America's past sins, from colonialism and slavery to the failures of Reconstruction after the American Civil War. Economic inequality, racism, nativism, xenophobia, mass incarceration, labor abuse, scientific distrust, the privatization of media, dark money in politics, and political polarization created the perfect preexisting conditions for the virus to spread rampantly. This is a written record of a year marked by mass death, grief, memory, and the spiritual power of our cultural losses. It is the story of dreams and hopes for America's future. It is also about American *after life*, both in terms of what is left behind and what lives on in the shadows and echoes of our nation's past in our customs, politics, and institutions that shape our daily lives.

After Life is divided into four parts. The first part, "American Exceptionalism: Colonization and Immigration," features essays that draw attention to the problems facing our nation stemming from white settler colonization, anti-immigration policies, and our inhumane penal system. It features essays by Monica Muñoz Martinez, Mary Kathryn Nagle, Philip J. Deloria, and Robert L. Tsai. Each confronts the idea of American exceptionalism by plumbing the deep roots of division and racial inequality in our society. Our penchant for a sanitized version of American history has contributed to the cycle of historical ignorance. As Gwendolyn Midlo-Hall writes in her essay on the Colfax massacre, "'Death' is a word modern-day Americans rarely use. Nobody dies here. They pass away."

In part 2, "Mass Death and White Supremacy: The Civil War and Civil Rights," the historians Stephen Berry, Martha Hodes, Tera W. Hunter, Gwendolyn Midlo-Hall, Rhae Lynn Barnes, and Peniel Joseph explore the numerous connections between our present political tribulations and the Civil War, the Civil Rights Movement, and even the Black Lives Matter protests of 2020. Peniel Joseph concludes that racial justice can only be achieved through a Third Reconstruction that completes the unfinished work of the First and Second Reconstructions.

Part 3, "Finding Light in the Darkness: Memory and Grief," reconceptualizes death and grief through personal narrative. Using history as a guiding force, Mary L. Dudziak, Ula Y. Taylor, Jacquelyn Dowd Hall, and Keith Ellison grapple with moments of loss in their own lives, from the AIDS crisis to the COVID pandemic.

In part 4, "The Reckoning," the historians Robin D. G. Kelley, Keri Leigh Merritt, Scott Poulson-Bryant, Heather Ann Thompson, and Yohuru Williams explore the convergence of COVID-19, poverty and inequality, and the power of perseverance. Although these essays evoke personal grief, they show how we are a nation of problem-solving survivors.

The conclusion of the book revisits the legacies of Trumpism, Russian aggression in the cyber age, and the existential threat of an attempted coup that played out during the first three Wednesdays in January 2021. While the end of this story has yet to be written, *After Life* ends on a note of hope, recognizing that we, the people, have the power to write the ending we desire. As Leon F. Litwack so aptly wrote, our country's crises arise when "Americans choose to think themselves immune not only to history but to the lessons of history."[12]

Two teachable appendixes supplement the book. "A Brief History of Public Health in America" provides an overview of the significant public health crises and moments of mass death in our nation. Rhae Lynn Barnes and Keri Leigh Merritt show how public health is inextricably tied to white supremacy's long history, intertwined with slavery, capitalism, immigration, and colonization. Finally, in the second appendix, Yohuru Williams opines on "Black Lives Matter and the Beginnings of the Third Reconstruction."

★ ★ ★

Over time, we hope *After Life* will make that transition from witnessing to a form of archival record, an early history, ensuring that the volume will be an invaluable and trusted resource for decades to come because of the historical lens the authors employ.

James Baldwin confessed that part of his democratic duty was to witness atrocity. "This was sometimes hard on my morale," he wrote, "but I had to accept, as time wore on, that part of my responsibility as a witness, was to move as largely and as freely as possible. To write the story and to get it out."[13]

After Life is a small slice of our American story. Thank you for helping us get it out.

THE PRESENT CRISIS

Rhae Lynn Barnes and Keri Leigh Merritt

Once to every man and nation comes the moment to decide,
In the strife of Truth with Falsehood, for the good or evil side;
Some great cause, God's new Messiah, offering each the bloom or blight,
Parts the goats upon the left hand, and the sheep upon the right,
And the choice goes by forever 'twixt that darkness and that light.

—*James Russell Lowell, "The Present Crisis"*

I can't breathe, I'm waiting for the exhale.
Toss my pain with my wishes in a wishing well.
Still no luck, but oh, well.
I still try even though I know I'm gon' fail.

—*Juice WRLD, "Wishing Well"*

M arquerita Donald was given a choice during the COVID-19 pandemic: did she want to live or die?

The forty-nine-year-old mother and sheep farmer had contracted *Dik'os Ntsaaígíí-19*, or "Big Cough-19," as locals called it in the Diné language she spoke. The gentle laugh lines around her brown eyes that radiated positivity vanished. She was fading fast. It was clear to her son Tyler that his mother was struggling as she took the few steps from their family home to his truck to head to the hospital.

1

It was tough for Tyler to watch the family's pillar of strength bow to the infection, a stark reminder that no one could escape the spreading disease: not rural families on remote farmlands, not the brother of Senator Elizabeth Warren, who was fighting to expand national health care, and not the president of the United States himself, locked behind barricades erected around the White House to keep protesters out.

For days, Tyler tried to nurse his mother back to health but to no avail. "It kind of felt like taking care of a baby," Tyler said as his voice quivered. "Seeing her vulnerable like that was hard." Marquerita was always the one taking care of everyone else.

The Donalds lived in needle and thread–grassed Shonto, speckled with Utah juniper and Gambel oak, in Navajo County (population 591), Arizona, an hour south of the iconic Monument Valley Navajo Tribal Park. Here, sheep outnumber humans.

Marquerita understood what would happen once she arrived at the hospital. She worked as a Navajo translator at the Tuba City Regional Health Care Center's respiratory care unit; she had seen it all. Marquerita loved her home and job. "It was the bomb!" she exclaimed. "It was great to talk Navajo to a lot of the elders, just to hold their hand. It made me feel really good and felt that I was needed. The interpreting was really fulfilling."[1]

While there was no confirmation that COVID-19 was airborne, everyone understood that health-care work was hazardous. States begged for anyone with tangential experience in health care— those retired, recently graduated, veterans, and volunteers—to report for duty. Marquerita went to work.

* * *

On January 20, 2020, the United States confirmed its first recorded cases of COVID-19. The new pneumonia-like virus was first observed in Wuhan, China. Rumors circulated that it was incredibly deadly. Over the next two years, Americans experienced their worst public health crisis in modern history. What accounted for the remarkable failures of America in responding to COVID-19? Why were our nation's death rates so high? What went wrong? The American people, including the generations to come, deserve answers.

We aim to provide the political and factual framework needed to answer these questions in this introduction and in our conclusion, but the heart of this book is a series of everyday stories of everyday people living through pandemic America. One day the facts of these years will be long forgotten, but our stories—the feelings, the narratives—will live on.

★ ★ ★

A large part of what went wrong in 2020 started with the 2016 election of Donald J. Trump. Best known for his NBC television show *The Apprentice*, the real estate investor built a following by humiliatingly firing a different contestant every week. Trump won the Electoral College but lost the popular vote to the former secretary of state Hillary Clinton. Trump became America's forty-sixth president under allegations of Russian election interference and viral disinformation. Through social media algorithms and manipulating cable "news" and talk radio, Trump seemingly won the culture wars.

By the start of 2020, after several years of Trump's incendiary rhetoric and policies that threatened to erode democracy, Americans were already worn down. When health officials in China declared they were investigating a mass pneumonia outbreak on January 3, 2020, American health officials took notice, but much of the public did not.

Shortly after the first US case was reported, Trump downplayed concerns, telling reporters on January 22, "we have it totally under control. It's one person coming in from China, and we have it under control. It's going to be just fine."[2] Within nine months, coronavirus had claimed nearly 200,000 American lives, leaving a trail of devastation in its wake.

By February 2020, American scientists, including many Asian-born immigrants who had firsthand experience of epidemics, warned the government that the key to containing a novel outbreak was mass testing—we needed to test, trace, and isolate. At a briefing on February 11, 2020, the World Health Organization (WHO) announced the new virus's name, COVID-19. At the press conference, it was announced that there were 42,708 confirmed cases in China and one thousand deaths. The WHO's director-general confirmed the disease was globalizing, with four hundred cases in twenty-four countries. He predicted a vaccine in eighteen months, by September 2021, but solemnly acknowledged that the window of opportunity to contain COVID-19 was small.[3]

Despite the sobering WHO report, American health officials squandered precious days. Trump discounted the threat, asking Vice President Mike Pence, an evangelical Christian with a questionable record on science, to oversee the issue with Trump's son-in-law Jared Kushner. Trump's handling of the pandemic highlighted his penchant for showmanship and his lack of governance and diplomacy skills. He oscillated between claiming the nation was caught off guard by the outbreak and taking credit for containing it.[4]

The administration continued to flounder. On Wednesday, February 26, 2020, Dr. Nancy Messonnier, the director of the National Center for Immunization and Respiratory Diseases at the Centers for Disease Control (CDC), alerted the nation to the severity of COVID-19, warning Americans to prepare to make short-term sacrifices for the good of the country.

Putting the threat of COVID-19 in the starkest terms possible, Messonnier shared: "I told my children that while I didn't think that they were at risk right now, we as a family need to be preparing for significant disruption of our lives." This wasn't kitchen table politics. Messonnier explained how and why person-to-person spread meant a tsunami of sickness was coming and "might include missed work and loss of income." While she communicated that she understood how overwhelming COVID-19 seemed, Messonnier didn't pull punches about what needed to happen: "These are things that people need to start thinking about," she sternly said. "Now."[5]

Messonnier's comments came two full weeks before any type of concerted federal response to COVID-19. On March 11, in a rare prescripted teleprompter speech, Trump fumbled through addressing the nation from the Oval Office. Earlier that day, the WHO officially designated COVID-19 a global pandemic. Squinting awkwardly into the camera with his hands folded on a binder, Trump continued to downplay the virus's danger. "The vast majority of Americans," he rasped, "The risk is very, very low. Young and healthy people can expect to recover fully and quickly."[6]

Despite Trump's attempt to ease concerns, uncertainty ruled. On March 13, 2020, Trump declared a state of national emergency, marshaling limited federal resources to assist public health agencies in their efforts to combat the spread of the virus.[7] Three days later, the stock market tanked three thousand points, causing the New York Stock Exchange to suspend trading.[8]

To deflect personal blame, Trump began referring to COVID as the "kung flu virus," reviving anti-Chinese "yellow peril" rhetoric with American roots as far back as the California gold rush. As he continued lying about COVID-19 only being deadly to the elderly, millions of college students partied over their spring breaks, returning to their communities, spreading the COVID virus all over the country.[9]

By April 7, 2020, at least thirty-nine states issued some form of a shelter-in-place order to mitigate the spread of COVID-19. Adherence was uneven. Antimaskers, antivaxxers, conspiracy theorists, white supremacists, and a profit-driven media disseminated deadly rumors, convincing millions that the virus was a "liberal" hoax. Nearly 40 percent of all misinformation circulating about COVID-19 originated from the Trump administration.[10]

Much to the chagrin of Dr. Anthony Fauci, the director of the National Institute of Allergy and Infectious Diseases (NIAID),

Trump suggested outlandish remedies on national television—from injecting bleach to taking the antimalaria drug hydroxychloroquine.[11] Emergency calls to poison control skyrocketed. In May, Trump shocked reporters by admitting he took hydroxychloroquine as a prophylactic, touting it as a possible "game-changer." His dubious claims gave credence to conspiracy theorists, who would soon be dangerously inhaling hydrogen peroxide through nebulizers, injecting and ingesting bleach, and taking Ivermectin (a horse, cow, and sheep dewormer).[12]

Some Washington politicians used the occasion to line their pockets. In February 2020, the Republican senator Rand Paul of Kentucky, who sat on the Senate Health Committee, was briefed that Gilead Sciences had started an initial trial for an antiviral drug to fight COVID-19 called Remdesivir (which Trump would later take). Paul's wife purchased significant stock in Gilead the following day.[13]

Senator Paul wasn't alone in grifting during America's crisis. After an intelligence briefing, the Republican senator Richard Burr sold off a vast quantity of stock, unloading somewhere between $628,000 and $2 million worth of stocks the week before the market plummeted. The Georgia Republican Kelly Loeffler did the same, while buying up stock in the telecommunications company Citrix, an online platform used during the pandemic. Burr explicitly warned the well-connected constituents at the Capitol Hill Club that COVID-19 was "much more aggressive in its transmission than anything that we have seen in recent history."[14]

Trump's cries of "fake news" undermined faith in information and media, odiously undercutting public health efforts. One of the most problematic tools at the president's disposal was Twitter. Trump routinely suspended formal press conferences regarding COVID-19, instead inciting fear, racism, and xenophobia in his often-incoherent early morning tweets.[15]

With as much as Trump used social media, his administration never embraced it to disseminate accurate public health information. Trump did the exact opposite, tweeting out quack cures. In October 2020 alone, Trump sent out or retweeted 1,415 tweets to his 88.7 million followers.[16] "Don't be afraid of Covid, Don't let it dominate your life," he wrote and later falsely claimed the flu was more deadly.[17]

Five significant issues exacerbated COVID-19 in America without coordinated federal help. First, travel was "restricted" (not banned) from China, but international flights from every- where else remained in place until March 11, 2020, when Trump abruptly announced a ban on flights from Europe, sending citi- zens abroad frantically scrambling to reenter the United States. When their flights landed, passengers were packed together in tightly confined customs without temperature or symptom checks. They spread the virus, including new strains, throughout the na- tion while returning home.[18] This was in stark contrast to nations like New Zealand and Australia.

Second, there was no preemptive national lockdown. Instead, lockdowns and regional travel bans were uncoordinated, roving, and in reaction to already spiking cases. Due to the lack of federal guidelines, state and local governments devised their own. Other nations like Spain, Germany, and the Netherlands provided ample cash payments so citizens could stay home, containing the spread of disease and thus, death. America did nothing to ease the pan- demic's financial burden for several months.[19]

Third, the federal government did not create a reliable national testing and tracing system like South Korea or Israel. In Britain, a family could get a pack of seven rapid tests each day—for free. In the United States, people had to pay for the tests (and they were expensive, ranging between twelve to fifteen dollars). There were shortages, making tests challenging to find until the Biden admin- istration made them available via the US Postal Service in Feb- ruary 2022. While the delta variant was ripping through India, Abbott Laboratories, the US makers of rapid tests, destroyed their supply, judging COVID-19 to be "over."[20] The United States opted to use testing centers—that people frequently needed cars to access—with laboratory backlogs that sometimes took days. This time contributed to the spread of the virus while people waited on their results.[21]

Fourth, under both the Trump and Biden administrations, the US government did not issue a national masking mandate (except on flights). Recommendations from the CDC were unclear. There was a nine-to-ten-month refusal by the organization to publicly disclose COVID-19 was an airborne disease. As late as October 2020, the CDC vacillated, changing its stance on COVID-19, arguing that it was only "sometimes" airborne.[22] Once the WHO declared the virus airborne on May 4, 2021, the CDC acknowledged that fact three days later.[23] A week later, on May 13, 2021, the CDC, along with President Biden, triumphantly announced that vaccinated people no longer needed to wear masks, a deadly message, especially given the concurrent rise of the delta variant in other parts of the world. On July 27, the CDC reversed course yet again, recommending masking due to the rapid spread of delta.[24] Many American people lost faith in the CDC as a reliable authority.

Finally, the fifth blunder that exacerbated COVID-19 concerned America's inadequate stockpile of medical supplies and personal protective equipment (PPE) and the bungling of the vaccine rollout.[25]

* * *

Despite wealth and connections to white-glove medical services, well-known Trump supporters began getting sick, even dying. On July 30, 2020, former presidential candidate Herman Cain succumbed to COVID-19 after attending a Trump rally in Tulsa (held on the ninety-ninth anniversary of the Tulsa race riot of 1921). Attendees were maskless and ignored social distancing guidelines.[26]

One month before the 2020 election, Trump announced that he, along with First Lady Melania and their son Barron, had tested positive for COVID-19. The nation held its breath, waiting to see if the president would die in office from the same virus he downplayed. But Trump was treated with experimental care denied to most Americans at Walter Reed National Military Medical Center, and he returned home a few days later.[27]

A cluster of COVID-19 cases were linked to a reception Trump hosted on September 26 for Supreme Court nominee Amy Coney Barrett. More than 150 attendees packed together, indoors and maskless, prompting health officials to label the gathering a super-spreader event. Over the coming months, nearly fifty people affiliated with the White House contracted the virus, including Stephen Miller, Chris Christie, Kellyanne Conway, Hope Hicks, journalists, and White House cleaning staff.[28]

★ ★ ★

The president and his inner circle could expect top medical care, but in Indian Country, COVID-19 was a different story. Tribes knew what to expect from their long history of tribulations with novel diseases. In March and April 2020, sheets of plywood went up, with spray-paint lettering that read "CLOSED UNTIL FURTHER NOTICE," blocking nontribal members from entering.[29]

Diana Hu, a Navajo pediatrician who worked with Marquerita, bluntly summed up health workers' tasks. There was no medicine to cure COVID-19, and there was little way to predict who would flatline. "When people get sick, they crash and burn. They crash and burn," she repeated.[30]

A Navajo woman named Dorothy Scott lost her husband of forty-five years and her son to COVID, days apart. She was at her son's grave when she found out her husband died. "I got a call and I just stand there. I couldn't move. I said, 'What's going on?' It's my husband, I know he was okay when I left. He was the one telling me to go to the funeral." Returning to her hogan, she felt her home was still occupied. "My husband is still in there," she sobbed, feeling his spirit.[31]

At times during 2020, the Navajo Nation had the highest coronavirus infection rate in the contiguous United States.[32]

Fifty-seven-hour curfews—strictly enforced by police—were implemented every weekend, with access blocked for nonresidents starting at 8:00 p.m. each weekday. There was also a shelter-in-place order for all Navajo residents to quarantine and isolate.[33] The Navajo Nation surpassed both New York and California in both positive cases, and deaths per capita, with 32,528 confirmed positive cases and 1,403 confirmed deaths out of a population of 173,000 people. Unironically, COVID-19 peaked in the Navajo Nation on November 27, 2020, the day after Thanksgiving, a notoriously fraught holiday for Native Americans.[34]

Marquerita had to suit up in multiple layers of PPE. The Navajo Nation, much like the rest of the United States, had been scrambling to find not only PPE but basic hygienic equipment like hand sanitizer and Lysol.[35] For so many frontline workers like Marquerita, their worlds became dominated by staying protected: by single-use examination gloves made of latex, nitrile rubber, or chloroprene; hairnets; goggles; an entirely impermeable bodysuit; fluid-resistant polyester surgical gowns; and the infamous N95 respirator masks that had to be hazardously reused and stored in paper bags.[36] Some nurses put them in microwaves to try and decontaminate them. Others laid them on their cars' dashboards to sun bleach. Hospitals used ZipWall Magnetic Dust Barriers made of plastic for makeshift contamination units.

News stories cropped up about nurses wearing trash bags into medical units. The lucky ones had rubber boots, hazmat suits, and respirators. There weren't enough adequate safety supplies, and everyone was improvising in the fog of war. There was no hazard pay. There was no social distancing. One survey found that 61% of health workers "felt high fear of exposing themselves or their families to COVID-19 while 38% self-reported experiencing anxiety or depression. Another 43% suffered from work overload and 49% had burnout." They were walking through the valley in the shadow of American death while citizens fought over whether COVID-19 was even real.[37]

* * *

Nurses and other frontline workers were taxed to their limits. Other laborers across America felt this frustration, too. After the government shutdown on March 15, thirty-three million workers applied for unemployment insurance. But millions of the country's lowest-paid workers, designated as "essential workers," were required to continue working. Fed up with low wages and no health care, and now facing the added threat of pandemic caretaking, they finally had enough. They walked off the job en masse.

From the Golden Arches and Burger King to late-night Taco Bell, cooks, custodians, and counter workers reported understaffed and unsafe workplaces. With 1.7 million unfillable jobs in leisure and hospitality, paper signs went up on glass doors and marquees in 2020 and 2021 reading "Closed: We All Quit," to cheers from Americans who supported their stand.[38]

Labor economists began referring to this phenomenon as "the Great Resignation," and a year and a half after COVID-19 changed our world, there were ten million vacant jobs that applicants chose to turn down. In August 2021, 4.3 million Americans quit their jobs, pushing the monthly quit rate to a new high of nearly 3 percent.[39]

Asked to put their lives on the line for unlivable wages, often with no benefits like health care, it seemed as if America had entered into the most significant de facto labor strike since the end of slavery. W. E. B. Du Bois argued that the American Civil War was the most significant labor strike in American history. The enslaved rose up, stopped working for their enslavers, fled plantations, and eventually comprised one-tenth of the US Army, freeing themselves—and America.[40]

Yet even before the pandemic took its first fifty thousand lives, America was in a financial tailspin. The Dow tumbled a troubling 20.3 percent between February and March 2020, and businesses began closing in droves. By April 2020, the unemployment level was at a staggering 14.7 percent, with more than twenty-three million unemployment filings. Workers did not have a social safety net and human rights—like universal health care—that people in all other wealthy nations enjoy. Where was the accountability?[41]

When the Black Detroit bus driver Jason Hargrove died of COVID-19 that he contracted on the job, he became the spokesman for essential workers left to fend for themselves. His final social media posts included a video about a woman coughing on his bus without a mask or covering her mouth. Hargrove dramatized the risks and dangers of workers left unprotected without mandates, laws, or PPE. "I feel violated," he said. "I feel violated for the folks that was on the bus when this happened. To those who are watching, this—this is real. And y'all need to take this seriously."[42]

Daily life changed for the majority of Americans. Seventy-nine percent of American grocery shoppers adjusted where they shopped that first month. As early as March 15, 2020, online shopping apps like Instacart, Walmart Grocery, and Shipt skyrocketed 218 percent, 160 percent, and 124 percent respectively, with mass disruption in product availability. Supply could not keep up with demand: 84 percent of all would-be online shoppers experienced technological or supply chain issues. Newly unemployed people risked their lives as personal shoppers.[43]

In the twentieth century, the Sears catalog helped get supplies to every corner of America through the US mail. Amazon.com put brick-and-mortar stores and their paper catalogs out of business in the twenty-first century. With millions sheltering in place, online shopping became the top way Americans consumed goods from books to clothing to food.

Amazon *delivered*. Amazon Prime subscribers could receive almost any product, including groceries, within two hours to two days. Amazon became the new commercial hub of the nation with its iconic logo—a smile and a forward-moving arrow—cropping up on cardboard boxes on nearly every doorstep, producing mass waste.

Part of America's supply chain issues were due to domestic workers getting sick. The virus ravaged meat and poultry plants. As Olivia Paschal reported, among northwest Arkansas's Hispanic and Marshallese populations, one-third of all COVID cases were among poultry workers, comprising 40 percent of first cases in household-wide outbreaks. Megacorporations infected their laborers and the children, partners, parents, and siblings of their workers.[44] "We're not essential," said one poultry worker. "We're *expendable*, and that's the truth."[45]

By November 2020, the meatpacking industry was stricken with COVID-19. Over forty thousand workers tested positive. Half worked at the four corporate giants of the industry: JBS, Smithfield, Tyson, and Cargill, which collectively process 80 percent of all American meat. Just half a year into the pandemic, two hundred meatpacking workers died. Half of all counties in the United States with the highest per capita infection rate had meat processing plants. Why?[46]

Killing floors are enclosed airless spaces designed to expedite death. Working "the chain" is exceptionally hazardous work. One mistake can result in the loss of an eye or limb, or death. During the Great Migration, the gruesome task of killing and butchering inspired some of the best-known blues songs, like Skip James's "Hard Time Killin' Floor Blues" in 1931 and Howlin' Wolf's "Killing Floor" for Chess Records in 1964.

Today killing floors are often worked by immigrants. Just like ninety years ago, these workers have few rights and are subjected to coercion as corporations use Immigration and Customs Enforcement (ICE) and Homeland Security to keep laborers "in line." Months before the COVID-19 pandemic, the nation's largest raid on immigrants began at seven poultry processing plants in Mississippi, and 680 people suspected of being undocumented were detained.[47]

The infrastructure of meatpacking plants made COVID-19 spread. Disposable face masks became soaked in animal blood and the workers' sweat, making it impossible to breathe. Workers, who were not given time off for being sick, removed their masks to breathe in the blood-soaked infernos, shoulder to shoulder their entire shifts.

One immigrant laborer told his supervisor his eyes burned—he was showing all the symptoms of COVID-19. Management told him to "fuck off and go back to work." His wife, who also worked at the plant, became sick. "They think we are like slaves, not workers," she said. "You're not allowed to get sick." They were bedridden for seven weeks, locking themselves away from their young children, who had to care for each other.[48] In twenty-three states reporting COVID-19 outbreaks in meat and poultry processing facilities, 87 percent of the sick were racial or ethnic minorities.[49]

The situation was dire. The Occupational Safety and Health Administration (OSHA) took little action. By the summer of 2020, "essential" workers filed over twenty thousand complaints about their safety and work conditions with OSHA. Only one citation was ever issued.[50]

Trump put his disregard for American workers' lives on full display while visiting the Honeywell Factory in Phoenix, Arizona, in May 2020, to watch the production of N95 masks (the kind Marquerita and health-care workers needed). Trump walked in maskless, putting all the factory employees' lives in danger. In protest, the workers overtook the factory public address system to blast Paul McCartney's 1973 song "Live and Let Die."[51]

The first stimulus checks were authorized on March 27, 2020, but they would not be available until well after mid-April 2020, when some Americans had been without wages for over a month.[52] It seems that many consumers used these $1,200 payments for shopping online, boosting Amazon sales $108.5 billion in the first quarter of 2021, with a 220 percent profit increase. Jeff Bezos, Amazon's founder, became the second wealthiest billionaire globally. But for the one out of 153 Americans who work for Amazon in warehouses, as sorters, packagers, or delivery people, the work is challenging, risky, and underpaid. "It affects your nerves, your mental state, your way of thinking—because you have to be cautious in everything you do now. It's like I'm risking my life for a dollar. It's twisted," said Rosie, after learning her coworker, a man in his twenties, died of COVID-19.[53]

Global supply chain issues left Americans in disbelief as many experienced, for the first time, the types of product shortages they believed only happened in communist countries during the Cold War. Images of large shipping containers stacking up at dockyards in Long Beach, California, became commonplace.[54] Recognizing the potential impact this could have on American consumers, David J. Lynch observed, "The commercial pipeline that each year brings $1 trillion worth of toys, clothing, electronics and furniture from Asia to the United States is clogged and no one knows how to unclog it."[55]

Unable to get essentials like toilet paper, meat, or wood in the early days, and electronics, car parts, and appliances a year later, the scale of disruption threatened traditional retail, an industry already weakened by online competitors. Deliveries that would typically take hours or weeks to ship suddenly required waiting for half a year. As Dawn Tiura, the head of the US-based Sourcing Industry Group, explained, "All roads lead back to China, and that has a major effect across the entire supply chain."[56]

China's labor strikes and shortages were not alone in compromising logistics. Labor strikes spread through America. In April 2021, dockworkers in Los Angeles walked out in support of striking port truck drivers, effectively shutting down one of the seven primary terminals at the port that processes about a fifth of all US imports.[57] Residual bottlenecking in retail and food services is expected to continue for years to come, driving prices up and leaving consumers angry and frustrated.[58]

One year into the pandemic, three-quarters of the 22.8 million confirmed cases of COVID-19 in the United States affected working-age groups (sixteen to sixty-four). As of February 2021, the hours lost by full-time workers due to their own health, childcare, or pandemic-related reasons hit $138 billion. As prices continued to climb and inflation rose to a multiyear high, US household debt broke a new record of $15.24 trillion in September 2021.[59]

Lawmakers responded with the $2 trillion Coronavirus Aid, Relief, and Economic Security (CARES) Act. It included a foreclosure moratorium that allowed more than seven million homeowners to remain in their homes temporarily. It also provided short-term financial aid to individuals through stimulus checks and grants to businesses.

These aid forms were not without hurdles: there were mail delays, bank closures, and bureaucratic hoops to jump through. Conversely, some of the largest (and richest) corporations qualified for governmental "loans," which eventually became free money. Individual working Americans came second to big businesses that prospered.[60]

Mass isolation, confinement, and stress took a psychological and physical toll. Chronic diseases like addiction spiked in quarantine. Thirty-four percent of Americans reported binge drinking, increasing every additional week spent in isolation at home.[61] Drug overdose deaths reached an all-time high of ninety thousand for the year ending in September 2020, and a significant number of those were tied to fentanyl.[62] Murder rates rose, too, skyrocketing 29 percent, the largest increase since the start of record keeping in 1960.[63]

Finally, one of the most striking aspects of the pandemic was how men and women experienced COVID-19 differently. In January 2020, two months before the pandemic began, the US Department of Labor declared that women held just over half of all payroll jobs. This was only the second time in America's history this happened. Then COVID-19 hit. The recession was an anomaly in that more women than men lost their jobs. By June 2021, there were 1.8 million fewer women in the workforce than before the pandemic. Women composed most of the service sector jobs that disappeared in early 2020, partly because they bore the brunt of care work, as children stayed home for "virtual school."[64] Many families made the difficult choice to bring parents or grandparents back into the home from nursing homes, because 40 percent of COVID-19 death cases originated there.[65]

Of course, none of this caretaking work was paid. Whether doing the laundry, cooking, cleaning, grocery shopping, paying bills, ordering medications, or handling the family calendar, women are still responsible for the vast number of tasks in the 2020s. This fact, along with the additional caretaking responsibilities caused by COVID-19, only served to worsen the state of gender equality in America.[66]

★ ★ ★

The pandemic arrived amid, and *accelerated*, a national reckoning with racial disparities and injustice. The nine-and-a-half-minute video of a Minneapolis police officer mercilessly draining the life out of George Floyd—despite Floyd's desperate cries of "I can't breathe"—was a tragic confirmation of the importance of the national Black Lives Matter (BLM) movement.[67]

The documentation of extralegal and police killings of Black and Brown Americans has long been facilitated by new technology, reaching back to the days of abolitionism when lithography, journalism, and photography captured the horrors of whipping, lynching, and family separation. Rodney King's beating was filmed on a camcorder in the late twentieth century. In the twenty-first century, anyone in the world can instantly record police with cell phones, going directly to the people via globalized platforms like Facebook, Twitter, Instagram, and TikTok.[68]

This confluence of technology and activism brought African Americans' excruciating pain and suffering to the world's attention. After its founding, Black Lives Matter dominated the national stage, impacting all aspects of life, from sports to politics. Athletes like Colin Kaepernick and LeBron James and other members of the Miami Heat, who had initially donned hoodies in solidarity with Trayvon Martin in 2012, began wearing BLM T-shirts and "taking a knee" during the performance of the national anthem to raise awareness of police brutality.[69]

Floyd's murder ushered in a wave of protests, the likes of which had not been seen in the United States since the 1960s. His tragic last words, "I can't breathe," were the same words gasped by Eric Garner, who was choked to death by police on Staten Island, New York, in 2014. Those three words took on new meaning as millions of Americans suffered through the suffocating respiratory symptoms of COVID-19.[70]

Floyd's murder came just months after the high-profile killings of Ahmaud Arbery by a pair of would-be vigilantes in Georgia and Breonna Taylor by police in Louisville, Kentucky. Arbery was hunted, shot, and killed while out for a Sunday afternoon jog in Brunswick, Georgia, on February 23, 2020.[71] Just a few weeks later, Breonna Taylor was murdered in the hallway of her home in Louisville, Kentucky, the victim of a bungled raid executed by plainclothes police after midnight. Utilizing a controversial no-knock warrant, police gained entry to the apartment, startling Taylor's boyfriend, who fired a single warning shot, unaware the intruders were police. Police, in turn, fired thirty-two shots into the residence, striking Taylor six times.[72]

Given this rapid succession of public murders, the BLM movement increased exponentially in 2020, expanding globally and reanimating Black internationalism reaching back to the human rights campaigns of abolitionism. Protests were documented in at least forty countries, focusing on global anti-Black racism. As the South Africa-based journalist Lynsey Chutel explained, "There is a George Floyd in every country."[73]

Igniting into a full-fledged civil rights movement of a different order, possibly as many as twenty-six million Americans of all races—who had not left their homes since March 2020—risked their own lives during the pandemic, taking to the streets, joining BLM protests, and demanding justice. The near-daily marches and demonstrations seemed to pick up where the tumultuous year of 1968 left off: this time with a much more diverse group of people. A natural narrative emerged, linking the Civil Rights Movements of the 1950s and 1960s to 2020, complemented by a desire to claim a double victory over the viral spread of both COVID-19 and white supremacy.

* * *

The pandemic had begun to transform cultural norms and practices in dramatic ways. Much like in Black America, losses were systemic, structural, and devastating in the Navajo Nation. By May 15, 2020, Indians accounted for 18 percent of all documented COVID-19 deaths. In the Navajo culture, you are not supposed to talk about death. "Now, it's gotten routine," Michael Begay, a Navajo mortician, said as he pushed a body draped in a white sheet through the Valley Ridge Mortuary. Entire families disappeared. "We have a mother and a son that passed. Two sisters that passed."[74] An external refrigerated trailer sat outside with the victims of COVID-19. Begay was in a race against time. Navajo bury their dead within four days. "There is a time period of when the spirit will start its journey, so we have to get it done within that time period."[75]

Seeing all the loss "just broke my heart," the stressed-out mortician recalled between tears, adjusting his glasses and mask yet unable to wipe away tears or touch his mouth or nose safely. He choked up thinking about processing and storing his friends lost to the disease.[76]

The Navajo Nation made a digital flowchart outlining the costs of COVID-19 funerals for burial assistance: a standard adult funeral was $2,500; a traditional Native funeral without a casket was $1,000; and funerals for stillborn babies were $100.[77]

COVID-19 decimated the Navajo Nation for historically rooted reasons. Despite the urbanization of the Indian American experience throughout the twentieth and twenty-first centuries, impoverished rural and remote intergenerational homes are a feature of the Navajo Nation (and were historically crucial to the tribe's cultural survival). The elderly ate at the table with their grandchildren during the pandemic and shared the same living spaces. Grandparents passed on tradition; grandchildren passed on contagion.

Poverty and water insecurity were repressive drivers of the rapid spread of the disease. Thirty-eight percent of Navajo live below the poverty line. The Navajo president estimated that 40 percent of the Navajo Nation does not have indoor plumbing or clean water, a travesty exacerbated by man-made droughts resulting from climate change. Without running water, hand washing becomes a herculean effort.[78] While the average American uses eighty-eight gallons of water every day, someone in the Navajo Nation might be lucky to access ten gallons.[79]

Finally, half of the Navajo Nation lacked access to broadband internet. This cut them off from up-to-date information about COVID-19. To highlight the disparity, both the European Union and the United States had to ask Netflix to reduce its broadband because so many people watched series like *Tiger King* on these streaming entertainment services that it could disrupt government and online education.

Like many low-income Black and Brown Americans, many Navajo live in a food desert. In March 2020, 38 percent of Americans became food insecure, including 52 percent of Hispanic households and 48 percent of Black families.[80] During the first two months of the pandemic, 169.9 million breakfasts and lunches distributed by the National School Lunch Program and School Breakfast Program went unserved. Schools closed; children went hungry.[81]

By April 2020, the St. Mary's Food Bank in Tuba City, Arizona, distributed 100,000 pounds of food to two thousand Navajo Nation families in three hours. This lifeline was only available to those with cars, gasoline, and time to wait. Recipients were instructed to not roll their windows down, to press their photo IDs against their car window, and to remain inside.[82]

* * *

The experiences of the Navajo Nation, George Floyd, and Breonna Taylor put racial disparities into clearer view for millions of Americans. The United States now stands at a momentous precipice: the possibility of a Third Reconstruction. When activists talk about abolishing the police, they conjure the momentum of movements past, from the abolitionists who shut down the transatlantic slave trade to civil rights leaders from the 1960s who dared to imagine a more just America. Envisioning a country free of racism and bigotry means creating new political and economic systems, as well as new power dynamics. There are infinite ways to make this nation a better place. The question is not whether we *can* make a difference, but whether we *will*.

America can continue to be a country ridden with violent white supremacy; it can continue to invest in an even-more-heightened police state; it can continue to be the only developed nation in the world to force our people to weather a deadly pandemic with no universal health care. Or, conversely, we can light a new path forward, revolutionizing society from the bottom-up—taking back power as a people through collective effort.

Visionary optimism is at the heart of the abolitionist project. As the prison abolitionist Mariame Kaba said, "I'm a deeply, profoundly hopeful person. Because I know that human beings, with all of our foibles and all the things that are failing, have the capacity to do amazingly beautiful things." While working in the darkest corners of America, advocating for the freedom of those locked away in jail cells, Kaba still sees rays of light, beaming through the darkness.[83]

The Constitution clarifies from its first three words: the United States is "we the people." The people are the power. The people are the government. *We* the *people* can create that more perfect union. No one else will do it for us.

★ ★ ★

In Marquerita Donald's world, there was work to be done. While "the Donald" idled away the precious days of 2020 raging at less-than-favorable news coverage, Marquerita Donald was putting her own life on the line to save the lives of other Americans.

But the PPE Marquerita used made both translating Navajo and caring for patients challenging. Masks and face shields concealed smiling or sympathetic faces behind a protective layer of plastic. More importantly, they made lip-reading impossible for the deaf and hard of hearing.

Marquerita could tell those elderly Navajo ICU patients were frightened; they did not understand what she was saying. She admitted, "There was a couple of times I took my mask off," like when she was explaining a do-not-resuscitate order to a dying elder. "Her oxygen machine was, like, really loud. She kept saying, 'What? I don't understand. I don't understand.'"[84]

Marquerita removed her mask to communicate with dying patients a few times to show respect to her elders. She thought she would be fine because she had a robust immune system. She was doing important work: the Navajo language is not only sacred to their tribe but has also been credited with being a vital tool in America's victory during World War II.[85]

But one day everything changed for Marquerita. "It started out with congestion. Then it became excruciating. Then came the fever, the vomiting and the shortness of breath."

Tyler watched as his mother lumbered to his truck, gasping for air. Desperate to breathe, she flung open her son's truck door and crawled in. She turned on the air conditioner full blast, and panically affixed her mouth to the vent to fill her lungs with air.

As Marquerita wheezed and gulped at the vent, she had what some people call a near-death experience. The Navajo call it a vision. Suddenly everything went white. She found herself in a hallway.

"In the distance a horse was saddled," Marquerita remembered. "With the bridle and everything. The horse didn't move, it just looked at me.". She and the horse held each other's stare for what could have been moments or an eternity. Its barreled chest breathing peacefully, it hoofed at the ground. In Navajo culture, horses symbolize one of the most powerful forces of nature.[86]

Her family was also in the dream. "They said that, if you were to get on, that would be the end of your life." By climbing upon the horse, she could rejoin her husband who died young in a car accident, as well as two of her adult children, and the late father she had cared for.

Marquerita had decided she needed to live by the end of the vision. She had a purpose and a job to do. She fought until morning, desperately swallowing the air-conditioned oxygen, and then called 911. Local hospitals were at capacity, so she was airlifted over three hundred miles to Scottsdale, Arizona. Marquerita stayed in the hospital for six weeks as a critical patient.

Marquerita survived. In the process, she realized a greater purpose. "I look at my life differently now," she explained, "I am not messing around," she said, vibrantly laughing. "I don't think anything's going to stop me now."[87] She even enrolled in school to become a licensed nurse.

In many ways, what Marquerita experienced was the quintessential story of Indigenous survival in North America over centuries. Her story represents those who, despite overwhelming odds, have fought to survive, found ways to remain resilient in trying circumstances.

"Once more darkness descends upon our people and this land," an Athabascan elder lamented. "It bears many names: smallpox, the flu, measles, typhoid, TB. Today . . . a virus. Suffering and death always follow." Still, faced with so much sorrow, he held onto hope: "But our traditions shine brightly, casting light to guide the way."[88]

* * *

Working for the Farm Security Administration during the Great Depression, the journalist Sanora Babb noticed a common phrase in legal notices nailed to the doors of vacant American homes after families were evicted. They were addressed to "John Doe and Mary Doe Whose Names Are Unknown."[89]

Now, in 2020s America, nearly a million Americans are dead, whose names are unknown, and whom we could not take the time to mourn properly. One of the most startling features of the COVID-19 era was losing so many people that we never even learned their names.

They were numbers. Then statistics.

As lives extinguished by COVID-19 mounted, newspaper obituaries could not keep up with the deaths, often only offering a simple sentence or phrase to encapsulate entire lifetimes. Ironically, as thousands of Americans were dying by asphyxiation with COVID-19, the beginnings of a major civil rights movement arose around George Floyd's final words, "I can't breathe." Out West, wildfires raged in every single state, ravaging Oregon and California, filling the skies with dark, poisonous smoke.[90]

It felt as if America itself was suffocating.

Yet here we are—the survivors. Struggling, but still breathing—ready to share our stories.

PART I

AMERICAN EXCEPTIONALISM:
COLONIZATION AND IMMIGRATION

ONE

EL PASO IN MOURNING

Monica Muñoz Martinez

El Paso City, by the Rio Grande
A voice tells me to go and see
Another voice keeps tellin' me
Maybe death awaits me in El Paso.

—*Marty Robbins, "El Paso"*

Recuerdo ranchero y ganado
sonrisa y orgullo de ayer
Mi altarcito salado de llanto
por tantas Marías que hemos de ser
Yo rezo a mi madre tierra
La vida y libertad
Yo busco a mi hermana justicia
la paz, la cultural, y felicidad.

—*Tish Hinojosa, "Las Marías"*

There seemed to be a century's worth of hard days in 2020. One of the most haunting was August 3, the first anniversary of the El Paso massacre, a horrific and devastating hate crime perpetrated against Latinx people. An anti-immigrant white supremacist entered a crowded Walmart with a semiautomatic weapon, deliberately targeting individuals who looked ethnically

27

Mexican. He murdered twenty-three people and wounded twenty-three others.[1]

On the massacre's anniversary, cars and trucks slowly rolled past drive-through memorials commissioned by the city and created by volunteers, a way for the community to experience a new type of socially distanced collective mourning during the COVID-19 pandemic. Forty florists from El Paso and neighboring towns in New Mexico created twenty-three human silhouettes of mosses and dried sunflowers, zinnias, roses, and larkspur, one for each victim. For the youngest victim, fifteen-year-old Javier Amir Rodriguez, the florists covered the shorter silhouette completely with flowers, to acknowledge the years of his life that never bloomed.[2]

In many ways, young Javier is not a bad metaphor for El Paso itself: Both the innocent boy and the beautiful city were so full of promise, yet their ability to thrive was impeded. For centuries in the American Southwest, white Americans have criminalized, policed, and forcibly removed people of Mexican descent near the frequently expanding US border. From the early 1800s to Donald Trump in 2020, politicians have used anti-Mexican rhetoric to fuel fear of the border and suspicion of the people who live there. For communities like El Paso, loss and grief in 2020 was twofold. People simultaneously had to protect themselves against COVID-19 and the rise of hate crimes fueled by xenophobia.

There are three striking similarities between the long, sordid history of US-Mexico border relations and the crises of 2020. First, Latinxs living near the border have long been portrayed as threats to white Americans and their property. Racist depictions of Mexicans as revolutionaries, bandits, murderers, rapists, drug dealers, and thieves proliferate in American culture and have left Latinx people vulnerable to racist violence by local law enforcement, state police, US soldiers, and vigilantes.

Second, Latinxs were painted as dirty, disease-ridden carriers. Latinx people were conflated with nonhuman forms, from animals to insects to viruses. Eugenicists, doctors, and local officials created dehumanizing immigration practices mandating quarantining and "disinfecting" Mexicans, sometimes with toxic chemicals. This dehumanization was repopularized under Trump, culminating in one of the deadliest attacks against Latinxs in US history.[3]

Third, in this climate of racial terror, social control, and intimidation, ethnic Mexicans were denied space to mourn the loss of their loved ones according to their preferred religious and cultural customs. Unresolved grief and trauma have been passed from one generation to the next, affecting everything from the social ills that often accompany poverty to measurable epigenetic changes. These facts are a stark reminder: time does not heal all wounds.

* * *

My last professional research trip as a historian in 2020 was to El Paso in late January. I gave a public lecture at the Border Network for Human Rights and learned from families advocating for social justice on the border. With a group of delegates from the Ford Foundation, we listened to refugees, migrants, and American citizens who had been impacted by US detention and deportation policies.

Advocates called for family reunification and a restoration of human rights at the border. The visit included a tour with border patrol agents of a segment of Trump's border wall. We also toured memorials at the site of the Walmart massacre in east El Paso and nearby parks to commemorate the lives lost less than six months before. The city was persevering, but it was stricken by grief that continued to be reignited by tragedy. Months after my visit, Guillermo "Memo" Garcia, a beloved thirty-six-year-old soccer coach, died on April 25, 2020, from fatal injuries sustained on the August 3 massacre.[4]

El Paso had already been experiencing a humanitarian crisis even before the massacre. Doctors, lawyers, religious leaders, and teachers had raised alarms of the devastating effects of inhumane immigration detention and deportation policies, which had compounded over decades. But during the Trump administration, El Paso was used as a staging ground to advance a white nationalist immigration agenda. In May 2018, to drum up support for "the wall," Trump ramped up his racist rhetoric, baselessly claiming, "You wouldn't believe how bad these people are," crossing the border. He infamously corrected himself: "These aren't people. These are animals."

In pithy lines, Trump managed to dehumanize all people of Mexican descent, reviving language and tactics that white supremacists have used for centuries. El Paso was selected to pilot the inhumane family separation policy that eventually removed nearly 5,500 children from their guardians. The children ranged in age from teenagers to newborns, some taken from their mothers while they were still nursing.[5]

When news of this policy broke and images of children being hurried into windowless vans to be transported by bus and by plane to undisclosed locations circulated, the people of El Paso, heartbroken by what was taking place in their hometown, responded with protests and offered to provide refuge for the children. When reports leaked that babies were negligently left in soiled diapers while under the care of border patrol facilities, El Pasoans donated clean diapers, formula, and toys for the children, but the border patrol agents refused to allow their distribution. When news broke of children being imprisoned in a tent city in nearby Tornillo, elected officials from El Paso, like Texas state senator José Rodríguez, called for accountability. Linda Rivas, the executive director of Las Americas Immigration Advocacy Center described the experiences of 2018 and 2019 as a series of attacks on El Paso.[6]

The people living in El Paso and in border towns all along the US-Mexico border have carried the unfair burden of calling out injustices. In this context, while in a state of physical and emotional depletion, the people of El Paso had to weather the COVID-19 pandemic in 2020.

According to the Centers for Disease Control (CDC), as of December 23, 2020, more than 54,000 Latinxs died from their battle with COVID-19. Latinxs were dying at a rate three times as high as white Americans. In Texas, more than half of the people who died from COVID-19 in 2020 were Latinxs. By the end of 2020, Latinxs were also overrepresented in the deaths of working-age adults, making up almost 50 percent of the people aged thirty-five to forty-four years old who died.[7]

But the deaths from the pandemic were not the only losses Latinx communities faced. According to the FBI, anti-Latinx hate crimes rose from 430 in 2017 to 485 in 2018 to 527 in 2020. In 2019, the FBI reported that anti-immigrant sentiments had become a top perceived threat fueling hate crimes. Of the fifty-one hate-motivated murders reported that year, almost half of the victims were from the El Paso massacre.[8]

The simultaneous crises can perhaps best be understood through the separate efforts of Angel Gomez and Bishop Harrison Johnson to bring aid to mourning families in El Paso. Gomez's nonprofit, Operation HOPE (Helping Other People Endure), hosts annual back to school events for families in El Paso and Ciudad Juárez. On August 3, 2019, more than eight hundred families were expected to attend. Families were gathering when news broke that there was an active shooter at Walmart. Panicked, parents and children cleared the park. Operation HOPE switched from helping families plan for the school year to helping twenty-two families plan funerals for their loved ones. In the aftermath of the massacre, Bishop Harrison Johnson, a minister who also directed a funeral home, helped organize a funeral for one of the victims, Margie Reckard. Antonio Bosco, Reckard's surviving husband, asked the funeral home to invite the public to the service, because he had no family and did not want to mourn alone. In a time of need, Bishop Johnson modeled care and empathy, and he created space for collective mourning and repair. He organized a moving memorial attended by over three thousand people. "This is about a community coming together to be there for him," Johnson said.[9]

On the anniversary of the El Paso massacre, Gomez and Operation HOPE had helped more than 160 families plan funerals for relatives that died from COVID-19. When burial relief from the Coronavirus Aid, Relief, and Economic Security Act (also known as the CARES Act), started to run dry, the nonprofit provided funeral assistance. Two months after the first anniversary, on October 15, 2020, Bishop Johnson died from complications of the novel coronavirus. His surviving family, and the city of El Paso, mourned an important community leader who had helped them manage their collective grief.

Unfortunately, the humanitarian work of Angel Gomez and Bishop Harrison Johnson is not new to people living along the US-Mexico border. Generations of people have had to mourn victims that died at the hands of white supremacy. They have also been subjected to violence and abuse by doctors and medical officials who saw them not as patients, but as "diseased criminals."

These disparaging stereotypes with devastating real-world consequences echoed in the twenty-first century when Donald J. Trump launched his first election campaign arguing that the border wall was needed because "when Mexico sends its people, they're not sending their best . . . They're bringing drugs. They're bringing crime. They're rapists."[10]

Although he had mastered racist rhetoric, it is unclear if Trump understood how closely he adopted language from a century before. But members of his cabinet had publicly praised racist policies created in that era.[11] The decade between 1910 and 1920 was a period of racial terror. Mushrooming nativist sentiment shaped how Anglo Americans viewed both ethnic Mexicans and the US-Mexico border, inspiring calls for violent policing. Hundreds of people were murdered—men, women, and children. People who witnessed this era frequently referred to it as *la matanza*, the massacre.[12] Simply put, this was an era of state-sanctioned racial violence. In 1919, US congressman Claude Hudspeth of West Texas described hordes of Mexican bandits just south of the border as an ever-present threat. He publicly justified state police officers shooting Mexicans on sight. He testified under oath, "You have got to kill those Mexicans when you find them or they will kill you."[13]

But politicians went beyond rhetoric. They militarized the border. Mexican revolutionaries were seen as a threat to Anglo control and American capital. Residents worried that the revolution to overthrow the Porfirio Díaz dictatorship, redistribute land, and reclaim natural resources from foreign mining companies in Mexico could spill across the border and threaten Anglo property or even US control in the Southwest. As conflicts between federal and revolutionary soldiers reached the northern Mexico border, Texas governor Oscar Colquitt dispatched over one thousand state militiamen and the Texas National Guard to appease El Paso and Brownsville residents. By 1916 the Wilson administration had deployed approximately 100,000 National Guard troops to the US-Mexico border between Yuma, Arizona, and Brownsville, Texas. The Texas legislature budgeted to hire more state police. In 1915 the state police included only twenty-five rangers. By 1919, nearly 1,350 rangers policed the state.[14]

During this era, local law enforcement, Texas Rangers (who held investigative jurisdiction across Texas), US soldiers, and vigilantes alike enjoyed impunity. In 1915, Texas governor James Ferguson ordered the state police to "clean out the nest" near the border with Mexico of ethnic Mexicans, and he openly offered his pardoning power to Texas Rangers who committed crimes. Rangers initiated a revenge-by-proxy policy, killing ethnic Mexicans, regardless of evidence of guilt, merely for being near the location of a crime. They profiled any ethnic Mexican as a Mexican bandit, made arrests, and then left prisoners vulnerable to mobs. Vigilante groups formed with euphemistic names, like "Home Guard" and "Law and Justice League," inflicting fear and violence.[15]

★ ★ ★

Three cases from just over a century ago show that neither class, age, gender, nor citizenship protected people who "looked" ethnically Mexican in Southwest Texas.

In September 1915, two landowning American citizens, Antonio Longoria and Jesus Bazán, reported to state police that they had been robbed. While returning home, the two men were shot in the back by a posse that included a state police captain. Captain Henry Ransom then warned people that witnessed the double murder not to bury the remains. They defied his orders and buried Bazán and Longoria. There were no investigations. No one was ever prosecuted.

In January 1918, a group of Texas Rangers, US soldiers, and civilians traveled to Porvenir in West Texas and arrested fifteen ethnically Mexican men and boys. The Texas Rangers then opened fire, massacring the fifteen prisoners. The massacre survivors loaded the bodies of their loved ones onto a wagon, crossed the border south into Mexico, and buried the remains in a mass grave. No civilians or officers were ever prosecuted.

In April 1919, nine-year-old Concepción García was shot by a US soldier when she crossed the Rio Grande south into Mexico on a raft with her mother and her aunt. A military court found the soldier guilty of manslaughter, but President Woodrow Wilson ordered that the soldier be freed and reinstated to military duty.

Despite the climate of violence and intimidation in each of these cases, and knowing full well that the aggressors who murdered their loved ones were still free, armed, and cloaked with legal authority, surviving family members persevered. Antonia Longoria and Epigmenia Bazán, the widows of Antonio Longoria and Jesus Bazán, refused to leave their property and stayed with their children on their family ranch. Twelve widows, grandparents, and children of the victims of the Porvenir massacre testified as witnesses, called for investigations, and filed a claim against the

United States government for failure to prosecute. The parents of Concepción García also filed a claim against the United States for the death of their daughter by a soldier. An international tribunal through the US-Mexico General Claims Commission awarded the family a financial indemnity. The commissioners found that states should be punished for "such offences as unnecessary shooting across the border without authority." The commission obligated the US government to pay an indemnity on behalf of Teodoro García and Maria Apolinar Garza. "An amount of $2,000, without interest, would seem to express best the personal damage caused the claimants by the killing of their daughter by an American officer."[16]

State-sanctioned anti-Latinx violence did not always result in death. Refugees that crossed into the United States fleeing the conflicts of the Mexican Civil War were denied humanitarian aid. In 1914, Mexican federal soldiers suffered a defeat at Ojinaga. Both soldiers and panicked civilians crossed into West Texas as refugees, but they were met with growing nativist hostility. White residents in Presidio, Marfa, and El Paso called for them to be apprehended.[17]

The US military detained refugees at the border town of Presidio and forced them to walk nearly seventy miles across the unforgiving desert to Marfa, where the imprisoned were boarded onto trains and "shipped" west to Fort Bliss outside of El Paso. Under guard by US soldiers, the refugees built a prison camp that stretched across forty-eight acres of land. It was enclosed by an intimidating barbed wire fence stacked ten strands high and secured to the ground by a hog wire fence. Some reported that electricity charged the barbed wire with a lethal current.[18]

The prison was unforgiving. Prisoners lived in canvas tents that provided little reprieve from the extreme desert temperatures. They were completely reliant on the US military for food, water, and firewood. As many as five thousand prisoners reportedly lived without running water or adequate medical attention. Despite the dire conditions, both the local and national press described the imprisoned as a danger to residents and an expense to all Americans, callously tallying the costs of detaining these refugees. Some residents in El Paso, whether friends and relatives of the imprisoned or simply generous strangers, passed the refugees food and clothing through the barbed wire fence.[19]

The stress of war, exhaustion from traveling on foot, and exposure to extreme cold took a toll on the refugees. Dozens died from pneumonia, dysentery, and acute gastroenteritis. Young children and pregnant women were especially vulnerable. Two pregnant mothers, Maria Lehandra and Luz Garcia, both gave birth to stillborn babies in prison. Pedra Mareno gave birth to her son Anacleto Esquibel, but the baby died eight days later. His death certificate notes that he died "without medical attention." Luz Rodriguez gave birth to a baby girl who died five days later. Shortly after escaping a civil war only to be imprisoned, the grief and loss suffered by these mothers should be hard to fathom a century later.[20]

These grieving mothers were detained at Fort Bliss, a United States Army post with its headquarters in El Paso, until May when they were again boarded onto trains and transported nearly four hundred miles to Fort Wingate in New Mexico. The refugee prison may have closed in El Paso just months after it opened, but the controlled expulsion of imprisoned Mexicans continued.

Ethnic Mexicans living in El Paso, regardless of citizenship, were treated as harbingers of disease. The El Paso mayor Tom Lea telegraphed the US surgeon general Rupert Blue asking for help to prevent the spread of illness from "diseased criminals" coming from Mexico. "Hundreds of dirty lousy destitute Mexicans arriving at El Paso daily[.] [W]ill undoubtedly bring and spread typhus unless a quarantine is placed at once."[21] In the El Paso County Jail, prisoners were "disinfected" by bathing in solvents like kerosene, a known carcinogen often used for illuminants and in jet fuel. This policy led to a tragedy in March 1916, when a prisoner struck a match igniting the kerosene and causing an explosion.

Approximately twenty prisoners, some suspected of supporting Mexican revolutionary Pancho Villa, died and fifteen others were seriously injured in what was reported by the *El Paso Herald* as the "city jail holocaust."[22]

The United States public health surgeon Claude C. Pierce swiftly initiated an "iron clad quarantine" against anyone from Mexico entering the United States. Pierce built the first quarantine and disinfecting center in El Paso. At the quarantine center, described as a "disinfection plant" by German scientists who took inspiration from these practices, Mexican migrants were stopped, inspected, and if deemed necessary by immigration officials forced to strip naked and take toxic baths. They were sprayed with a hazardous mixture of gasoline, kerosene, sulfuric acid, DDT, and even Zyklon B, the major agent used in gas chambers by Nazi Germany during World War II. These quarantine procedures quickly spread to border checkpoints in other towns. Soon after El Paso, sanitation procedures were put in place in Laredo, Eagle Pass, and Brownsville, and later in border towns in Arizona and California.[23]

Racist caricatures and dehumanizing language conflating Mexicans and Mexican Americans at the border with infestations and viral contagions have long institutional roots stemming back to the nineteenth and twentieth century. The year 2020 showed that these issues still mobilize our political discourse, justifying unjust detentions and encouraging extreme white supremacist violence.

As months passed in 2021, it became clear that dangerous patterns would continue. The second anniversary of the El Paso massacre was bookended by three damning whistleblower accounts that raised the alarm about conditions at the Fort Bliss Emergency Intake Center, where unaccompanied children were being detained in tents. The reports provided evidence of patterns of abuse and gross negligence. They described inhumane conditions that put children at risk of physical, mental, and emotional harm. They reported hundreds of cases of COVID-19 due to overcrowded, unsafe conditions, and insufficient access to clean water, food, clothes, or basic sanitation. One report also warned that children suffered symptoms of severe depression, prompting staff to remove objects like pencils and nail clippers.[24] Under the Biden administration, children seeking refuge in the United States continued to suffer from being incarcerated at Fort Bliss.

When it became clear in the summer of 2021 that COVID-19 variants would continue to fuel the surge of infections, the Texas governor Greg Abbott returned to an old scapegoat; he blamed migrants as the cause. Despite evidence that the resurgent pandemic was "a pandemic of the unvaccinated," he and other pundits repeated rhetoric that continued to inflame anti-immigrant and anti-Latinx sentiment.[25] These dangerous efforts, however, could not deflect attention from the governor's own actions that arguably made Texans more vulnerable to infection. In 2021, in defiance of recommendations from the World Health Organization and the CDC, governors like Governor Abbott signed orders and passed laws that prevented mask or vaccination mandates by local or county officials or by state agencies, including public schools.[26]

In the face of state policies that would hamstring local efforts to implement preventive public health measures, border communities made use of the greatest protective measure available: vaccinations.

Border residents had seen enough death and devastation, so when there was a medical solution to one of the pandemics that they faced, they pushed misinformation about vaccinations aside and proactively protected themselves and their communities. In this regard, border communities stood second to none. In August 2021, the city of El Paso hit an important milestone. The city vaccination rate for eligible residents was over 70 percent, and for people over sixty-five years of age the rate was nearly 90 percent. Less than a year before, the city had been a nationwide hotspot for COVID-19.

By the time the delta variant was filling hospitals and mobile morgues were arriving in other Texas cities, hospitalization rates remained relatively low in El Paso. Experts believed that that was thanks to the high vaccination rates. Other border communities similarly confronted the resurgent pandemic with the highest vaccination rates in the state. At the end of August 2021, Cameron, Hidalgo, Starr, and Webb counties all had vaccination rates over 72 percent, with Starr and Webb counties recording 80 percent and 82 percent vaccination rates, respectively. Border communities were the highest vaccinated counties in the state, even compared to counties with urban centers that offered incentives for vaccination, like Harris County. The sharpest contrast lay with more than ten Texas counties with a vaccination rate of less than 30 percent at the start of the school year that same month.[27]

The children growing up in border communities will learn the hard truths of the recent past in due time. When they do, they should also learn that border communities collectively worked to protect them in the face of forces that attempted to malign them or make them more vulnerable to death. It is a long tradition that they should no longer have to bear, but for centuries *fronterizos* have shown a commitment to remembering their lost loved ones, repairing broken humanity, and building a more just future.

TWO

2020

A Year for Epic Victories amid Historic Loss

Mary Kathryn Nagle

D ue to COVID-19 and federal court cases, 2020 was a time of historic celebration encapsulated by historic loss for both our families and our tribal nations.

We took our first family vacation since the pandemic began and hit the road in the summer of 2021. It had been a family tradition, each summer, to pick a part of the country our boys have not yet seen and to travel, by car, stopping at as many goofy and serious destinations as possible. Destinations have included emu farms, national parks, dinosaur bones, the grave of Billy the Kid, sacred sites where we respectfully engaged in ceremony and prayer, reservations where friends have opened their homes and welcomed us, world-renowned ice cream parlors, and impromptu rest stops when bathrooms cannot be located for what seemed like hundreds of miles.

We canceled our trip during the summer of 2020 due to coronavirus, but in 2021—with all of us except the youngest now vaccinated—we decided to drive from the Pacific Northwest through the Dakotas to the Muscogee (Creek) Nation Reservation. Our boys had not been able to travel home to see the Muscogee (Creek) Nation Reservation since the Supreme Court issued its historic decision in *McGirt v. Oklahoma* on July 9, 2020, announcing to the world that their nation's reservation remains in existence. While the import of this event may seem theoretical or academic, it is anything but that. Justice Neil Gorsuch began his decision in *McGirt* proclaiming: "*On the far end of the Trail of Tears was a promise.* Forced to leave their ancestral lands in Georgia and Alabama, the Creek Nation received assurances that their new lands in the West would be secure forever. . . . Today we are asked whether the land these treaties promised remains an Indian reservation for purposes of federal criminal law. Because Congress has not said otherwise, we hold the government to its word."[1]

Less than one year before the Supreme Court issued its decision in *McGirt*, our boys lost their grandmother, and my husband loss his Mamagee, our beloved Aunt Rich. She was the matriarch of our matrilineal family, and for our family, she was the last of a generation born speaking her Mvskoke language and living a connection to Mvskoke culture that the United States had tried, unsuccessfully, to eradicate. Just four months before the United States shut down and quarantined for COVID, and just eight months before the Supreme Court issued its decision in *McGirt*, we traveled back to the family's allotment, where Mamagee was born in 1945, and with the boys, we spread her ashes. My husband, Muscogee (Creek) Nation's ambassador, Jonodev Chaudhuri, penned an op-ed in the *Washington Post*, stating: "For me and for thousands of other Muscogees, the court's ruling is more than legal confirmation of a treaty. It is confirmation that the sacrifices of my mom, my Mamagee and all of our ancestors were not in vain. That my children won't be erased in their own home. That we are still here."[2]

As Joy Harjo, a citizen of the Muscogee (Creek) Nation and the first-ever Native US poet laureate, wrote in the *New York Times*: "Justice is sometimes seven generations away, or even more. And it is inevitable."[3]

For our boys and my husband, the return home once vaccinated was bittersweet. Since our family's last trip home in 2019, the United States Supreme Court had rejected Oklahoma's attempt to destroy their nation's treaty-created reservation. And since our family's last trip home in 2019, the Muscogee (Creek) Nation has lost several first-language Mvskoke speakers. My husband's ceremonial grounds lost their *mekko* (the Mvskoke word for the leader of a traditional ceremonial grounds). Many more ceremonial leaders and culture bearers have been lost to the pandemic.

But COVID-19 is not the first time our tribal nations have experienced this kind of profound loss. As my family and I made our way through the Dakotas on our way to the Muscogee (Creek) Nation Reservation in Oklahoma, we stopped to visit friends from Standing Rock, and then Ogalala. As we continued our drive to the Ponca Tribe's homelands, at the confluence of the Missouri and Niobrara Rivers, I couldn't help but notice we were driving right along the Missouri River, where the Standing Rock Sioux Tribe, Cheyenne River Sioux Tribe, and Yankton Sioux Tribe fought to defend their treaty rights, drinking water, sacred sites, and burials from the Dakota Access Pipeline and Army Corps of Engineers just a few years ago. And two hundred years before that, these same tribes were visited by the Army Corps' predecessor, the Army Corps of Discovery (1804–1806), led by Meriwether Lewis and William Clark after the Louisiana Purchase—a payment that went, of course, to the colonizing French at a reduced rate due to the Haitian Revolution. The colonized, meanwhile, got nothing.

On a happier note, 2020 was a critical year in the federal courts for tribal nations. While most non-Natives have heard about or know something about *McGirt*, and while many know about the protests that took place at Standing Rock in 2016 and 2017, very few remember that the Standing Rock Sioux Tribe (and many others) sued the Army Corps of Engineers for illegally granting Dakota Access the easement they need to construct their pipeline across the Missouri River.

On March 25, 2020, District Judge James E. Boasberg issued a historic decision in this case, concluding that the tribes were correct and that the Army Corps violated federal law when the agency granted Dakota Access the easement it needed to construct its pipeline in treaty lands without considering the treaty rights of the nations that today comprise the former Great Sioux Nation. I filed an amicus brief in this case (as well as in *McGirt*) on behalf of my client, the National Indigenous Women's Resource Center (NIWRC).

Judge Boasberg ordered the Army Corps to "prepare an EIS (Environmental Impact Statement) because the pipeline's effects on the quality of the human environment are likely to be highly controversial." As NIWRC's amicus brief explains, the impacts on the human environment from the pipeline—namely, the fact that increased oil production in the Bakken will bring an increase in violent crimes being committed against Native women and children living in the region—is a factor the Corps must consider with in-depth analysis in the EIS it has been ordered to prepare. As we noted in the brief:

> The connection between increased oil extraction from pipelines, such as Dakota Access, and violence against Native women has been well-documented. The Army Corps' decision to permit a pipeline that nearly doubles the amount of oil extraction taking place in North Dakota, without undertaking an Environmental Impact Statement that considers the public health and safety impacts the agency's final action will have on Native women and children, has only exacerbated what was already a crisis. If the pipeline is not vacated and an actual EIS undertaken, there will be real life and death consequences for the Native women and children living on or near tribal lands in North Dakota.

Although the case then went back up to the DC Circuit Court of Appeals and back down to the district court for further consideration, the pipeline has yet to be shut down. Judge Boasberg refused to grant an injunction ordering that the pipeline be shut down pending the outcome of the Army Corps' EIS review.

As we drove the boys to the site of the camp where thousands stayed for months in solidarity with the youth at Standing Rock who started the movement, I shared the story with our boys. The movement began on March 26, 2016, when a group of Standing Rock youth ran from Wakpala, South Dakota, to Mobridge, South Dakota, to raise awareness about the proposed pipeline. Their tribal leadership had provided comments to the Army Corps regarding the significant damage the pipeline would cause to sacred sites and the graves of their relatives if the pipeline was constructed along its proposed path just one mile north of the Standing Rock Sioux Reservation border. In addition to their run, several Native youths created a petition in opposition to the pipeline that ultimately garnered over half a million signatures. In their petition, young Natives explained why they were exercising their constitutional right to free speech in opposition to the Dakota Access Pipeline. As one thirteen-year-old from Standing Rock wrote:

> I've lived my whole life by the Missouri River. It runs by my home in Fort Yates North Dakota and my great grandparents' original home was along the Missouri River in Cannon Ball. The river is a crucial part of our lives here on the Standing Rock Reservation.
>
> But now a private oil company wants to build a pipeline that would cross the Missouri River . . . and if we don't stop it, it will poison our river and threaten the health of my community when it leaks.
>
> My friends and I have played in the river since we were little; my great grandparents raised chickens and horses along it. When the pipeline leaks, it will wipe out plants and animals, ruin our drinking water, and poison the center of community life for the Standing Rock Sioux.
>
> In Dakota/Lakota we say "mni Wiconi." Water is life. Native American people know that water is the first medicine not just for us, but for all human beings living on this earth.
>
> The proposed Dakota Access Pipeline would transport 570,000 barrels of crude oil per day, across four states. Oil companies keep telling us that this is perfectly safe, but we've learned that that's a lie: from 2012 [to] 2013 alone, there were 300 oil pipeline breaks in the state of North Dakota.

>With such a high chance that this pipeline will leak, I can
>only guess that the oil industry keeps pushing for it because
>they don't care about our health and safety. It's like they think
>our lives are more expendable than others.
>
>So we, the Standing Rock Youth, are taking a stand to be the
>voice for our community, for our great grandparents, and for
>Mother Earth. Join us, and sign to ask the Army Corps of Engi-
>neers to stop the construction of the Dakota Access Pipeline.[4]

These young activists decided to open a prayer camp in Cannon
Ball, North Dakota, to protest the planned construction of the pipeline where their relatives were buried. The organizers of this movement were not radical environmentalists or ecoterrorists, but young
citizens of the Standing Rock Sioux Tribe and the Cheyenne River
Sioux Tribe, fighting to ensure a livable homeland for present and
future generations and to protect the graves of their ancestors.

The youth named their camp Sacred Stone—where, before the
Army Corps's damming of the Missouri River in the 1950s, the
river's natural current spit out perfectly spherical stones that looked
like cannonballs. From the beginning, the youth focused on prayer.
"Days began with a water ceremony; the sacred fire had to be regularly fed; meals began with prayer and a 'spirit plate' served for the
ancestors; alcohol and drugs were strictly forbidden."[5]

On April 26, 2016, when it was clear that the Army Corps
was moving toward granting Dakota Access the necessary easement to construct the pipeline across the river, Standing Rock and
Cheyenne River Sioux youth ran from Cannon Ball to Omaha,
Nebraska, to deliver a petition to the Army Corps. The petition
the youth carried from Cannon Ball now contained 457,000 signatures and demanded that the Army Corps refrain from granting
Dakota Access the easement the company needed to construct the
pipeline across the river. Once again, the petition included the
words *mni Wiconi*—water is life.

Despite their efforts, the colonel of the Army Corps refused to
even meet with the Native youth who had run so far to peacefully

deliver their message. When the Army Corps ignored their request, the youth then ran from their camp at Cannon Ball all the way to Washington, DC. In July 2016, thirty young runners ran over two thousand miles to the White House and demanded that President Obama stop the pipeline. While in Washington, DC, they delivered a petition with more than 160,000 signatures to the Army Corps asking that the pipeline not be built next to their reservation.

Just two days later, the Army Corps granted Dakota Access the easement they needed, under the law, to build their pipeline across the Missouri River. And three and a half years later, as the world shuttered its doors and went into a panicked quarantine in response to COVID-19, Judge Boasberg issued a powerful forty-two-page decision declaring that the youth were correct. The Army Corps was wrong—and they had violated federal law.

We showed the boys Facebook Hill, where everyone at camp walked to gain a tiny bit of cell service and post their selfies on the social media website Facebook. We drove past the sign indicating where the Standing Rock Sioux Reservation begins, and we took them to the spot where, on September 3, 2016, Dakota Access employed bulldozers to destroy the twenty-seven burials that Standing Rock Sioux Tribe's former tribal historic preservation officer Tim Mentz had identified for Judge Boasberg's court the day before.[6]

As we drove up and down the Missouri River with one of our family friends from Standing Rock, she reminded us that when Lewis and Clark traveled the Missouri River, they had a vaccine for smallpox, but they didn't share it with any of the tribes.

Just think: Only two hundred years ago, smallpox decimated the population of tribal nations from the Delaware Lenape, the Comanche Nation, and the Great Sioux Nation to the Mandan, Hidatsa, and Arikara Nations. Lewis and Clark traveled up and down the Missouri and could have shared the vaccine with tribal nations, thereby preventing thousands of needless deaths. But they didn't.

History has a way of repeating itself. Progress is when hundreds of years of a historic wrong is finally identified and labeled as the wrong that it is. I don't consider it ironic that Lewis and Clark's Army Corps of Discovery eventually became the Army Corps of Engineers, and that the same federal agency that viewed the Missouri River as the doorstep of "manifest destiny" later granted permission to a private pipeline company to destroy burials, human remains, sacred sites, and the drinking water of tribal nations that predate the United States.

Yet 2020 was also a historic year for tribal nations in the United States federal courts due to the victories of *Standing Rock v. Army Corps of Engineers*, as well as *McGirt*. For Natives in the United States, 2020 is the year we won our own *Brown v. Board of Education*.

Just as *Brown* rejected a legal regime designed to preserve white entitlement to segregation by race, *McGirt* rejects a legal regime that has, until now, catered to white expectations that tribal nations, and their reservations, will someday simply cease to exist. Just as *Brown* declared *Plessy v. Ferguson*'s "separate but equal" unconstitutional, *McGirt* rejects the notion that a tribal nation loses its treaty-created reservation simply because white Americans decided they wanted to live on it.[7]

And 2020 is the year we lost Supreme Court Justice Ruth Bader Ginsburg (1933–2020). For many in Indian Country, the passing of Justice Ginsburg in the fall of 2020 was bittersweet. Although she had become an iconic superpower of justice and righteous dissent for American women and other disenfranchised populations, her jurisprudence in Indian law was, at times, quite problematic.

It is a bit ironic, then, that the final opinion bearing her name was *McGirt v. Oklahoma*, issued on the last day of the last term in which she sat as a justice. However, it is only ironic if you do not consider the entire arc of her Indian law jurisprudence.

In 1997, Justice Ginsburg authored *Strate v. A-1*, a case brought by non-Indians challenging the inherent jurisdiction of tribal courts over non-Indians. In *Strate v. A-1*, Justice Ginsburg concluded that "the civil authority of Indian tribes and their courts with respect to non-Indian fee lands generally does not extend to the activities of nonmembers of the tribe."[8]

Justice Ginsburg's opinion in *Strate* has caused great harm to tribal nations seeking to regulate the conduct of non-Indian individuals and corporations doing business on tribal lands, as non-Indians began to cite Justice Ginsburg's opinion in several tort lawsuits where non-Indians engaged in harmful behavior, but hoped to escape the consequences, on tribal lands. Time and time again, bad actors relied on *Strate* to argue against tribal jurisdiction. Time and time again, lower federal courts applied Justice Ginsburg's decision in *Strate*, thereby allowing non-Indians to engage in tortious conduct on tribal lands with no consequence.

But in 2015, everything changed. The Dollar General Corporation relied on Justice Ginsburg's decision in *Strate* to argue that the Mississippi Band of Choctaw Indians (MBCI) Tribal Court did *not* have jurisdiction over the corporation—whose non-Indian store manager had repeatedly sexually assaulted a thirteen-year-old Choctaw boy on the reservation while working at Dollar General's store—because, under *Strate*, tribal courts do not have jurisdiction over non-Indians who sexually assault Native children on tribal lands.

According to Dollar General, citizens of tribal nations are the only Americans who do not have a right to seek justice in the courts of their own government but must instead turn to a foreign government in the quest for justice. This argument, of course, has been repeatedly used against Native women and children victims of domestic violence and sexual assault with great success—causing severe harm. Imagine if citizens of Kansas had to go to Colorado to seek justice when they have been raped. Very few could afford the time off from work, representation, and travel needed to seek justice. That is the outcome—but of course, that is also the desired result of those who seek this discriminatory rule of law.

Today Native women and children are more likely to be raped, murdered, sexually assaulted, and abused than any other segment of the American population. The challenges to the inherent jurisdiction of our tribal nations come with real life and death consequences for our people.

Dollar General v. Mississippi Band of Choctaw Indians was argued in December 2015, and by all counts, many expected the court to follow Justice Ginsburg's decision in *Strate* and strike down the MBCI's exercise of jurisdiction over a non-Indian (in this case, sexually assaulting a Choctaw child on tribal lands). The National Indigenous Women's Resource Center, and many other Native women advocates and organizations, came to the steps of the Supreme Court to pray for justice. I think I speak for all of us when I say our prayers were heard.

At the end of the 2015 Term, the Supreme Court issued a one-line opinion, upholding the judgment of the Fifth Circuit Court of Appeals in a four-to-four vote. The court was at a standstill: Since the passing of Justice Scalia in February 2016, there was not a ninth justice to break the tie. This tie upheld the lower court's judgment, which favored the MBCI and tribal jurisdiction.[9]

How did Justice Ginsburg vote? We will never know for sure. But everyone at the Supreme Court that day who heard the argument and listened to the questions is pretty sure she was one of the four who voted in favor of tribal jurisdiction—and against the application of her own decision in *Strate*.

What changed? What took Justice Ginsburg from the justice who authored *Strate* to the justice who joined Justice Neil Gorsuch and the majority of the court to affirm the continued existence of the Mvskoke Reservation?

By the end of her time on the court, Ginsburg had taken the initiative to visit Indian Country. A massive fan of opera and theater, she had seen plays written by Native playwrights—including one specifically that focused on the impact of the restored tribal criminal jurisdiction in the 2013 reauthorization of the Violence

Against Women Act (Justice Ginsburg went to see *Sovereignty* at Arena Stage in February 2018). She toured the Indian Art Market in Santa Fe, where she visited with tribal leaders and witnessed the incredible work of Native artists.

In her final days, Justice Ginsburg understood sovereignty and safety for Native women is not the result of an excellent legal education. It is the result of our advocacy, our perseverance, and the power of our true stories. If anything, the revolution of her jurisprudence demonstrates our resilience. Rest in power, Justice Ginsburg.

The year 2020 will forever be remembered as the year the promises of the United States were finally held up in the courts. Not that they won't be broken again. They are broken every day in this country. But, for quite possibly the first time in US history, we have a Supreme Court case stating that, under the US Constitution, they shouldn't be.

When we finally reached the Mvskoke Reservation at the end of our road trip, our boys had lots of questions about what it meant that their nation's reservation had been "affirmed" by the Supreme Court.

"Wait, is it new?" our youngest asked.

"No," answered his father. "Our reservation has been in existence since the Treaty of 1866."

"Then why did we need the Supreme Court to tell us that?"

"Because Oklahoma wanted to destroy it. But thankfully, the court wouldn't let them."

THREE

GUITARS, DREAMS, DOGS, AND TEARS

Grieving Hard Histories

Philip J. Deloria

When reality shatters a young person's dreams, there's usually a bystander or two. One of mine was Jerry Jeff Walker, a Texas singer-songwriter who died in October 2020. Jerry Jeff has been wrapped up in my emotional life for almost five decades, and when I heard the news of his death I cradled my guitar tightly, playing his songs and pausing on this verse or that chorus to lament. I was grieving for Jerry Jeff, to be sure, but for more than that: for the pileup of losses that cursed 2020, for the ones yet to come, for the hard histories conjured by all the death and destruction.

A good song has magical powers—a certain line can knock you down and make you cry for no reason. Of course, the reasons are always there, emotions pushed down and waiting to be sprung loose. By the time October 2020 rolled around, a year of pandemic, violence, racial reckoning, brutal repression, and disastrous politics had created an excess of sorrow, pressurized and ready to explode out of a song. My friend Bobby Bridger, an accomplished Austin songwriter and treasured bystander, once set me straight on the song question. "You have to write fifty songs to get a good one," he said. "Catching a truly great one is a matter of luck and good fortune that most don't see."

Jerry Jeff Walker was one of the chosen few, crafting a truly great song early in his career. It crested his wave and gave him a good long ride. Listen to the deftness of the internal rhymes, the ability to humanize a character with a few quick strokes, and the way harmony, melody, and words paint the picture:

> He danced for those in minstrel shows and county fairs, throughout
>   the South
> Spoke with tears of fifteen years, how his dog and him traveled about
> The dog up and died, he up and died
> After twenty years he still grieved

A hit for the Nitty Gritty Dirt Band in 1970, "Mr. Bojangles" has been recorded hundreds of times. I learned the song as a kid in the midseventies and always loved it, in large part because—thanks to its limited range—I could actually sing it. And there is evidence for its greatness: sometimes, even on a good day, when you hit that line about twenty years of grieving for a dog, you can't help but break down yourself. The fifty-year-old song spoke directly to 2020, reminding us that we'll be lamenting this year for another twenty, and more. And so, on an October afternoon in 2020, I played that song and I cried.

* * *

But what was it about Jerry Jeff? After all, during 2020, the world had already lost John Prine, Bill Withers, Little Richard, Charley Pride, Kenny Rogers, Eddie Van Halen, Charlie Daniels, and Helen Reddy, among others. Another Austin legend, Billy Joe Shaver, would sound his last chord only a few days after Walker moved on. Prine, most would insist, was the better songwriter, Little Richard more outrageous, Charley Pride more pathbreaking, Rogers more successful, Daniels more representative. My mom, balancing family and working on a life-changing degree in library science, used to smile quietly and look more determined when "I Am Woman" came on the radio in 1971; I've got a great soft spot in my heart for Helen Reddy. Who didn't adore Bill Withers or watch Van Halen in awe—but Jerry Jeff Walker?

Maybe it was a moment like this: It's the summer of 1975 and I'm sixteen, wide-eyed, and backstage at Red Rocks Amphitheatre in Colorado. Seals and Crofts are on the other side of the stage, and they've laid out a garden of large potted plants and established a laid-back Bahai groove. On our side, Jerry Jeff Walker is lurching around with a large cup, into which various forms of alcohol are being poured. The crowd is filing in, and we're hanging out with the members of the Lost Gonzo Band, Walker's crack backup group, and Bobby Bridger, who has introduced my dad to the Austin music scene. My father, the Dakota intellectual Vine Deloria Jr., is smack in the middle of a writing streak jumpstarted by his 1969 book *Custer Died for Your Sins: An Indian Manifesto.* It's cool to mingle together Texas cosmic cowboys and Indians—everyone agrees on that. It's also true, though, that my dad grew up on midcentury country, with Gene Autry–inflected song-and-guitar dreams of his own. He loves the Red Rocks scene, hobnobbing with half-crazy mountain men and big-time pickers, but he is also here for the music.

Gary P. Nunn, one of the head Gonzos, has a new camera. He leads my dad out to the stage, drapes Jerry Jeff's guitar over my father's shoulder, and lines up a picture. He looks pretty damn comfortable out there, and the image becomes one of my dad's most cherished possessions. After the show, we'll all head back to our house and hang out on the back

*Vine Deloria Jr., early 1950s
(image in author's collection)*

Vine Deloria Jr. at Red Rocks, 1975 photograph by Gary P. Nunn (image in author's collection)

patio most of the night. There will be guitars and songs, beer and pot, a little cocaine. Nothing like this has ever happened to me, and nothing will ever be the same.

Or a moment like this: It's the Kerrville Folk Festival, 1976, and I've gotten on an airplane—flying solo for the first time in my life—to travel to Austin and attend, under the appropriately watchful eye of Bobby Bridger. We camp at the festival and listen to the greats of Texas music. I get tick bites and hang out with the symphonic genius and jazz French horn master David Amram. We stop on the way home in Luckenbach, Texas, meeting Texas fixture Hondo Crouch, who bought the tiny old town in 1971, made it into a rural happening, and himself into a gray-bearded rustic sage. 'Twas holy ground, Luckenbach, the spot where Jerry Jeff and the Gonzos live recorded the legendary album, *Viva Terlingua*, a sonic tapestry of human ambience and occasionally boozy songs. My life, already divided into two parts, widens out a little more. Dreams are awaiting here—and yet there is also Mr.

Bojangles, a broken-down street dancer plagued by drink and jail, his own dream mangled and barely recognizable.

Jerry Jeff always insisted that Mr. Bojangles—a real dancer, encountered (as the song says) in a cell in New Orleans—was white. But you can't hear the name without thinking about Bill "Bojangles" Robinson, the pathbreaking African American performer—the first to reject blackface makeup, to perform solo, to headline Broadway, and to do an interracial dance scene (with Shirley Temple). Robinson had his own dreams too, and they suggested something powerful: the transcendence of a structure of racism and exclusion.

And so, Jerry Jeff's song explodes, not only with literary and personal grief but also with a kind of existential uncanny—with the pain of past confronting present, of Bill Robinson greeting George Floyd, of a permeating structure of anti-Black violence demonstrating the impossibility of Bojanglian racial transcendence. Was Jerry Jeff Walker just a simple man committed to the historical truth of his own experience of a cell in New Orleans? What if that commitment meant denying the larger world of meanings that clung to the name Bojangles, meanings that refused to sit quietly in troubled New Orleans, but instead steamed north up the Mississippi River to Minneapolis, and then spread beyond? A world of meanings and histories that led a white dancer to adopt the nickname of a Black one, a tribute to Bojangles, to be sure, but also yet another species of theft? The defining social triangulation of 2020—George Floyd, Donald Trump, and unevenly distributed pandemic death—made that kind of denial impossible. Any grieving for Jerry Jeff had to be accompanied by a cold-eyed look at the world that made not just his historical subject white, but also whitened the social imaginary conjured around the dancer, the song, and the cell. That imaginary was part of the river of white supremacy conjured by Trump, enacted on Floyd, and visible in the nightly COVID death count.

★ ★ ★

I remember the first time I heard of Jerry Jeff, sometime in 1974, from my guitar pal Dan Schisler. We were in ninth grade, had nailed down most of the chords, and were trying to learn the playable acoustic classics of that era, songs by Cat Stevens, James Taylor, Jackson Browne, America, the Eagles, John Denver. This music was for rangy tenors, though, and we were unrangy baritones with wobbly voices. In genial torment, Dan's brother used to blast at us a song called "Up Against the Wall, Redneck Mother," full of besotted humor, country two-beat, a little genial sloppiness. "Who would ever have a name like 'Jerry Jeff?'" Dan would shout back. "They don't go together. That's the stupidest thing I've ever heard!" And we went back to learning "A Horse with No Name." In the end, though, it was "Up Against the Wall, Redneck Mother"—recorded in Luckenbach—that would win out and become part of a repertoire that moved ever more toward outlaw country rock, just as Jerry Jeff himself was riding high.

Jerry Jeff was born Ronald Clyde Crosby in 1942. He came out of upstate New York, a basketball player, like Dan (who was the tallest kid in our class and graciously carried me through junior high hoops). Unlike either of us, though, Jerry Jeff seemed to have no fear. He went AWOL from the National Guard. Almost on a whim, he took off for Florida with a guitar, learned the art of busking, moved to the clubs, traveled about, found himself in jails and bars, and wrote songs about the life. He passed through the Greenwich Village folk scene, and bounced between bands, collaborations, and solo work. "Mr. Bojangles" set him on his way, and he moved to Austin, becoming a fixture in the "Redneck Rock" world of Willie Nelson, Waylon Jennings, Michael Murphey, Guy Clark, Townes Van Zandt, Ray Wylie Hubbard (who actually wrote "Up Against the Wall, Redneck Mother"), the Threadgills, and so many others.

Walker emerged victorious in a local struggle to sign the Lost Gonzos as his backup band, and together they put together a mid-1970s run of fabulous music, frenetic touring, and successful albums, including *Ridin' High* (1975), *It's a Good Night for Singin'* (1976), and *A Man Must Carry On* (1977). Walker was indeed riding high: wild life, good-time music, drunken fun, and an occasional smashed guitar. That's how it looked to me as a kid, and I think my perception was probably about right. The concerts were unpredictable. The music felt besotted and gloriously loose, though the band quietly kept it tight and focused. I learned a lot of those tunes over the years.

And then came the inevitable crash and the rebuild. Jerry Jeff proved, in the end, to be much more interesting than just another faded figure of seventies excess. He got healthy, became a runner, and established an independent label and management and booking companies with his smart and savvy wife, Susan. They became pioneers in online and social media marketing. He kept recording and performing, on his own terms, one of the surviving sages of the Austin 1970s, until at seventy-eight he booked a gig at that great roadhouse in the sky. I don't hesitate to celebrate his life.

★ ★ ★

But there's also my teenage sense of that world, at least as I remember it today: Austin was a white liberal oasis in a complicated but basically racist Texas starting down the road that would lead the place to COVID denial, antivaxxers, and antidemocratic Trumpism in 2020. Redneck rock was a rebellion against Nashville, which relied on a renarration of southern good old boy tropes that could not escape their casual racism and class politics. The communal bonding of guitars, booze, and song was—for all its joyousness—segregated and white. Even as a talented collection of musical refugees made Texas the antithesis of mainstream country, they reproduced old social structures in new locales like Austin, Kerrville, and Luckenbach.

The participants knew it, but they didn't quite know what to do about it. I look at the cover of *It's a Good Night for Singin'* and am captured by the fun of it all—a bunch of folks closing down a bar, singing songs, and howling at the moon. The challenge is not that it's just all white people; it's the normalizing of that whiteness as it was paired with the utter goodness of collective bonding over song. And while it was cool that my father could quasi-indigenize a Jerry Jeff concert, no one thought to put together Marty Robbins, Spade Cooley, Jesse Ed Davis, Redbone, Jimi Hendrix, Tom Bee, Buffy Sainte-Marie, Robbie Robertson, and even Wayne Newton—among others—and recognize a cohort of Indians bringing my dad's musical dreams to some kind of fruition. Just as "Mr. Bojangles" had traction in a world not entirely friendly to Bill Robinson, Indians occupied the imaginary terrain of Johnny Cash's "Bitter Tears" and Paul Revere and the Raiders' "Indian Reservation," not the real world of guitars and records.

When I played "Mr. Bojangles" after hearing the news about Jerry Jeff, I was lamenting it all: the loss of a person, the failure of music to solve the problems of political collectivity and social hatred, the loss of my own dreams of connecting up songs and people, and the realization of the manifold complicities to be found in my own desires and memories.

★　★　★

If life and dreams fit seamlessly together, each sustaining the other, then death's junior partner might be the broken dream—the busting up of futures, loves, lives, the planet itself. Dreams shatter in different ways. Some break over the short term—a goal unfulfilled. Others take time, producing long lives full of regrets and unrealized possibilities. Too many shatter abruptly, lives ended too soon by a knee or a bullet, or gasping, strung out on a ventilator, or just drunk in a cell in New Orleans. Could it be that the griefs that spring from deathly loss and broken dreams are of a piece, a question not of essence but of scale? Is that why a single line from a song can suddenly transcend its form and magically call up a feeling of world-historical despair? Is that why so many of us burst into tears during 2020, devastated by some particular song that unaccountably captured the fullness of the year's losses, from human lives snuffed out to smaller—but still cherished—dreams broken down by violence, illness, despair? And how weird was it that "Mr. Bojangles"—a tune complicated by the very forces it was prompting me to lament—could be that song?

When I graduated from high school in 1977, I told the student newspaper that my ambition was to move to Austin and try to eke out a musical life. In no way whatsoever was I qualified. I was a mediocre guitar player, a weak singer with limited range and no distinguishing style, and I had written a handful of utterly pedestrian songs. My performance experience was limited, and I lacked the bold fearlessness of someone like Jerry Jeff. I did not follow my Austin dreams. I headed instead to the University of Colorado to play trombone—though I kept my guitar close at hand.

My musical dreams bifurcated. There was intellectual work, centered on the trombone. The figuring out of modal scales, voice-leading harmonies, and intricate musical histories carried over into Bobby Bridger's Alan Lomax–influenced studies of folk music, his love of the Nebraska poet John Neihardt, and his commitment to bringing historical scholarship into his music. Down the other road waited my friends and their guitars—Dan Schisler and his Epiphone, Paul Chan and his Ovation, to say nothing of Frank Okoren and his mandolin and Ben Bowen and Ed Fenner and their banjos—and that was all about fun, emotion, possibility. It was a good night for singing, indeed. There was driving around on warm summer evenings, serenading girls, one of whom I ended up marrying. Such things let me imagine a world beyond 1977, beyond Colorado, a world of *more*—of turning a side yard into a stage, a listener into a love, music into a calling and a vocation.

Jerry Jeff had made the *more* seem possible. If Bobby Bridger's voice (and Jackson Browne's and James Taylor's and everyone else's), was too high, Jerry Jeff's was, if anything, too low—but I could work with that. Jerry Jeff let me sing, as best I could. My voice wasn't much, but it was mine, and I've never let go of that gift. He also had a way of writing simple songs, using only three or four chords, and performing them with an enticing looseness that made you think you might not be all that far off. You looked at the goofy pictures of him, cigarette dangling from his mouth or sitting sheepishly on a horse, and figured that you at least had the musical smarts to keep up with *that* guy. And when you really got into his repertoire, you found—as with all songwriters—that some of the great songs were paired with some not-so-great ones.

And then the dream falls apart. In my case, it was the recognition that talent is an objective reality. It may not be quantifiable, but it is measurable. Jerry Jeff had a full measure, my own was woefully insufficient, and that was just a fact. No matter how much you repeat the mantra of the American dream—working hard and never giving up, and all that—the truth will win out. For me, music could be a hobby at best; a vocation, never. Likewise, no matter how often Americans repeat our other mantras—equality before the law, the content of character rather than the color of skin, honor and decency, liberty and freedom—the real measure of these things, objectively viewed, always comes up lacking. When you're born, we used to be told, the doctor would slap your behind to start you crying, and thus breathing, and thus living and proving your aliveness. But the real slap comes later, for people and for nations, when in a flash you suddenly see yourself as you are: a wannabe musician, a country with a grifter president, a murderous strain of white supremacy, a broken social world, impending end-times for human presence on the planet.

★ ★ ★

Fifty years on, at the very beginning of the COVID-19 pandemic, the Nitty Gritty Dirt Band posted a Facebook memory of their 1970 album *Uncle Charlie and His Dog Teddy*, which reminded me of (Mr.) Bojangles and led me to revisit the racial anxieties of a project that once seemed pure innocence. Their version of Jerry Jeff's song begins with a scratchy interview with "Uncle Charlie," recorded in

1963, that has all the trappings of Alan Lomax or some other folk-lorist recording an old Black blues master. "I was born in Kaufman County, Texas, in 1886," Uncle Charlie says, and then, after some reminiscences, tries to get Teddy the dog to sing along with him: "Chord by this now . . . sing, Teddy, sing!" Cut to a hypercrisp guitar and "Mr. Bojangles" begins, transporting you instantly from associations with Parchman Farm, Angola, Huntsville, and into the new white world of country-bluegrass-Americana rock. The transition echoes Jerry Jeff's sense of things and directly connects the two: Charlie is something like Bojangles; Teddy is something like the dog who up and died. Like Bojangles in a New Orleans cell, Uncle Charlie initially codes as Black, and that Blackness suggests a politics of racial authenticity and cross-racial sympathy. The photos on the album cover—and the folklore surrounding its music and imagery—dashes the possibility. It's not that Uncle Charlie is somehow less valuable, or less authentic—he is said to be a relative of producer Bill McEuen's wife—but that the whole exercise is a species of appropriation, a borrowing not of image or music, necessarily, but of idea and association.

Here's a different appropriation. Out of all the performers who recorded "Mr. Bojangles," the one who made it most decisively his own was the one who knew the reality of Bill "Bojangles" Robinson's song-and-dance dream—Sammy Davis Jr., who very deliberately turned Walker's white Bojangles Black. Abused by the Rat Pack and cursed by his biggest hit, the horrific earworm "The Candy Man," Davis's version of "Bojangles" reveals him as deep, a master stylist aiming to sing that one line (for him too, perhaps, the dog that up and died) that caught his audience by surprise, that moved them to tears, that made them see things they preferred not to see, that called them to grieve the largest things. He transformed Walker's folky lament into a combination of talk-sing storytelling and ultrasmooth vocals, with hat play and dance moves that would later inspire Michael Jackson. Like Walker, though, Davis also denied that he sang the song about

Bill "Bojangles" Robinson. He had larger aspirations. He sang it, he said, for "all the Black hoofers who never made it." He sought to widen the circle: Not just a man and a dog. Not just a life that didn't pan out. Not just the hoofers who didn't reach Bill Robinson's heights. But all those things, and what they said about the hurts and haunts of history. In that sense, the song returns yet again, with a new set of possibilities.

And so, out of all the losses of 2020—five friends, more than a few acquaintances, hundreds of thousands of fellows, the dream of a democratic United States, the possibilities of justice, a future for the planet—it was Jerry Jeff Walker that broke me down and let me grieve for all of it. He died of throat cancer, not COVID-19 and not racial violence. It was a painful sad irony for a songwriter with a rangy voice that savored the low notes. But what mattered—what my tears spoke to—was not the man or the irony. It was the recognition of what the tattered remnants of the pandemic, the election, the violence and killings, the protests, and the repression promised for our collective future: *for twenty years he still grieved.*

FOUR

SOMEWHERE, USA

Robert L. Tsai

S he comes to me in the night, her jeans tucked neatly into her scuffed brown boots. I can hear the soft crunching of the gravel underfoot, though I'm focused elsewhere: her shining green eyes, her red-blond hair waving.[1]

Katie glances over one shoulder, beckoning me to accompany her down a familiar dirt road and into the darkened wood. Her white shirt billows gently in the breeze. She smells faintly of strawberries.

Katie was thirty-five years old when she killed herself. It wasn't hard to spare a bullet in a region full of guns collected for deer hunting and home defense. I didn't know her as an adult. Only as the teenager—frozen in youthful mystery—who visits me from time to time.

I actually saw Katie in the flesh a few years before she ended her life. I had returned home to see my folks and ran into her on a street corner. In the days before social media, that's what you did when you came home: drive around town slowly or visit all the usual haunts by foot, hoping for spontaneous reconnections.

We met up for drinks at a waterfront saloon located in a Victorian building that had once contained a sporting goods store. I used to spend hours there as a kid, mentally laying away fleeces and waterproof boots I wanted to purchase. Now the place was covered in dark wood and lacquer, trying hard to impress out-of-towners, but never quite successful at disguising its sea-shanty feel.

Katie and I had met as school children. As teenagers, we traded winks and nods, and shared furtive kisses under an old blanket. But we had grown apart, tugged in opposing directions by the swirling waters of public education that sent strivers in one direction and others content to float in another, until it became undeniable that we shared little in common when we would bump into each other at bonfires. She had discovered a group of teenagers who accepted her without reservation and cherished having a good time over collecting resume-stuffing experiences. I, on the other hand, figured out that my ticket out of town depended on collecting good grades and marketing myself as one of the town's finest exports.

Seated together at a small table, we now caught up. I summed up college in a few bland stories and made sure to brag about the interesting classes taught by renowned professors.

The rain began to fall softly, tap-tapping on the window.

Katie regaled me with the tale of her marriage, which had gone zero to a hundred, from delirious infatuation to suffocating responsibility. She pulled out pictures of her two kids, a boy and girl. Unmarried and without children of my own, I smiled and mouthed, "They're beautiful. You must be so happy."

Outside, the seagulls shrieked.

Katie had finished high school just as her family expected but no further. She described her daily routine, which was dominated by going to work every day at a clerical job she despised. My mind wandered.

During our conversation, I sensed she was probing for a way out.

I didn't offer one. Instead, I excused myself, fetched us more drinks.

That night, I dropped her off early, not realizing it would be the last time I would ever lay eyes on her. I sped away from her house, though in truth I had already left years ago.

★ ★ ★

What ties a person down to a place? I turned this question over in my mind as I sat outside a coffee shop overlooking the waterfront. More than a decade had elapsed since Katie's passing. I had come home again to check on relatives, as sickness and deaths from the novel coronavirus piled up. With elderly parents, it was too risky to be in the same room, so I settled for being nearby.

Fog hovered over the brackish water that gently lapped the pebbled beach below. I glanced up when a familiar horn broke the morning stillness to announce the arrival of the ferry, painted white and green and black. Snowy cliffs hugged the skyline.

When a gull called out—once, twice—other gulls answered.

There was more than one gas station in town, three in fact, but little industry to speak of. The largest employer was the paper mill. Built in 1927 by a San Francisco conglomerate, the mill had jumpstarted a town whose heart had stopped beating, drawing thousands of people to work in construction and supply companies like a sudden rush of blood. A generation before that, the economic downturn of the 1890s had led to an exodus of inhabitants who left doors swinging on their hinges as they abandoned their homes and businesses.[2]

A few of my friends had worked at the mill gratefully during the summers, and then they glumly took up permanent positions after graduation, when other kinds of steady, honest work became hard to come by. Toiling for long hours, laborers operated gigantic machines that cut, sorted, and pulped the trees that had been chopped down elsewhere. Inside the mill, steam and sweat filled the air as wood chips were turned into giant sheets of paper.

You could spy the mill on the hill that overlooked the bay from different vantage points around town. It was the community's heart and soul, though you'd never know it by how hard people pretended that it didn't exist. Day or night, plumes of smoke curled skyward—the only thing that changed was the color, from

gray-blue to purple to crimson-orange. As you passed it on the
way in or out of town, the mill would announce its rancid presence
by itching your nose hairs and clinging to your coat.

To keep the mill going 24-7, workers built a new water system
to bring fresh water from nearly thirty miles away. Before that
innovation, settlers had to catch rainwater or rely on wells. The
problem wasn't just insufficient clean water to support a thriv-
ing community; the quality of the water was also so poor that
it rusted pipes, caused appendicitis, and drove people to turn to
harder stuff.

In town, people who no longer fit in anywhere else mingled
freely with people who ached to escape. There was roughly an
equal proportion of hippies, yuppies, and yokels, but the hippies
and the yuppies long ago brokered a truce and now ran the place
together.

Nothing brought the denizens closer than a common enemy.
Word that a multinational corporation wanted to establish a chain
store or fast-food restaurant inevitably inspired various factions
in the community to show up in force and unleash a deluge of
concerns. In turn, officials would weigh down development plans
with so many permit conditions that most of the time corporate
leaders abandoned their plans and selected a different city in
which to expand.

On every crisp Friday evening in the fall, residents would
assemble and cheer on the high school football team. Its name
alluded to the Indian nations forcibly relocated to tiny plots of
land, something that happened so long ago that most people
didn't bother to remember. A few townspeople were mortified that
a mostly white population chose to honor once proud and sov-
ereign peoples, who roamed the region freely, through displays
of athletic prowess. Most folks barely gave any of this a passing
thought, whooping and hollering as they had always done.

The achievements of the town's children were tallied, ranked,
and broadcast across the land by adults. Gridiron conquests and

heartbreaking defeats survived long afterward in the breathless chitchat of parents and boosters. There was always next year.

Developers razed inexpensive homes and replaced them with ever-fancier structures that could be presented to urbanites seeking a tiny slice of fantasy, pricing families who had lived there for generations out of the housing market, because the basic structure of the economy never changed. The jobs never got much better or the wages much higher.

Historical preservation and the encouragement of tourism served as the twin pillars of economic gospel. City leaders, working hand in glove with the chamber of commerce, dreamed up festivals, enticing travelers to marvel at the town's charms. There was the "Great Boatbuilding Festival," "Jazz Weekend," the weeklong "Historic Homes Tour"—and other events I've forgotten. Tourist dollars were gratefully accepted, like donations to a collection plate that kept the faith in local prosperity going.

Grumbling broke out among the locals each season as a festival neared. A few partook of the festivities, but the rest stayed hidden as outsiders infiltrated their cafés and stores. But all understood that ritualized consumerism was the price of progress.

Those who stayed put said they had fallen in love with the town or partied too hard. Both choices led to the same destination. The first represented the absence of imagination; the second, its withering. It always seemed unfathomable to me that a single place could capture the full scale of one's dreams. For me, the only way to truly live was to leave.

* * *

As I thumbed through the newspaper laying on the table next to me, I reflected on the human and economic wreckage of COVID-19 since late 2020. Day after day, the coverage of mass suffering revealed cleavages in age, income, and race. But the attention was also relentless, full of sorrowful detail, dripping with moral outrage. I couldn't help but think about the kinds of death that got less attention. I was curious how people would react once their callousness toward less visible forms of suffering was revealed. Will the response be to do better? Or will we try to justify a concern for some but not for others?

I stopped at a fascinating science story. Apparently, researchers had discovered that a small temperature rise was causing behavioral changes among the wildlife in the region. Seagulls were resorting to eating their young. Scientists called this "egg cannibalism," but every so often a gull could be spotted swallowing another gull's chick whole.[3]

Rising sea temperatures were causing tufted puffins to spend so much time hunting for food that they were starting to abandon their nests from exhaustion. Fatigue also meant the puffins were not incubating their eggs. Changes to the environment, in other words, were causing shifts in animal behavior. In adapting to their context, some were turning on their own species. Others were spending so much time on short-term survival that their actions threatened the community's future.

I wondered: did the birds even notice the changes to their world or were the changes to their environment so gradual as to be imperceptible? And why did some birds prey on the weak, while others embraced solidarity to confront an existential threat?

* * *

It was always easier for me to shake free from the invisible shackles of the town. After all, my family had immigrated from Taiwan and had wound up in Port Somewhere out of serendipity. A restless precarity pervaded our days no matter where we laid our heads at night. You had to be ready to go wherever work could be found.

My father, who gave up a secure position as a judge to pursue opportunities in a strange land, had to acquire new survival skills when he arrived in America. Restarting a legal career from scratch proved to be too much, so he put away his past life like a childish thing. In the big city, he landed a job working in a hotel kitchen.

A friendly Black chef taught my dad how to make a few American dishes: nothing special, but tasty and reliable. From that point on, until the day he retired, my father was known as Joe the Cook.

One day, my parents noticed a newspaper ad announcing a small café for sale in Port Somewhere. After a few phone calls and a pleasant ferry ride, a deal was struck with the owners. My parents had saved just enough to make a down payment on the place. We packed our bags and set off on our next adventure.

My mother, a middle-school dropout, had been taught to cook by her parents. During the day, the café would serve American fare; at night, a few Chinese dishes appeared on the menu. Mom could also sew and make clothes. My mom outfitted my sister and me in the colorful garments she had constructed or the gently used items she discovered in a thrift store. When the restaurant did better, clothes came from the mall, an hour's drive away.

This immigrant experience made my identity pliable, my childhood a paradox: most of the time, I longed to be accepted by others; and yet, I didn't plan on spending the rest of my life there, so why did it matter whether I fit in?

One of my worst acts of self-abnegation involved wearing yellowface during a school play. I had gotten a bit role in the musical and decided to turn the part into something memorable. I put on a fake Asian accent and spoke my lines in broken English for cheap laughs. The director clapped and said it was brilliant.

I'll never forget the night my parents attended the performance. When I shuffled out, the lights were so bright I could barely recognize anyone. I noticed only white faces given up to ecstasy as the packed auditorium roared its approval. My mom and dad didn't know what to make of it all but chuckled as if they were in on the joke.

No one asked me to do what I did. I chose to turn that role into an act of minstrelsy all on my own. I came to hate the pathetic part of me that was so desperate for approval. When I would later dream of that moment, things would unfold in slow motion, except I am watching my younger self while seated in the crowd, enveloped by humiliating laughter. I do not laugh along.

Members of the audience toss gold coins at my sneakered feet. I see myself bend down and scoop up the coins, but they turn out to be arcade tokens. The spell is broken.

As I got older, it dawned on me that in order to make it elsewhere, I would have to kill this part of myself. The innocent, obsequious self would have to be throttled, so that a wiser version might have a chance to live.

★ ★ ★

The story of the founding of our adopted hometown seemed like a giant cosmic joke. A handful of eager white settlers raced ahead of the pack and built cabins along the water in the early nineteenth century, praying that the spot would become a major territorial seaport. If it did, and Congress converted the territory into a state, their improvements of the land would pay off handsomely.

But things didn't quite work out that way.

What the settlers underestimated were capitalism and inertia. As a result, the railroad tracks, laid down at an overly plodding pace by Chinese migrants working alongside white laborers, took too long to reach the tiny civilization founded among the Douglas firs and maple trees. The tracks headed to where rich people lived, and the town's inhabitants were assuredly not rich people.

In 1857, the state legislature incorporated the Northern Pacific Railroad but raised no capital. The more populous communities took the lead and built railways connecting themselves to other large communities, mostly out of private resources.[4]

Every time the residents of Port Somewhere felt their hopes raised that the next round of construction would integrate their town with the rest of the world, those aspirations would be dashed by bankruptcy or plans torn up in a corporate boardroom. Economic investments by the townsfolk in anticipation of a boom would be lost each time. During this period of its history, as isolation was being imprinted upon the DNA of the place, the town died many times over.

In March of 1889, all the townsfolk gathered in an enormous display of civic pride as work began on their own railhead. The people had crowdfunded the project, each donation signifying a tiny down payment on the future. But money and excitement petered out after a single mile of track was laid. The severe nationwide depression during this period soon took its toll, as the town's population, roughly seven thousand people, plummeted to two thousand.

Efforts to attract the attention of investors would continue, and even result in the incorporation of a local railroad company, but the town was not connected by train to the rest of the nation until 1916. By then, white residents had no more use for cheap Chinese labor, and though some of these migrants had also become enamored with the place, they were told that they must go.[5]

When war came at last and claimed a family's firstborn son as tribute, or disease threatened to decimate the population, genuine bursts of communal feeling would fill the air. But the fanfare with which lives were noted was not universal. Some deaths—of those deemed less worthy—barely registered.

Why such secrecy about the unfortunate? The thought of people struggling to keep their heads above water disrupted the local narrative of unspoiled contentment. Port Somewhere was proudly billed "The City of Dreams," not a place where dreams came to die. When every life became refracted through the prism of progress and achievement, there could be no such thing as undeserved misfortune. Unhappiness had to be banished.

During the summers, I volunteered at the county courthouse. One day, I recognized someone from high school. Bobby was in court that morning because he had violated a condition of probation and had to stand and face the judge for his punishment all over again. The original charge was possession with intent to distribute. His head was bowed. I looked away, avoiding eye contact.

Gathering some papers, I hastily departed before the judge pronounced his sentence.

Was I embarrassed on his behalf or mine? Did it make me uncomfortable to watch someone I had grown up with being judged by the law, or did it feel like I, too, was being judged?

I had experienced my own brush with the law as a teenager. When I was about fourteen, a few friends and I had the bright idea to drink some beers in the woods behind the elementary school.

We ran screaming through the trees to let off steam. The next thing we knew, cops were chasing us through the brush, gathering empties as evidence. The police didn't have much to do in town, but they sure cracked down on underage drinking.

I was lucky, maybe luckier than I deserved. In those days, a first-time offense for minor in possession still led to diversion. A genuine show of contrition landed me community service.

After being mortified at having to ride in the back of a patrol car with its red lights flashing and then judged by adults known to my parents, I was scared straight. Picking through stinking trash and wet recyclables cemented the lesson.

I've often thought back to that time and wondered how life might have turned out differently for me. Since my parents were out of town, what if I had to spend the weekend in a juvenile detention center instead of being released to a friend's father? What if the charges had been more serious? What if it had been my second infraction?

I never bothered to learn what sentence Bobby received. Years later, I heard that he wrapped his car around a telephone pole on the highway on the outskirts of town. One night, he had too much to drink. His car veered across the median, struck another vehicle, and flipped over. The four passengers in the oncoming car suffered chest injuries but miraculously survived.

Bobby wasn't so lucky. He was pronounced dead at the scene, age thirty-five. His dog, thrown clear from the car, hadn't been lucky, either.

Bobby's fateful drive was part of a three-month spike in car crashes in the county: nine of the fifteen traffic fatalities involved drinking and driving. Police officers expressed disbelief at the sudden string of misfortunes but offered no explanations. They shrugged and chalked it up to God's infinite wisdom.

For weeks I was haunted by the image of Bobby's poor dog, flying through the air.

★ ★ ★

Every kid in Port Somewhere partied. The only meaningful distinction we could discern was between those who partied and those who partied harder. Not just blowing off steam on the weekends with a few beers or a fifth of vodka, but using a broader range of drugs: marijuana, acid, heroin, meth. Some of the kids you partied with eventually became adults who partied—sometimes with other people's kids.

Now, putting it *that* way made it sound like everything hinged on the individual choices a person made, good or bad. Even the language of "partying" obscured the differences between celebrating joyous moments and gathering in rote fashion to dull the pain.

But what if the town's entire economic and social structure created haves and have-nots that folks refused to acknowledge, leading to an increasingly stifling range of choices for some residents? If being an adult was nothing more than a high-stakes version of the games we played as children, then there would finally be consequences as winners were sorted decisively from the losers.

For meritocracy's losers, it meant trying to reconcile themselves to their lot in life: bouncing from one low-wage job to the next, with little prospect of a meaningful rise in income or improvement in material well-being. In town, that meant the kids who didn't go off to college and had no access to capital to start a business felt like failures. Their struggles to pay their bills seemed to be proof of a painful social judgment. For the winners, it meant cobbling together a comfortable lifestyle that reinforced their triumphant sense, however flawed, that personal achievement led to deserved social status for the winners.[6]

At some point, winners just stopped partying with losers.

Once you'd lost your sense of place in the community, the only option left was exit. That exit could come by leaving the only home you'd ever known and starting over. Or, when daily existence became intolerable, but you had no better prospects elsewhere, exit could come by finding little ways to check out. Partying every weekend, as Bobby did, suddenly took on a whole different meaning.

Then there was Lorraine, who had been partying harder and longer than anyone else I knew. We'd catch her at reunions wasted, slurring her speech as she struggled to remember people's names.

Lorraine got married after high school and took over the house in which her mother had raised her. But relations became unbearable between husband and wife. Their split was ugly. The two fought over everything from the run-down Pontiac Grand Prix to the chainsaw. Compounding Lorraine's humiliation, a judge awarded her childhood home to her former husband, as she was unable to pay the mortgage.

Enraged as the day approached to turn over possession of the house, Lorraine set about making the place uninhabitable. She tore every door from its hinges. Lorraine got rid of all the appliances. She cut a giant hole in the wall of her bedroom to remove a beloved mural.

After ripping up the carpet, she smashed in three windows. And then, for the coup de grâce, she spray painted a giant penis on the bathroom wall in gold paint and left her husband a message: "If this were U cockroach."

"This house is mine," she explained to the sheriff's deputies who showed up. "I've lived in it all my life."

Lorraine's revolt against her circumstances led to a conviction for third-degree theft. She spent ten days in jail and faced two years of probation. Worse, she was branded a "domestic violence perpetrator," had a no-contact order entered against her, and was forced to undergo counseling.

The bad news continued to pile up. Lorraine got word that a close friend who struggled with a drug addiction had hanged himself in the county jail. Then, last year, Lorraine was diagnosed with a virulent form of cancer. A few months later, as her friends struggled to process the devastating news of her condition, she perished in a single-car accident. While driving on a lonely stretch of highway, she had a heart attack. Her car slid off the road and came to rest in a giant brush.

Lorraine was found still wearing her seatbelt. She was forty-nine.

What linked these seemingly disparate endings was more than just that infernal, glorious place. It was also a shared experience that, unless somehow interrupted by drastic policies or personal choices, often led to what researchers Anne Case and Angus Deaton call "deaths of despair." Case and Deaton observed that for the last several decades, the rates of suicide and deaths by drug overdose or alcohol poisoning have been rising dramatically among white Americans without a college degree. Their point isn't that a secondary education guarantees a golden ticket to wealth or fame; rather, it has simply become a marker for a widening gap in wages, opportunities, and quality of life for those left behind by the country's prevailing economic order.

Only years later did I realize that my classmates' lives ended in tragic ways that were entirely foreseeable.

* * *

On my way out of town, I visited Katie's grave in Greenwood Cemetery, located one town over. The cemetery was established in 1892 after a few residents donated land and $750. Before that, the dead were scattered by the living in different places, including "dead man's gulch."

Thousands of miles away from us, the seventh hour burned and the world inclined toward shadow. As the light began to fade, my eyes turned again to Katie.

I found a modest memorial. Next to her name, a small inscription read, "If Tears Could Build a Stairway, And Memories a Lane, I'd Walk Right Up to Heaven, and Bring You Home Again."

Why did you feel so hopeless, I wondered? Did other people's memories feel unbearable? Or had your own expectations become too light?

The pine trees swayed as the winds began to gust. Gray clouds rolled by, promising rain.

I hopped back into my rental car. Flipped on the radio.

"Will you still love me for the rest of my life?" Jason Scheff wailed plaintively from the speakers. "'Cause I can't go on."

"No, I can't go on,"

"I can't go on, if I'm on my own."

I floored the gas pedal and disappeared into the cool night.

PART II

MASS DEATH AND WHITE SUPREMACY

The Civil War and Civil Rights

Insurrectionist carries a Confederate battle flag inside the US Capitol on January 6, 2021. Photo © Saul Loeb via Getty Images.

FIVE

CONFEDERATES TAKE THE CAPITOL

Stephen Berry

I am a white male Civil War historian of a "certain age" reared and raised in the American South. Like many of my ilk, I began my life as a well-intentioned white-boy who, at a pre-ternatural age, managed with misguided pride to memorize the back-of-the-baseball card version of a war. I knew how many died on which side at Shiloh, on which day, in which copse of trees. I could recite with indecent precision which regiments suffered what losses on which day at Gettysburg. I knew that slavery caused the war, but I managed not to focus on that fact. I was too focused on war as a man's calling. *Red Dawn* made me want to piss into a radiator. *Rambo II* sent me to a local knife and gun shop where—not yet old enough to drive and too young to buy anything—I childishly cut my thumb and manfully bled all over the store. God help me, I collected Desert Storm trading cards.

Gradually and by degrees, I became a student not just of the Civil War but also of war itself. I should have learned lessons from teachers who were still teaching Americanism vs. communism. I later learned them from W. E. B. Du Bois's *The Souls of Black Folk* and *Black Reconstruction*.[1]

Like anyone's, my perspective comes from a particular place, and I own it from the outset. I was, born and raised, a Florida boy—a "Florida man" in training. Sandspurs, bull thorns, and cockroaches were once my great nemeses; Slurpees, disc golf, and flippy-shoes were once my great compensations. Coming of age in South Florida public schools, all of my early friends were Black, but I didn't see it that way. We were just kids cutting up and playing kickball on scorched sand, avoiding like the plague the playground "tower" where a thirteen-year-old had supposedly hanged himself. We knew that race was a thing, but racism belonged to the adult world, looming on the horizon like puberty or lost innocence. Racially we existed "before the Fall." I was called a "cracker" a hundred times before I realized it was an insult because it had always been meant fondly.[2]

And then, in that way particular to the South, we were pulled apart. I didn't have the words for it then—self-segregation, peer pressure, cliques, structural racism, social sorting. All I knew was that something profoundly sad was happening. I saw my friends as across a great divide, tethered to me still by a solid silver cord. "The South" would never be my friend because it had never been a friend to my friends. Whatever we once were, we shared a common enemy—the same white kids who called them racist names and kicked me in the kneepit when I was playing *Defender* at the arcade just because I was a "long hair."

I remember especially the long days on "safety patrol," spending time directing younger kids across the crosswalk after school. I remember we were charged with bringing the school's flag down every day. I remember standing at attention as someone burst upon the flag ceremony to shoot us with a squirt gun full of what turned out to be piss. I remember learning that the "shooter" was one of my best Black friends. I remember feeling wretched to learn that he was paddled, as the saying went then. Paddling, I should say, was something we all accepted, even venerated, as a school tradition. My fourth-grade teacher had a paddle with its name

burned lovingly into the wood—Old No. 47—supposedly because forty-six paddles had been broken on the asses of forty-six
unfortunate children. And did we complain? Worse. We built him
Old No. 48 in wood shop with holes in it to be more aerodynam-
ically designed. So did I care that my best friend had effectively
pissed on me in that flag ceremony? Honestly, I was proud of him.
Someone had to strike a blow. I was just sorry it wasn't me, and I
was sorry he was paddled.

I say all this as a way of explaining how convoluted it was to
grow up a nascent Black ally in the South before such language
was known. I hope it explains in some small way why it broke my
heart to see a Confederate flag flying inside the Capitol on January
6, 2021. As a child, I had always believed that there was some far
off somewhere where things were different, where I hadn't lost
my Black friends, where I hadn't needed to be pissed on, where
I hadn't been so weak. Instead, forty years later, I watched on
television as the all-too-familiar banner of my childhood wafted
freely through Statuary Hall. Kevin Seefried, the man holding the
flag, was gleeful and paunchy—receding hairline, baggy clothes,
bad beard, bad boots—and I instantly knew him, not literally but
autobiographically. "Our look was as if two . . . deadly enemies,"
said Annie Dillard in a far different context, "met unexpectedly on
an overgrown path when each had been thinking of something
else: a clearing blow to the gut."[3]

Instantly iconic, the image of Seefried's flag captures the whole
of the day, the whole of American history, in a single tableau.
Seefried is frozen in place between the portraits of South Carolina senator John C. Calhoun and Massachusetts senator Charles
Sumner. Calhoun had pioneered the "positive good" defense of
slavery, claiming "there never has yet existed a wealthy and civi-
lised society in which one portion of the community did not . . .
live on the labour of the other." To Calhoun it was obviously better
for the permanent laborers to be Black, and Northerners' failure
to recognize this was a sign of their depravity and unwillingness

to compromise. "It is easy to see the end," Calhoun said in 1837. "By the necessary course of events . . . we must become, finally, two peoples."[4]

Sumner adhered to a different philosophy. "We are one people," Sumner said, "under one sovereignty, vitalized and elevated by a dedication to Human Rights." For Sumner, the United States was not just a country but an idea. "Here [is] a new Nation," he said, "with new promises and covenants, such as had never been made before. . . . The rights which it promise[s] [are] the equal rights of all; not the rights of Englishmen, but the rights of man. [And] on this account our Nation [will become] a source of light to the world."[5]

Growing up on scorched sand in segregated Florida, I believed in Sumner long before I had heard of him, long before I could express in words so pretty the world he believed in. But the whole of my childhood came home to me when I saw *that flag* in *that space*. I became vertiginously ill. *My* citadel had fallen: The House I had counted on; the House where things were different; the House where Abraham Lincoln had taken a stand against the Mexican-American War in the 1840s; the House that had passed the Civil Rights Act and the Voting Rights Act in the 1960s. My old nemeses had literally taken a shit on all of it, smearing excrement on the walls, snapping triumphant selfies, banging on doors in a futile search for the highest-ranking woman in the United States: "Bring Nancy Pelosi out here now. We want to hang that fucking bitch."[6]

Staring at the television, my mind somehow recurred simultaneously to childhood and to 9/11 in a familiar sense of revulsion, violation, and impotent rage. History wobbled on its axis, and all that I cared about, all that I believed in, died just a little.

* * *

The Civil War was inaugurated, basically, because one side refused to recognize the legitimacy of an election. For decades, the "slave power" had been the masters of minority rule, but with the ascension of Abraham Lincoln to the presidency, first seven, then eleven, Southern states took their ball and went home—pulling out of the Union to form the Confederacy. By 1864 the Confederacy was teetering toward defeat, and the Confederate general Robert E. Lee decided the only thing that could save the day was an invasion of Washington, DC. He gave the assignment to General Jubal Early, affectionately known by his troops as "Old Jubilee" but known to Lee as the "Bad Old Man." Early had made his bones in the Gettysburg campaign. Marching north, he had levied $220,000 from the cities of Hagerstown and Frederick; when Chambersburg had refused to pay a half-million-dollar ransom, he had burned it to the ground. (He had also burned the house of the postmaster general.) Early's 1864 invasion of Washington (narrowly) failed. On July 11, 1864, a hastily mobilized force of government clerks, raw militia, and convalescing veterans held his invasion at bay.[7]

What Jubal Early only dreamed of doing, Kevin Seefried and his accomplices carried out in an afternoon. In the ultimate example of white male privilege, goobers were allowed to o'erstorm our ramparts, meeting a federal response at once individually heroic and collectively pathetic. We don't even need to speculate what would have happened if the Capitol had been overrun by Black Lives Matter protesters; we already know. Trump had already given the order: "Just shoot them," he said of the peaceful protesters exercising their First Amendment rights in the wake of George Floyd's murder, or at least "beat the fuck out" of them.[8]

* * *

The day before the assault on the Capitol, January 5, Kevin Seefried had pulled down the oversized Confederate flag from the front porch of his Laurel, Delaware, home, in a county that is 40 percent Black. He and his son clambered into their car for a gleeful road trip to Washington to hear their leader speak:

Trump: "All of us here today do not want to see our election victory stolen by emboldened radical-left Democrats. . . . We will never give up, we will never concede. . . . Our country has had enough. We will not take it anymore and that's what this is all about."

Audience: "Fight for Trump! Fight for Trump!"

Trump: "We will not let them silence your voices. We're not going to let it happen, I'm not going to let it happen."

Audience: "Fight for Trump! Fight for Trump!"

Trump: "We're gathered together in the heart of our nation's capital for one very, very basic and simple reason. . . . Republicans are constantly fighting like a boxer with his hands tied behind his back. . . . We want to be so nice. We want to be so respectful of everybody, including bad people. [But] we're going to have to fight much harder. . . . Anyone you want . . . but I think right [now], we're going to walk down to the Capitol. . . . Because you'll never take back our country with weakness. . . . The radical left knows exactly what they're doing. They're ruthless and it's time that somebody did something about it. . . . So today . . . we fight. We fight like hell. And if you don't fight like hell, you're not going to have a country anymore."[9]

We all know what happened after they broke through the windows: Hunter Seefried with his fist, punching a hole in democracy, others with two-by-fours and flagpoles. Chanting "Whose House? Our House!" they and their ilk desecrated halls formerly walked by John Adams and Abraham Lincoln, looking for someone to hang from the Home Depot gallows they had constructed on the Capitol grounds.

Yes, a lot of them were "tailgaters of treason" engaged in a "Beer Pong Putsch." But this *entirely* misses the point: Virtually every unmitigated disaster that has ever befallen the United States has been facilitated by clueless chuckleheads.

Take the crack squad of turtleneck nihilists who inaugurated World War I, resulting in forty million deaths worldwide. With

five of them strung out along the route of Franz Ferdinand's motorcade, the first would-be assassin lost his nerve and watched the
car go by. The second also lost his nerve and watched the car go
by. The third misthrew his grenade, bouncing it off the trunk and
watching glumly as it exploded ten seconds later because he'd also
missed the timer. He then swallowed an (expired) cyanide capsule
and tried to drown himself in a river that was four inches deep.

The sole successful assassin, Gavrilo Princip, was more lucky
than skilled. The archduke's motorcade took a wrong turn and
stalled right in front of him. Standing on the running board of an
open-topped car, he managed to hit Franz Ferdinand but somehow missed his second target, the governor of Bosnia, and instead
shot Ferdinand's wife through the bowel. Princip then turned his
gun on himself but failed to get a shot off. (In prison, he also failed
to hang himself with a towel.)

There is nothing funny about any of this, but there is certainly
something farcical. Throughout history, devastating events have
been augured by, even triggered by, total imbeciles. The doofuses
who caned Charles Sumner on the floor of the Senate in 1856
were the Matt Gaetz and Jim Jordan of their age. Preston Brooks,
the man who lashed Sumner until he "bellowed like a calf," was
described by his own friends as "a mal-apropos young man of
little talent, fidgety to be doing . . . always moving in the wrong
time and place." Laurence Keitt, the megalomaniac who massaged
Brooks's shoulders and egged him on, was described, again by
friends, as likely "to founder his [canoe] in *smooth* waters." And
yet Mary Chesnut, the great diarist of the Lost Cause, understood
perfectly that these two goobers had helped precipitate a war that
cost the lives of 750,000 men and consigned her husband to the
porch where he nightly drank himself into a gray haze. "What
an awful blunder that Preston Brooks business was!" she wrote
in her diary.[10]

* * *

Students of history and politics make two fundamental miscalculations in their theory of political change. First, they assume that a majority of people act in their material self-interest. Especially in the American context, they don't. They act in their cultural self-interest. Any government program that benefits everyone (whether Obamacare, mask mandates, or vaccines) benefits outgroups relatively more, and America's traditionally dominant class (white male Christians and their allies) like winning less than they like watching other people lose. They're not actually cynical about government; they know it works, but they want it to work for them particularly, perhaps exclusively, as it usually has, or they want it not to work at all. And they're not actually wrong—the government programs envisioned by today's Democrats are precisely calibrated to benefit everyone while also closing gaps in achievement, performance, and wealth, especially along racial lines, which is precisely what many Republicans seek to resist. This is what Thomas Frank gets profoundly wrong in asking *What's the Matter with Kansas?* There is nothing the matter with Kansas if we assume that they—the majority of white Kansans—vote to protect their relative cultural status.[11]

The second wrong-headed assumption historians (and the general public) make is more subtle but more germane to the grave threat posed by chuckleheads: They tend to focus on *why* things happen when they should focus on *how*. Darwin got one thing wrong; evolution, like history, does not proceed gradually. Both proceed in punctuated equilibria—periods of stasis shattered by sudden periods of change.

Our politics has always been a contingent stew of fantasy, apocalyptic vision, and political grandstanding, but in periods of political plasticity the Overton window can shift dramatically. Sometimes this rare elasticity works to the benefit of humankind: "It is extraordinary how completely the idea of *gradual* emancipation has been dissipated from the public mind everywhere, by the progress of events," marveled the *New York Times* in 1864. "Before the rebellion, it was accounted the very extreme of Anti-Slavery fanaticism to believe in the possibility of immediate emancipation without social ruin. . . . But all these gradual methods are now hardly more thought of than if they had been obsolete a century." Sometimes the elasticity works to our collective detriment, as in the case of secession and World War I, when chuckleheads run amok met the event horizon of a historical inflection point and set everything (awful) in motion.[12]

Kevin Seefried unfurled his banner in *my* House to declare his "freedom." But as a Florida boy, I know these crackers in my nose. At the base of most contemporary American conspiracy theories is a white male sexual fantasy that indulges the feeling of being aggrieved, abused, dominated, or violated, precisely to justify the legitimacy of the ensuing white male vengeance and demonstration of power and control. Nothing tastes better in the white male mouth than indignation—not a job and not a paycheck. The historian Gordon Fraser calls it the "libidinal pleasures of paranoia" and traces the impulse from the "Illuminati Crisis" in 1798 to Pizzagate in 2016.[13]

Even as Mitt Romney skedaddled away from potential hanging or hostage taking, the federal women in the building knew the stakes. "I didn't think that I was just going to be killed," said New York representative Alexandria Ocasio-Cortez. "I thought other things were going to happen to me as well." Ocasio-Cortez didn't choose that moment to admit to the whole world that she is an assault survivor. The moment chose her because she's an honest person and the body keeps the score. "Indelible in the hippocampus is the laughter," Professor Christine Blasey Ford said in September 2018 to the United States Senate Judiciary Committee in response to Senator's Patrick Leahy's question of what she remembered most from her summer of 1982 assault as a high schooler in Bethesda, Maryland. She was in a formal hearing about Brett Kavanaugh, Donald J. Trump's Supreme Court nominee. "The uproarious laughter between the two [Kavanaugh and his friend,

Mark Judge], and they're having fun at my expense. I was underneath one of them, while the two laughed. Two friends having a
really good time with one another,"[14] she responded.

Kevin and Hunter Seefried, along with the rest of the rioters,
had a really good time on January 6. "I didn't know something
could be so terrifying and embarrassing at the same time," tweeted
the comedian Jess Dweck. The riot may have been a saturnalia
of stupid, but we need to take it seriously. There is abroad in the
land an entitled minority, marinating in grievance, convinced that
something is being stolen from them. What is being "stolen"—an
election, a "way of life," a "birthright," a "Lost Cause," Christmas,
Mr. Potato Head, Dr. Seuss—doesn't matter. Always it is a defensive white male fantasy, based on insecurity, helplessness, and rage.

And yet there is exactly one relief from the events of the Trump
years: we get to meet our old enemy on an open field. Today 66
percent of southern Republicans support seceding from the Union.
As a Civil War historian, my reaction is as simple as it is unprofes-
sional: Are you fucking kidding me? Are we really going to do this
again? Yes, we're going to do this again and, if we have to, again
and again, because "the destiny of the colored American . . . is the
destiny of America," said Frederick Douglass. Can a multiracial,
multiethnic democracy actually work? As Americans, it is our task
to figure this out. America isn't a country; it's an idea. And when
the idea dies, we all die with it.

★ ★ ★

Lincoln's 1838 Lyceum Address is remembered most and best as
a premonition of the Civil War. "If destruction be our lot," he
famously warned, "we must ourselves be its author and finisher."
What always gets forgotten is that Lincoln was *not* predicting
America's descent into a war over slavery; he was predicting America's descent into fascism.[15]

In the speech, Lincoln returned time and again to the fear that
the loosed passions and petty grievances of America's multitude

of (white male) morons might be weaponized by an unscrupulous con man, calling them to a crusade against the "others" in their midst. "Is it unreasonable, then," he asked, "to expect that some man possessed of the [craftiest] genius, coupled with ambition sufficient to push it to its utmost stretch, will at some time spring up among us? And when such a one does, it will require the people to be united with each other, attached to the government and laws, and generally intelligent, to successfully frustrate his designs. Distinction will be his paramount object, and although he would as willingly . . . acquire it by doing good as harm, yet, that opportunity being past, and nothing left to be done in the way of building up, he [will] set boldly to the task of pulling [us] down."[16]

Rereading these words in the era of Trump and Trumpism, I have come to realize that Lincoln had impossibly predicted the "reality war" in which we currently find ourselves. Lincoln may have devoted his personal life to the pursuit of self-education, but he spent his political career wrestling with his fellow (white) Americans' arrogance, ignorance, and roll-your-own reality approach to argument, which he knew all too well growing up in rural white poverty amid the self-appointed pontificators of the plains. When it comes to virtually every dimension of historical causality, we need to remember deeply what Lincoln very clearly understood—that a small but significant percentage of Americans are and have always been thoroughgoing assholes: small, scared, selfish, sadistic, ignorant, and mean.

These white Americans are driven most by a desire to deny the "undeserving" and protect what is "theirs." "I hope I am over wary," Lincoln mused in his Lyceum Address, but "there is, even now, something of ill-omen amongst us. I mean the . . . growing disposition to substitute the wild and furious passions in lieu of sober judgment."[17]

Sober judgment was what Lincoln consistently found most wanting in his fellow Americans. Calling for 100,000 troops in June 1862, Lincoln lamented to Secretary of State William Henry

Seward that the act would surely result in a "general panic and stampede" even though it was only what was logical and necessary to bring the war to a more rapid, triumphant close. "So hard is it," Lincoln said, "to have a thing understood as it really is."[18]

So here's how it really is: things are going to get worse. As the historian Heather Cox Richardson and others, including myself, have pointed out, political conditions are tracking eerily toward a pattern last seen in the 1850s, when entrenched minority rule was forced to adopt ever more extreme and then violent antidemocratic tactics to stay ahead of demographic realities.

The comparison is so apt that it warrants review: From 1789 to 1861, the South had twenty-three of thirty-six Speakers of the House, twenty-four of thirty-six presidents of the Senate, twenty of thirty-five Supreme Court justices, and always a majority on the court. For forty-nine out of seventy-two years, the president of the United States had been a white Southerner and enslaver; for twelve more years and for most of the 1850s, the president had been a Northern Democrat sympathetic to the South. How had the slave power so completely dominated the federal government despite always having a diminishing minority of the population? The answers will seem familiar.

In 1850, when the number of free and slave states was equal at fifteen, the free states had 60 percent of the population and 70 percent of the voters but only 50 percent of the senators. The three-fifths clause gave the slave states an average of twenty more congressmen after each census, which gave them outsize power in the House and the Electoral College. And by dominating the Electoral College (and therefore the presidency), along with the Senate, they had the power to control appointments to the court. And when even these antidemocratic loopholes in our political process proved inadequate to hold back the tide? Violence.

Today's entrenched minority uses updated tactics—gerrymandering, voter suppression, the filibuster, etc.—but the point and the effect are the same: antidemocratic minority rule. And in both cases, when that minority started to lose power, it had to go to ev-er-greater lengths to maintain it, first engaging in bad faith debate, political grandstanding, and fearmongering, before moving on to openly antidemocratic policies and ultimately to violence.

If another war does come (and I deeply hope it doesn't) the thing that heartens me most—and I say this as a white Georgian—are the words of the Union general William Tecumseh Sherman, written to a friend from his post at the Louisiana Military Academy (later Louisiana State University):

> You [white] people of the South don't know what you are do-ing. This country will be drenched in blood, and God only knows how it will end. It is all folly, madness, a crime against civilization! You people speak so lightly of war; you don't know what you're talking about. War is a terrible thing! You mistake, too, the people of the North [and their allies within the South]. They are a peaceable people but an earnest people, and they will fight, too. They are not going to let this country be destroyed without a mighty effort to save it.[19]

Historians aren't antiquarians; we're not interested in old things because they are old. We exist to tell you when the engine of time throws a rod. Like Cassandra, we are doomed to tell you what you should already know. Like canaries in a coal mine, we sound the alarm, not when the past repeats itself, as Mark Twain supposedly said, but when it rhymes. And I'm here to tell you: the past and the present are starting to rhyme. Time is becoming elastic, and, old as I am, I'm ready to piss into a radiator. My old friends, and my country, are calling.

SIX

TWO CATASTROPHES AND TEN PARALLELS

Lincoln's Assassination and COVID-19*

Martha Hodes

T wo catastrophes, a century and a half apart. One, a pandemic engulfing the globe for more than a year, in an era of instantaneous worldwide reporting. The other, the murder of a single man at a time when it took months for news to reach all corners of a single nation. In a thousand ways the two are incomparable, but what would happen if we thought about COVID-19 in the United States in tandem with the assassination of President Abraham Lincoln? In both times and places, the world changed, and people struggled to cope.

★ ★ ★

1. In early 2020, it feels as if the COVID-19 pandemic comes out of nowhere, suddenly sweeping through the United States. It has claimed more than 5.7 million deaths worldwide, and more than 900,000 in the US, by early February 2022.[1]

---

* Parts of this essay are drawn from Martha Hodes, *Mourning Lincoln*, published by Yale University Press, copyright © 2015 by Martha Hodes.

In the spring of 1865, the American Civil War was drawing to a close. On April 14, five days after the Confederacy surrendered, President Abraham Lincoln and his wife, Mary, went to Ford's Theatre in Washington, DC, to take in a comedy. There, John Wilkes Booth, the well-known actor and aggrieved defender of slavery, entered their box and fired a single shot into the back of Lincoln's head. As the nation's first presidential assassination, Lincoln's death was singular indeed, but for many it symbolized the losses of a far larger toll. Historians now count 750,000 deaths in the Civil War. That was perhaps 2 percent of the nation's population, which means that a similar number of deaths today would amount to more than seven million lives lost. By the spring of 1865, almost everyone knew someone who had died, whether husband, son, father, brother, neighbor, or friend.[2]

★ ★ ★

2. COVID-19 feels entirely unimaginable until it happens.

When word of Lincoln's assassination arrived, some simply could not believe it was true. "What a terrible calamity has come to us by the Murder of our beloved President," one man wrote to his wife. "I can scarcely realize it, it seems too horrible to be true, yet true it is." *Realize*: that was a favored nineteenth-century locution, meaning *to make real*, and over and over again people invoked that word, the same word they invoked in trying to make sense of the unfathomable number of deaths from the war. "I cannot realize it," wrote a young woman to her sweetheart the day after Lincoln died, for "it seems like a horrible dream." John Nicolay, Lincoln's private secretary, found the news "so unexpected, so sudden, and so horrible even to think of, much less to realize, that we *could* not believe it." A white captain of a Black regiment was astounded that such a thing could happen in the present day. "I thought the time for such things had passed," he wrote.[3]

★ ★ ★

3. With COVID-19 raging, anxiety and dread fill our days and nights. We hope for the well-being and safety of those we love.

"We have fallen on Evil times and anarchy," a Maine businessman wrote to a colleague on the day of Lincoln's death. "Who is safe in such times?" A Pennsylvania woman felt like "anarchy & destruction" were "coming upon us," wondering when it would all end. "O! for a word from my dear husband," she wrote in her diary—he was away in the Union Army. "Hope he is safe & well." On the day of Lincoln's death too, a Vermont woman wrote to her son with "deep feelings of anxiety," imploring, "If I could feel assured that you are alive and well our fears would be calmed for the present."[4]

Listlessness and depression swept over Lincoln's mourners. "Do not feel like doing anything," wrote a young girl who had to attend to her sewing. For a Union soldier stationed in Alabama, the news made him feel "so bad," he wrote to his wife, "that I went to bed and I have not felt like getting up since." For some, it was just the opposite. "Sleep was out of the question!" wrote a disconsolate Englishwoman. For others, feelings manifested themselves as bodily symptoms. Upon learning of Lincoln's death, an army captain trembled all morning; meanwhile, the minister Edward Everett Hale wrote in his diary, "Splitting headache and no wonder."[5]

★ ★ ★

4. COVID-19 undeniably hits certain populations harder than others.

When President Lincoln died, African Americans claimed for themselves a special place in the outpouring of grief. Their "Father Abraham," as author of the Emancipation Proclamation and commander in chief of the victorious Union Army, held a special place in their hearts and minds for his role in making possible the seizure of their freedom. A New Orleans minister asserted that his

people felt "deeper sorrow for the friend of the colored man," and
Black clergymen in the North allowed that their people felt the
loss "more keenly" and "more than all others." Journalists singled
out the "dusky-skinned men of our own race" as the "chief—the
truest mourners," and Black soldiers maintained that "as a people
none could deplore his loss more than we." Abolitionist and fugitive slave Frederick Douglass, speaking extemporaneously, told an
overflowing crowd that he felt the loss "as a personal as well as
national calamity" because of "the race to which I belong." Even
the most stricken white mourners conceded the point. As one minister told his congregation, "intense as is our grief," no white person could "fathom the sorrow" of Black people. As another white
mourner wrote in her diary, "How I pity the poor colored people,
who share *perhaps most* deeply in our *great calamity!*"[6]

* * *

5. During COVID-19, we find new ways to connect. On our electronic devices, we gaze upon faces we can no longer see up close
or unobscured by masks. We open our windows to ring bells
and cheer for frontline workers. We place signs in our windows:
"Sending love from a distance." "Patience. Fortitude." "Don't be
afraid. We can do this."[7]

As news of the assassination arrived, by telegraph or newspaper, Lincoln's mourners gathered in cities, towns, and villages,
searching one another's faces for verification of the terrible tid-
ings. Mourners read the meaning in eyes, brows, lips, and com-
plexions, offering proof of alarm and woe. Tolling church bells
across the landscape helped confirm the news too. Signaling
their belonging in a larger community, mourners draped their
homes and shops in black. Washington was shrouded, a federal
employee observed, in "miles upon miles of material," and another resident found that the drapery went "on and on," the day-
time streets presenting "only the blackness of darkness." People

drew signs to place in the windows of homes and shops: "Such a death saddens every victory." "Liberty's last martyr." "God moves in a mysterious way."[8]

* * *

6. Instead of the crisis uniting the country, the pandemic only further divides an already polarized nation, people turning on one another with fury.

Some of Lincoln's mourners hoped in the immediate aftermath of the crime that the war-torn nation would unite. "North & South are weeping together," said one. "The whole nation is shocked & horrified," said another. But after four years of bloody conflict, nothing of the sort came to pass. Not even North and South, as sections, were of one mind, since Lincoln's mourners encompassed Black Northerners, Black Southerners, and most white Northerners, while Lincoln's antagonists encompassed the vast majority of white Southerners and a vocal minority of white Northerners.[9]

Accordingly, Lincoln's enemies cheered at the terrible event. "Hurrah!" a seventeen-year-old South Carolinian wrote in her diary. "Old Abe Lincoln has been assassinated!" In a Florida town, the vanquished Confederates brightened at the news, "taunting the colored people" about reenslavement. In Kentucky, a white man assaulted a Black man, crying out, "Old Lincoln is dead, and I will kill the goddamned Negroes now." Racist white Northerners celebrated too, like the drafted Union soldier who incensed his comrades with the words, "Hip, hip, hurrah, Lincoln is dead," adding, "it served him right," since "he had allowed so many white men to be slaughtered for the n-----."[10]

While mourners mourned, they fumed at their gloating enemies. A woman who clapped and cheered at the news was a "dirty low-minded ignorant disloyal contemptable *Thing*." A mourner looking on those unaffected by the loss wanted to "knock every one of the mean, nasty, slimy, reptiles into the dust." Along with the window signs of communal mourning came messages of anger. "Death to the assassins." "Death to Traitors."[11]

* * *

7. Even as COVID-19 seems to stop the world, turning streets ghostly empty in lockdown, everyday life persists, and going through the motions of daily life can serve as comfort.

To Lincoln's mourners it felt as if the world had stopped. Men abandoned their plows in the field, intoned the minister who spoke at the president's graveside. Merchants closed their doors, and the hum of factories ceased. Or as another minister put it, "all things stood still when the President was killed." But everyone well knew that if the assassination interrupted everyday life, then everyday life also intruded on the process of mourning.[12]

Everywhere, grieving women continued their domestic labor, darning socks, ironing clothes, dying cloth, sweeping chimneys, and tending to children. One wife and mother wrote in her diary about the journey of Lincoln's body out of the capital, sandwiching the news in between two mundane incidents: "Tom ploughing to day. The Presidents body is to be taken to Baltimore to day. Fan coughed nearly all last night, & seemed very cranky." Another woman captured the mixture of obligation and emotion, writing, "We are cleaning house, but I don't care." Men kept working too. A farmer squeezed a notation of "funeral of president Lincoln" in between his record of planting peas and potatoes, oats and grass seed. A writer asked his publisher, "How about my 3d novel? Shall I commence it, or wait for a more favorable season?"[13]

Romance could serve as special solace. Edgar Dinsmore, a member of the Black Fifty-Fourth Massachusetts Infantry Regiment, was both deeply dismayed over Lincoln's death and at once engaged in a serious flirtation. How, Dinsmore wrote to a young woman, could he "express the pleasure that I experience this evening at the reception of your inexpressibly welcome and more than sweet letter?" He continued in the same vein at considerable length, until after many pages he pronounced, "We mourn for the loss of our great and good President as a loss irreparable."[14]

* * *

8. People struggle to find solace in faith, in the face of the pandemic's overwhelming upheaval.

Longing to make sense of what felt incomprehensible, Lincoln's mourners turned to God. Grief without faith was impossible for most nineteenth-century Americans, but the graceful acceptance of such a cataclysmic event proved challenging. The line between acceptance of God's will and the effort to understand divine will was a fine one. A white captain in the Twenty-Second US Colored Infantry (the men of his regiment had welcomed Lincoln to Richmond, the Confederate capital, when it fell) wondered if God had forsaken them all. The loss of Lincoln, the Black minister Jacob Thomas told his congregation in upstate New York, was "more than we can bear," even as he reminded his flock that "in God is our consolation," asking them to "hope for the best." As a white woman in Boston wrote after church on Easter Sunday, "Everybody here seems trying to remember that God will bear us safely through this new & terrible trial, if we are faithful."[15]

Uncertainty crept in everywhere, though. "It must be all right as God permitted it," reflected a Black woman in North Carolina, before allowing that "it does seem very hard to us." For a white northern Quaker, Lincoln's death was such an "incredible atrocity" that she could not tell "whether love & mercy still reign in Heaven." Steadfastness of faith seemed to be the key, and Jewish mourners made the same point: "stricken with sorrow," the members of a California synagogue strived "most resignedly" to bow to "divine decree."[16]

* * *

9. Living through COVID-19 makes for a palpable sense of living through history. "People will be talking about this decades and decades and decades from now," says Dr. Anthony S. Fauci, chief medical adviser to President Joseph R. Biden. Survivors are urged to preserve our experiences, as libraries and museums seek to collect records of this historic moment.[17]

In the wake of Lincoln's assassination in the spring of 1865, Americans felt themselves immersed in the unfolding of epic events, of history-in-the-making. The assassination, mused a Massachusetts lawyer, "will go on resounding down the ages for thousands of years to come." The physician Elizabeth Blackwell put it this way: "It is not often that one lives through such months as these last have been," during which "private lives have all become interwoven with the life of the nation." A Unitarian minister echoed her sentiments, noting in his diary, "It is history, not to be forgotten by the world, & our own sad feelings not likely to be forgotten by us."[18]

Americans kept scrapbooks to confirm the catastrophe, to write themselves into the history they were witnessing, and to enshrine the past for the future. A New England woman began a scrapbook on the day of Lincoln's death, snipping and pasting national and local newspaper stories about the assassination, mourning rituals, and the president's funeral, alongside related poems, drawings, and musical compositions. Within two weeks, she began a second volume, this one home to a fifty-page section entitled "Round the World," with coverage from Canada, England, France, Italy, Germany, Russia, Prussia, Austria, Belgium, South America, and Africa. She would later give the two-volume set to her son as a birthday present.[19]

★ ★ ★

10. COVID-19 will have changed the world forever.

For many there would never be closure after the assassination. Mary Lincoln would long remain emotionally unstable, unable to recover from the trauma of witnessing her husband's death, most especially after having already lost a three-year-old son and an eleven-year-old son, both to illnesses (a third son would later die, also of an illness, at the age of eighteen, leaving only a single son to survive her). Henry Rathbone, the young man who sat with the Lincolns in their box at Ford's Theatre on the night of April 14, 1865, never recovered either. Years later, he would lose his mind and murder his wife, ending his life in an asylum. Years later too, when another of Lincoln's mourners was admitted to an asylum for "chronic mania," doctors listed the cause of her breakdown as "Lincoln's Death."[20]

Many never stopped thinking about how the assassination had permanently changed the world, and none more so than African Americans who lived through the racist reign of Lincoln's successor, the impeached President Andrew Johnson, followed by the post–Civil War decades of Jim Crow violence and the destruction of equal rights. Decades later, when formerly enslaved people thought back to the assassination, their lamentations still felt fresh. The elderly Ann Edwards, in Texas, recalled the sense that "everyone had suddenly experienced the death of their most beloved child." Louis Meadows, in Alabama, believed firmly that "things was hurt by Mr. Lincoln getting killed," and John Matheus, in Ohio, imagined what would have come to pass had Lincoln lived. "He would have done lots of good for the colored people," Matheus said.[21]

★ ★ ★

In the spring of 1865, ministers had spoken of Lincoln as the last casualty of the Civil War, but that was true only symbolically. That spring, more intimate sorrows both accompanied and competed with grief for the slain president. After surrender and the assassination, after the funeral and the funeral train, soldiers kept dying, in hospitals, in camp, and back at home from disease, infection, and mortal wounds. "President Lincoln assassinated last night," wrote a soldier in a Washington hospital. Over the following weeks, he added to his diary: "Five died in this ward," "The man next bed to me died," and "Another poor fellow relieved from all suffering." As a minister observed weeks after the assassination, cemeteries everywhere were filling up, creating "a world of death" all around.[22]

Yet even after four years of a war that had claimed hundreds of thousands of lives, including that of President Abraham Lincoln, survivors could still scarcely believe it when loss touched them personally. Months after the president's assassination, a young soldier suffered the death of his brother, both men still serving in the Union Army down South. "It's very hard for me to bear," he wrote in a letter home, for this was "a sacrifice I little dreamed of." Asking why God had taken his beloved brother, the man confessed, "Little did I think this war was to strike me so near." Grief undiminished a month later, he wrote home, "I can not realize it."[23]

Two catastrophes, in which the lives of bereaved survivors offer us oblique parallels: There was the scale of loss, and the unimaginable nature of each and every one of those losses. There was the anxiety and dread, and the public rituals that offered comfort even as the end of grief felt utterly impossible. There was the bitterly polarized nation, the compounded losses for people of color, and the march of everyday life for all, as hope mixed with uncertainties of faith. There was the sense of living through history and the utterly irrevocable change wrought everywhere, every day.

In a thousand ways the two catastrophes are so different as to be incomparable. Yet in both times and in both places, people would never forget the terrible loss and grief that changed their lives, and the world, forever.

SEVEN

COVID-19

A New "Negro Servants' Disease"

Tera W. Hunter

R ace has had a significant impact on all aspects of American life and culture, including disease classification. Racializing maladies has not only exacerbated health disparities but compromised the speed and manner with which physicians and scientists have responded to mass outbreaks. Most Americans were exposed to an internationally known deadly disease in the nineteenth century, though they did not know it. The disease could not be discerned on the basis of outward appearances alone. It mimicked other maladies, which did not make diagnosis easy. By the time slow-moving symptoms like chest pain, coughing up blood, or extreme fatigue revealed themselves, those infected could be on the brink of death. It spread from individuals as the germs were coughed up, spit out, and became airborne, to be inhaled or absorbed from dried droplets deposited on particles of dust and objects. Not everyone got sick or died from it, but it killed more people than any other ailment in the colonial era, and by 1900 it was the third most common cause of mortality after cardiovascular disease and influenza pneumonia. And yet, despite the prevalence of tuberculosis (otherwise known as TB) across the nation, it was called the "Negro servants' disease" in the Jim Crow South by the early twentieth century.

The perception of TB and the discourse surrounding its spread offers significant insight into how we are coming to terms with a new infectious airborne disease, COVID-19, and racial disparities in the United States in the twenty-first century. We are approaching two years into an ever-spiraling pandemic with grave racial consequences we have yet to grapple with fully. The Centers for Disease Control (CDC) released data documenting this trend because of a successful Freedom of Information Act lawsuit filed by the *New York Times.* The CDC was forced to release data on the 1.45 million cases that were reported to the agency as of the end of May 2020 at a time when substantial data on demographic differences were not readily available. The paper's analysis of the evidence showed that racial disparities occurred across 974 counties that comprise 55 percent of the country's population.[1]

Scholars of social medicine have long argued that diseases are more than epidemiological events. How we name, analyze, and respond to them are deeply informed by cultural scripts that guide our responses to outbreaks. It is not surprising that many of our reactions to COVID-19 are pulled from a historical playbook of ideas about race and socioeconomic standing.

TB has been around for millennia. Humans have grappled with it and inscribed it with different meanings, using the cultural idioms of their times. The discovery of germ theory in 1865 confirmed that microbes were causative agents of diseases, and the discovery of the tubercle bacillus in 1882 generated new misgivings. Germ theory ignited anxieties about everyday interactions between people as they learned and accepted that TB was transmitted through close physical contact, which opened up possibilities for assigning blame based on prejudices.

One writer for the *Richmond Planet* in 1914 found a predictable target in the age of racial segregation: "In our Southern civilization the Negro comes into closest contact with the white race. In the streets, on the cars, in offices restaurants and homes this contact persists. The Negro is porter and sweeper, cook waiter, laundress and nurse." The writer zeroed in on the most troubling concern about the intimacy of contagion, scapegoating the most vulnerable and marginalized citizens in the process. "Servants emerge from squalid, neglected, and congested dwellings to prepare and serve your food and to care for your children. Perhaps each week your clothes are laundered amid just such surroundings, inviting and hospitable to every contagious disease, but more than all others to tuberculosis." By 1880, 98 percent of all Black female wage earners in Atlanta, Georgia, worked as domestics who cooked, cleaned, cared for children, and tended to the household economy and daily needs of white people.[2] The ubiquity of Black women workers crossing the thresholds of white homes led to a common perception that they were the ones spreading TB.

It is curious that while the reputations of all Black service workers were tarnished, white residents, health-care professionals, and politicians trained their ire most especially on Black washerwomen. A typical commentary like this one appeared in newspapers like the *Atlanta Constitution*: "In negro communities in every section of the city washing for the white families is being done in the same room where lie victims in the last stages of tuberculosis." Another commentator was more unequivocal: "there seems little doubt that much of the spreading of diseases is due to this source alone."

These ideas about Black women as the source of contagion were reflected in a plethora of articles and racist cartoons in mainstream white newspapers and even professional studies in regional and national medical and public health journals. Let me be clear, the notion that germs only moved in one direction from Black households to white ones was absurd. TB cannot be spread through the laundry. TB requires frequent and direct contact with a person with the active ailment, whereas washerwomen had minimal interactions with white people. They kept their distance, at their own insistence, by working and living in their own homes. They picked up the laundry in baskets and took it home to wash outdoors in communal settings, weather permitting. Household workers, in general, safeguarded employers by performing the elaborate chores of cleanliness and sanitation necessary for good health that involved substantial time and physical effort before the electrification of cleaning tools. Privileged white people who could afford to hire Black domestics reaped their well-being benefits by having someone else perform their "dirty" work.

It is important to distinguish the racist rhetoric that named Black women as primary, even the sole, carriers of TB from the fact that African Americans suffered disproportionately because of poverty and Jim Crow. The distribution of public resources was driven by the interests of businesses and wealthy residents. The lack of running water and sanitary conveniences, mucky and unpaved streets, and the use of Black neighborhoods as dumps for the garbage and sewage drained down from the affluent hills were optimal conditions for poor health. Household workers' pitiful wages also deprived them of good-quality food, clothing, and housing that imperiled their families' capacities to ward off illnesses of all kinds.

None of these considerations preempted the mostly punitive responses directed at the perceived vectors of feculence and contagion, however. Tuberculosis offered a persuasive vehicle for justifying and rationalizing harsh reprisals in the name of public health. In 1904 the city of Macon, Georgia, passed a law to require washerwomen to buy badges that "resemble those kept on hand for the city's canines." Sanitary inspections of the homes of washerwomen were mandated. But the badges were also designed to keep tabs on washerwomen, to regulate their movements in town as was often done during slavery using "slave passes" and to prevent stealing. White residents in Atlanta spent years debating various draconian proposals of a similar kind that criminalized Black women through surveillance, arrests, fines, and jail. But it turned out that no special law was needed, as the police were increasingly integrated into public health infrastructures there and elsewhere.

Critics spent far less attention addressing the real causes behind the spread of disease that victimized Black people, although the anti-TB campaigns set off alarm bells. The slogan, "germs know no color line," was invoked to rouse self-concern among white people, if nothing else, to take precautions to protect themselves.[3] African Americans launched their own grassroots public health campaigns to address the dereliction of sanitation in their neighborhoods and to counter these negative portrayals. Black women such as Lugenia Burns Hope, social worker and activist, in Atlanta, Georgia, were among the most stalwart leaders demanding attention to the lack of adequate infrastructure that compromised their health.

So, what was behind the racist narrative? As one Black writer argued in response to accusations hurled at domestics at a health conference in Dallas, Texas, in 1915: "It seems very strange that doctors are beginning to charge Negro servants up with white folks' disease." In the wake of emancipation from slavery, TB stimulated a fresh round of panics about an age-old affliction. White Southerners were troubled by what freedom had wrought in releasing Black people from what they proclaimed, falsely, were prophylactic white oversight and bucolic plantations. They were ambivalent, too, about the new social order. Segregation was theoretically supposed to separate the races, but it did so only selectively and in public spaces while Black women worked in intimate ways in white homes. It subordinated African Americans on white terms, requiring them to be available at beck and call in a range of low-wage service work. The "Negro problem" was loathed as a frequent visitor in white homes, though allowed to lurk as the price to be paid for dependence on labor that bolstered their beliefs in superiority.

Blaming Black women for TB was also a convenient scapegoat to displace blame for regional deficiencies. The South had a reputation for high morbidity and mortality, for disorders like malaria, yellow fever, hookworm, and infant mortality. Whites in the region were ridiculed as a backward and inferior breed of Anglo Saxons because they fell short nationally on social indicators of progress, such as literacy and education. African Americans, the most despised race, were a convenient target, though immigrants (associated with "strangers' disease") and poor whites (identified with "diseases of poverty") received some share of finger-pointing too.

In 2020–2021 we are grappling with the most dangerous contagious disease of our own times in which the past still resonates. COVID-19 disproportionately impacts African Americans and Latinos nationally and Native Americans, especially those living on reservations. According to the CDC, African Americans and Latinos are 3 times more likely to become infected and die at younger ages and higher rates than white Americans. According to the Indian Health Service, American Indians and Alaska Natives suffer infection rates at 3.5 times higher and hospitalization rates at 4 times higher than non-Hispanic whites. They are also more likely to die, and at younger ages, than non-Hispanic whites.[4]

A similar kind of racial "othering" from the past is inflicting perceptions and responses to COVID-19. President Donald J. Trump kicked off the first round of epithets using his Twitter platform to amplify "the Chinese virus." In defiance of criticism, he has continued to use racial slurs to stigmatize Chinese people and Chinese Americans as unique carriers. This has licensed a host of hate crimes toward people who look Asian, regardless of nationality or ancestry, and the resurgence of gross stereotypes of filth and contamination that harken back to earlier eras of anti-Asian xenophobia when Chinese immigrants were stigmatized as carriers of syphilis, smallpox, and bubonic plague in places like San Francisco.

The disparagement has also landed on "essential workers" not unlike yesteryear's vast army of domestic workers. The postindustrial US workforce is overwhelmingly concentrated in the private sector service industry, accounting for 129 million jobs. Essential workers are predominantly Black, Brown, Indigenous, immigrant, and female. Seventy percent of them are paid minimum wages, less than fifteen dollars per hour, typically without health insurance, paid sick leave, or other benefits. Many are undocumented and cannot complain about ill treatment or poor working conditions without endangering deportation. They have jobs that put them at risk to catch the virus—they are, for example, nursing aids in hospitals and home care facilities, transportation workers, janitors, store clerks, grocery shoppers, farm workers, warehouse employees, and meat-packers. Vice President Michael Pence told these workers, "show up and do your job" for the sake of the country, as if we are fighting a war and their sacrifices should be made because of "military necessity."[5]

The pandemic makes visible economic and racial disparities in the US workforce, between essential workers on the frontline of the crisis and affluent white-collar (and predominantly white) employees able to work from home. Essential workers are compelled to continue life as before, taking public transportation that is insufficiently sanitized and crowded with others like themselves, with few choices to get to work or face being fired for not showing up, even if they were sick. Meanwhile, white-collar employees bring work home, transforming their private residences into telecommunication pods, mimicking scenes from science fiction. These simultaneous trends are not coincidental; they were mutually interdependent. Affluent employees rely on the labor of essential workers to brave the perils of contracting the virus to harvest crops, shop for groceries, process meat, or pack goods in megaplants such as those run by Amazon. Delivery services like Instacart and Grubhub link the demands for goods made by better-paid consumers to the lowest-level workers in the "gig" economy. These precarious jobs are made more vulnerable by the whims of customer rating systems that track worker performance via electronic apps, giving workers little recourse when they fail to make the right impression.

Public officials throw up their hands when asked what they think should be done about the growing evidence of racial and socioeconomic inequities. The common refrain is to note that the workers have preexisting comorbidities so entrenched that there is not much that can be done about them. The CDC data show, however, that people of color in the workforce are bearing the brunt of dangerous face-to-face working conditions that make it impossible for them to work from home. Very little lip service is given to compensating them with hazard pay in any way that is commensurate with their extra burdens or addressing the toll of working in biohazard environments, often without proper protective gear.

Some like the US secretary of health and human services from 2018–2021, Alex Azar, bluntly expressed contempt for the most disadvantaged laborers who are imperative to the functioning of a robust economy. The stock market has soared, despite the loss of thirty million jobs by April 2020 due to the lockdown caused by the pandemic, which provides few incentives for corporations to address how laborers are harmed. The highest rates of outbreaks in the workplace have occurred in the meatpacking industry, which Azar said should be blamed on the "home and social" environments of the workers, not their jobs. Azar was simply doing the bidding of corporate leaders like those at the Smithfield Foods pork processing plant in South Dakota. A spokesperson for the company stated that the "living circumstances in certain cultures are different than they are with your traditional American family" to explain the dramatic numbers falling ill from the virus. Meanwhile, poultry and meatpacking plants in nearly half the states reported tens of thousands of cases of outbreak of COVID-19 as of July 2020. Eighty-seven percent of the deaths identified were among racial and ethnic minorities.[6]

COVID-19 is the new "Negro servants' disease" insofar as both are imagined spreading in one direction, from fetid Black and Brown homes to immaculate factories—and in which corporate heads bear no responsibility whatsoever for the petri dish shop floors they have fabricated. It justifies prioritizing profit margins over the lives of the workers expected to risk body and soul to keep churning out racks of swine, poultry, and beef to meet insatiable consumer demands.

Blame-the-victim style rhetoric was also articulated by the US surgeon general during the Trump administration, Dr. Jerome Adams, who is himself African American. Black and Brown people, Adams said, need to stop drinking, doing drugs, and smoking to protect themselves and one another. He urged them to practice social distancing, "if not for yourself, then for your abuela. Do it for your granddaddy. Do it for your Big Mama. Do it for your Pop-Pop." Adams invoked age-old caricatures associating obesity with Blackness in a public health address. But it's a funny thing when no other groups have been singled out for "tough love" lectures of this kind. Black Americans drink and do drugs less than white Americans. Everyone should be more vigilant about social distancing and wearing face masks, despite efforts to politicize conformity to these protocols as anti-Trump. Though Adams said he meant no offense, he reinforced the stereotype that Black people's own behaviors dictate their physiological states. It lends credence to hand-wringing, that these are innate problems that simply require more self-control.

We have also seen echoes of the racial response to TB in the stark comparison between how white people are extended the sympathetic hand of public health resources, while many Black people are treated with indifference or given the boots by police. At the outset of the virus, we heard stories of Black people presenting with known symptoms of COVID-19 being turned away from hospitals and social services after multiple tries for admittance, by healthcare providers who minimized their conditions, sent them home, where they ended up dying for lack of timely care. There are abundant research studies that show Black patients are often not taken seriously when describing pain more routinely accepted and diagnosed when presented by whites. According to research in the *Proceedings of the National Academy of Sciences,* a substantial number of white medical students and laypeople falsely believe that there are biological differences that cause Black Americans to experience less pain than whites, which influences how they are treated.[7]

As we have turned our attention to other police abuses, we should not forget incidents in which officers in New York City handed out masks to white people not wearing them lounging and walking around Central Park when bursts of spring weather drove the quarantined multitudes outdoors. Meanwhile, Black people were beaten down to the ground and put in headlocks for walking down streets without masks. These were not mere anecdotal examples. Data show that in New York City 80–90 percent of the arrests related to social distancing enforcement have been of Black and Brown people.

Disparate police treatment was on full display in contrasting scenes of armed and unmasked white protesters at places like the Michigan Capitol and Huntington Beach, California, who called for an end to stay-at-home directives, being given the leeway to spit and scream in the faces of officers with nary a hair on their bodies being touched. Should we be stunned that the state legislature in Michigan shut down in response to white militias protesting in their halls, bowing to their First and Second Amendment rights? Officials chose not to confront them, exercising disciplined restraint that should be used with everyone.

The cool deportment of law enforcement signals special standing of certain citizens and complements racial narratives invoked at those largely white events. Some protesters' choice of symbols, like Confederate and Nazi flags, indicate that the dog whistles once de rigueur in post–civil rights politics have lost their cachet to more brazen messaging in the age of Trump. A placard noticed at a rally in the spring of 2020 in front of a Humboldt County, California, courthouse enunciated this vividly. "Muzzles are for dogs and slaves. I am a free human being," the sign read, along with an iconic 1839 drawing of an enslaved man with a neck coffle and iron bit (face mask) used for punishment. Some of you people deserve a kind of treatment, others of us not so much.

Unarmed Black, Brown, and Indigenous people who protest against systemic oppression have historically been denied protected constitutional rights to express their discontent undisturbed by officials. We have been witnessing something very remarkable and urgent and growing since the violent murders of Breonna Taylor and George Floyd. Millions of multiracial, multigenerational, and overwhelmingly peaceful protesters are taking to the streets against state-sanctioned killings of unarmed African Americans, supporting the Black Lives Matter (BLM) movement. But they have frequently been countered with militarized retaliations across the country. Some white allies are experiencing a kind of disregard by proxy, as "race traitors," similar to what occurred during the Civil Rights Movement but on a national scale. Federal troops pepper sprayed and brutally beat a fifty-three-year-old white navy veteran and tear-gassed several hundred white mothers wearing bike helmets and locking arms last summer while peacefully protesting in support of BLM in Portland, Oregon.

Meanwhile, we are still reeling from an unprecedented pandemic with an upward curve, new variants more dangerous for children, and no end in sight. We must continue to be vigilant about COVID-19 and not let our concerns about those racial disparities recede. The lives of Black, Brown, and Indigenous people are at stake in this recognition too. As we discuss the underlying inequities, let us also remember the history of derisive ideas that have shaped our responses to common maladies. Chastened by this knowledge, we must ask ourselves if we have the courage and will to abandon the racial and socioeconomic scripts and change the conditions that have nourished them for far too long.

EIGHT

FROM THE COLFAX MASSACRE TO THE 2020 ELECTION

White Supremacist Terrorism in America

Gwendolyn Midlo-Hall

Mass death is a new experience for post–World War II generations in the United States. "Death" is a word modern-day Americans rarely use. Nobody dies here. They pass away. But the COVID-19 pandemic, along with its racial disparities, forces us to acknowledge death and its harsh realities. Hopefully, as Americans begin to discuss mass death and personal experiences of loss, we will also begin working on preventing mass death on this scale from ever happening again.

This is a story about mass death in America, but it is also a story about fighting for political freedom in the face of white supremacist terrorism. The modern groundwork for racial inequality was laid in the American Civil War's cultural, political, and legal aftermath (1861–1865) and Reconstruction (1863–1877). Yet most Americans have never heard of one of the most important stories of mass death in our history—namely, the Colfax massacre of 1873, in which white terrorists horrifically slaughtered over 150 Black men in Louisiana's Red River Valley. It was an assault on both American democracy and free Black life. It is part of the long history of the blurred lines between violent white terrorists, law enforcement, armed forces, and ex-military personnel, and it shows how these groups have frequently engaged in open rebellion against the state. In 2020 and early 2021, we saw a similar scenario unfold, as white supremacists, upset by their perceived loss of power followed by Trump's electoral loss, tried to cripple America's legislative branch.

While it is hard for the average American to recognize the highly organized networks white supremacists systematically use to disenfranchise Black voters, some of their terroristic ways were exposed on January 6, 2021. Court documents revealed that one in five insurrectionists were actively serving in the United States military or in veteran militia units. Historical events like the Colfax massacre and January 6 are portrayed as isolated tragedies, but historians know better. Even the social media footprint of the January 6 insurrectionists argued they were gearing up for a second Civil War: They came to finish the job they had started in the mid-nineteenth century in places like Colfax.[1]

To me, an activist organizing even before the Civil Rights Movement of the 1950s and 1960s, and as an elder historian who is now in her nineties, the events of 2020 and January 2021 have relevant connections to both civil rights organizing and white supremacist terrorism during Reconstruction. If, as many historians have argued, 2020 is the birth year of a new civil rights era or a Third Reconstruction, then we must go back to the leaders of the original Reconstruction to learn from both their triumphs and their tribulations.[2] Perhaps the most important point about southern history is that the Civil War did not end in the Deep South in 1865; it was almost the opposite. In many ways, the proslavery, pro-Confederate South won the war.

Colfax was the single largest massacre in Louisiana, and it led to one of the worst legal decisions in Supreme Court history: *United States v. Cruikshank* (1876). *Cruikshank* gave control of constitutional amendments and laws protecting civil rights back to the Confederate states that had recently seceded. This awful decision effectively ended Radical Reconstruction by prohibiting the federal government from using the Enforcement Act of 1870 to prosecute men who engaged in paramilitary actions; including actions orchestrated by the Ku Klux Klan (KKK), the Knights of the White Camelia, and the White League (other terrorist organizations that helped Democrats regain power in states like Louisiana). *Cruikshank* nearly erased all Black political gains made after emancipation, reempowering the local white oligarchies.[3]

The Colfax massacre is a perfect example of "whitewashing" history. Despite an inaccurate historical marker for the "Colfax riot" erected over half a century later that served as the only headstone for the over 150 dead, Colfax was never a riot. As LeeAnna Keith has argued, in the 1870s, the term "massacre" was usually reserved for white captives during the Indian Wars—not the Black or Indigenous captives or victims of white supremacist violence. But today we recognize Colfax for what it really was: a racist massacre, a hate crime slaughter, a violent political message to potential Black voters throughout the South. Described by historian Eric Foner as the worst instance of racial violence during Reconstruction, the Colfax massacre ended Black hopes for autonomy and self-governance, and ultimately restored the state of Louisiana to white conservative Democrats, many of whom were former enslavers.[4]

Located in the heart of the Red River Valley, Colfax was a highly prosperous area in the global cotton economy prior to the Civil War. But flush times ended abruptly for the planters along this river soon after secession. New Orleans fell to the United States Army early, in April 1862. During 1863, after Lincoln's Emancipation Proclamation freed those enslaved in Confederate-occupied territory, the United States Army conducted a ten-day raid up the Red River to Alexandria, where the Confederate governor of Louisiana, Thomas Moore, owned a large plantation.

A neighboring planter wrote to Moore in Shreveport: "The arrival of the advance of the Yankees alone turned the Negroes crazy . . . everything like subordination and restraint was at an end . . . the *drivers* everywhere have proved the worst Negroes. . . . All business was suspended and those that did not go with the army remained at home to do *much worse*. . . . You need not in the least be uneasy about the Negroes. They will get fully as much as they deserve, if not more."[5]

An Alexandria newspaper called for a military commission to carry out executions swiftly, creating an atmosphere of "wholesome terror. Its example will long be remembered. Here and there the life of a slave forfeited by his crime will entail a loss," the paper concluded, "but a great and good result will be attained . . . engraving a wholesome lesson on the minds of this impressionable population."[6]

With the beginnings of Radical Reconstruction, the former enslavers of the Red River Valley no longer controlled a home guard, a military patrol, or a military commission. Political, judicial, military, and police power were up for grabs. No longer manifested by the ownership of land and the enslaved, the character of wealth changed, as access to goods, supplies, and credit became paramount. Within this shifting landscape, a new group of merchants emerged, competing with each other through violent, insurrectionary means. The Red River Valley transformed into a highway of militarized desperados and warring factions, with no clearly established governmental authority. Murder, gun violence, and terror were the order of the day. This was concerning given the region's proximity to both the state capital in New Orleans (a two-day journey upriver) and to Texas.[7]

During the Civil War, the enormous US Army included over 200,000 armed Black troops (composed of formerly enslaved men, refugees, and free Blacks). They were charged with maintaining order, ensuring peace, and protecting polling places. By the fall of 1867, the numbers had precipitously dwindled to only

20,000 soldiers in Louisiana. The US government had decided to redistribute its military might instead to colonize the West, fighting the subsequent escalating war against Indigenous tribes.[8]

Louisiana's new Radical Reconstruction Constitution of 1868 created an enclave of Republican power along the Red River, an area that was majority Black and deeply divided. With so few troops to counterbalance the power of the former enslavers and their kin, laws enforcing the Fourteenth and Fifteenth Amendments, providing citizenship and the right to vote to all men, regardless of race, were applied with timidity and little effect. Federal election supervisors in rural areas had no police power and were reduced to poll watchers. Grant Parish was carved out of Rapides and Winn Parishes and named triumphantly for President Ulysses S. Grant. The parish seat, Colfax, was named after his vice president Schuyler Colfax Jr.

That same year, to help keep peace in the region, the Louisiana state legislature authorized a five thousand–man militia, half white and half Black. The white troops were mainly Confederate veterans, and the Black troops were Union veterans. During bitter struggles over control of the state government, the militia fragmented along racial lines, with one sector becoming the military arm of the terrorist organization called the White League after 1873. The boundary line between these white terrorists and Black Republicans was Bayou Darrow, located seven miles north of Colfax. The KKK had vowed to drive out or kill Black farmers living in this Republican stronghold. Much like the sentiments of organized white supremacist organizations that attacked the United States Capitol on January 6, 2021, these white Confederate veterans united through a race-based polity and wielded their military training to defend it. Believing their way of life was under attack by federally backed minorities, they felt fully justified in brazenly waging war against the state itself. Whether during Reconstruction or in 2020–2021, white supremacists' purported fear of losing status, wealth, and, most importantly, political power has always been part of what drives racial violence in this country, from riots to lynching to police brutality.[9]

Despite the rhetoric of a federally sponsored race war, the handful of federal officials and Republican officeholders along the Red River were left to their own devices without sufficient federal or state intervention. Violence quickly enveloped the region. The brutality was primarily carried out by two groups of white political terrorists in Grant Parish: the Knights of the White Camelia and the KKK. Organized and led by F. W. Howell, the Knights claimed a membership of three hundred men, nearly one-third of the white men in the parish, who pledged to maintain white political control. The Klan was more secretive. Klan members disguised themselves in robes and hoods. Both groups actively supported the Democratic Party, particularly during the presidential election of 1868, when the candidate Horatio Seymour promised to end Radical Reconstruction, restoring their power.[10]

During the wave of terror unleashed before the 1868 election, the political assassination rates among both Black and white Louisianans were staggering. There were 1,081 politically motivated murders, 137 shootings, and 507 other outrages *verified* within the state. Most of them took place right before Election Day in November. A congressional committee reported that the KKK had killed or wounded "over two hundred Republicans, hunting and chasing them for two days and nights through fields and swamps." After thirteen men were taken from one jail and executed, "a pile of twenty-five dead bodies were found half buried in the woods. Having conquered the republicans, killed or driven off the white leaders, the Ku Klux captured the masses, marked them with badges of red flannel, . . . led them to the polls, [and] made them vote the democratic ticket."[11]

The violence peaked in September of 1868, when two hundred Black citizens in Bossier Parish armed themselves during a conflict over land. In a commonly used right-wing power grab tactic, white supremacists arrested Black Louisianans for doing the same things as white men. They ultimately tried and convicted twenty-one Black men of insurrection. A few weeks later, several Black citizens were shot to death by a white mob, leading to a group of Black men arresting and killing two white suspects. Tensions escalated, reaching a fevered crescendo as over two hundred white terrorists indiscriminately slaughtered at least 150 people.[12]

White supremacist violence intensified, as former Confederates and poorer whites banded together in solidarity to "retake" the state. The racist tension during these tumultuous years of Reconstruction was not unlike Donald Trump's presidency. Trump was particularly effective at inciting white terrorism, from the infamous Unite the Right rally in Charlottesville, Virginia, in August 2017 (described as "the largest and most violent gathering of white supremacists in at least a decade") to the insurrectionist attack on January 6, 2021.[13] Much like in Reconstruction Louisiana, at Trump's "Take Back the Vote" rally and subsequent riot, disparate white militia groups; paramilitary; highly trained ex-military commanders; war veterans who fought in Vietnam, the Gulf War, Iraq, and Afghanistan; active duty service men and women; and police chiefs sought to assassinate legally elected political rivals.[14]

Still, as horrifically brutal as the 1868 election had been in Louisiana, the 1872 election and its aftermath were even deadlier. Not only was the gubernatorial election disputed, but several of the local elections were too. Just like four years before, the real political strife seemed to center in the Red River Valley, with Grant Parish as the eye of the storm. In tiny Colfax, the county seat, the local elections were hotly contested. A group of armed Black Republicans began occupying the county courthouse, claiming political victory. White terrorist Democrats overthrew them in a bloody slaughter. Historians know that only three white citizens perished during the attack, but the number of Blacks murdered is much more difficult to ascertain, as most witnesses were slaughtered. Evidence was lost as bodies were buried in the trenches in front of the courthouse in mass graves or dumped into the Red River. We do know that nearly all the dead were brutally slain *after* they had surrendered. We know that almost fifty human beings were callously murdered *after* being held as political prisoners for hours.[15]

Even before the 1872 presidential election, the Red River Valley was already deep in the throes of a local power struggle; Grant Parish had dueling governments. The previous Republican governor had appointed a full set of local parish officials upon Grant's creation, including Radicals who were unpopular with local white Democrats. The appointed sheriff Delos White was a Black Union Army soldier who also worked as an agent of the Freedmen's Bureau. In 1871, White became a white supremacist political assassination victim, just like so many other Radical leaders in the Reconstruction-era South.

More hated than Sheriff White was Judge William Phillips, a "scalawag" from Alabama who earned a reputation by openly fathering a child with a Black woman and by rallying Black voters around promises of land, horses, and tools as part of reparations for slavery.[16] The Knights of the White Camelia were incensed and demanded the removal of both men. The governor relented, replacing the Radicals with conservative Republicans (one a Confederate veteran), while the Radicals banded together with a group of Black Union veterans, including a former cavalryman named William Ward. Under the joint leadership of the white William Phillips and the Black William Ward, local African Americans coalesced around "a new type of militant Black politics."[17]

By 1872, Louisiana's Republican Party had split into factions at the state level, with a "returning board" ultimately voting on the validity of election returns. Politically divided, the returning board fractured along two main branches. One branch declared Confederate Colonel John McEnery, the Democratic candidate for governor, the winner. The other claimed Union colonel and Republican William P. Kellogg the rightful winner. A federal judge would ultimately declare Kellogg the victor, but not before the conflict spilled bloodily into the countryside. Both gubernatorial candidates held swearing-in ceremonies, and both began appointing and certifying men for local patronage positions, including in Grant Parish. For many in Louisiana, open warfare seemed imminent.[18]

In her book-length treatment of the Colfax massacre, LeeAnna Keith used new evidence from the site and eyewitness accounts to piece together the events from that terrible day. With dueling local governments in the Red River Valley, the power struggle in Colfax turned deadly in April of 1873, when a band of white supremacists murdered a Black man in his front yard. William Ward, the state representative, local Radical leader, and militia captain, ordered his company to muster immediately. About three hundred Black militiamen, along with their families, flocked to Colfax's town center, occupying the courthouse (a "repurposed" plantation stable). Ward, who had grown up enslaved as a carpenter in Virginia, began drilling the men openly in the town's streets, organizing watches to keep families safe. Armed with guns, they quickly dug entrenchments, erected breastworks, and "posted sentries" around their commandeered area.[19]

As expected, whites in the Red River Valley used these events to incite as much racist fear as possible. Three hundred white men poured into Colfax from Grant and surrounding parishes, forming an all-white paramilitary counterforce. Under the leadership of C. C. Nash, a former captain of the Confederate Army (who was also a well-known terrorist), they ordered the Black militia and their families to leave Colfax under threat of violence. With more manpower and weaponry than the Republicans—including a small cannon—the white supremacist Democrats began the battle just after noon on Easter.[20]

After hours of skirmishing, the white men found a gap in the levee on the riverbank and positioned their single cannon there. While the cannon continuously fired upon the Black freedom fighters, a former plantation overseer led a group of thirty whites in a direct attack against the Black militia. One group instantly surrendered and was taken prisoner. Although the former Confederate commander promised to free the men in the morning, a younger band of white terrorists executed the prisoners in cold blood under the cowardly cover of the night.[21]

Roughly sixty Republicans flooded into the courthouse, exchanging fire with the white militia, who finally compelled a Black captive to set fire to the courthouse roof. Some of the Black Radicals perished in the fire. The men who tried to surrender, numbering between fifty and seventy, would ultimately be shot to death by these bloodthirsty white supremacists. As a steamer pulled into Colfax the night of the massacre, one of the terrorists climbed on board, "armed to the teeth," offering to give the passengers a tour of "dead n-----s . . . for there were a hundred or so scattered over the village and the adjacent fields."[22]

★ ★ ★

Was Colfax a spontaneous uprising of white vigilantes against Black citizens as it is usually portrayed? No indeed. So how were these white terrorists mobilized to attack Colfax? It appears that while many white men in Grant Parish refused to be mobilized at all, some white men came in from neighboring parishes, convinced that their survival was at stake. They spread rumors of an impending race war, alleging that Black men were breaking into coffins, robbing and desecrating the dead. The defense in the Colfax trial claimed that "During the succeeding five days . . . Colfax was filled by Negroes, who threatened to kill the white males and hold the white females for the purpose of creating a new race. The whites fled and the work of rapine began."[23] Yet not one scintilla of evidence was presented that any of the Black men who defended the Colfax courthouse ever committed a single crime. They were simply freedom fighters, assassinated during their heroic quest for autonomy and political power.[24]

Unfortunately, many vestiges of Reconstruction reemerged in Trump's America (2017–2021). White supremacy has always assured elite whites' place at the top of society. Stoking racism and hatred, they have successfully prevented lasting interracial coalitions and have been able to keep Black Americans at the bottom of a type of caste system. While Reconstruction originally was an era of hope and incredible change, after a few short years white supremacists had regained nearly all their power, nullifying most of the hard-won gains made by Black and Brown Americans postemancipation. Today, the white rage following Donald Trump's 2020 election loss demonstrates just how badly this country still needs to reckon with and learn from its past. Just like their Confederate ancestors, the insurrectionists of January 6 indignantly rejected legitimate election results, vowing vengeance through racist violence and terrorism.

Still, one of the best things about history is that it can be used as a balm, as a healing agent. From finding inspiration in the actions of forebearers to feeling connected with a larger sense of purpose through the civil rights movements of the past, history has always been a powerful force that some have smartly tamed and some, to their own peril, have ignored. A new generation of activists are using civil rights, labor, and movement histories to help the country progress. But we face an uphill battle. Everything from the names of events to the counting of the dead remains inaccurate, written by the victors, all of them—until very recently—elite white men, all of them with a pointed narrative. Even more dauntingly, we are still deep in the fight of protecting Black Americans from white supremacist violence. Whether due to "lone wolf" gunmen, chaotic hordes of insurrectionists, or the police, it is still open season on Black America. As W. E. B. Du Bois said in 1946, it is well past time to put an end to this terrible system.[25]

NINE

MAN OF MEANS BY NO MEANS

King of the Road

Rhae Lynn Barnes

This story ends with me still rowing.

—Anne Sexton, "Rowing"

"**D**rive as fast as you can."

My neighbor's lanky voice shook like a jittery mother giving a dire warning to their child after a too-close call—the kind of concerned pleading that bursts out all at once in a tangled knot. We used to say hello while juggling packages and down coats as we fumbled for our elevator buttons, but I hadn't seen her since February 2020. Now it was late March. Like everyone else in the building, I assumed she had abandoned her apartment, was tethered to Zoom, or had died.

"Don't stop. Don't go into cities. Stay on the perimeters," Neha lectured. I nodded obediently as the streetlight glinted and hummed.

We were standing ten feet apart. We weren't allowed in the elevator. We didn't know if the confined air or elevator buttons could kill us. A day earlier, the building manager barricaded himself by flipping the couches on their arms to block tenants from getting to his office or his stockpile of bleach. A new sign went up: "No rent checks or cash," it read. "Digital only." I didn't blame him. He didn't want to die for his job any more than I did.

A deserted drum kit, weatherworn Ikea furniture, and a sea of bulging trash bags filled with mismatched clothing were heaped on the cracked sidewalk from residents who disappeared. They dumped everything and left. We were tripping over the littered remnants of one of the largest migrations in recent United States history.

Around 420,000 people left New York City during the first two months of the COVID-19 pandemic. More people moved out of New Jersey in 2020 than any other state.[1] "The golden rhythm was broken," as Joan Didion put it when she left Manhattan for the Golden State in 1967. Hundreds of thousands were now saying, "Goodbye to all that,"[2] but in 2020 *all that* was fatal.

The well-heeled sought greener pastures in the Hamptons or the Catskills and inundated resort towns in Pennsylvania and Vermont, carrying the virus to places with Indigenous names where viruses devastated Indigenous inhabitants long ago. Those without means, cars, or financial cushioning—the elderly on fixed incomes, those caught in the quicksand of American poverty, essential workers, and renters making under a $90,000 household income—stayed in the perilous epicenter during New York and New Jersey's first wave. I was one of them.

Before the second wave crested, I needed to get out. I needed to pack up my apartment and drive across the country—alone—on Route 66 to reunite with my family in Los Angeles. It should have been a joyride, the kind of American dream road trip they make movies about. But there was a plot twist. I had to get across the United States without interacting with a single person to avoid contracting or spreading COVID-19. If I made it back to California without contracting COVID, a prize was waiting for me: a one-year residential research fellowship at Stanford worth multiple years of my graduate school fellowship in a single paycheck. With my hometown at 17 percent unemployment, I was terrified a new depression was hurtling toward us to decimate the stability we had hobbled together since the 2008 subprime mortgage crisis. My new gig required me to show up in person. I was terrified.

Ironically, I had to risk my life like millions of other Americans to secure health insurance. Despite my fear, I was grateful to have guaranteed work. Haunted by the financial crisis my family endured during the 2008 layoffs, I thought the gamble could protect both my family and me from a spiraling economic downturn, keep us housed, and keep us fed for another year if the market crashed. I had to try.

It was like a classic American western: I had to survive the journey from the East Coast to the Pacific to get the gold. But this road trip wasn't going to be *Travels with Charley*. I wasn't revisiting Highway 61 with a raspy-throated Dylan in Ray-Bans or rambling with the Merry Pranksters on the psychedelic FURTHUR. Sal Paradise was nowhere to be found. What I was in for was more like Thelma and Louise staring down the canyon in their Thunderbird convertible or Duke and Gonzo swatting at swooping hell bats; only the terrors that flitted around me weren't the hallucinatory winged mammals many claimed were the origin of COVID-19 in Wuhan. And the kicks I got on Route 66 were *not* what Nat King Cole sang about. I had to dodge COVID deniers touting Trump flags on their pickup trucks and the scraggly bearded bros who cussed me out at a gas station on the fringes of Joplin, Missouri, because I wore a face mask near a pop-up corner store of Trump paraphernalia.

Before leaving, I stretched out a map on my brindle cowhide rug alongside Google Maps on my laptop, tracing a route that would allow me to stop every six hours to rest. My task was daunting. I was 2,811 miles away from my family. My best friends were 996 and 3,462 miles away. Downtown was the person who caressed my face and told me they were falling in love with me. The distance between me and all of them now felt the same. I was alone. No one was coming to help me, and I could not go to help them. To protect each other, we had to stay apart.

My best chance at survival in an airborne pandemic, I decided, was to use the mid-nineteenth century's infrastructure of mass death. I would pull over to eat, stretch, or rest in Civil War battlefields and rural or garden cemeteries. Rural cemeteries were built on the outskirts of major cities in response to mass urbanization, stretching across the nation from Mount Auburn in Cambridge, Massachusetts (1831), to Bellefontaine in St. Louis (1849) and Mountain View in Oakland, California (1863). They were designed in antebellum America with lavish gardens and curving paths for strolling, glens for picnicking, and massive marble hillside mausoleums so the living could enjoy green space beyond congested city streets and convene with their beloved dead. Here, grieving could happen in an Edenic setting while avoiding "miasmas."

Miasmas were a public health obsession in the nineteenth century. It was widely believed that noxious stinky air or poisoned vapors from filth, garbage, sewers, pollution, and the swampy stench that radiated off stagnation stewed in human bodies caused pestilential diseases we now attribute to germs. To escape airborne dangers, I would travel among those dead. And most surprising, even to me, I did something millions of American women did during and after the American Civil War in the era of spiritualism, table turning, and séances while racked with inconsolable grief, longing to reconnect with loved ones who passed in faraway places: I contacted a psychic.

The countdown was emblazoned in my brain. I would need to survive 172 days in my six-hundred-square-foot apartment before extricating myself and driving like mad to Los Angeles. I would then go another 145 days alone without ever intentionally touching another human being. The isolation was mind-numbing; it played tricks on my sanity and was physically painful. On day

331, I would finally be in a room with my family, indoors *and unmasked*. We would momentarily relax. Then came the second wave, which decimated Los Angeles after the virus mutated in the UK and circulated before the B.1.1.7. strain knocked out California. And we received an emergency phone call that launched a new phase of pandemic grieving for my family.

Miraculously, on day 370, I would receive my first dose of the COVID-19 mRNA vaccination, in the back room of a San Francisco Walgreens on the corner of Gough and Fell, that would protect my life.

★ ★ ★

Neha specialized in the globalization of disease. She looked worn down and Argus-eyed as she told me about aerosol transmission through respiratory droplets. This was new to me. The CDC would not confirm COVID-19 spread this way for over half a year in late September 2020. I listened to her canting as if my life depended on it, because maybe it did.

"Absolutely no public restrooms on the road!" she admonished grimly.

I laughed at the absurdity of our situation, but this was no joke; it was the definition of deadly serious.

"It goes airborne if some asshole flushes in a stall near you or uses the automatic hand dryer," she interjected before I could even ask.

We discussed the delicate geometry of female "urination devices" designed for camping as we watched our building manager laboriously drag a blood-stained mattress down the street. He tried to keep his distance. It seemed pointless. His face had already been smashed against its quilted top as he clumsily carried the wobbling deathbed outside. He tried to ignite the mattress four times unsuccessfully. Finally, he started a dumpster fire and flipped the bed on top of it. The edges burned first, hollowing out the foamy cakey layers that curled up like book pages. Open burns were illegal, but no one said anything. I stood ten feet away from Neha, watched it go up in flames, and prayed for its previous owner as the smoke swirled above us. We would repeat this ceremony a few days later. I never told my friends or family they burned mattresses infested with COVID-19 outside my window. It would terrify them, and what could they do?

Neha and I found a phone app that rerouted directions to gas stations and restaurants with private unisex bathrooms. The only problem was restaurants were all closed. And then there was the problem of lodging: should I sleep in the car? Bring a tent and risk public showers? Use biodegradable wet wipes for bathing? Major hotel chains were unrolling "touchless check-in." I could pick a room on the floor plan next to the first-floor exit and enter from the parking lot to avoid tourists. I could unlock the door by hovering my phone over the key plate, break the "clean room" Lysol-sponsored seal, open windows, air out the room while I sat outside on the curb, and return to disinfect light switches and remote controls. The best option would have been a Griswold family–style RV, but companies were sold out nationwide. For nourishment, I would pack enough canned, boxed, and preserved food to get me across the country plus ten days if I became sick and had to stop. There was so much to think through.

I was baffled, afraid, and morbidly amused. How in the hell did we get to the point that this mildly vulgar, farcically weird, and incontestably dystopian conversation was critical to my rugged survival in the United States of America in 2020? Just three weeks before, everything was normal. I quickly learned this is what happens at the peak of a pandemic—everything you do with your body, physical space, and your social world transforms if you want to survive.

"Wear gloves at the gas pump. If you can't find latex, bring your leather winter gloves, rubbing alcohol, and remove them at the wrist so you don't recontaminate yourself," Neha rattled off. She had thought about this.

"And stay on lighted highways," she added, "where someone can find you if something goes wrong." We both knew she didn't mean if I blew out a tire in Arizona or cracked the windshield or any grisly "true crime" anecdotes a curvy woman like me might fret about while driving alone on a desert highway in a summer dress with all her belongings teetering like a Jenga game in the rearview mirror.

In the distance, I could hear the crosswalk signal chirp "Walk" to no one. There were no cars and no people except an occasional jogger who ran down the middle of the street. Sound carried eerily over the vacant intersection in the unrelenting silence that characterized our brave new world. I preferred this over the pandemic's other nightmarish soundtrack: ambulance sirens all day and all night.

Neha pulled up the surging positivity and death rate on her iPhone. I already knew the numbers from Governors Cuomo and Murphy's daily press conferences that vacillated from heart-stoppingly traumatic to surprisingly hilarious with Cuomo's bizarre PowerPoint slides simply reading, "Younger people not fully complying" in a yellow banner followed by the bullet point "YOU ARE WRONG."

"The numbers" was now the first and last thing I looked at every day, like a gambler itching to check their fate on lotto tickets. It made me dizzy with adrenaline and nausea, imagining thousands of people around me wheezing for air, convulsing, alone.

My last "normal day" in the "before times" Manhattan hinted everything was about to shift. I almost got into a fight with a stranger who refused to be serviced by an Asian American aesthetician at a Lash Loft, where my friend Sandylee worked. Sandylee told me the customer's vile insults, parroted from the vitriolic racism Trump spewed. Disgusted, I walked through Union Square and Washington Square Park. Both were empty.

I made my way to Monte's Trattoria on MacDougal Street. As I clomped down the steps, Chef Pietro Mosconi called out,

"Professora!" I spent many Friday afternoons with him, sipping Montepulciano wine, asking about Chef's childhood in Piacenza, memorizing how his mother baked befanini cookies for Christmas, or about his ship voyage to America while writing. He said I reminded him of his daughter, an author in Malibu. The iconic Italian restaurant was next door to the Comedy Cellar; it opened in 1918 at the end of World War I and the start of the influenza pandemic. Now it was empty. Chef said, "Everyone is too scared to come in because of the outbreak in Italy," as he handed me a basket of bread. Some of the stories the staff told me from that week while leaning on the bar echoed the anti-Italian immigration terror their families experienced a century ago when the restaurant first opened. In the early twentieth century, anti-Catholic Klan members targeted Italian immigrants. Caricatures saturated dime novels and films in America, and Italians were cast as dirty criminals and mobsters.

When I left, Chef hugged me goodbye and suggested, "Come back next week. I'll teach you how to make the tortelloni you like."

I held him close as he kissed my cheek. We both knew I was not coming back.

I walked through a vacant Penn Station at 3:00 p.m. and was delighted to discover the Walgreens on the Amtrak level restocked antibacterial hand wipes. Score! I bought three for $5.34. Unknowingly this would be the last time I would shop in a store and exchange pleasantries with a checkout clerk for over a year.

On March 10, 2020, a conductor I befriended approached me on the platform and quietly said, "Don't get on the trains anymore. Go home." His tone frightened me. I don't know what he knew. Later I wondered if he knew Peter Petrassi, the first of 157 MTA workers killed by COVID-19.[3]

* * *

"De Blasio announced they need three thousand ventilators by next week and fifteen thousand by May," I said, muffled behind my leopard print mask. My hot breath fogged my vintage sunglasses. I hadn't yet figured out glasses need to sit atop masks at the bridge of your nose.

Neha rapidly flicked her index finger against the glass screen. She was scrolling through the county death charts, pulling up ours. She wanted to see if the burning mattress was in today's numbers or if it would post tomorrow.

"There is a refrigerated truck outside my friend's apartment on the Upper West Side. She said it's a portable morgue for the elderly care facility." Neha was too zeroed in to react to anything I was saying.

She was running mathematical equations for exponential growth, checking each state's peak estimates against her own, trying to guess the trough when I could try to get to California. She suddenly looked up, resuming a conversation aloud she must have been having in her head.

"This is the kind of disaster rich people spread, but poor people pay for with their lives. This is only the start. We're in a blip. By the end of the year, you'll *wish* we were at today's numbers," she said bleakly. She slung her phone back in her messenger bag.

A blip? I shuddered with a gut-wrenching pang of despair for our country. It was ghastly. I also sensed she was right.

There was no hope for true leadership. Trump was a comorbidity to America's ills. He treasonously encouraged rebellion to "liberate" Michigan, Minnesota, and Virginia, claiming they were "under siege" by public health lockdown measures.[4] He ignored blue states' governors' pleas for federal help. New York and New Jersey stood on the front lines of a political slaughter, masquerading as political theater.

Every day I learned more acquaintances were sick than I could keep track of, and others died—thirty-year-old Zoe Mungin, a social studies teacher in Brooklyn, who was turned away from

hospitals likely due to racism because emergency medical technicians assumed she was just having panic attacks, and ninety-three-
year-old Ruth, who mailed me cakes on my birthday.[5] I watched
on Zoom as my friend pushed dirt on her forty-one-year-old as-
tronomer husband's grave while sobbing, "I'm sorry, Andy just
really loved life." I thought about how Andy said we were all made
of stars.

Neha told me to go back into my apartment and lock myself
away while the numbers spiked. "Six months. Wait out your lease."

While she recited medical facts about pulmonary embolisms
from blood clotting, upper respiratory blood vessels, and overac-
tive immune responses that made victims drown in their lungs, my
mind meandered through murky family history.

The only thing I knew about my great-grandmother was that
she contracted the 1918 flu in Texas and was stricken with mysterious maladies for the rest of her life. The only time I met her, she
was blind and said, "The good Lord doesn't want me. The devil
doesn't want me. So I just sit here and wait." I thought about my
grandma, who went into Yellowstone National Park alone before
her wedding so she would always know she could survive without
anyone's help, and the cross-country trips she made as a military
spouse. I could hear the sounds my grandfathers made while dying of congestive heart failure and how the same year they both
died my father and I were exposed to tuberculosis somewhere
between Los Angeles and Austin on my first plane ride. I had to
get chest X-rays and take pills every night for a year. The memory
of their bitter taste flooded my mouth as I took a deep breath in
2020 just to make sure I still could.

"Drive as fast as you can!" Neha hollered again as she dashed by
me, heading to lock herself inside. "Wait until mid-August. Then,
make a run for it."

★ ★ ★

Two years. Two years. Two years.

I whispered it to myself in a convoluted jumble of disbelief and determination as I stared at the apartment ceiling. *Two years.* I knew from history what we were in for if this was a pandemic. Two years. Two years. Two years *at best.*

March and April 2020 crept into an eternity. I was now in a new state of consciousness, and time was no longer linear. It was an endless golden childhood summer of no school and no alarm clocks; "School's out forever" was true. I was also on high alert. My hair fell out in clumps, and I developed a stress rash. My senses attuned as if in a slow-motion car crash, as I was inundated by the coughs and terrified gasps for air that came through the paper-thin apartment walls that surrounded me.

After two weeks indoors, my legs ached from inactivity. In my solitude, I turned to history for strength, reminding myself how lucky I was to be an educated, independent, employed, and free woman in twenty-first-century America. The empathy I felt while given the slightest peek into the lives of historical figures I taught overwhelmed me. I marveled at the enslaved Harriet Jacobs crouching for seven years in a crawl space under her grandmother's roof, so low she could not stand, so she could watch her children through the floorboards. On week three without groceries, I thought of the World War II hero and Olympian Louis Zamperini floating in the Pacific on his rapidly deflating raft as shark fins encircled him as he recited his mama's recipes to stay awake. I thought about John McCain and how Donald Trump said he only liked war heroes who were never captured. I realized I was the same age as Florence Owen Thompson, the "migrant mother" photographed by Dorothea Lange when she too fled to California during a national catastrophe.

I wasn't enslaved. I wasn't a soldier. I wasn't a prisoner. I wasn't a migrant mother with starving babies, picking peas for other people to eat during the Great Depression. I had virtually nothing in common with these Americans except their descriptions of confinement, hunger, and fear of a deadly threat—descriptions that moved me through the nights as I struggled with my fear and isolation. Despite all the visual rhetoric, country songs, folk music, blackface tunes, and road trip movies portraying American freedom as a vast open road, the other side of the coin was true. America was a place of mass incarceration, immobility, deprivation, and captivity. America had a consistent history of family separation. I was now peering into the emotional depth of those histories too.

* * *

The Federal-Aid Highway Act of 1956 was created to protect and defend Americans. It linked military bases and cities, allowing easy mass transport of weapons or civilians in the case of an attack during the Cold War. But American roads were not safe for all Americans in the past, nor are they today. One of my best friends from high school, Darlene, said she would drive back across the country with me, but she vowed never to drive through Texas. She is Black and the same age as Sandra Bland. I thought of *The Negro Motorist Green-Book* and about how so many Black leaders were lost or injured or terrorized in cars: Bessie Smith, James Weldon Johnson, Jack Johnson, Recy Taylor, Sammy Davis Jr., and James Byrd Jr. Entire communities in Los Angeles were razed to make highways. Cars themselves had become weapons of mass destruction during the Trump administration after the Charlottesville attack that left Heather Heyer dead in 2017. America's streets were also not safe for my friend's handsome older brother Jermaine. One of the most heartbreaking photos I have is of my friend cradling Jermaine's service flag in the same national cemetery where my grandparents are buried.

Jermaine was a proud US Navy vet who served in the Persian Gulf. In 2012, a white drunk driver hit him while he was walking home with his groceries in Miami. He was supposed to make dinner with his kids. Witnesses said Jermaine was thrown thirty feet and wrapped around a bus stop. The judge reprimanded, "Some of the allegations are very disturbing," in court, she read aloud that the driver "got out of his car. He went over to the pedestrian and yelled at the pedestrian and left" in his white Chevrolet Impala. Officers were stunned by his indifference to human life. Jermaine went into hospitals and rehabilitation centers but didn't come back out until years later. His official death date was June 6, 2016. When my friend showed me his flag, I whispered, "He waited until D-Day to go." His perfect timing awed us. But we both knew it wasn't his timing.[6]

As a classical concert pianist, Darlene was obsessed with knowing what Jermaine heard that evening. She kept asking me every few minutes after it happened. She recorded her concerts. She made playlists for him. Always Rachmaninoff.

"Do you think he heard the people on the street trying to help him?" she asked. I responded, "We know he heard the songs you played for him in the hospital." I prayed that he had not heard the hateful words of the man who ultimately took his life. In 2020, when she heard about Ahmaud Arbery and the truck, Darlene's shaking came back.

Many of us stood silently in our living rooms for eight minutes and forty-six seconds as Mr. George Floyd's funeral baptized us in our screens' glow. Darlene called me and talked about the look in George Floyd's eyes. "They bulged. He was so scared." She ran to throw up. She said, "I wish they would call him Mr. Floyd. I call him Mr. Floyd. I don't know why. He could have been my dad."

Conversely, my dad was once unknowingly given a counterfeit hundred-dollar bill at one of his art shows. When he tried to deposit the shows' proceeds, the bank discovered the fraudulent currency. The bank teller apologized *to him* for the inconvenience. It was a strange anecdote we remembered after George Floyd's public execution. It was a bizarre memory, not a death sentence for my white father.

Darlene was driving somewhere in Las Vegas. Millions of Americans were in the streets protesting. The casinos reopened. New York and New Jersey were under curfew. I called her at three o'clock in the morning when the helicopters stopped hovering overhead. She was cussing at the neon signs. She was scared her students would get *it* and told me how to disinfect piano keys.

"I just don't know what to say or think anymore," she said. I didn't either.

"I think Jermaine can hear the people on the street trying to help him now," I told her. "They're finally loud enough."

We stayed on the phone as millions of Americans flooded the streets demanding racial justice and just listened, alone, together.

★ ★ ★

It was mid-August and time to go. I couldn't get packing material. I folded dishes into quilts and photographs into clothing. For half a year, the only way I could make space was to rearrange my apartment's furniture. Now, all of America was in front of me. I wanted to count the cars on the New Jersey Turnpike, but it seemed no one had gone to look for America in the summer of 2020 except me. The freeway was empty except for Amazon delivery trucks.

I was in a rented Nissan Rogue with Minnesota plates. I was glad. Minnesota could go either way politically, so the plates gave me cover in both red and blue states.

The first night I made it to Wheeling, West Virginia. At a rest stop, a Greyhound bus pulled in. The passengers streamed off. Few had masks, but they were required to get into the bathroom. I saw a man wrap a T-shirt around his face. A mother tried tying a bandanna on her children, but they kept sliding down. I pulled out three of my disposable masks. "Don't take these off," I told her. She looked at me as if she wanted to cry while standing by a sign that said "BE SAFE! BE SMART! STAY SIX FEET APART!"

In Ohio, I stopped in my first cemetery. I finally saw other cars after long stretches on the highway by myself. They weren't pulling in to grieve or stretch their legs like I was. They were living there. Likely evicted, they were sleeping in their cars. Thirty minutes later, I turned a corner and found hundreds of cars split into two lines that backed up for miles as I sped by. One lane was for COVID-19 testing. The other lane was for a food bank.

In Buckeye Lake, I noticed that the McDonald's posted a sign: "We are currently offering a limited menu," it said in bold. When I skimmed the menu, I noticed what was missing: McDonald's had no beef.

I followed highway signs to Abraham Lincoln's tomb at Oak Ridge Cemetery in Springfield, Illinois. It was another rural cemetery from the 1850s with 365 acres of rolling green hills. Springfield had magical golden light at sunset and enormous old trees. The lawns? "Green Grass of Home" vibes. Lincoln's burial site was a point of contention. Politicians wanted his remains in downtown Springfield, rightfully predicting Americans would make pilgrimages to his burial site. Still, Mary Todd Lincoln wanted her husband in the new rural cemetery, Oak Ridge. A 117-feet granite obelisk and bronze sculpture of Lincoln's face towered over the perfectly manicured cemetery. Henry McNeal Turner, a Black minister and state representative in Reconstruction-era Georgia, proclaimed, "Every colored person that can visit this monument ought to do it." When it opened to the public, 25,000 people came.[7]

As I entered the utterly abandoned cemetery and memorial, a park ranger reminded me to keep my mask on. He was the first person to speak with me for days. Of course, I would, but I laughed to myself—to protect Lincoln from COVID-19? He was already dead. Famously so.

As I stood in the awe-inspiring shrine to the Great Emancipator, I gravitated to his wife's memorial. Mary Todd Lincoln was one of the millions of Americans in the Civil War Era of mass death who identified with spiritualism (a burgeoning religious movement that argued the living could communicate with the deceased as souls lived on).[8] For some, it was hokey entertainment. For others, it was their desperate lifeline to their beloved while bereaved.

Mary Lincoln held at least eight séances in the Red Room of the White House after her charismatic son Willie died of typhoid in 1862. Mary claimed her son came to the foot of her bed each night. After her husband was assassinated beside her at Ford's Theatre, she locked herself inside a small room in the White House. Mary paid for a portrait by the "spirit photographer" William H. Mumler (often considered a huckster fraud) that depicted an apparition of Lincoln hovering behind her.[9] Mary wrote to the antislavery politician Charles Sumner, "only a slight veil separates us from the loved and lost. To me there is comfort in the thought that although unseen by us they are very near."[10] She wasn't alone. Queen Victoria held séances in Buckingham Palace to communicate with her husband, Prince Albert.

People thought Mary Todd Lincoln was insane and ridiculed her. I could not imagine the kind of PTSD she must have lived with. As I looked at her memorial that read 1818–1882, I remembered how in April 2020, when my best friend's husband fought for his life against COVID-19, I also engaged with spiritualism. My best friend screamed, "He looked so scared!" repeatedly into the cell phone while she was in a hospital parking lot beside a COVID tent. I had never heard that tone in her voice. *She* was so scared. *I* was so scared, but I couldn't let her know that. I tried to piece together everything she had to do, from turning on humidifiers to getting him vitamin D.

I was readying myself psychologically and financially for what I would need to do to step up and support her if my newlywed best friend suddenly became a COVID widow. I could never tell her that. I never did. After we had done everything on the checklists the doctors gave us, I told her that I had called a psychic. Her husband would have found this foolish, like Lincoln did. The psychic told me to imagine all of their deceased loved ones surrounding him, protecting him in his sickbed, and holding him in a protective healing seal of green light. Ultimately, she was telling us to visualize recovery and pray. We could do that.

Spiritualism was usually women's work regardless of race or class. *The History of Woman Suffrage* edited by Elizabeth Cady

Stanton and Susan B. Anthony claimed, "The only religious sect in the world . . . that has recognized the equality of woman is the Spiritualists."[11] The idea of talking with the unseen dead was not far fetched. The United States Postal Service, lithography, telegraphs, and the advent of photography (especially portrait studios) let Americans connect with, see, and talk with their loved ones searching for gold in California or fighting for racial justice and a new world in the Civil War.[12] Much like reality television shows where globally famous mediums talk to the dead, in nineteenth-century America, conjuring, trance lecturing, spirit rapping, and mediumship shows for thrilling entertainment were commonplace.[13]

Entire industries cropped up surrounding the materiality of the dead. This allowed the bereaved to immerse themselves in a sensory world of grief. There were mourning ritual books that gave systematic accounts of how to properly observe death in the home and society. Mourning fashion was retailed, stereotypes commemorated funerals, memorial quilts were sewn of the dead's clothing, there were death masks, sheet music for home parlors, and locks of hair were made into jewelry so the dead could adorn the living.

Gazing upon, touching, and vigilantly watching the dead was a part of mid-nineteenth-century mourning practices that could include routinely exhuming the dead from tombs. Ralph Waldo Emerson, who lost his twenty-year-old wife to tuberculosis, wrote in his diary that he wanted to lie down in her tomb with her. On March 29, 1832, he wrote a single unsettling sentence: "I visited Ellen's tomb & opened the coffin." She had been dead a year.[14]

Westward expansion and the Civil War meant loved ones could not engage in this kind of physical grieving with their dead. America turned to new technologies, belief systems, and urban landscapes to reconnect. I would relate to this anguish when my eldest aunt died unexpectedly in February 2021. Because we feared the specter of COVID-19, her son was shuffling outside their apartment, clutching his chest in shock, unable to go inside.

I could not hug him. I could not go inside and respectfully prepare her body how I wanted: to cover her with a sheet, to put flowers around her, and fix her blond hair one last time. Instead, my dad and I contacted a funeral home. We played my aunt's favorite music as we waited. The sun was shining. Los Angeles was so inundated with COVID-19 deaths, my aunt's body was stored in a refrigerated truck, the same invention that came about during the Civil War. Her autopsy and cremation did not occur until several weeks after her death. There was never a funeral. Los Angeles that winter lost so many people in the second wave of COVID-19; the crematoriums were running 24-7 despite the environmental damage. If you looked closely, it was raining ash.

During COVID-19 we communicated with our distant loved ones in new ways. We attended funerals on Zoom, said goodbye to those in the hospital on FaceTime, and text messaged videos and photographs back and forth that shot around the world in a second. Our cities, physical spaces, and environments were reconstituted just like they were during the Civil War.

★ ★ ★

Before leaving Springfield, Illinois, I sat on a bus stop advertising Mr. Lincoln's Souvenirs facing the Lincoln Home National Historic Site. I then walked to the Capitol, where Lincoln worked. I thought about the Springfield race riots. I sat in an empty plaza and tuned into Barack Obama's speech at the 2020 Democratic National Convention while seated where he announced his presidential candidacy years ago. A timid woman named Rachel approached and asked if she could listen too, six feet away. She was also alone, trying to get home. While I absorbed the historical spectacle, she was terrified by the plaza's emptiness. She asked if she could follow me on Route 66. We left the parking lot by Lincoln's home. She stayed behind me, visible in my rearview mirror, until I pulled over in Oklahoma to look at the site of the Tulsa riot, the Woody Guthrie Center (closed, of course), and, later, the memorial to honor the Oklahoma City bombing.

In Indian Country, I saw signs reading "NON RESIDENTS, NON TRIBAL MEMBERS: KEEP OUT CURFEW, 8PM–5AM" and the closed-up fry-bread stops and Native American art trading posts.

I stopped in Amarillo and Albuquerque, and I dipped down off Route 66 to see Sedona. I savored the glory of the purple skies radiating from behind the majestic red rocks and prayed. The manzanita in the light rain smelled like childhood family campouts. Something about that place bellowed deep inside me and gave me peace beyond my understanding.

The drive through the California desert was scorching. The temperature reached 116 degrees, and it was hard to find gas out among the Joshua trees.

I cried when I saw the first green road sign pointing toward Los Angeles. I did not know what disease might be lurking in my body, but no matter what, I made it far enough that if I got sick, I would make it home to my loved ones and see them one more time.

★ ★ ★

My family would survive. My best friends who contracted COVID-19 survived. Vaccinated and back in Manhattan 562 days later, I sat in an outdoor tent on MacDougal Street and waited anxiously to find out who at my favorite restaurant had survived.

Suddenly I heard a familiar voice yell "Professora! You're here!" and Chef hugged me. He told a bystander, "She's like family." Everyone who worked in the restaurant survived.

We sat on the bustling city street, still unable to eat indoors but vaccinated during the delta surge, poured a glass of wine, cheered, and said a prayer of thanks that God had seen us through and brought us back together. This time he said, "You tell *me* a story, I eat," and I picked up where we had left off.

TEN

THE AFTERLIFE OF BLACK POLITICAL RADICALISM

Peniel E. Joseph

The police killings of George Floyd and Breonna Taylor in 2020 sparked a movement that cast a spotlight on systemic racism, white supremacy, and Black rebellion in the face of political catastrophe and personal heartbreak. Dizzying juxtapositions abounded over a year that seemed to encapsulate, with each passing day, the grandeur and travails of American history.

Black people form the beating heart of the American story, even as their presence remains viewed as pathological. In many ways 2020 and the age of Black Lives Matter 2.0 represents the answer to W. E. B. Du Bois's "unasked question" of "how does it feel to be a problem?" Black political rebellions that reverberated around the world turned that question on its head, asking instead: What kind of society revels in the public torture, arrest, and execution of human beings who are Black?[1]

BLM 2.0 began in the immediate aftermath of George Floyd's public execution, transforming a social movement rooted in the 2012 death of Trayvon Martin that took on national significance in the wake of the 2014 police killing of Michael Brown into a global phenomenon in which an estimated 15–26 million Americans took part. Around the world, from the United Kingdom to Germany and Nigeria, solidarity demonstrations turned BLM into a metaphor for human rights and social justice movements internationally.

The racial disparities accompanying the COVID-19 pandemic disproportionately gutted already vulnerable Black communities beginning in the first weeks of March 2020. Black folk confronted premature death in new and terrifyingly familiar ways as winter turned to spring.

As a Black man raised by a single mother in New York City during the late 1970s and 1980s, I watched the scenes of suffering unfold with the suffocating intimacy of a familial tragedy. From my adopted city of Austin, Texas, I observed with increasing horror news of pandemic outbreaks in my hometown of Queens, New York.

Elsewhere, parts of America made famous by the Civil Rights Movement experienced the devastating shock of pandemic-related death. Albany, Georgia, birthplace of a movement for racial justice that attracted Dr. Martin Luther King Jr. and the Southern Christian Leadership Conference in 1961 and 1962, became ground zero for premature Black death. The most vulnerable Black folk— the elderly, immunocompromised, the poor who lived in tightly packed, racially segregated housing projects, the housing insecure, and the incarcerated—caught the illness quicker and died sooner.[2]

Black frontline workers employed in warehouses, hospitals, nursing homes, meatpacking plants, post offices, emergency services, and other exposed spaces faced a morbid catch-22: they could risk exposure to COVID or face losing their already precarious livelihoods. Black folks residing in America's lower frequencies confronted the pandemic in lost wages, the inability to pay rent, food insecurity, illness, and death.

I counted myself among the most fortunate Black people in America. Able to continue my university teaching via Zoom classes, I could spend more time with my daughter whose prekindergarten classes were all online. My entire family, including my mother in New York and my emergency room doctor brother in Maryland, were all safe.

As the "Pandemic Spring" continued, I tried to sound the alarm about how systems of structural racism, violence, and white supremacy were exacerbating both the impact of COVID-19 on Black America and the national response—including a federal bailout authored by the Trump administration—amplified inequities so deeply baked into the nation's DNA as to have become normal. Black businesses were more likely to close and less likely to receive government assistance. Black workers across the nation were underrepresented among the labor force who could work from home. Black students were more likely not to have internet access for virtual school. The Black poor were in a double bind with widespread school closures impacting the ability of millions of children to access a nutritious breakfast, hot lunch, tutoring, and after-school care, not to mention the mental, physical, and wellness resources normally provided by public schools.

In my role as a scholar-activist and public intellectual, I argued that America's civil rights legacy—while fully aware of that legacy's contradictions, shortcomings, and failures—was at risk in the face of a pandemic that upended myths of racial progress that endured well into the first two decades of the twenty-first century.

What happened to Black politics? How had dreams of Black citizenship that soared in the wake of Barack Obama's watershed 2008 presidential election curdled into a community under open siege amid the presidency of Donald Trump, an unapologetic white supremacist? Why did it seem that large parts of the Black community seemed destined to experience suffering, misery, and premature death?

When I think back to the first four months, three weeks, and five days of 2020, what stands out is the silence—not from Black people but from the nation in the wake of Black death. The carnage the pandemic wrought on Black communities that spring took place within a rapidly transforming historical context.

COVID-19 appeared like a lightning storm in unexpected places, where its greatest harm befell the most vulnerable.

And then we heard the rolling thunder.

George Floyd's public execution on May 25, 2020, telescoped one hundred and fifty-five years of American history into an agonizing nine plus minutes that found a Black man being murdered by a white police officer in Minneapolis, Minnesota. The viral video, released at the exact moment prevaccination pandemic restrictions nationwide were easing, helped spark American history's largest social justice movement.[3]

Floyd's murder came on the heels of another viral video of a white woman, Amy Cooper, in New York City's Central Park, calling the cops on a Black man, Chris Cooper (no relation), who requested she put her dog on a leash. Cooper became the year's most notorious "Karen"—the new moniker for white women who casually weaponize racial privilege, the racialized fear of sexual violence, and police violence against Black people for occupying spaces they supposedly should not. That Chris Cooper, the Harvard-educated bird-watching Black man, shared the same surname with Amy Cooper, the white woman who casually wielded the police as her personal hit squad, is one of the subtle reminders of racial slavery and the often-silent role white women played in upholding the peculiar and cruel institution. The vulnerability of being Black while walking, shopping, barbecuing, swimming, or even just *breathing* played out more acutely than ever in the wake of the pandemic and Floyd's death.[4]

The next days unfolded in a dizzying blur as protests in support of justice for Floyd grew exponentially around the nation, spreading to cities in Europe and Africa. Floyd's death helped to fuel what I call Black radicalism's afterlife.

Black radicalism is most easily identified with the Black Power–era politics of the 1960s and 1970s, with images of Malcolm X jabbing his finger in the air during a Harlem rally to make a particularly emphatic point, or the Black Panthers marching, with swashbuckling bravado, on courthouse steps in Oakland, California, vowing to defend Black people against a police state it identified as fascist. Angela Davis's and Kathleen Cleaver's towering afros have become more iconic than the political movement they represented.[5]

The Black Power Movement represents a high point in a larger historical tableau. A mélange of radical Black activists, including feminists, Marxists, and liberal integrationists, attempted to fundamentally transform Black people's relationship with the state.[6]

Black radicalism is a central tenet of America's three periods of Reconstruction. The first, which took place in the shadow of the end of racial slavery and the catastrophe of Civil War, featured the abolition democracy of Black activists who became the unheralded architects of a second American founding. The Reconstruction Amendments opened up new political worlds. Black men and women stepped into civic arenas and helped reshape American democracy, from rural southern hamlets to the nation's capital. They sought to fundamentally alter Black people's relationship to their own bodies, prizing autonomy, independence, family reunification, legal marriage, education, land ownership, and dignity above all else. Political citizenship claims grew in tandem with the personal dignity that always existed, even during chattel slavery, even if it remained unrecognized by white supremacist violence, terror, and intimidation structures.[7]

America's First Reconstruction, from 1865 to the 1898 massacre in Wilmington, North Carolina, laid the groundwork for mass incarceration, racial segregation, and anti-Black violence and terror as well as movements for radical Black dignity and citizenship in the face of regimes of political, economic, social, environmental, and cultural terror, degradation, and death.[8]

The modern Civil Rights Movement, between the May 17, 1954, passage of the *Brown v. Board of Education* Supreme Court decision that declared the "separate but equal" doctrine unconstitutional and the April 4, 1968 assassination of Dr. Martin Luther King Jr., was directly inspired by the radical Black internationalism of the 1930s and 1940s. The Depression-era and Second World War freedom dreams found Black radicals confronting racial capitalism through Popular Front organizations, the Communist Party, Black nationalist and Pan-African groups (many of whom owed a major debt to the Universal Negro Improvement Association and the political organizing of Marcus and Amy Jacques Garvey), labor, and civil rights networks. Activists including the ever-inspiring Ella Jo Baker (the future founder of the Student Nonviolent Coordinating Committee), the multitalented Paul Robeson, and the brilliant W. E. B. Du Bois embarked on a campaign to fundamentally transform American democracy. The Cold War dimmed but did not extinguish the era's radical antiracist and anti-imperialist politics, which found new life during the 1960s in the respective movements for Black dignity and citizenship innovated by Malcolm X and Martin Luther King.[9]

Malcolm X's notion of Black radical dignity and Martin Luther King Jr.'s conceptions of Black radical citizenship are especially crucial to this particular historic era. Malcolm defined Black dignity as the recognition of humanity inherently denied in America. From Malcolm's perspective, citizenship could never be realized without Black people having a deeper understanding of their intrinsic worth, beauty, and intelligence. This required a deep appreciation of history, both in America and elsewhere, a project Malcolm spent his entire short life trying to complete.[10]

King defined citizenship as more than just voting rights and racial integration. He defined citizenship as more than merely the absence of racial and economic oppression. For King, citizenship meant redistributive justice that allowed Black life to flourish. Good jobs, a living wage, food justice, health care, and the end to domestic and global violence structures encompassed the aspirational citizenship King called for. Malcolm X's call to transform struggles into an international human rights movement dovetailed with King's call for a beloved community free of militarism, materialism, and racism.[11]

We are living in the midst of America's Third Reconstruction, a period marked, thus far, by four important hinge points: The 2008 election of Barack Obama; the 2013 eruption of what I call BLM 1.0; the 2016 election of Donald Trump; and the racial and political reckoning of 2020.

The Black Lives Matter hashtag that became a movement in 2013 transformed once again seven years later. Seasoned by its efforts to build a national consensus on Black life in America and globally, BLM emerged as a sprawling, panoramic movement for Black dignity and citizenship. Shaken by the wanton murders and casual political cruelty of a criminal punishment system run amok, BLM 1.0 argued that the misnamed justice system was, in fact, a gateway to multipronged structures of racial and economic injustice in America. These structures invested in institutions that punished, tortured, and murdered Black people instead of providing high-achieving schools, good jobs, environmentally safe neighborhoods, housing, and health care.

The very phrase "Black Lives Matter" sparked controversy then, inspiring a white supremacist and law enforcement backlash—"All Lives Matter" and "Blue Lives Matter"—whose very existence reflected a bad faith adherence to color-blind racism that infected the entire national discourse around race.

BLM laid the groundwork for the defense of Black life in the age of Trump. The Movement for Black Lives, a group of dozens of nonprofits including the Legal Defense Fund, that formed in 2014 released a bold policy agenda two years later, anticipating the revolution that would be required to achieve dignity while pressing for citizenship in America's searing racial wilderness.[12]

BLM 2.0 reached unprecedented heights in 2020. In the wake of Floyd's public execution, Black radical activists, who organized under the BLM banner, transformed America's racial and political consciousness. Black feminists would prove crucial in this regard. Ayọ Tometti, Alicia Garza, and Patrisse Cullors—the trio of grassroots Black feminist organizers who founded

BLM—stood on the shoulders of earlier generations of radical activists. This included Kimberlé Crenshaw, the legal scholar, critical race theorist, and activist whose African American Policy Forum started the #SayHerName campaign to cast a spotlight on the Black women and girls who were murdered by the police but too often left forgotten in the roll call of Black martyrs capable of inspiring community action.[13]

Breonna Taylor, a Black medical worker who was shot by police in her apartment during a botched drug raid in Louisville, Kentucky, almost two and half months before Floyd's murder, became one of the global faces of BLM 2.0. Taylor's story captured international headlines, her murder was the subject of long investigative pieces in the *New York Times* and other mainstream newspapers, and her image posthumously graced the cover of a special *Vanity Fair* issue edited by the Black writer and journalist Ta-Nehisi Coates.[14]

The political rebellions unfolding across the nation reflected centuries of struggle for Black dignity and citizenship. Black radicalism, from the abolitionist democracy urgings of Frederick Douglass to the crusades to reform American racist ideas of punishment by Ida B. Wells, represents the wellspring of national political transformation. If radicalism involves going to the root of a problem, Black radicals have confronted racial capitalism, patriarchy, misogynoir, queerphobia, transphobia, and structures and regimes of violence against the incarcerated, immigrants, people with disabilities, the housing insecure, and those forced to live in environmentally toxic neighborhoods within and outside of the United States.[15]

BLM 2.0 represented a kaleidoscopic reimaging of the Black radical tradition. Crenshaw's notion of intersectionality—a concept inspired by almost two centuries of Black feminist activism—became one of the core frameworks of a global movement for Black dignity and citizenship. Recognizing that so-called identity politics that acknowledged how race, class, gender, sexuality, geography, and ability impacted communities in America and around the world proved both controversial and liberating.[16]

COVID-19's blatant inequities, therefore, proved a point a long time in the making. The pandemic impacted everyone, but differently. The more than 900,000 Americans who have died as of this writing experienced the pandemic in vastly distinct ways from those who survived.

Black Lives Matter represents the continuation and afterlife of the Black radical tradition. That tradition combated racial slavery, sought to make Reconstruction a second American founding capable of turning the nation into a multiracial democracy, and demanded reparations for slavery, recognition of Black humanity, and a reckoning with the institutions of white supremacy that flourished long after the Civil War.

Massive rebellions, ones that were truly global in scope, unleashed by the combination of the pandemic, the George Floyd protests, and the violence of racial capitalism were decades— centuries—in the making. But the response proved remarkably coherent, framed by an intersectional political analysis and policy demands authored by a contemporary generation of Black and queer feminist activists and organizers who represent an essential part of the Black radical tradition.

In 2020, statements such as "abolish prisons" and "defund the police" became mainstream. Movements nurtured for decades, at times over a century, in networks of Black radical and feminist organizations, nonprofits, informal policy advocacy groups, churches, schools, and social media were ready when the time came. The 2016 BLM policy agenda proved vital in this regard, offering the most granular policy recommendations for investments in Black people over punishment, reparations for slavery, a universal basic income and living wage, free health care and education and housing for Black communities, and an understanding that in order to build a new world vestiges of the old order needed to come tumbling down.[17]

The beauty of the Black Lives Matter rebellions of 2020 is found in how concepts of radical Black dignity and radical Black citizenship have converged into a comprehensive movement that recognizes the depth and breadth of racial capitalism, the violence of white supremacy, and the genius of ordinary Black folk who turned the world upside down against the backdrop of relentless state violence, a global health pandemic, and a society hell-bent on denying this reality.

Angela Davis, the Black Power–era revolutionary activist, is one of the foremost prison abolitionists in the world. That movement is rooted in the abolition democracy that Du Bois historicizes in *Black Reconstruction*, his 1934 masterpiece that reinterpreted the period after slavery as a missed opportunity to create a new and just America. This perspective refuted the Dunning school of history that charged Reconstruction as a failure thwarted by Black pathology, sexual violence against women, and incompetence and corruption. Davis contributed new layers to Du Bois's notion of prison abolition, through both her own historical reflections on Black women's pivotal role in shaping concepts of dignity and citizenship during racial slavery and her real-world activism in making the abolition of prisons and systems of punishment the central tenet of an effort to remake American society and the entire world.[18]

Black radicalism's afterlife unfolded in bold, brilliant, and unexpected ways during 2020. Like an episode of *Lovecraft Country*—the Black science fiction, horror, fantasy, racial allegory that mashed up Jim Crow racism within a space- and time-bending milieu—a year of protest, politics, and pandemic featured striking juxtapositions that recalled the first and second periods of Reconstruction.

Between fifteen and twenty-six million people protested in support of racial justice, the largest number in American history. Millions of white people joined in protests that were organized, led, and conceived, in large part, by Black radical feminist and queer organizers. Most of the demonstrations were peaceful, and displays of police violence against nonviolent demonstrators exposed the political cruelty of a system that Black folk had been fighting against since the beginning of the republic.[19] Black activism transformed itself into a living archive; a sinuously expressive organism demanding bodily autonomy, creative expression, displays of the ecstatic mixed with mourning rituals. Our grief and pain animated the streets of America even as our joy and resilience forecast alternative modes of thinking, breathing, questioning, living, and being human. In 2020, millions of Black bodies assembled in cities, rural hamlets, suburbs—from farms to factories—and presented themselves as witnesses and participants in an unfolding political revolution. They embodied a living archive of resistance, courage, fortitude, and, most central of all, love.

Clear-eyed demands for justice from below upended Black politics from above. Faded memories of gnarled Black hands reaching for blood-stained ballots fueled a modern-day voting rights movement that stood on the broad shoulders of an unbowed and unbroken line of precious Black ancestors. Stacey Abrams, the former gubernatorial candidate from Georgia, turned a 2018 defeat marred by allegations of voter suppression into a coordinated movement for Black political power. Abrams's voting rights organizing helped elect the first Black senator from the Peach State, Raphael Warnock, who presided over Dr. King's former pulpit, Ebenezer Baptist Church. Warnock in turn dragged Jon Ossoff, a thirty-three-year-old Jewish American candidate, to victory, giving the Democratic Party a slim majority in the Senate.[20]

Black voters, especially Black women, helped to save democracy by rescuing the former vice president Joseph Biden's candidacy in the South Carolina primaries. Some of the same Black voters pushed in some quarters to choose Biden over more left-wing candidates, particularly Senators Bernie Sanders and Elizabeth Warren. Unspoken in such castigation is the knowledge that

Black Democratic primary voters in South Carolina could trace back a genealogy of fighting for Black citizenship that went back to Reconstruction when Black folks were the majority.[21]

In 1895, the South Carolina delegate Thomas Miller, at a state convention organized expressly to disenfranchise the Negro vote in the wake of "redemptionist" backlash, lamented about the "eight years in power" Blacks enjoyed in the state during Radical Reconstruction. From 1868 to 1876, Black South Carolinians led the way in creating a politics that built hospitals and invested in public schools, roads, bridges, and anti-poverty efforts that found a way to bring universal healing to a state scarred by violent civil war. Those voters who chose Biden did so with the memory of a not-so-distant past that continues to inform the present.[22]

Kamala Harris, the first Black woman vice president in American history, proved a beneficiary of this Third Reconstruction, even as her past choices as San Francisco district attorney, California attorney general, and senator made her an unlikely vehicle for the radical change the times and the BLM movement demanded.[23]

The January 6, 2021, white riot at the United States Capitol proved to be, not an aberration, but a central part of American history. Donald Trump's "Big Lie" in the aftermath of his defeat at the hands of Black America's overwhelmingly supported candidates—Joe Biden and Kamala Harris—continued the "Lost Cause" narrative upholding white supremacy as the nation's true moral guide and political soul. Since the rioters, and the president, cited voter fraud in Black cities that helped Biden win Georgia, Pennsylvania, Michigan, and Wisconsin, the assault on the Capitol represented a denial of Black citizenship.[24]

Yet instances of Black joy flowered against assaults on Black humanity. The BLM protests inspired local political battles that led to concrete policy changes, including the reallocation of millions of dollars intended for punishment to restorative justice, education, mental health, and anti-poverty programs. Black folk danced, sang, chanted, yelled, screamed, and channeled the hopes and dreams of generations who dared to imagine an America beyond the confines of punishment, prisons, and premature Black death.

Black history emphatically took center stage throughout 2020, anchored by the radical pedagogical impulses of *The 1619 Project* that delineated racial slavery's central role in creating American capitalism, revealing the production of supply chains of power and privilege for whites—and grief and misery for Blacks. Books dealing with antiracism, white supremacy, and deep-seated histories of racial oppression climbed the best-sellers lists.

Corporate America made grandiloquent promises to invest in racial justice initiatives. Confederate monuments and flags came tumbling down, literally in certain instances, as millions received a crash course in the history of Reconstruction, how slavery's afterlife haunts and shapes the present, and why racism is the origin story of the republic's more than cherished notions of freedom.[25]

As the proud son of Haitian immigrants who came to America in 1965, I watched these events with profoundly mixed feelings. I participated in numerous interviews, gave countless virtual seminars, wrote more op-eds than ever before in my life, and engaged in promoting my recent dual biography of Malcolm X and Martin Luther King Jr.[26]

Suddenly Black scholars mattered, perhaps especially those of us who engaged in the history of the Black radical tradition. That tradition proved at once enduring and, in certain instances, malleable. The flexibility of racial capitalism could be seen in its effortless accommodation of once fugitive knowledge production that could be comfortably reinterpreted as intellectual property capable of turning radical organizations and political actors into more comfortable economic elites.

I cried as I watched George Floyd's life slipping away in May, and I shed new tears during the trial of former police officer Derek Chauvin, whose infamous knee to the neck of yet another Black person made history in 2020. I wept between these events as well. The year 2020 changed me as a person, as a father, a partner, and a human being.[27]

I have always used history to make sense of the world, a gift bequeathed to me by my mother, who remains the most intellectually curious person I have ever known. My study of history bloomed into a vocation under her tutelage, with C. L. R. James's *The Black Jacobins* read in elementary school, courtesy of Mom's personal library. The histories of rebellion against slavery, Jim Crow, and white supremacy, whether in Haiti or Harlem, New Orleans or Nigeria, Bandung or Brooklyn, always left me feeling more exhilarated and empowered than defeated and depressed.[28] History became my central anchor personally and professionally; it offered a way to build community, restore a sense of belonging, and recover lost worlds.

Yet in 2020, the rapidly expanding list of Black martyrs dying under regimes of brutal state-sanctioned violence, ritualized political cruelty of elected officials, and the casual malice of quotidian structures of governance left me, during the pandemic, feeling hollowed out and in need of replenishment. My family nourished my heart, but my normally optimistic political soul needed further healing.

Hope dawned, slowly, as the year progressed. The striking juxtapositions contouring the search for Black dignity and citizenship in the face of a relentless onslaught of violence, misery, and death were not aberrations. These were integral facets of American history made plain before millions and in such a public way for the first time. This is, at least in part, who we are. The lessons we were learning together were rooted in the Black radical tradition I spent my entire life studying. The creation of communities of solidarity required shared sacrifice and disciplined political commitments, but most of all it required the recognition that our search for public justice for George Floyd, Breonna Taylor, and the many more thousands who have perished before them represented an urgently fierce act of love. As a student of this history, I recognized 2020 as a high point in a longer-running drama.

If the 1963 March On Washington, where Martin Luther King delivered his famous "I Have a Dream" speech, hoped to turn America, for one afternoon, into a mass movement meeting, 2020 did one better: It transformed the American project into a global seminar on Black dignity and citizenship, complete with soul-shattering public lynchings, life-affirming Black-led multiracial demonstrations, intellectual reimaginings of the very meaning of democracy, public displays of Black genius whose most fulsome architects proved to be Black women so long denied acknowledgment of their world-historic achievements. There was so much more. Like I have since I was a boy, much of the public now sought to better understand the present by carefully studying the past.

The afterlife of Black radicalism very much resembles our present. The political vision animating BLM forcefully expanded upon Black radical traditions to make the case that all Black lives matter. True liberation is achieved only by centering the least of these within global Black communities, and dignity is a prerequisite to citizenship. BLM activists and their fellow—local and global— travelers amplified historic concepts of dignity and citizenship deeply rooted in the Black radical tradition. They democratized Black radical visions on an unprecedented scale.

The Black Trans Lives Matter March in Fort Greene, Brooklyn, in June 2020 stood out as a testament to this. Over fifteen thousand people came out to oppose the killing, sexual assault and trafficking, incarceration, and unpunished murders of Black trans women in a rally that purposefully echoed the 1917 Silent Parade against lynching in St. Louis, during another mean season of anti-Black violence and death. The gathering channeled James Baldwin's efforts to serve as a "witness" to an unfolding struggle for Black dignity. Their presence helped to dislodge oppressive barriers with the Black freedom struggle that have divided potential allies, weakened our collective spirit, and crushed the souls of too many brilliant Black activists. BLM's ability to walk the talk by centering parts of the Black community that have remained fugitives from a politics of racial solidarity thought to be based on empathy, dignity, and love perhaps best represents Black radicalism's political afterlife.[29]

Until all Black lives matter, none will. That simple declaration became, in 2020, actualized in street demonstrations, policy advocacy, and mutual aid and wellness networks that sought to provide aid, comfort, and material and spiritual resources and nourishment to allow segments of the Black community that have never received love, compassion, and mercy from anyone to have the opportunity not just to survive but to flourish.

I feel more hopeful and cautiously optimistic now than in the heat of the historical events that unfolded in the wake of George Floyd. This is not because I see a clear path toward victory in toppling systems of racial violence and death that reproduce themselves with uncanny sophistication at every level of American society as well as around the world. My hope lies in the recognition that more people than ever, led by Black people, are engaged in the same search I am. A journey to better understand history by remaining an attentive student of it and recognizing the invisible strands of power that, more often than not, shape competing narratives capable of being easily digested by the public. The aspirational world was large enough to sustain the abolition democracy that Du Bois recounted in his stunning account of Reconstruction. My hope lies in the genius of Black women, who Angela Davis reminds us were some of the key theoretical and practical architects of Black survival during slavery and after. The indefatigable brilliance and courage of Black women activists and organizers who spread a message of Black dignity and citizenship across the land that, like Promethean fire, became the flame that lit political rebellions capable of toppling political regimes, Confederate monuments, and a redemptionist political order that refuses to die.

These fellow travelers may never discover the answers, but in seeking to ask more complex, difficult, and challenging questions, we come closer, I believe, to fashioning the freedom dreams that possess the power to liberate the entire world.

PART III

FINDING LIGHT IN THE DARKNESS

Memory and Grief

ELEVEN

THE GRIEF THAT CAME BEFORE THE GRIEF

A Home Archive

Jacquelyn Dowd Hall

The title of this essay comes from the *New York Times* columnist Margaret Renkl's observation that "if any good is to emerge from all of this grief, it will only be because we have finally addressed the grief that came before the grief." She was talking about the detonation of a bomb in the heart of Nashville on Christmas Day 2020. But she also had in mind the flaws and failures in our society that have been thrust into the light by a catastrophic pandemic, a blaze of climate change disasters, a democracy-threatening presidency, and a racial reckoning blunted by foot-dragging officials, calculating Koch brothers–style operatives, and a strain of rabid white nationalism that has a long history in American life.[1]

As I watched our country descend into political madness and fail so spectacularly to rise to the challenge of the Black Lives Matter movement and a predictable, lethal global onslaught of disease, I cycled through feelings that I struggled to name. I was angry. I was afraid. But it was grief that overwhelmed me. That was not because I experienced the searing personal losses that so

many people endured. It was because I have never felt more impli-
cated in the suffering that I read about every day and sometimes
dreamed about at night. I had never been so cloistered while, at
the same time, the membrane between self and others, inside and
outside, was stretched so thin. Likewise, the plague year tore apart
the fine wall between past and present, laying me low with personal memories of "the grief that came before the grief," which is
what I want to write about here.

* * *

I was a firstborn, World War II child. My father was in the United
States Army. He did not see me until I was two. My mother carried
all the keepsakes from my earliest years with her. I, in turn, saved
those and every artifact after that, carting from attic to attic boxes
of the long, handwritten, heartfelt, agonized letters my family,
friends, lovers, and I used to write. This home archive had been
sitting in my current attic for decades when the pandemic shut
everything down.

Stuck inside, I found myself obsessed with organizing or dis-
carding the detritus of a lifetime. On that impulse, I hauled those
boxes down and began sorting hundreds of letters by people and
period, trying not to read them but randomly reading them nonetheless. I was driven by what drives me as a historian. Here was a
cache of relatively uncensored, detailed traces of a family of farmers who immigrated to this country from Ireland, Scotland, and
Quebec. These good-looking, silent men and talky, vivid women
joined the ranks of the hardscrabble rural poor. Then, swept along
by the relentless force of settler colonialism, they converged on
Pauls Valley, Oklahoma, a small county seat in Indian Territory.
There they grasped the lower rungs of the white middle class,
and, in my generation, ended up scattered across the United States.
Here also was a story about how I was formed within the crucible
of that history and then, along with a cohort of scholars that came
of age in the 1960s and 1970s, found a home in women's and

southern history—a community that both echoed and departed from the one in which my life began.

I have never doubted that, like all lives, mine and my family's are meaningful when viewed through a meaning-making lens. Yet I quickly realized that taking a hard look at myself, my family, my friends, and the times I lived through was not at all the same as trying to reconstruct and recount the lives of the people I have written about. Those people might have obsessed me, but they did not fill me with longing and regret. Still, I persisted, subjecting myself to memory, allowing (really, *inviting*) the ghosts of the past to deepen the pain of a global disaster. Of course, the obverse was true as well. Would I have been so overwhelmed by these artifacts under other circumstances? Of all the ways in which the pandemic crept into my psyche, this one surprised and disoriented me the most.

Among the letters that confronted me with a sharp, unshakable sense of loss were dozens of exchanges with two friends written during a period when to openly identify as gay was fraught with danger. Both were brilliant. Both were in love with straight men I knew well. One of these gay friends was a Rhodes scholar. The other was my constant companion during a pivotal and enlightening year I spent as a Delta Air Lines "stewardess" (in the parlance of the day). I would bid for flights to Chicago, where he was living with his blue-collar parents and dreaming of graduate school. He would meet me when I got off the plane. We would walk and talk all night, eat breakfast in a twenty-four-hour diner at dawn. He took me to the first art museum I ever visited, the first symphony I ever heard. His company was one of the reasons I could perform Delta Air Line's signature brand of southern hospitality and navigate its sexist culture with my sense of self intact.

I had not forgotten those friendships. But I had forgotten how intimate they were, how deeply I had been involved in these two men's two different worlds. Reading these letters, I was struck by how easily I seem to have folded same-sex desire into the general angst of first love, the outsize joy and piercing hurt of young romance. At the same time, I am embarrassed by how oblivious I was to the devastating structural and cultural pressures that were bearing down on my friends. For me, at that time, the personal was not yet political enough.

The "grief that came before the grief" is deepened by the fact that, of all the people whose friendships were essential to me and whose letters I have carried with me, these are the only two who seem to have disappeared completely. Our correspondence stops in the 1970s, and my attempts to locate them have been to no avail. That failure leaves me with the regret of broken bonds, the haunting feeling of an unfinished past, the guilt of being not only a friend who moved on but also a historian whose limits, along with the silences and distortions of official records, have allowed these and other histories to be erased. Did these young men find the love that we were all searching for and that eluded them in our youth? Did they survive the scourge of the AIDS epidemic, that earlier era of callous government inaction, which, in combination with crushing stigmatization, cut short so many precious and promising lives? Were their fates shaped by the fear and hatred of difference that is coursing through the right wing of American politics as we speak?

Following the trail of these friendships led me into other confrontations with the pressure and unreliability of memory. My mother, who died twenty years ago, welcomed those young men, along with countless other strays and children's friends, into her home. She had been a girl who lived in books. Too poor for college, she was married at nineteen to a handsome, bullheaded, deeply conventional man. I have written before about how my life in women's history was inspired by her: her fierce backing of her children, her thirst for knowledge, her political instincts, her late breakthrough into a life of her own. But I was mostly writing from what I remembered, the narrative I had constructed in my mind over the years. I was not prepared for my encounter with the flood of letters we exchanged.[2]

My mother was a listener. She was usually the quietest person in the room. So I was struck—really struck, as in stunned, struck down—by her writing voice: her sharp-as-life observations, the rhythm of her language, her grasp of narrative, her distinctive, trust-inspiring point of view, her quotable way of putting things. She thought I idealized her, but I now think I underestimated her. Worse (here is where the grief creeps in), I overestimated myself. I forgot how much I took for granted. If I am being generous, I could say that I had the perspective of a daughter fully absorbed in the drama of her own ascending life, gaining experience, thrilling to the new, assuming a mother's unconditional support. If I am owning up to my own current feelings, I'm shocked that I didn't find more ways to lift the weight of poverty that dogged my mother and at how long it took me to realize how sick she was during her last descending years. It was not news to me that I will always mourn my mother's death. But subjecting myself to this home archive reminded me that I will always grieve the lost opportunity to give back something approaching what she gave to me.

As for money and motherhood, reading these letters made me realize how hard I have had to strive to write working-class and women's history without letting grief laced with anger be the driving force. In 1961, I was the first person in my family to go to college. I had a scholarship from the school and a loan from the federal government and worked full-time every summer and part-time during the year.[3] Still, I was always on the verge of having to drop out for lack of what seems today like a minuscule amount of money. "Don't worry," my mother wrote to me at one point, there remained "an infinite number of hours" she could put in at her mind-numbing job at Perforating Guns Atlas Corporation. She was still married to my father at that point (they would soon separate and divorce). Yet she assumed—and was assumed to have—responsibility for every aspect of raising five children born across nineteen years, ranging in age from me to the baby who arrived the year I left for college, while *also* working full time as a secretary and using *her* earnings to keep me in school. According to this letter, I was overdrawn on the account she had created for me by $6.72. She had covered that and was working nights and weekends to "add to the fund."[4]

In the summer of 1963, a few months after she wrote that letter, she left my father, taking with her almost nothing but us children. Most people around us saw the breakup of a family as an almost unheard-of tragedy. I saw liberation, adventure, and possibility. (The memory of that state of mind was almost as piercing during the plague year as were the more overtly melancholy or infuriating ones my home archive conjured up). I can see myself clearly back home at the end of that consequential summer, sitting on the steps of my mother's dilapidated rented house in the brutal Oklahoma heat, devouring her copy of Betty Friedan's just-published *The Feminine Mystique.*

By then the seismic shifts of the Civil Rights Movement were upending not just the iconic spots that now serve as touchstones of that era's story but also obscure, out-of-the-way places like my hometown. They did so not in dramatic confrontations but in small acts of resistance, reaching out, and speaking up. Some of those found their way into the family stories we still tell, retell, and treasure. But reading these letters in the atmosphere of the present moment cut two ways. It made me grateful to have been raised in a family that, within limits, was awake to the history it was living through. It also reminded me of what the movement was up against and how provisional so many of its triumphs turned out to be.

One example: the time my mother and my sister, her second child, organized an integrated "mixer," complete with the dramatic *Friday Night Lights*–worthy arrival of the star football players, Black and white, much to the chagrin of the white parents who were circumventing *Brown v. Board* strictures by holding private, off-campus, segregated dances. That mixer marked the end of that particular vestige of segregation in our town, at least as we remember the story. But those white parents' ploy was echoing and continues to echo through the country in everything from the closing of public swimming pools to the ongoing, indeed intensifying, campaign to destroy public education and elevate private schools.

By 1964, my mother, now a single parent of five, was girding herself for whatever it would take to send my sister to Cornell University while also trying her best to keep me in school. In the fall, just before the last semester of my senior year, when somehow we had scrounged up enough money to get me through to graduation, she wrote: "Talking with you last night was reassuring. . . . That sort of thing is the only time I really worry about money. As far as we are concerned here, if I can't pay the rent we'll move. If I can't make the furniture payments, they can come and get it—but you have to go to school."[5]

There is so much packed into that letter. My mother was determined that her children were going to have opportunities that she had been denied—that was axiomatic. Also, she was notoriously indifferent to money and the material possessions that money can buy. But give up that furniture? I had no memory of that! Those beds and tables and chairs carried so much symbolic weight. She had bought them, on time and at interest rates she could not afford, in an exuberant gesture of independence from my father. In the end, I graduated from college and she kept the furniture. But as this letter seems to predict, she spent the rest of her life moving from one rental apartment to another. When she died, we still had remnants of those furnishings, paid for many times over. Almost everything else she owned could fit in one box.

Reading these and countless other exchanges, I am filled with gratitude for the gift of being born into my particular family, place, and generation. I am also filled with grief and, yes, anger over the knowledge of how my mother and countless women like her have assumed such burdens, have lived in a society that gave them so few opportunities and so few social supports. Did we really need this pandemic to reveal, yet again, how much responsibility this individualistic, stingy country thrusts upon mothers and how they keep on rising to the occasion, using their own backs as our safety nets?

At a certain point, I had to box up those traces of the past, shove them in a closet, and shut the door. But I hope and trust that I will find my way back to them. For this excavation into my one "wild and precious life" and the lives of my friends and family did have benefits.[6] Yes, it stirred up memories of struggle and loss, but it also reminded me of how flawed and vulnerable human beings can—at least sometimes—stumble forward, stay together, survive, grow, and find hope and happiness even in the wake of personal and political sorrow. And it left me believing as fervently as ever in the necessity of reckoning with our personal and political pasts, even as it drove home how wrenching that reckoning can be and how impossible it is to imagine what the future is going to mete out.

TWELVE

AN UNCOUNTABLE CASUALTY

Ruminations on the Social Life of Numbers

Mary L. Dudziak

My last sight of my brother may have been in a fundraising video. A man with longish gray hair lay face down on the walkway of a park in Southern California. The wheelchair behind him was like the kind my brother would have had. It was draped with a green sweatshirt and a bag of belongings. A medical worker knelt down and spoke to him about a motorized wheelchair, which he was hoping for. "He has refused help," the narrator said to the camera. The film was otherwise filled with earnest medical workers providing care to people who lived outdoors. That head of hair on the ground looked like the one I remember from the time my brother turned up in a Nevada hospital after decades of silence. I cut his hair and beard with little fingernail scissors—the only implement at hand.

Some months after the video was filmed, my brother spent the last day of his life on a street in Southern California. Through his six decades of sobriety and addiction, he always loved to be outside. Several weeks after his passing, the coroner's report was not yet filed. Without a cause of death, it was impossible to know what column of figures to put my brother in.

Death is personal, but it is also a matter of state. This begins with the body itself, for the state takes possession of the body when a cause of death is unknown. The coroner's office does its work and then "releases" the body to a funeral home designated by next of kin. At that point, privacy cannot fully envelop the dead, for they live on in public life as data. A cause of death assigns the dead to various categories that enable the state to draw conclusions: the death rate, the leading causes, and the quantity of death over time.

It is unclear whether my brother has become a statistic of a regular death or whether he belongs in a perilous curve upward on a COVID-19 graph showing the latest pandemic surge. During the pandemic, the dead have gained significance for the broader public as we are daily confronted with numbers of new entries on COVID mortality tables.[1] In essence, the dead reenter society through their categorization. Appearing as a statistic of a great threat, however, the COVID dead themselves cannot reassure their public. They cannot say: "I now exist as ashes and cannot harm you."[2] Instead they are required to serve as a specter, a threat. They are like Dickens's Ghost of Christmas Future—a silent, shrouded, and terrifying figure, a reminder that death is not only inevitable. It can be cloaked with regret.[3]

When deaths are represented in numbers on charts, the path of the disease becomes the story. The historian Jacqueline Wernimont writes of the seventeenth-century plague that numbers are thought to show something bigger, "a view of the whole." When aggregated, however, the dead lose their individuality and are "rendered meaningless to the state in their own moment."[4]

Counting deaths enables the public and the state to ascribe their own meanings to them. In war, for example, the enemy's deaths are usually thought to be an accomplishment.[5] Nonenemy deaths by the United States require explaining. The bodies of children were found after a drone strike during the US withdrawal from Afghanistan in 2021. Their age kept them out of the category of enemy combatant—a presumptively lawful target—so that instead they might be "collateral damage," which is what we now call civilian casualties in war.[6] An investigation soon revealed that the entire strike was a mistake, so that all of the dead, adults and children, reinforced a narrative that the withdrawal was brutally chaotic.[7]

Categories matter, for death can drive politics, public policy, and philanthropy. Mass casualty events—hurricanes, fires, school shootings—are often thought to require a response. Numbers alone do not give rise to concerted action, however. The nature of response is informed by the way the deaths are understood. For example, the terrorist attacks on September 11, 2001, killed 2,977 people (just under the number of COVID-19 deaths in the US per day in December 2020). September 11 was not one moment but an era that that continued to spiral into darkness. Aircraft crashing into buildings followed by toxic clouds of debris sweeping through lower Manhattan after the Twin Towers fell was just the beginning. Long after, the nightly news would show the illuminated New York crash site, with rescue workers first looking for survivors and then searching for bodies that could not be found.[8]

Having been turned into dust, the 9/11 dead had no agency in how they were remembered. A contested set of narratives congealed into a national message, as President George W. Bush grabbed a bullhorn at Ground Zero and enlisted the dead in a war on terror. American planes were soon bombing Afghanistan.[9]

It may seem, to us, unfair that the dead were drafted into war without their consent. The dead are often called into service, however, for the purpose of war, peace, or the passing desires of those left behind. Joining the ranks of the dead makes one eligible for this kind of involuntary labor. Their memory is invoked to goad the living into action, even, in the case of war, for the expansion of the ranks of the dead themselves. That we call upon the memory of the dead for our most important objectives is just one example of the cultural work the dead do for the living. The very way societies treat dead bodies, the historian Thomas Laqueur has shown, does not arise from the needs of the dead themselves. Instead, even as we lay them to rest, our practices serve the needs of the living.[10]

In 2020, the Black Lives Matter movement issued a powerful call to action in the names of Black people killed in senseless police violence. In 2020 alone, this list included George Floyd, Breonna Taylor, Ahmaud Arbery, Rayshard Brooks, and Daniel Prude. Videos revealed, for example, the callousness of Derek Chauvin, his hand nonchalantly in his pocket as he spent nine minutes asphyxiating George Floyd by kneeling on his neck on a Minneapolis street. The BLM movement kept Floyd's killing in the public eye, and protests erupted around the world.[11] The sight of Floyd's face on the pavement, the sound of his voice—"I can't breathe"—made his humanity and individuality inescapable, even as he came to represent a history of similar lost lives. Statistics alone could not have this power, for they subsume humanity into an anonymous whole. It was these named deaths that generated mass politics, although the ultimate outcome of the political moment is yet to play out.

Contrast this with the absence of an effective call to action in the memory of COVID dead. For example, there was no mass movement to protest the Trump administration's failure to immediately expand the production of personal protective equipment. Instead of marches demanding lifesaving, there were angry protests against mask wearing. Embracing the rhetoric of "liberty" to demand an end to safety measures was a strange perversion of the idea of a right to die. Meanwhile, Donald Trump's effort to dismiss the pandemic led to an absence of public memorialization. The dead were potentially toxic to his political image.[12]

As the nation retreated behind closed doors, daily life during the pandemic was enabled by shielding the sight of the dead and of brutal conditions in hospitals, to protect privacy. Meanwhile, burials of unclaimed dead at Hart Island, New York, increased fivefold. Simple pine caskets were neatly stacked on top of one another. When a journalist used a drone to photograph the site, believing that others should know of it, he was arrested for the obscure crime of using an aircraft outside of an airport, and his drone was confiscated.[13] This inability to see the carnage was not unlike the way terrible World War II casualty photographs were censored, in part to avoid generating an anti-war movement.[14]

. To be shielded from suffering was a privilege of those like me who could stay home. Others could not. "Essential workers" in health care and other life-sustaining industries, like food production, were on the front lines. In April and May 2020, COVID-19 surged through poultry and meatpacking plants in the United States.[15] Meatpacking workers often labor indoors, side-by-side, in crowded conditions. Farmworkers were also vulnerable—three times more likely than others in Montgomery County, California, to get the virus in the spring of 2020. "I think the average American has no concept of how food reaches our table," Dr. Max Cuevas, CEO of Clinica de Salud del Valle de Salinas, told *Frontline* producers. "We don't know how meat is processed. We have no idea where lettuce comes from. We have no idea how it's harvested." Those sheltering in place could not understand "how those people work, and how much they have to work to make a living."[16]

American culture became a version of the workings of a slaughterhouse. Brutal actions produce dead animals that are neatly packed for American supermarket shelves. The operations of the slaughterhouse are hidden from view. They would be too shocking for meat eaters to see. That very shock, political scientist Timothy Pachirat writes, is "predicated on the operations that remove from sight, without actually eliminating, equally shocking practices required to sustain the orbit of their everyday lives."[17] For most of us, life in the twenty-first century United States is enabled by practices it would be unbearable for us to fully understand.[18] Perhaps a lesson that the rest of the country could draw from the Black Lives Matter movement, and the sight of George Floyd dying on the ground, is that there is power in seeing and showing what carnage actually looks like. Mamie Till taught the nation this lesson long ago when she revealed the battered face of her fourteen-year-old son Emmett, who had been lynched by two white supremacists in Money, Mississippi, in 1955. She opened his casket for viewing, leading *Jet* magazine to place his disfigured corpse on their cover, shocking the nation.[19] It is uncomfortable to view such deaths, but preference for comfort fuels ignorance and complacency.

Whatever category my brother belonged to, he died in public, but was not seen, at least by nearly all passersby. A bus driver who had noticed him regularly did see him that day. When the driver looked again, he saw that my brother had not moved. He stepped out of the bus, and walked over to him, and he could see that life had left my brother's body.

I like to think that this kind person's eyes were the last to rest on my brother, and that his spirit—if there is such a thing—left at that moment to find its place in the ocean, or among the redwoods. As time passes and the coroner's report remains unfiled, I like to think that my brother is confounding the categorizers. He is refusing to render himself into a tidy statistic. His final power was to deny the state a complete numerical accounting. He even defied the fundraisers, who have removed the video from their website after a complaint. The only way to see him was to have been there, on the street. And to stop, and look.

THIRTEEN

SOMETIMES I FEEL LIKE A MOTHERLESS CHILD

Keith Ellison

I will never forget when my mom called my congressional office in Washington, DC, on Thursday, June 23, 2016, and asked my assistant to pass me a note directing me to join a civil rights protest.[1] I ended my business meeting immediately. I did what Mom said.

Clida Cora Martinez Ellison, my mom, was watching a televised livestream of an old-fashioned sit-in, civil disobedience at its finest, occurring in an unusual place: the floor of the US House of Representatives, where it was my job to represent Minnesota's Fifth Congressional District. This daughter of Frank Martinez, a farmer, teacher, mechanic, and NAACP activist from Caddo Parish, Louisiana, wanted her son there. So I went.

The late representative and civil rights icon John Lewis (1940–2020) had led some members of Congress to the House floor to protest congressional inaction on mass shootings. This time forty-nine souls were murdered and fifty-three more were wounded at Pulse, a gay nightclub in Orlando, Florida, making it the deadliest attack on LGBTQ and Latinx people in United States history. My mom wanted me to support human life and peace. By the end of the day, 170 lawmakers joined in the protest. And that is a memory I now cling to because the year 2020—the same awful year that took John Lewis from the nation—also took my mother away from me. On the morning of March 26, 2020, my mom died from COVID-19.

I wish I still had her to call me with her demands, her jokes, and her stories, but I have my memories. And that's what all of us have, our memories. That's part of what loss is about: the realization that all you have is memories, but what wonderful memories. Much like my own family, by September 2021, over 660,000 Americans and over 4.4 million people worldwide have been left with just their memories—because COVID-19 has taken their loved ones. And each one of those memories is unique and special. My memories have spawned a whole new level of appreciation for my beloved mother. I suspect the families who've lost their loved ones all feel the same way. My mom had five boys within ten years, and my brothers and I were all extremely close to her. But now that she has become part of history, we see her more clearly than we ever have.

My mom would have been shocked and disgusted by the murder of George Floyd, an unarmed Black man who was brutally suffocated by police officer Derek Chauvin in my home state of Minnesota. More importantly, she would have wanted her son to help right the wrongs that caused it. She would have empathically felt Floyd's pitiful, final cries for his own mother as he suffered and died under the weight of Chauvin's knee.

Yet a poignant thought came to me only after my mom passed away: she also would have felt compassion for Chauvin's mother, who testified at his sentencing hearing. I can hear her voice in my mind and see her placing her hand over her heart saying, "Oh, his poor mother." That was Clida. The perfect blend of passion, humor, attitude, and empathy—for *everyone*. If I had thought more about who my mom was before she died, I would have known that she had a heart big enough even for Derek Chauvin and his family. She had a heart big enough for everyone.

My mom was a social worker. For years, she led court-referred juveniles in sex offender group therapy. She was proud of her work and the kids she served. She was the first person to tell me about the devastating effects of childhood trauma. Some of "her" kids (as she called them) had committed horrible offenses, some of them carried great shame. But my mother tried to help them heal themselves. Only a few of them came back for repeating the behavior that brought them to juvenile court in the first place. She tried to help them become successful in the world.

Though the world scorned these troubled children, my mom cared about them and their families. She had the rare capacity to love people who the world deemed undeserving. So, I know how she would have seen Chauvin. She would have wanted him held accountable, but she would have argued anyone to the ground who said he was beyond redemption.

How could I have ever thought she was naive, especially after all the grace she extended to her own children? But I did. We worried about her and the difficult, psychologically draining work she did, but she was never afraid of her clients. While she was with us, I didn't always understand how her upbeat positivity blended with her street smarts. That misunderstanding led me to believe that she didn't fully understand the dangers of her chosen profession.

But *I* was the naive one. She got it; she always got it. *I* didn't get that she got it because she was never cynical or judgmental. My mom could look horror in the face and still possess hope. I see that now.

★ ★ ★

I remember when I first read *Manchild in the Promised Land, The Autobiography of Malcolm X, Black Like Me,* and *Stride Toward Freedom*—all within about a month at the age of about fourteen. It was winter in Detroit, where I grew up, and the miniseries *Roots* was on ABC. I was glued to the TV during January 1977 when *Roots* was on the family TV screen, and when *Roots* was not on I was devouring books on race in America, sometimes to the detriment of completing my homework. I was reading a book per week.[2]

Once, when I was in the ninth grade, I was feeling persecuted by a teacher who happened to be white. When my classroom deportment came to my mom's attention, she confronted me. My response was, "Mom, you just don't understand. This teacher only picks on us Black kids." In her Louisiana drawl she quipped, "Ah don' understand?! Did you say, Ah don' understand?! Honey, I was raised in Jim Crow. You have no idea what I understand."

This was probably the first time I realized what living through Jim Crow might have been like for her, and I was shocked by it. My fourteen-year-old self was outraged by the books I had been reading and the films I'd been seeing on the screen. Somehow, I found it hard to believe that my very own mom faced "whites only" signs. She lived under state-sponsored hate, terror, and apartheid. I asked her, "Mom, why didn't you tell us about it?" Her answer: "Ya know, I suppose I didn't want y'all growing up angry, or feeling like you couldn't overcome the odds, or making excuses for failure. But, hey, I see what you've been reading, and I'm happy you're interested."

Then, one day, she finally started talking. "They tried to lock us out, and hold us down, but we made our own world," she said. "We had our own churches, schools, and other things. And we held our heads high, and never let anyone convince us that we were less than anyone, no matter what a stupid sign said." Self-sufficiency was big for her, and I occasionally joked with her about being a conservative. She would laugh and reply, "there's nothin' about Jim Crow I want to conserve!" And then, as she often would, she started singing Billie Holiday's song written in 1939:

> Mama may have
> and Papa may have
> but God bless the child that's got his own
> That's got his own.

She had a message in the music.

★ ★ ★

Roots sparked conversation around our house, and my mom would lead it: "It might sound weird to you, but we knew lots of white people, worked with them, and got along well with many. It wasn't all conflict all the time. We knew who the 'good old boys' were, and we avoided them, but for so many people, it was more complicated than a TV show. At the end of the day, people are people, and that was true in Natchitoches (her hometown in Louisiana) too." She wasn't bitter, and I was a little surprised by this in the midst of learning about America's racial history.

But my mom shared stories about terrorist mobs too. "Your grandpa Frank was active in the Civil Rights Movement in Natchitoches. He was active in the local NAACP chapter, and he would work with other local leaders doing voter registration. And the local racists were awful. They wouldn't sell my daddy gasoline, and he had to use Uncle's [Carroll Balthazar's] tractor fuel to put in his car. They would call the house and say that they had him tied up to a tree, even when they didn't. It was all about terrorizing us," Mom lamented. "One time they burned a cross on the other side of Lee Street, near our house." Violence and threats of violence were so bad that my grandfather ultimately could not convince his mother-in-law, my great-grandmother, Cora Marinovich Balthazar, to register to vote.

Mom didn't only tell us about her father's activism. She talked about her own civil rights rebellion as a college student at Xavier University in New Orleans. She laughed about joining her friends to take down the movable Jim Crow signs on public buses. "We would stick 'em in our purses or coats or whatever. We must have had dozens in the dorm room," she laughed. My mother carried her activism into adulthood, as a PTA parent, a youth sport parent, and a social worker. She walked her talk, with hopefulness, despite everything her eyes saw.

My mom was the first person who told me Trump could win. Sitting in the kitchen in her Detroit home, she said casually, probably while she was cutting okra or shelling peas, "They better not play that man cheap. For a whole lot of people, he's a dream come true. A lot of people resent sharing this country with anyone except who they consider 'the real Americans,' and that ain't us, by the way. Especially after a Black man won the presidency—twice." I can't claim that I really reflected on her words; I just soaked them up. Despite her incurable optimism, it is another example of how aware and in tune she was to American history and its racial temperature.

In July 2015, I was on *This Week with George Stephanopoulos*—the same TV station I devoured *Roots* on as a young man—and I predicted that Donald Trump might win the Republican nomination and then the American presidency. Veteran journalists doubled over in laughter. One very experienced *New York Times* reporter said, "Sorry to laugh."

Trump won in 2016, but my prediction was not luck or clairvoyance. In fact, based on logic and reason, these journalists were probably right to laugh. My prediction was not based on minute electoral statistics, polling, or projections. It was based on being Clida Ellison's son.

Clida was not shocked by Donald J. Trump. She told me that he was not the first politician to say "Make America Great Again," and he also wasn't the first to say "America First." "Read your history," she told us. "George Wallace pledged he would never be 'out-n-----ed' again. Manipulating race is old thing in politics." And she reminded me that Trump was far from the first to use race as a wedge.

★ ★ ★

The way Mom managed the loss of her hero, her grandmother Cora "Co" Marinovich Balthazar, taught us something about carrying on, long before Mom passed away. Of course, my mom loved and admired her own mother, Doris, but everyone on Cane River looked up to Co, the matriarch. I doubt she was even five feet tall. But she was funny, very tough, and resolutely sure of herself. I loved being around her and so did everyone else—not that she wouldn't scold you if you deserved it.

Co would get on your case, but she would also love you up too. And she would feed you. In the morning, she'd stuff you with grits, eggs, bacon, ham, fried chicken livers, biscuits from scratch, and fresh orange juice. Lunch could be anything, but dinner might be gumbo, okra, red beans and rice, jambalaya, shrimp creole, boiled crawfish, catfish, or some other type of fish. She was *the* best cook ever. And when Co died, my mother assumed her title.

My mom was a wonderful cook. She even appeared on *My Grandmother's Ravioli*, a Cooking Channel show hosted by Mo Rocca. Thanks to YouTube, you can check out her recipes even now. And even when I converted to Islam and the pork came off my menu, it didn't change much for my mom. We never had any arguments about religion. Turkey replaced ham hocks for the greens, and she still served ham, but I just avoided it. That was fine by her. "Keith, I'm glad you're a Muslim," she'd laugh. "More ham for me!"

My mom never actually taught my brothers or me how to cook, but we all watched her and learned. My brother Tony is probably the best cook, but I cook too. Tony grilled some red snapper for the family one evening in the summer of 2020, right as we were preparing Mom's house for sale. It was the house we grew up in. My parents raised five boys, a bevy of dogs, goldfish, and even a few cats there. When Mom died, my aunt Thelma, who was living there, moved in with her daughter, my first cousin Cheryl. And my dad Leonard, at ninety-three years old, moved in with my brother Leonard Jr.

As we were cleaning and clearing the house, going through decades of pictures, clothing, old greeting cards, and holiday decorations, it was emotional for all of us. No one noticed, but I got misty eyed as I sorted through the world my mom had created. When Tony, after a hard day of washing, mopping, lifting heavy furniture, and sorting precious family items, fixed dinner for everyone, I could feel my mother's presence, and I could feel Co's presence too. Tony was stepping in, being responsible—just like Mom did when Co died. Loss does that. Loss makes you step up. It helps you to realize that it's up to you now. It was a beautiful evening after a tough emotional day, and we finished the way mom and Co would have wanted us to: over good food—together.

★ ★ ★

The loss of my mom has been instructional. Of course, I have a lot more to learn. I will, without a doubt, lose a lot more in the days to come. If I am lucky, I will lose my youth, naivete, and illusory belief that somebody else will take care of it. If I am not so lucky, I will lose my hair, my good looks, and my bladder control. But living life means losing. Hopefully, losing helps to teach us something about value, about truth, about what really matters. I wish I would have had the presence of mind of realize these things while Mom was physically in our midst.

Losing Mom means that my brothers and I are now going to have to figure out holidays, family problems, homemaking for our kids and their kids, and caring for our ninety-three-year-old father, like Mom did. It means taking some responsibility for more than just myself. It means losing the collective illusion that a higher power—Mom in our case—was always going to be there to "take care of it." Having lost her, we must become more responsible for each other and the rest of the family if we're going to maintain family unity as she would expect.

I had to lose Mom to realize that she was operating on a sense of duty. It's clear to me in hindsight that she was facing physical pain in her final year. She wasn't debilitated, but I could see the pain in her face. She was working. She was keeping on keeping on, even when she wasn't always feeling good. But she never complained. She just kept going to work because she saw it as her job. It's clear now that duty kept her going, because at eighty-two years old she was carrying too much. She considered herself responsible for taking care of my dad, providing a home for my aunt Thelma, for all of it. Maybe she figured, "who else is going to do it?" It occurred to me that maybe cooking Thanksgiving dinner for thirty people at the age of eighty-two wasn't just pure enjoyment for her, but she did it. And, other than my brother Brian, I doubt any of us ever understood how much pain she may have been in. But she had a sense of responsibility and a deep maturity. Her death taught me this: her sense of duty didn't excuse me from helping more, from doing my part. I wish I would have done more.

Here's what I know for sure: my mother taught us well. She could leave this earthly place in peace because she did her job. It's up to us now. She taught us about love, faith, resilience, and brotherhood. She taught us, but did we learn? The training wheels are off, and we have to ride that two-wheeler all on our own now. Mom's final life lesson is that we can survive loss. Losing a loved one is not doom; we are not supposed to go to the grave with our loved ones. It's *our* job to carry on. What else did she teach us but to carry on? She taught us to survive and thrive despite odds, with a full and open heart. Mom gave us everything we needed.

Our society is going through trying times. COVID-19, Trumpism and its legacy, resurging white supremacy, and the horrific murder of George Floyd and so many other Black and Brown Americans. The United States may be the world's oldest democracy, but it's a young civilization. We've ended slavery, survived the Civil War, and stopped Jim Crow.

Now, we are confronting a bold, violent racism, which is still raging. With Confederate flags being waved inside the US Capitol building side by side with men wearing "Auschwitz" T-shirts, it's clear that our society has not yet outgrown some of the ugly attitudes of the past. The assault on the Capitol was revelatory. It exposed that so many of our fellow Americans are violently devoted to lies and delusions. They clung to the illusion that their false prophet of racial privilege would make everything great for them again.

But those of us who are aghast and appalled by the storming of the Capitol and everything that led up to it have our own illusion. And the storming of the Capitol hopefully destroyed some of our illusions, too. Active citizenship is necessary for democracy to function and survive. It's up to us. Somebody else isn't going to take care of it.

My daughter Amirah, Clida's granddaughter, once said to me, "You know, Dad, loss of an illusion is not loss of hope." I absolutely agree. Dropping the myths of American exceptionalism doesn't mean that we drop hope for a better future for our nation. We don't have to cling to the idea that George Washington told the truth about cutting down that cherry tree, that Columbus "discovered" America, that America is a post-racial society, or even that justice inevitably improves over time.

Yet we do have to stay optimistic and street smart. Optimism about racial and economic justice and democracy does not mean that we don't apprehend the dangers that accompany them. We still have the hope President Barack Obama spoke of so idealistically. But maybe our hope is now based on more solid ground.

Illusions and assumptions based on national myths about American history are not static or stable. Things do not get better just because of the passage of time. The truth is that every institution is fragile and, under certain conditions, unpredictable. Social stability is an illusion. During 2020, a sensible COVID-19 response was anything but assured; the shared commitment to democracy was a farce. It turns out that everything Americans counted on and assumed is completely dependent on what courageous and public-spirited people are willing to do and sacrifice to make them happen.

It turns out there is no consensus on democracy. But loss of illusion and loss of hope are not the same. In fact, loss of illusion may be the foundation for deep hope—a more assured hope. It turns out that loss can help you see the world and people in it much more clearly. And in these troubled times when so many are facing so much unfathomable loss—when one in five hundred Americans have now died of COVID-19 and so many others have been lost to state violence—it's a good moment to take stock.

Take stock of what really matters. Mom taught me that.

FOURTEEN

LOSING MY STARBUCKS TABLE

Ula Y. Taylor

To say that I am a creature of habit is a huge understatement. My local coffee shop is a Starbucks, and I always order a tall soy latte—no foam—and a reduced-fat turkey bacon sandwich. If someone is sitting at "my" table in the most secluded corner with an electrical outlet, I usually hover around them like a pigeon waiting for breadcrumbs until they leave. It's only then that I sit, relax, unpack the workhorse laptop, and get into my thinking rhythm. I never imagined not having access to this space.

Losing my Starbucks table is all I can write about at this time because the avalanche of death and illness directly related to the COVID-19 pandemic is too much for me to handle emotionally. I've had my share of personal loss, and my heart breaks for those who have buried their loved ones unceremoniously.[1] Distancing myself from the pandemic climate of hurt and sorrow by focusing on a seat at a café serves as an example of how to cope, and be hopeful, in a world of frightening uncertainty.

My coffee routine began in college, and to this day I cannot function properly without caffeine in the morning. It is an addiction I share with millions of others. The habit-forming ritual brings all kinds of people into Starbucks. A 2018 Reuters study, for instance, found that 64 percent of people in the United States age eighteen or over begin their day with a cup of coffee. A 2018 Nielsen Scarborough survey suggests that 37.8 million individuals visit the over fifteen thousand Starbucks stores daily in the United States.[2]

As of October 29, 2020, Starbucks is the largest coffee chain in the world, with a total of 32,600 locations in the United States and globally. The coffee giant frames its multinational capitalism as "environmentally friendly." Banning plastic straws and recycling coffee grounds, along with selling some fair-trade products and donating leftover food to food banks, Starbucks brands itself as a socially responsible corporation. All this PR translates into mega money! The Seattle-based company reported a net worth of $137.37 billion as of August 12, 2021.[3]

Given my reputation for penny pinching, I never imagined regularly paying for a pricey specialty coffee. Moreover, I try to support small local businesses, yet Starbucks is the epitome of a capitalist monopoly. Nevertheless, this corporately produced zone near my home has generated a delightful opportunity for me to engage with community folk, organic intellectuals, and working-class baristas.

The first time I went to a so-called urban Starbucks was in Los Angeles, California. Known as the Magic Johnson Starbucks (or affectionately, Starblacks), there were so many Black folks drinking coffee, reading books and newspapers, playing dominoes and chess, and chatting and laughing it up that I fully embraced the atmosphere, despite my reservations about the capitalist takeover of the coffee market.[4] Years later, when Starbucks landed near my Oakland neighborhood, I was again drawn to the lively meeting venue.

Initially I would take my drink to go. One day, however, I ran into a campus colleague. We were both surprised to see each other, having no idea that we lived on the same turf. All of the inside tables were occupied, so we sat outside under a trademark heather green Starbucks umbrella. Our conversation vacillated between campus gossip, politics, and his colorful sneakers. As I walked to my car, I thought about how we would have never had a comparable conversation at work. We often bump into each other when I am putting closure on my teaching day, and he is beginning a night shift as a lead custodian in the building that houses my department at the University of California, Berkeley. Since that day, Starbucks is the spot where we touch base. It's never a planned meeting—which makes the fellowship a nice surprise.

Perhaps this is how it begins for many of us who enjoy camaraderie at our local cafés. There is something about seeing a familiar face outside of your usual engagement. I still haven't figured out why I am always shocked to see a friend or colleague and then question what brings us to the same place. Every new encounter made me feel more and more comfortable at my local Starbucks, and over time I transitioned from ordering a drink to go to bringing my laptop and books inside the café to work.

Before the COVID-19 pandemic, whenever I was intellectually stuck, needed to catch up on writing student letters of recommendations, or wanted to read outside of my house, I would go to the local Starbucks. For years this is how I prepared to teach, tinkered with sentences, and fleshed out academic projects. Thus, losing my Starbucks table was not simply about a loss of privilege or convenience but something that had become essential to my identity as a person and a scholar. Undoubtedly, the closure of barbershops, beauty salons, and soul food restaurants and lounges (nonessential businesses) brought a comparable feeling of loss to those who regularly build community in these spaces.[5] These are unique institutions for African Americans that generate social identities, cultural intimacy, and a constellation of happenings centered around Black life and joy. Not having my Starbucks table plucked me out of my unique space and fostered the beginning of a downward spiral of losses that I had never fully counted as bringing meaning to my life until they were gone.

When my neighborhood Starbucks temporarily closed because the California governor Gavin Newsom issued a strict shelter-in-place order, I immediately thought about the baristas who worked there to support themselves and their families.[6] I was particularly concerned about two women, Jennifer and Rosie, who opened the store so they could return home in time to get their children ready for school.

When the café was not busy, Jennifer and Rosie shared their children's school experiences and growing pains with me. Their income helped stabilize their home life, and they always asked me about my great-niece who accompanied me into the café on the weekends. We often laughed about how she learned to spell her name out loud in the café when ordering a kid's hot chocolate. Together in harmony, we would say, "L-e-e-n-a-h, Leenah, four years old."

Our conversations reminded me that raising children should not be done in isolation, that parenting strategies and tips are to be shared, and that there is no substitute for face-to-face dialogue and laughter. When the café opened back up for minimal take-out-only hours and no seating close to a month later, I was so glad to see Jennifer and Rosie. And for the first time I met their young children. The closing of school districts and the tectonic shift to virtual education had translated into parents becoming teachers and families scrambling for ways to supervise their children. Huddled in "my" corner and sitting at "my" table with the hidden electrical outlet, their jumbo knocker-ball ponytails and beautiful eyes shined above their kid-sized masks.

Google Chromebooks had replaced my laptop, and neon-colored pencils and LOL dolls took the place of my African American history tome. Practicing social distancing and doing their best to serve customers as they supervised their children through the corner of their eyes, there was no time to chat. Even amid their masks I could see that they were overwhelmed. The look of fatigue showed across their tired eyes and slumped shoulders.

Parents with school-aged children have come up against what can best be described as a "colossal boulder" during this pandemic.

In particular, as noted in the United States Census Bureau data, "Mothers carry a heavier burden, on average, of unpaid domestic household chores and child care, which, during a pandemic that draws everyone into the home, disrupts parents' ability to actively work for pay."[7] The baristas were living this "disruption" before my bespectacled eyes, and similar to many mothers working outside the home, the already cumbersome pressures were magnified. News headlines about the "maternal misery" experienced by countless mothers whose employment radically switched to remote work underscore how the pandemic didn't start their struggle, but it did make it "impossible to ignore."[8]

Moreover, the mothers who are frontline workers (the media has zeroed in on physicians, nurses, and emergency medical technicians) don't have the option to juggle their job and childcare exclusively in the comfort of their homes.[9] While the baristas were not working in hospitals, they were still serving customers and continually coming into contact with people who might be asymptomatic. Given that COVID-19 transmission can occur before symptom onset, this reality had to heighten their stress.[10]

Still another barista that I worried about, Tyre, worked at the Starbucks near the UC Berkeley campus. He was a former student whose smiling spirit always warmed my heart. Newly married and excited to share with me the celebration of his and his wife's first anniversary, I often thought about how they were making ends meet. Economic hardships are noted to have the most devastating impact on couples' relationships. The American Academy of Pediatrics reports that the pandemic exacerbated financial hardships for low-income families and wreaked havoc on their quality of home life.[11]

Kourtney McGowan shared in a *New York Times* interview that "The relationship with her longtime partner quickly crumbled under pressure. They broke up 'due to mental health issues' that she said started to appear with both of them being stressed out inside all day."[12] Even before the pandemic, "housing crowding in adults has been linked to social withdrawal, stress, and aggression."[13]

Not surprisingly, the long periods in close quarters because of the stay-at-home orders have increased domestic violence.[14] Top-notch journalism kept me informed about the destructive nature of pandemic stressors. Report after report advised people to go for daily walks in the fresh air to maintain balance. I reluctantly took the advice because the critic in me determined that it would only be an illusion of balance so why play! One year after the start of the pandemic, however, I was elated to see Tyre while walking around Lake Merritt in Oakland. He was with his wife and pushing a stroller occupied by their gorgeous infant child. Now working as a full-time youth minister in his church, he and his wife both appeared to have weathered the pandemic storm with a Christian faith.

In all likelihood, these three baristas had challenges working at Starbucks. Most working-class service employment is filled with varying levels of exploitation. Yet it seemed to me that they were able to navigate the corporate minefield. Many employees at Starbucks saw their jobs disappear instantly after stores closed. When the temporary closing of the café that Tyre had worked at became permanent, the windows boarded up; I best understood how the COVID-19 pandemic had impacted a spiderweb of college-town economies. The financial solvency of this Starbucks café, which was always packed with student traffic, was directly linked to their monetary footprint. This café was not alone in relying upon students' cash for the livelihood of its business.

The ripple wave of what happened when the student population vanished from Berkeley was startling. When the campus closed the dorms and shifted to virtual classrooms, all residential-life staff (cafeteria workers, maintenance, residence hall managers, landscapers) were impacted. The empty classrooms closed buildings; thus, custodians' and building managers' hours were reduced. Eateries, bars, snack shops, and small grocery stores that also relied on the student population went under. Cashiers, cooks, waiters, bartenders, and shelf stockers lost their jobs. And then there are all the catering businesses that supported campus events. The buses that the students rode to campus were now empty and soon the service was stopped, releasing drivers from their jobs. Ubers, Lyfts, and GIG Car Share were nowhere in sight. The fading away of street vendors from Telegraph Avenue sealed the end of iconic Berkeley. None of the above includes how the university coffers were diminished by no income from collegiate sports enterprises and artistic performances.

As COVID-19 cases soared, employers across the nation furloughed employees in startling numbers. By May 2020, the National Bureau of Economic Research announced that the United States was officially in a recession. It's one thing to read the reports about the rise in unemployment; it's another to know people who are unemployed because of COVID-19. The domino effect of unemployment hits individuals and families in uneven ways—not to mention the unprecedented depression and anxiety of individuals.[15]

As a professor, I am blessed that my employment transitioned onto the Zoom platform with only a few hiccups. Prior to COVID-19, Tuesdays and Thursdays were my nonteaching days, and thus I would often go to Starbucks to work around others. Academic work can be so isolating, and unless I am under a pressure-filled deadline, I become easily distracted at home (I can give Marie Kondo a run for her money when it comes to organizing a drawer!).

Before the digitalization of books and archival holdings, libraries had served me in the capacity to work in the company of people I don't know. Although I still love libraries, laptop computers provide academic mobility and the freedom to have a hot drink and food while studying or working. Talk about a quadruple threat—drink, food, books, and neighborly people—the combination puts me in an intellectual comfort zone!

The communal factor—the crowds of people circling in and out of the Starbucks—keeps me alert. I can be a bit nosy and will lean into old-fashioned drama. If ear hustling were a sport, I would be a highly paid professional.[16] I am convinced that my right ear has a bionic superpower. Talk about being entertained at Starbucks! Whether overhearing what happened at a club the night before, why the NBA Warriors would lose steam if they left Oakland, or which church has the best gospel choir, eavesdropping on other peoples' conversations kept me grounded in the social worlds of my community.

In the midst of this stimulating cornucopia, I most loved listening to, and occasionally engaging with, the organic intellectuals, the retired elders who have the time to keep up on just about everything happening in the world, who gave me insights that I otherwise would not have. Their informed opinions vacillated between what academics would label conservative, pan-African, neo-liberal, and progressive Christian. Always layered with humor that de-escalated heated debates, the elders' conversations were a constant reminder that we can respectfully engage different opinions.

At the beginning of the pandemic, the elderly were identified as the most vulnerable to COVID-19. As I worried about my older friends from the café, I will never forget the news reporting that close to thirty thousand people living in nursing homes across California had tested positive for COVID-19, with close to five thousand dead by November 2020.[17] The gurneys in front of buildings and the families waiting outside trying to see their family members brought tears to my eyes.

By losing my Starbucks table I lost my weekly routine and my world beyond the academy and my family. Honestly, I failed to realize how much this space brought lovely meaning to my life. The café is now open full time, with seating, but the folks I enjoyed are not there. Ninety percent of the seats are now vacant. I, too, am hesitant about sitting down and working. The delta variant of COVID-19 has breathed new life into the devasting virus.

The vaccination provides protection, but hesitancy, politics, and new variants have limited its efficacy. I wish I could write a happy ending to this essay: describing getting rerooted in my seat and sitting at my Starbucks table, surrounded by friends, neighbors, and elders. We all want to come full circle; it can make us feel whole and gives the fallacy of success through crisis. Given the human loss linked to the pandemic, the recent past feels like a lifetime, and the continued vulnerabilities make getting back to "normal" unimaginable. More than anything, however, the COVID-19 pandemic has displayed how we should never take for granted our interconnectedness.

PART IV

THE RECKONING

FIFTEEN

BURIED HISTORY

The Death and Life of Donald S. Kelley

Robin D. G. Kelley

I only had one job to do—write the obituary. His wife, Freddia, arranged the church service for him in Boston, and my sister, Makani, took care of everything else. She flew from Jackson, Mississippi, to Albuquerque to identify the body, arrange his cremation, pay bills, close accounts, pack up his things, clean out his apartment, and inform friends and family that our father had transitioned. None of our father's other three children went to New Mexico to help out, myself included. Writing his obituary was to be my contribution.

Donald Sheralton Kelley officially died on February 29, 2020, although two or three days passed before someone found his body.[1] He was eighty-two years old, alone, and wheelchair bound. I never saw him in this condition because we had been estranged for over two decades. He called me occasionally, usually on my birthday, but I rarely answered the phone. In sixteen years, I think I picked up twice. Both times I began with a contrite explanation for losing touch. I blamed my busy schedule, deadlines, the time difference, travel, among other things, and then I listened in silence for the next hour to an earful of misogynistic and xenophobic rants, conspiracy theories, random biblical passages, a critique of how I'm ruining my children and why they need to be saved. There was a lot of crazy talk about his "number one son" (that would be me) and "your father" (that would be him). I never disclosed what I really thought about anything because I was afraid of him. When I learned that he had passed, I shed no tears and felt nothing except, perhaps, a sigh of relief followed by a slight pang of guilt for feeling this way. My therapist released me from the guilt but gently reminded me that I still needed to grieve, and that writing his obituary might be a way to begin the grieving process.

I started gathering material the first week of March 2020. The service was scheduled for mid-March 2020, so I had very little time to write an uplifting, respectful narrative about a father I didn't like, didn't exactly know, and yet knew all too well. I reluctantly made plans to fly from Los Angeles to Boston, thinking that mourning with family and friends might help me grieve. As I wrestled with my dad's obituary and waited for word about the funeral arrangements, the World Health Organization declared a global pandemic and the federal government declared a state of emergency. All flights were canceled and his funeral service postponed indefinitely.

Family on my father's side were disappointed; I was relieved—at first. Two weeks had passed and all I had to show was a sorry, equivocal opening paragraph. I knew how to write an obituary. I'd published many such tributes on accomplished figures and delivered my fair share of eulogies. But an obituary requires a certain kind of artifice, a kind of narrative cleansing not unlike the undertaker's work of preparing and dressing a corpse for public viewing. Many of the most basic facts about my father's life concealed traumas—mine, my siblings', and his own. I longed to tell the truth just to release years of pent-up anger but worried that it would only open old wounds and make new ones. So I set it aside for the time being.

Meanwhile, spring 2020 became the season of death. We sheltered in place as hospitals overflowed with COVID-19 patients, and the nightly news led off with mounting numbers of infections and deaths. The pandemic became a pretext for the Trump administration's death-dealing policies, allowing the government to accelerate border closings, impose more barriers to asylum seekers, expand immigrant detention, ignore or abrogate laws protecting vulnerable workers. Indian country and prisons predictably became the epicenter of the COVID-19 crisis in the US, and cases of domestic violence spiked, as many survivors were forced to choose between homelessness and "sheltering in place" with abusive partners. And while all of this was happening, the world witnessed what could only be called a public lynching in Minneapolis. Thanks to Darnella Frazier, the courageous seventeen-year-old who captured the police officer Derek Chauvin pressing his knee into the neck of the handcuffed George Floyd Jr. for over nine minutes, the world watched a forty-six-year-old Black man beg for his life. "Please, please, please I can't breathe," he moaned, hoping that courtesy and compliance might save him. When it did not, we watched him summon his dead mother minutes before joining her. For Frazier, bearing witness to Floyd's execution was traumatic. "It changed me. It changed how I viewed life. It made me realize how dangerous it is to be Black in America."[2] The video of Floyd's public execution circulated on the heels of other spectacular killings of Black people—notably, twenty-five-year-old Ahmaud Arbery, fatally shot by vigilantes while jogging in Brunswick, Georgia, and Breonna Taylor, a twenty-six-year-old medical worker gunned down in her bed by Louisville police during a "no-knock" raid. It was Floyd's murder that lit the fuse. Twenty-six million people took to the streets across the country and around the world, risking their health and safety to face down riot police, tear gas, rubber bullets, and the COVID-19 pandemic to demand justice for Floyd and an end to state-sanctioned racial violence.[3]

"Black Spring" had arrived, and I did what I always do in times like these—I protested, spoke to the press, participated in countless forums, and wrote. I wrote emotionally about the killing of

Rayshard Brooks in a Wendy's parking lot in Atlanta. I mourned the deaths of Dijon Kizzee and Daniel Prude and so many others killed by police. But I had yet to mourn my own father. I found it easier to write about the state killing Black people and the dream of abolition than to come to terms with my father's death—or more precisely, his life. As 2020 drew to a close, my inability to perform the one task my sister asked of me remained a cloud hanging over my head. And then a week before Christmas 2020, I contracted COVID-19.

I dodged the dreaded ventilator, but the time I spent in the hospital hooked up to half a dozen machines and an intravenous drip, or at home coughing uncontrollably and gasping for breath, left me wondering if my time had come. All I could think about was having to confront my father—a completely incongruous image for a person who doesn't believe in the afterlife. My therapist explained in no uncertain terms that my father was haunting me *now*, in this life, and that the only way to free myself was to face him. I had to write his obituary and confront his painful and often tragic journey if I was ever to confront my own.

★ ★ ★

My father was born during the Great Depression on August 9, 1937, in Winston-Salem, North Carolina. He wasn't a Kelley—not initially. When I looked him up in the 1940 census, he was listed as Donald Bost, sharing the same last name as his mother, Lottie.[4] I had never heard this name before, nor had my sister who kept up with family lore and had a pretty good grasp of the family tree. Lottie is listed as a domestic worker and married, but her "husband" is nowhere to be found. (My mother recently confirmed that Mr. Bost was, indeed, my paternal grandfather.) Lottie and my dad were living in a small house on West Twenty-Third Street with three of her sisters—fourteen-year-old Florence Hodges, seventeen-year-old Emma Hodges, and twenty-seven-year-old Allien (pronounced Ay-LEEN) Kelley. (Another sister, Lena Mae, was liv-

ing on her own). Allien was married to the Reverend Rafe David
Kelley, head of the household and my father's uncle. The R. J.
Reynolds Tobacco plant had employed Allien and Rafe both for
over ten years—she worked as a stemmer, he swept floors.[5] Reynolds was not only the city's largest employer but a leading killer
of Black people: tobacco is a chief contributor to heart disease,
cancer, and strokes—the three leading causes of Black mortality.[6]

There are a few things to untangle here. We grew up calling
Allien and Reverend Rafe Kelley Grandma and Grandaddy. We
called Lottie Nana and visited her occasionally in Brooklyn. Lottie
had two other children, who we affectionately called Uncle Jerry
and Aunt Loretta. I was in my twenties when I found out the "real"
story, though the version passed down to me was not entirely true,
either. This is how it went: The Hodges were from Darlington,
South Carolina. Joseph Hodges and Lottie Mae Richardson were
married and had nine children. Around 1928 or 1929, they moved
to Winston-Salem, and soon thereafter Lottie Mae died.[7] Joseph
was unable to care for the children who had not reached adulthood. Because Allien had married Rafe Kelley in 1927, she took
responsibility for all of her younger siblings. When Lottie turned
thirteen, she became pregnant with Donald, my father. Lottie was
considered too young to raise a child, so Allien and Rafe formally
adopted Donald. In this telling, Allien and Rafe are heroic for
caring for all of the Hodges children and sparing my father the
indignity of being raised by an unwed teenaged mother.

I never questioned this narrative before I had to reconstruct
my father's life. Turns out Allien and Rafe did not take in all of
the Hodges children. Allien's eldest brother, Leroy, was also married, and he and his wife took in their father and sisters, Lottie
and Emma. Rafe and Allien were responsible for the two youngest siblings, Lena Mae (age five) and Florence (age two and a
half).[8] Rafe and Allien and the girls rented a room from a family
in Winston-Salem, so they were hardly separated, although the
four youngest daughters lived in different households. Even more

shocking is that Lottie was *seventeen*, not thirteen, when she gave birth (she was born on Christmas Day in 1919).[9] The birth certificate filed five months after Donald's birth listed Allien and Rafe as parents, directly contradicting what I found in the 1940 census.[10]

For many Black families facing economic hardship, displacement, chain migration, housing discrimination, and the incarceration of parents, intrafamily adoptions were not unusual. Such adoptions were a legacy of Reconstruction, when formerly enslaved people tried to reconstitute families after generations of forced separation.[11] This was not the case with my dad, however. Lottie gave birth to another boy, my Uncle Jerry, a few years later, and she was perfectly capable of caring for both children. But the Kelleys had legal claim, so when Rafe—now Reverend Rafe D. Kelley—was dispatched to Massachusetts in 1943 to pastor a church, they took Donald with them. At age six, he was suddenly separated from his mother, making him feel like either the chosen one or the disposable one. I suspect he swung back and forth between the two, but he came away from that experience contemptuous of all women—his mother, in particular.

To those on the outside looking in, having Reverend Kelley as your father was a big deal. Born in Lee County, South Carolina, in 1906, Rafe David Kelley was tall, handsome, and so high yellow he could almost pass for white. He had the golden tongue, platinum voice, and stage presence that made him a legendary "singing" preacher. Raised Baptist, he converted to Methodist, and in 1938 he was called to pastor a Colored Methodist Episcopal Church (CME) in Kernersville, a small town just outside of Winston-Salem, North Carolina. Five years later, he was sent by Bishop L. Russell to pastor a CME church in Cambridge, Massachusetts.[12] He served for one year before setting out on his own and founding St. John's Congregational Church in the Black community of Roxbury. In 1947, he returned to his Baptist roots and renamed his church St. John's Missionary Baptist Church. Being the son of a preacher man did not mean my dad was privileged.

They lived in a multifamily dwelling at 22 Hollander Street in the Grove Hall neighborhood of Roxbury, and for several years Reverend Kelley shined shoes to make ends meet, and Allien worked.

Roxbury was overrun with storefront churches, and urban renewal and the city's strategic use of eminent domain made it difficult to hold on to a space of worship for very long. But in 1952, Reverend Kelley and his flock purchased a beautiful church on 135 Vernon Street in Roxbury that was once a synagogue and then an African Methodist Episcopal (AME) church. St. John's remained there for twenty-eight years, and we spent many summers there cleaning pews, landscaping, attending Sunday school, hearing my grandfather preach, and watching older Black women get the holy ghost.[13]

My father attended public schools in Roxbury and graduated from Boston Technical High School in 1955. He was admitted to Boston University, but according to my mother he never graduated. In 1958–59, I know that he and my mother, Audin Reid, ended up working at the same factory where she soldered wires together and he worked in the office. My mother was part of a wave of some fifty thousand Caribbean migrants who came to the US during and immediately after World War II. Just after Christmas in 1949, my grandmother Carmen Rodrigues, a young single parent, put her ten-year-old daughter on a plane from Kingston to New York to live with an aunt and uncle in Queens.[14] Six years passed before my grandmother made the trek to the US, and not long after she arrived, the two of them moved to Boston.

Reverend Kelley married my parents in December of 1959, and they practically fled to New York City to get out from under Rafe and Allien's judgmental eye. My sister was born in September of 1960, and I followed eighteen months later. We lived in Brooklyn briefly, until my father began working as some kind of an engineer and made enough money to buy a small house in Hollis, Queens. I was about two when we moved in and five when we left.

I remember having my own room, a dog, a backyard, and my mother sometimes cooking, sometimes making art. A self-taught sculptor, she created beautiful clay busts of John F. Kennedy and Dr. Martin Luther King Jr. I remember seeing my father dance in the living room once, but much of what I recall of those days is not fit for an obituary—like seeing my father slapping my mother hard enough to knock her to the floor or smashing her precious sculptures and hollering and spanking us when we disobeyed. I remember his long absence when he took a job in Seattle and how it felt to breathe, laugh, and skip without fear. I used to pretend to be a grown man, so my mother bought me a bottle of Old Spice after she caught me smearing toothpaste on my cheeks pretending to shave. And I try to forget the night he came through my mother's bedroom window as I slept next to her. He came home early to surprise us, found aftershave in the bathroom cabinet, and set out to kill my mother and the man to whom the cheap cologne belonged. That was my first encounter with a real gun.

My father was filled with rage. When he encountered defiance, dissent, disorder, or anything beyond his ken, he responded with violence. He beat his children, I assume, because his parents beat him. Reverend Kelley and Allien lived by Proverbs 13:24: "He that spares the rod hates his son, but he that loves carefully chastens him." Their love was prodigious, judging by how often my father got his ass whipped. I know this, having felt my grandparents' careful chastening firsthand. During our many summers in Boston, when we weren't in church our grandparents took us fishing and hunting and gave us plenty of chores to keep us busy. If we stepped out of line, however, a switch came out of nowhere, striking our naked behinds in quick succession. How many lashes depended on the number of syllables it took to explain your crime and the consequences of recidivism.

On my father's side of the family, beating kids made you a good parent, and being a parent made you worthy. A true man was a patriarch, and a true woman was a mother. My father learned early on that motherhood determined a woman's value, and he resented Lottie because she failed him as a mother. Aillen,

on the other hand, couldn't bear children, so adopting my father allowed her to fulfill her duties and attain value. This logic
carried consequences. Aillen's younger sister, my Aunt Florence,
lived in New York, worked full-time as a nurse, and wanted her
own children. In the early months of 1966, she announced to the
family that she was pregnant. She gained weight. She displayed
her protruding tummy with great pride. She bought baby clothes
and made plans for a nursery. As the delivery date approached,
she became reclusive. On July 5, 1966, just two days before her
thirty-seventh birthday, Aunt Florence took her life.[15] Turns out
she was never pregnant.

Not long after my Aunt Florence died, my father was recruited
into a program designed to increase "minority" representation in
the aerospace industry. After considering a range of opportunities, he accepted a job at Boeing in Seattle, Washington, where he
worked as an engineer on the team that built the 747 aircraft.[16]
My mother didn't want to move and he didn't encourage her. He
had already begun an affair with Revele Bishop, a single mother
with a young son. He divorced my mother, hastily remarried, and
the new Mrs. Kelley was carrying his baby, my half brother, in a
blink of an eye. With no money and two young kids to care for,
my mother moved in with her cousin and her family in Harlem.
My mother's mother lived on the same block (157th between Am-
sterdam and Broadway) and helped us out until we found a place
of our own in a neighboring apartment building.

Despite the roaches, rats, rusty tap water, shared rooms, cracked
linoleum, and underfunded, overcrowded schools of Harlem, life
was infinitely better than living in Queens under a dictatorial king.
And my mother gave birth to a baby boy in 1968 named Sean
Christopher, whom we called "Chris," turning our little trio into a
quartet. Meanwhile, my father had other plans. He wanted custody.
The issue wasn't money since he never honored his legal obligation
to pay child support. His new kingdom was incomplete without
his firstborn and first son, and he was urged on by his parents and

wife, who believed that our presence could help shore up their fragile marriage. When the custody battle failed, they kidnapped us. Revele, who worked for Northwest Airlines, offered to fly us to Jamaica to visit family during the summer of 1971 so long as we spent a couple of weeks in Seattle before returning home. My mother used our summer away to relocate to Los Angeles, fulfilling a dream we'd been talking about since I could remember. It was supposed to be a big surprise. Instead, my father dropped a bigger surprise when he wouldn't let us go. He was merely fulfilling his duty as patriarch, adhering to the same logic that made him a Kelley, caused him to hate his mother, and ultimately killed his aunt.

As with most kidnapping operations, there were glitches. Chris, who was not my father's child, got caught in the ambush. When my mother traveled to Seattle by bus to reclaim her children, my father handed Chris over and drew his gun to let her know that the rest of us were here to stay. I weakly suggested that my mother should get one of us but was popped in the mouth before finishing the sentence.

A standard obituary would tell us that Donald Kelley reunited with his children, briefly worked at Aerojet General in Redmond, Washington, where they made weapons for US military operations in Vietnam, and formed his own company, Effective Service Planners, which specialized in technical writing and consulting on engineering and maintenance matters. It could not include his long, humiliating bout with unemployment, a litany of business failures, and the many tales of brutality. I refuse to relive the horrors of being beaten with belts, sticks, hot wheel tracks, open hands, and closed fists. I will say this: I was a good son. I did everything he and his wife asked of me. I studied hard. I played sports, though not very well. I helped him fix his car. At age eleven, I did the grocery shopping and became my stepmother's private errand boy. I even worked at my father's office two weekends, doing something with blueprints. In middle school, I got straight A's on all of my report cards—a pretty big deal for a Black kid bused to a white school in what was then the lily-white suburb of Ballard. But fall semester in eighth grade, my usual perfect report card had no teacher's comments. My father looked at it, turned it over, and slapped me hard in the face. He noted the absence of comments as evidence that I was slipping. He demanded a meeting with my teachers and the principal, who incredulously tried to explain that my grades speak for themselves. The conference prompted the guidance counselor to check in with me about my home life.

I used to think my intense work ethic and blind obedience were driven entirely by fear. Now I see there was more to it. I was also seeking his approval. I wanted him to be proud of me. I wanted his love. My sister did, too, but she had had enough. In 1975 at age fifteen, she escaped the kingdom and made it to our mom's house in California. Her flight proved to be the final blow to my father's failing marriage. Revele split with her two children, leaving me alone with my father.

The year was 1976, and I was fourteen years old. I probably should have tried to leave, but I could not break with my role as a pleaser, the good kid, the loyalist, the master's errand boy. This invisible bond was shattered, but not entirely severed, on Christmas Day. That morning we drove to Revele's parents' house to pick up my half brother. As I sat in the car waiting, I heard shouting and scuffling. My father emerged, his face bloodied, ran to the car to retrieve his gun, and disappeared into the house. I heard several gunshots. I was afraid to stay, afraid to run, and unable to move. He came back out, jumped behind the wheel, and took off. We drove a few blocks to the home of Norman and Lea Proctor, family friends whom we referred to as our aunt and uncle. They had three daughters and a son I considered cousins. After a few hours, it became clear that we were not going back to my father's house and that my father had no intention of sticking around. I learned later that no one was hurt in the fracas, but assault with a deadly weapon was a serious charge. Uncle Normie and my father decided that night to take a trip.

Here is the part of the obituary that would praise Donald Kelley's love of travel and adventure: He was part of a proud tradition
in aviation history as a licensed Black pilot. He and his friend
Norman Proctor flew a single-engine Cessna to the African continent (making frequent stops, of course). Their flight was historic
and heroic, so long as we leave out why they left in the first place.
My father was running from the law, running for his life.

I moved in with Aunt Lea that night and found familial love
and peace of mind. It was like a yearlong exhalation, a space to
grow and come into my own. My father and Uncle Normie returned a year later after a truly spectacular adventure that ended
with their plane catching fire in the Canary Islands and my father
being hospitalized for trichinosis. Fortunately for him, he was
never charged for the Christmas Day shooting. Unfortunately for
me, he returned even crazier than before. Three weeks later, I fled
to California.

Reunited with my mother and siblings, I thought my ordeal was
over. But still I remained tethered to him. When he remarried a Jewish woman twelve years his junior in 1979, he asked my sister and
me to attend and appointed me best man. The marriage didn't last
long, but he did father another son who became the object of yet
another nasty custody battle. He remarried again in 1987 to another
white woman, this one seven years his junior. He had renounced
Judaism and reconnected with his Baptist upbringing, driven, I believe, by a desire to connect with *his* father—to please his father, to
be his father. He was called to the ministry, grooming himself as the
next Reverend Kelley. When my grandfather died on Easter Sunday,
1996, my father moved back to Boston to care for his mother (she
died in 2002), take over the house, and take what he believed was
his rightful place as pastor of St. John's Missionary Baptist Church.
Neither the current pastor, the deacons, nor the congregation were
interested, so his bid ended in humiliating defeat.

The idea of becoming pastor of his father's church was all my
father had left. He was a failed patriarch. Two of his children

literally ran away from home, and the other two had little or nothing to do with him. He finally won custody of his youngest son
and tried to erase his mother's Jewish heritage by enrolling him
in Christian schools. That son, my half brother, eventually joined
the military and broke all ties with our father. With no children
to lord over, how could Donald Kelley attain his rightful place as
patriarch, a role for which he had been groomed his entire life?

In 2004, he wed wife number five, a member of the church
who was the spitting image of Allien Kelley. My sister Makani and
I were his only kids who attended the wedding, and, once again,
he asked me to be the best man. I obliged and even delivered a
toast that acknowledged his mistakes without sounding critical or
judgmental. That was the last time I ever saw him.

My father left Boston and his wife in 2016 and moved to Albuquerque. He lost money from his parents' estate, a leg to diabetes,
and three sons who simply stopped speaking to him. Makani,
his firstborn, assumed responsibility for his care, kept him connected to his grandchildren, and gave him what he was unable
to give us—unconditional love. Her actions, as well as my futile
attempts at writing his obituary, taught me that Donald Sheralton Kelley was nothing but a man—a terrified little man whose
bombast and violence masked deep insecurities; a man trapped in
the prison house of patriarchy who spent his life chasing after his
father's love.

I stopped chasing long ago. I think I'm finally ready to grieve.

SIXTEEN

SUICIDE AND SURVIVAL

Deaths of Despair in the 2020s

Keri Leigh Merritt

The nightmares started again with the pandemic.
They were the same PTSD night terrors I've had my entire adult life, though now they came every night—stronger, more vivid, and with terrifying intensity. My husband would wake me during the worst parts, after hearing my muffled screams, or feeling me fight off the pillows and blankets surrounding me, as I tried to save myself from the murderous attackers invading my unconscious mind.[1]

These dreams of 2020—a mess of emotion and anxiety over a fascist president, a deadly pandemic, and the blatant reemergence of violent white supremacy—came hot on the heels of one of the most sorrowful years of my life, as I lost three people I truly loved within a whirlwind six months. As stressful and heartbreaking as the early 2020s would end up being, countless Americans—me being one of them—would enter the era already perilously close to their breaking points. The beginning of the decade only raised the stakes of the tumultuous ordeals so many of us were already facing.

On June 6, 2019, my paternal grandmother, Marilyn Mathilde Miller Morrison Merritt, finally passed—as peacefully as one can with end-stage Parkinson's—on her eighty-ninth birthday. Bed-ridden for nearly a year, her system shut down slowly and pain-fully. She finally stopped eating, and then drinking. Her wrinkled, worn hands, including the left hand that had begun it all, shak-ing slightly when I was a child, and moving with uncontrollable tremors by the time I was a teen, had seized up into clenched fists by the end, crossing her body in an oddly defensive pose. They looked so unnatural that my sweet aunt, who cared for both her and my papa in their later years, wrapped a soft blanket into Nana's tiny, shriveled fingers to make things appear, somehow, someway, possibly *better*.

Growing up, I had always felt incredibly connected to my grand-mother. She seemed to be the only one in my life who wasn't afraid to show me unconditional love. I certainly did not feel loved at home by my parents. And though we lived only a few hours away from her in metro-Atlanta, we did not visit the small town in the South Carolina Appalachian foothills where all my extended family lived with much frequency. As a cotton mill village sitting on an old railroad line, the town was already dying when I was a child. No other major industries were there; it was the first place I truly learned about poverty in America. Today, the mills sit idle, gut-ted—all their equipment bought out by Chinese firms in the 1990s.

The ambitious and lucky leave, like my parents did. But we hardly ever went back. My father was always working, traveling—he clearly did not want anything to do with us or his family of origin. Instead, he hid out, like the coward he is, under the facade of work obligations. Burying his head in the sand, he'd periodi-cally emerge only to remind us that my mother's abuse *was* love. To this day, he—ironically, a psychologist by trade—pretends not to understand why so many of his daughters ended up in abusive relationships early in their lives.

By the time I was in kindergarten, my mother had fallen deep into her illness. Although she was never properly diagnosed (the closest a doctor came was treating her for bipolar depression, and she consistently refused to take the medication anyway), after decades of research on the matter, my best guess is that she had borderline personality disorder (BPD). BPD is characterized by extreme mood swings and volatile relationships. "Inappropriate, intense anger," abusive tendencies, and threats of suicide are common in people with the disorder.[2]

My world was volatile, neglectful, and horrifically emotionally abusive. I had the Sisyphean task of raising three younger sisters while keeping my constantly suicidal mother from following through on her threats to kill herself.

I became an extension of my mother's own psyche—I existed as her protective bubble, shielding her from the outside world. I learned the hard way that I had to devote myself to fending off the smallest thing that might set her off, at least mitigating its blow as much as I possibly could. I became—out of an acute need for survival—my mother's emotional sieve. I absorbed all her wretched pain, all the world's troubles, allowing the good to pour straight through me to her so quickly I never got a chance to enjoy it. I had so naively hoped and prayed that something good might, possibly, defuse some of her constant, unprovoked anger.

Looking back, I finally realize what an impossible task this was for a young child. At the time, though, there was no thinking.

There was only surviving.

* * *

Witnessing the ravages of COVID-19 and how it robbed hundreds of thousands of families of the ability to say goodbye gave me a different perspective on these losses. I got to see Nana one last time before she died, about two weeks before she took her last breath. I am relieved that she and Papa, and my dear friend Cliff, suffering through stage four colon cancer at the young age of fifty-one, did not live long enough to see the horrors of this global pandemic. I am happy that they did not have to be hospitalized for days or weeks without visitors. And I am so incredibly grateful that they didn't have to die alone, in a strange room, hooked up to countless machines, struggling to breathe.

During that trip to South Carolina, I knew it would be the last time I would ever see her. She had been unconscious for the previous few weeks; death was hovering over her, waiting (excruciatingly) patiently. As I entered her room, her head turned ever so slightly toward me. To this day I still don't know quite how to describe it, but her sparkling blue eyes, always so lively and kind, slowly opened. They looked dim, shallow.

Suddenly, it was if her soul shot back into her body; I could see her coming back into herself. The light was there again, at least for a brief moment. I gently spooned some ice chips into her tiny, dry mouth, and she began struggling to talk. I told her everything I needed to tell her; I told her how much she meant to me, how she saved me, and how it was okay to let go.

Mustering every little bit of strength she had left, she looked deep into my own blue eyes—the eyes I inherited from her— and barely murmured what would be some of her final words: "I'm so happy."

I think about those three words more than I probably should. I think about how she could have said "I love you," words I used to long to hear (but did not) from my own parents, but she knew that I already knew she loved me. Instead, she chose to make me realize that despite being in horrific pain, despite literally dying, she was *happy* that I came to see her.

Happy.

A word I rarely, if ever, uttered—and barely understood.

* * *

Although she had a tragic background herself, Nana had been the only one of my four grandparents to not come from extreme poverty. Born in Asheville, North Carolina, in 1930 during the height of the Great Depression, Nana was the first and only child of my great-grandfather, Samuel Neely Miller, a bookkeeper and

CPA. Very likely due to the Great Depression ruining his business—and thus, his ability to provide for his new wife and child, my great-grandfather took his own life on May 30, 1933, six days before his thirty-first birthday—exactly a week before my grandmother turned three.

Nana never, ever talked about her father's death. I knew that she loved him deeply and admired him greatly, but it would not be until after her own death that I, a historian by trade, began digging. Samuel Neely Miller Jr. killed himself with a single bullet through his right temple. My poor, long-suffering great-grandmother found his body, his brains scattered across the floors of the McDavid Apartments in Greenville, South Carolina.[3]

"Gunshot wound of head, entering above" his right ear, his death certificate plainly states—right through his brilliant, troubled brain—"exiting" through the left. "When America caught cold, the South got pneumonia, and when the nation was really sick, as it was in the Great Depression, its colonial states below the Mason-Dixon line were on their deathbed," historian John Egerton wrote. He deemed 1932 "the cruelest year," as the suicide rate tripled in those twelve months alone.[4]

By the spring of 1933 my great-grandfather was nothing more than a statistic.

Perhaps he came to this place of seemingly unending despair because of the ruin of his business, savings, ability to support his family, and worth as a *man*. Or perhaps he, like my uncle, suffered from schizophrenia, constantly hearing voices and seeing apparitions and fighting off demons. With my grandmother's passing, I will never know. I only know what I managed to pull up online. I only know what strangers wrote about him, what they recorded on prefilled forms, about dates and times and addresses.

Sometimes I think about how my grandmother never knew her father's laugh, never knew his dreams or his fears, never knew the simple pleasure of him enveloping her in a hug, of seeing him smile, of hearing his voice.

★ ★ ★

My family's arduous history with suicide unfortunately does not end with my great-grandfather. It haunted me—quite ruthlessly—through my early childhood, persisted into my young adulthood, and still affects many of the decisions I make to this day.

My mother's story is a long and deeply sad one; I could write an entire book on it. Having grown up in extreme poverty in that small mill village in the South Carolina up-country, she came from a mother who had, at best, a partial fourth-grade education. This grandmother, Wilma Carrie Howard, came from such poverty that she spent her childhood alternatively picking cotton during bottle-neck seasons and working in the cotton mills. By the time I was a teenager I had started wondering why there were no newspapers or reading materials in her house. She had a few bookshelves, but they were filled with pictures and little figurines instead of books. By the time I was an adult I finally realized why.[5]

I only learned one of the most horrific stories about "Mama Wilma's" life well after her death, when I was in my thirties. To-day I can't—no matter how hard I try—remember how the topic came up, yet another manifestation of my PTSD. In my memory, the conversation emerges sharply, with no beginning and no end; it just hovers around this one aspect like a vortex of sorrow. For some reason my mother finally confided to me that her own mother, despite birthing eight children and miscarrying numer-ous more, could not bear to hear the cries of an infant—it sent her into a frenzied panic. This panic resulted from her gruesome childhood during the Great Depression, as she heard her baby brother die of starvation, crying for weeks on end as he could not get enough milk from his mother's breast.[6]

As with many poor white southerners, my mother grew up in a huge family—counting half brothers, she was one of ten—in a tiny mill village house. My grandmother lived in that tiny house, just two blocks from the cotton mill, until she died—early, of course, from cancer.

My mother's life had undoubtedly been more difficult than mine; looking back on everything, I know that while some parts of her mental illness were likely inherited, most of it was situational. Her father, a Cajun-Creole veteran of both World War II and the Korean War, died of a massive heart attack when she was seven, leaving my pregnant, illiterate grandmother destitute— with six hungry children to feed.

My grandfather, Clarence Joseph Constance, was gone within weeks of his forty-third birthday. When he began having chest pains, they immediately took him by ambulance to the local Appalachian hospital. But there was one problem: the hospital was Baptist, and he—born in New Orleans with Avoyelles Parish roots—was Catholic.

They refused to treat him based on his religion. My mother always told me that they had to drive to the next "big" town to find a hospital that would admit him. Until I found his death certificate, I would not realize that she was not referring to Greenville, South Carolina, but instead to Columbia—at least a four-hour drive back then, as it was prior to the current highway system. It was too late by the time they finally got him to the Veterans Administration hospital in the state's run-down capital.[7]

During my mother's trademark volcanic tantrums, she would often tell us about how she was forced to kiss her father's cold, dead lips as he lay in the casket. It was as if she could not be descriptive enough—the coldness of his body was what struck her to the core. She'd describe the experience again and again, reliving it in front of us, forcing us to share in her anguish.

It was always as if there was a contest for who had experienced the most pain and sorrow for my mother. Whatever we, her children, experienced, no matter how bad, she would constantly remind us that she went through far, far worse.

The few times I got a "whuppin'" from my own mother, it was done with wooden spoons and the backs of hairbrushes. I'd soon learn that her grandmother made her go out and choose the stick she'd "tear her ass up with." Later, I'd learn that the grandmother that had beaten her had been beaten by her own father with a buggy whip.

I suppose we have to call that progress.

★ ★ ★

Sometimes I catch myself slipping up, talking about my mother's suicide as if it had actually happened. Then I realize that it in many ways did. She *is* dead to me, has been dead, had died thousands of times in hundreds of scenarios. She died to me a little each time she so casually and callously threatened to end her own life. I lost some of her every time she triumphantly described in gory detail how she planned to murder herself.

By the time I was five years old, something had shifted. It was almost as if I could perceive a physical shift because I so profoundly felt the change in mood. Something dark and sinister and endlessly insatiable had taken over our household. It surrounded me, it consumed me. It suffocated me.

By seven years old, I was acutely aware of how to kill yourself by carbon monoxide asphyxiation: how to attach a hose to your tailpipe and snake it through the window of a running car, preferably in a closed garage. She described it in such detail. By the time I was nine, her use of imagery had become even more violent, with vivid, expletive-laden language describing the stark contrast of her blood and brains splattered against our pale kitchen walls. By eleven, I usually knew when to call her bluff, but I never did.

Certain risks are just too risky.

Perhaps even worse than my mother's frequent threats of suicide and her massive, soul-sucking mood swings were her words to us, about us. See, my mother wasn't just suicidal: she was angry, vengeful, and needed people to blame for her pain. She had no friends and isolated herself from anyone who tried to get close to her, and my workaholic father tried to stay away from her—and us—as much as possible. We, her children, were thus left as her only scapegoats, a captive audience for her theatrical tantrums: she'd throw things against the walls and scream for hours. This was generally followed by days of dark brooding, crying, and making my entire world seem like a gauntlet of suffering.

With no one else around to blame, my mother would explicitly tell us that we were the reason she did not want to live. We were dirty, filthy, and did nothing but create work for her—she was nothing more than an uncompensated, unappreciated maid and cook and driver. She'd call us "white trash" and "white n-----s," repeatedly screaming about how, by virtue of being born, we had ruined her life.[8]

This was a child's war, and I was a toy soldier. When I could see one of her tantrums coming on, I'd immediately go into action. To this day, when there's something wrong, I can't sit still—I have to clean, I have to make things better, I have to work myself into complete exhaustion because I can't ever—*ever*—relax.

My first task was to remove my younger sisters from the toxic situation. I knew from many past experiences that she wanted an audience to experience her pain with her, but when my sisters—just babies during many of these years—began crying as she shrieked in our faces, she would become increasingly enraged. Looking back, I think it was because the focus then was on them, not her. So I learned that when she started on one of her rants, I'd immediately get the next oldest to take the little ones out—to take them upstairs to their rooms and stay there, together, like silent captives, until I told them it was safe to come down.

Then I'd deal with her. I was her terrorized audience of one. I was her whipping boy. And when I became suicidal myself by the time I was ten or so, I instead learned to numb the psychological pain with physical pain, carving words into my left arm throughout my teenage years. Words like "vile," because that's what I was.

Today, at forty-one years old, I still have a scar of the "v." Yet I only employed physical pain to a point: I consciously chose to cut, not to kill. But why?

Because as much as I hated myself, and my life, I refused to allow myself the blissful peace of death. Because I had to care for my younger sisters. Because I had to be there—be alive and functioning—*for them*. I had to take her pain onto me and away from them. In my mind there was no choice.

Just survival.

★ ★ ★

Then 2020 hit. In this historically tragic year, it was only natural that we, the survivors, were the only ones fully emotionally aware of the depths of suffering the pandemic would bring. We fully realized how bad things might possibly get, how many people were about to experience deep, transformative pain—suffering on a scale most Americans couldn't fathom.

And aside from the death toll of those with COVID, we—the survivors—knew that "deaths of despair," a disturbing triumvirate of suicide, alcohol, and opioid-related deaths, would soon start to skyrocket, too.

In 2017 alone, three years before the pandemic, the Princeton economists Anne Case and Angus Deaton found that at least 158,000 Americans died deaths of despair. Unlike other developed nations, Case and Deaton argued, America never adopted the social safety nets that other democratic nations deem human rights, thus creating one of the most unequal societies globally.[9]

There is not yet enough data on post-COVID deaths due to alcohol and alcoholism, but we know that liquor, beer, and wine sales quickly shot up throughout the pandemic. Opioid overdoses were increasing long before COVID, and they began rapidly rising throughout March and April of 2020, peaking in May. But opioid deaths are entirely different from suicide: most are accidental overdoses, especially given the recent prevalence of deadly fentanyl.[10]

Meanwhile, the suicide rate in America is currently at its highest level since the Great Depression (1938), growing an astounding 36 percent in the twenty years since 1999. Herein lies America's true exceptionalism, as the United States' soaring suicide rate stands in stark contrast to the rest of the world.[11]

But Case and Deaton were surprised to find that suicides have not yet risen as much as they would expect during the pandemic. Unlike opioid deaths, suicides began declining in April and May of 2020, slowly reverting to the pre-COVID average by summer. "It is tempting, perhaps too tempting," they wrote, "to take the analogy between the pandemic and war, and to note the well-documented result that suicide falls in wartime."[12]

As for the suicide rate, only time will give us more answers. As a survivor, I know that there is a correlation between suicide and survival for some of us. For some of us, there are caretaking responsibilities that we just cannot escape, no matter how much we may want to.

See, resilience isn't always personal; in fact, it's usually dependent on others. We see this all the time in war; many soldiers commit to tour after tour not because they relish the fight but to save their friends and comrades.

Like so many countless others, I survived the hellish torture of my childhood because I had responsibilities. I had to protect other people.

★ ★ ★

We must learn to become more comfortable with the concept of simple survival—of making it through the next month, week, day, hour, minute. This is something most Americans have had the luxury of forgetting for nearly a century. Other nations have not. And we must focus on others—on the well-being of all sentient beings; on loving-kindness; on living in the moment; of being connected to the natural world on a very basic, molecular level; of being a part of the larger, the communal, the macro. Of not being so completely, hopelessly, tragically alone. We simply cannot think about the unbearable lightness of being.

There are some things in this world that therapy cannot fix. There are some deep psychological wounds that time will never heal. Some of us cannot shake our battle scars, no matter how hard we try, or how much we work on ourselves and our lives, whether through sacrifice or self-help, medication or meditation.

We, the wounded, are left to *live*, make sense of the senseless, preach to the deaf, and paint for the blind. We become empaths and healers and are more in tune with the natural world. We are closer to death, and because of that, we are closer to life. We are the people who carry our wounds openly, bleeding into the void. And while only some of us fully realize it, our awareness of that void is a form of enlightenment. We are the humanists: the artists, the musicians, the writers—*the translators of suffering*. For us, it is not about the passion.

It's about the survival.

SEVENTEEN

"HOW DO WE LIVE?"

A Journal of a Lost Year

Scott Poulson-Bryant

15 September 2020

Today, I can see the faces of twelve of my eighteen students. A couple of weeks in and I still don't know what five of them actually look like.

I thought a lot about teaching in 2020 during the COVID-19 pandemic and global uprisings after the murder of George Floyd.

Fall semester 2020 was my first semester teaching at one of the largest and most prestigious public universities in America, the University of Michigan, after four years at Fordham University, a Jesuit school in New York, and here I was sitting at my desk in Long Island while most of my students—freshmen taking my first year seminar—sat in dorm rooms in Ann Arbor, all of us staring across the virtual Zoom void, trying to connect. Connect, I should say, beyond the digital connection of 0s and 1s in our computers, which allowed us to convene as a class on the Zoom app which presented us to each other as faraway faces in a grid of little stacked black boxes. At Fordham, we'd gone remote rapidly in March 2020; then I taught a summer course—three hours twice a week—so by fall 2020, I felt equipped to stare at a computer screen, to teach across that digital Zoom void while discussing the African American popular culture texts that my classes focused on. I would even become technically proficient enough to broadcast a soundtrack of songs to play on the Zoom app as students' faces popped onto the screen—the online version of arriving to class. I didn't feel equipped though to introduce freshmen, straight from their parents' homes, new, like me, to the University of Michigan, to the university experience. So I did that elaborate dance professors must do, balancing the instructor with the guide, the authority figure with the partner-in-learning. However, the choreography for me (as I'm sure it was for others) was conceived in connecting with my students, reading on their faces (or perhaps in their nods of agreement or understanding) their responses to questions and comments, sensing their confusion or bemusement or fear. That didn't happen as readily on Zoom as it did in the classroom—it couldn't, could it? Unlike in a physical classroom, where students might be loathe to abruptly leave the room in the middle of a professor's lecture, Zoom teaching meant girding oneself for the sudden blackout of one of those small boxes, the disappearance—because of tech issues, because of mood, perhaps because of the understandable stress of trying to be "there" when the emotional capacity didn't allow it—of a student's face, sometimes never to arrive again, and as a result I found myself thinking a lot about teaching college students in 2020.

No one had ever taught me *how* to teach. It just wasn't part of the curriculum at the Graduate School of Arts and Sciences at Harvard, where I went to graduate school for a PhD in American Studies. I ran discussion sections for my superstar professors and advisers, guiding students through the readings that someone else had assigned. And we weren't allowed to create our own courses there, as I'd heard other schools invited their PhD students to do. I was however late in my graduate career, fortunately, given the opportunity to teach in the Program in History and Literature for a year. As a former journalist and current American Studies PhD student immersed in thinking about the cultural production of literature and film through the lens of historical inquiry, the invitation to teach in Hist & Lit (as we called it at Harvard) meant bringing this scholarly method to undergrads, creating a syllabus, assigning reading and papers, creating a dialogue with students based on my ideas and strategies for thinking them through. And as I did that, I also learned that perhaps no one taught me how to teach because no one really could teach me how to teach. I just had to do it and either get good at it or fail. By the time of my first job after graduate school, I had gotten good at it. I'd won awards for it. Other teachers came to me for advice.

But now here I was teaching new students during a pandemic, unable to continue a tradition I'd begun in graduate school, taking each of my students out for a cup of coffee, opening the conversation with a phrase I'd learned from a friend in college—"tell me your life"—eager to learn about them in a way we rarely get to know our students when you only know them as a face staring back at you from a movable desk in a classroom. I was a better teacher—or so I've told myself over the years—when I knew where they were from, when I knew what sport they played in high school, when I knew if sitting in a college classroom was *really* what they imagined for themselves if they had the chance to do anything. The pandemic changed that, snatched away the chance to make that early-semester connection. But it wasn't just the pandemic—or the distance created by it—that had taken that away. This was a semester following a summer inflected by, defined by, what the media was calling a "racial reckoning." And what the media often did not say, of course, is that for many of us, existence in the United States was always a "racial reckoning," that "racial reckoning" was part of our daily lives, seemingly bred in bone, the structural, systemic architecture of our history. But here I was teaching plays like the powerful *A Raisin in the Sun* and memoirs like the edgy *Down These Mean Streets* and films like the tragic *Boyz n the Hood* to nine white students, six Black students, and one student each of Chinese, South Asian, and Middle Eastern descent in a course about twentieth-century popular culture and the performance of racial and ethnic identity in the American urban space called Good Kid/Mad City: Urban Identity(s) in US Popular Culture.

Designed for first-year students, it was a seminar in the Department of Afroamerican and African Studies created with the pedagogical goal of introducing students to the nuances of college coursework, the heady blend of discussion and analysis they would encounter throughout their time in college. But it was also a course which, I knew, would also be for many of my students an introduction to discussing race and racism in the United States. But how does one teach "race" or how to talk about it during a "racial reckoning"? How does one corral the themes of struggle, of political and cultural shifts and uprisings, in a moment that feels so tense, so inchoately traumatic, in the wake of George Floyd's murder on May 25, 2020, in Minneapolis? How does one tiptoe through the potential minefields planted in the subject matter, especially when you can't even see students' faces, depending on the day?

Those are some of the things I was thinking.

1 October 2020

> Today, I can see the faces of eleven of my eighteen students. A month in and I still don't know what four of them actually look like. One of them came to office hours to ask about the first assignment, so now I know what he looks like. But his box is back to black today.

The course, Good Kid/Mad City, is named after the second studio album of Pulitzer Prize–winning rapper Kendrick Lamar. I chose it because I wanted the class to think not just about race and Blackness but also about the cities in the US where Blackness has so often been the ingredient giving those places their flavor, even as the bodies marked by Blackness so often find themselves un-

der siege. I wanted my students—many of them from suburbia—
to grapple with the formation and creation of what we call "the
ghetto" and the racialized implications of it, the material results of
the place so many of them, whether they'd admit or not, already
associate with a particular kind of racial and cultural experience.
The song title, the song itself, spoke directly to the themes of the
course, and it felt modern enough to reach them, to mean something to them. It was a seduction of sorts: some would expect hip
hop to be part of the curriculum, and it was important to relax
them into subject matter that would, for some, hit them hard, but
also teach them new things.

But I take them deeper on the first day. I open the class with an
older song: Stevie Wonder's "Living for the City" (1973), the second single from Wonder's brilliant *Innervisions* album. I tell them
the song is a kind of "ground zero" of rap music's grim beauty, a
sonic and lyrical origin text, for the cityfied, rough-and-tumble
narratives they'd encountered in hip hop, and I tell them to listen
closely to the lyrics, to the narrative that Stevie lays out with his
blend of passion and precision.

"Living for the City" is seven minutes and twenty-three seconds
long; in pop music terms, it is an epic. I choose to play it for them
because of Wonder's unsparing, unrelenting attention to detail.
It blends funk with the blues and with gospel, from the loping
rhythmic organ that opens the record like the opening of a church
service, which launches, with the drums or Moog bass, one of
those records—like much of the rap music that will follow it up
music charts many years later—that sounds like its subject matter,
where the music competes with the lyrics to make as much meaning for the listener as possible. Recounting the cautionary tale
of one young man's great migration from "hard-time Mississippi"
to big bad New York City, narrating the sad realization that his
American dream might be a nightmare, detailing through spoken
dialogue his run-in with hustlers and cops and the justice system, Wonder nonetheless envelopes the record in hope, using the

melodic, multitracked, octave-climbing vocalizing of a mythic and angelic-sounding gospel choir to provide nothing less than sonic Black history. But it's also American history. Because it is about loss: a loss of innocence, a loss of direction, the loss of spirit that has dogged so many Black communities across centuries.

As I was planning the course during the summer of 2020, I'd experienced loss, like so many other people in the United States. I felt infected by it; it became the thing I feared more than the illness circulating through our streets and homes. In my case, "home" meant sheltering with my aging parents and Molly, the old sad-eyed basset hound in the Long Island house in which I'd grown up. Once I'd decided not to move to Ann Arbor in the middle of a global pandemic to just sit in a new apartment and stare at a Zoom screen to teach, I stayed with my folks, hoping to be a help to them during this uncertain time. Of course, moving back home meant, at my age, a blend of the good and the not-so-good. I'd have little privacy; I'd be sleeping in the room I slept in as a teenager, where posters of the pop stars still hung on the walls. But I'd also be eating my mother's delicious home cooking; I'd get to spend time with my dad, hearing his stories and laughing at his accidental jokes. But also: I found myself, whenever I'd escaped my bedroom to head downstairs, eavesdropping on my mother's phone conversations. And often, she was chatting with relatives in states like Florida which had been hit so hard, and I sometimes caught the sound of her hushed, tear-stained voice as a cousin or an aunt described to her the funerals they couldn't have for the family members we'd lost. And it occurred to me those losses, especially for a church-going elder like my mom, also meant the physical loss of traditions which sustained her, flowers and fans, the prayer books, and the preachers who intoned not just biblical stories but a way of life.

I carried that loss into my syllabus building, and I knew that my students might be carrying that loss into our classroom, the virtual void where I wouldn't see as many of their faces as

I wanted to. And I knew that in many ways hip hop, despite its so-often raucous sonic rabble-rousing, was about a kind of loss, about the traumatic transactions that defined so many Black and Brown lives. And I knew that in its musical maneuvers and lyrical phrasings it also is a site of, as playwright Robert O'Hara describes in the subtitle of his play *Insurrection*, "holding history," a sonic cauldron of the deepest fears and frustrations, but also joys, of Black people. This legacy links the past to the present, which had invested in a kind of "racial reckoning" on vinyl since its earliest days. In his author's note to the play, which I assign to my students, O'Hara describes his work as the "Theater of Choke"—an intense word to encounter in this particular historical and political moment in the wake of George Floyd's murder. "I do not want my work to go down easily," O'Hara writes. "I want you to Gasp. To have to work what you see and read down into your Gut. . . . I had to *work* to create it, and you should *work* to experience it."[1]

I'd shared O'Hara's goal with my courses. I wanted my students to enter the space I'd created at the beginning of the semester, and by the end of the semester, not to have just read and listened and discussed, but to have *experienced* the texts we'd engaged, to experience, at least once, that gasp, that choke. But I was not quite sure I wanted to engage that way in the fall of 2020, in the deep end of so much loss, in the wake of a "racial reckoning."

But one of my students, an African American from Grand Rapids, listened to "Living for the City" and said, after I asked for thoughts about it: "Professor, that sounds so modern." I asked him what he'd meant by that, and he immediately answered: "It sounds like now."

22 October 2020

Today, I can see the faces of ten of my eighteen students.

That night after class, I went downstairs to the kitchen to look for a snack. My father sat at the table, one eye on the newspaper the other on the western playing on the TV mounted over the counter. He's eighty-two years old, and as I looked at him I said a silent thank you that I was able to spend this COVID year with him and my mom. Instead of moving to Ann Arbor, I am a middle-aged man sleeping in the room where I was a child and then a teenager before I headed to the Ivy League at seventeen and discovered politics and sex and theory.

I look at my father from across the kitchen, and I remember election night in November 2016, which I chose to spend with them because they are the first historians I knew, and sharing historical events with historians gives the experience of history an extra heft. But the history we'd hoped for didn't happen, we did not get our first woman president; history changed in a more malignant, unexpected way. But it was not unexpected for my father, or particularly new or special. "Of course all those white folks voted for him," my father said to me, reading the dejected look on my face. "I'm really not surprised that he won." And it was that night that I flashed back even further, to the George Zimmerman trial for the murder of seventeen-year-old Trayvon Martin in Sanford, Florida, when I was home that summer of 2013, feeling exhausted and frustrated and angry by the verdict but nonetheless safe (what a word for an adult to use). This was altogether different from the loss felt by people like my parents, Black people raised in the South in the 1940s and 1950s, who'd seen it all and had escaped north, living to tell the tale, as they had in fact done for me, educating my younger sister and me about the legacy of Emmett Till and the little girls killed in the bombing of Birmingham's 16th Street Baptist Church in 1963. I'd always understood my parents, and many of their friends who'd also migrated north in the 1950s and 1960s, as haunted souls fearful of sharing their ghosts with us, the next generation. But life had shown me that for Black folks, the ghosts, terror, and pain linger and often return in modern dress.

And it occurred to me that to my students, I am what my parents have been to me in many ways.

Earlier that day, the in-class discussion about the 1991 film *Boyz n the Hood* had evolved from a discussion of Cornel West's

chapter "Nihilism in Black America" into a discussion about how
the film updates and remixes the 1975 film *Cornbread, Earl and Me*,
which like *Boyz* depicts the violent death of an upstanding athletic
Black kid with dreams of launching himself and his family out of
the ghetto. It strikes the students that Cornbread was wearing a
sweatshirt and carrying an orange soda when the cops, mistak-
ing him for another young Black man who'd committed a violent
crime, shot him. It strikes them that Cornbread's situation—in
1975—mirrors in so many ways Trayvon Martin's murder in 2012,
and one of my students, fully making the connection between the
sartorial choices of Trayvon and Cornbread, fully understanding
the electricity of how such choices get racially politicized, says,
"It's like right now, Professor." And another says, "Nothing's fucking changed." And we're all silent for an entire half minute after
that before another student mentions George Floyd and of the ten
faces I can see, I can tell that they've all been affected. They all
have experienced the gasp.

But it's later, two classes later, discussing the 2015 film *Straight
Outta Compton* and Kiese Laymon's essay "Hip Hop Stole My
Southern Black Boy," that a student asks me about my own relationship to NWA, to gangsta rap, to hip hop. And I realize that
I teach hip hop to these eighteen-year-olds as history, a history
I'm a part of, a history, for better or worse, that I helped shape
and bring to the forefront of American culture as a member of
the 1990s media that helped hip hop become the official sonic
language for a slice of urban Americans through the musical and
aesthetic and social posturing of "inner city maestros" and what
I'd called in an essay their "breakbeat concertos."[2] My students
haven't just utilized me as a guide, as an authority figure in the
metaphorical room, as the cultural historian I was trained to be.
Because I'm teaching them texts created in the 1970s and 1990s,
I am a living embodiment of the culture they dance to and drive
to and are now studying. And that embodiment means that, like
my parents, I have seen and lived to tell tales about things they've

only read about. So the questions dig a bit deeper than I expect: Have I lost friends or family to drug or state violence? Do I feel as traumatized, more traumatized even, by the state violence of the summer because I've seen it happen so many times before?

I try to answer their questions as honestly and as directly as I can. But I often did it through music, using hip hop songs like "Fight the Power" by Public Enemy and "Fuck the Police" by NWA, trying to articulate to them through music the experiences I avoided describing with my own words. It occurred to me that my own experiences of loss had rendered me unable to recount *for them* my experiences of loss, and in the moment of that realization, I blessed hip hop for being able to stand in for me in these moments; I cherished that a genre of music which originated as party songs had been able to mature itself into, as Chuck D has famously intoned, "Black America's news channel."

But afterward, after class, standing in my parents' kitchen looking at my father, I'm remembering when I'd gone off to college and discovered politics and the world and asked them similar questions, about Emmett Till, about Malcolm X, about Medgar Evers. And I remember that when I was my students' age, perhaps a bit older, I experienced the impact of illness and politics together, marching to free South Africa, and a few years later, as sparked by the electricity of politicized sexuality as I'd been by racial injustice, inspired to act-up, in the moment in the 1980s when AIDS and a right-wing US government became the point of ire for an angry, radicalized generation of us on the margins, wondering if any kind of center would hold our history and enforce the change we demanded and fought hard for.

11 November 2020

Today, I can see the faces of nine of my eighteen students.

In the spring semester following Good Kid/Mad City, I will teach Hal Ashby's 1970 film *The Landlord*, a film I considered teaching in Good Kid/Mad City but rejected as being potentially too sophisticated for freshmen, and during one of the final classes of the semester, I think about Ashby's film and the cinematically self-reflexive and narratively self-reflective moment when a teacher asks her suburban all-white elementary school classroom, "How do we live?" before Ashby cuts away to a montage of his lead character—one of the white children in the classroom—exposing the shallow, self-directed ways in which he does live in his adult life. By the end of the film, this character will have moved to a ghetto, impregnated a Black tenant of his building, dated a biracial woman, and realized how racist and insular his family and world has been. The film is both a deep dive into the coddled life of a limousine liberal waiting at the stoplight of life and an evocative, historical take on late sixties American race relations and the kind of "racial reckonings" that happen in the small, tight one-on-one interactions between Black and white when the masks of race are forcibly removed.

"How do we live?" was a question that lingered alongside my questions about teaching, about how it got done in 2020. It's a question that lingered with those other questions because it occurred to me that my teaching was as much about teaching my students how to live as it was about teaching them how to read, historicize, process, analyze. They would soon go home for Thanksgiving, and I knew that some of them would go home to places that may have shared their language but didn't share their politics—or shared their politics, only now their politics had been inflected by their time away, by their time out in the world, by, potentially, my class. And I knew this because of the faces I could see: the idea that neither the ghetto nor the suburb were natural or accidental spaces, that they both resulted from racialized, systemic choices made by powerful people, was a complete and utter surprise to many of them. Based on many of their faces, it was clear that most, if not all of them, had never considered that race itself is made, created for and through the experiences of their ancestors. Based on their faces, it had never occurred to them that hip hop might be a site of historical analysis, that the sample, the hot loop from an old record upon which so many hip hop records are built, is a kind of historical memory, a kind of historicizing, a history of race and sound sutured into the text of their present tense.

We live in history, and through it, and we hold it within us, even as we do sometimes, when we're not our most careful, lose the thread of it along the way. And there is loss embedded in history, always inflecting it. And I had to realize that there is loss embedded in the texts I teach and in the experiences we all bring to the room and the study of them. That loss is not always traumatic. That loss is not always painful. But there can be, should be, learning in loss, with the precision and passion of a Stevie Wonder record from 1973 played in a classroom in 2020, a year of loss for so many of us. That is the real reckoning I want my students to take away from my classroom.

In 2020, we didn't have a choice.

EIGHTEEN

THE PERMEABILITY
OF CELLS

Vulnerability and Trauma in the
Age of Mass Incarceration

Heather Ann Thompson

The fear that hovered over the United States by the end of March 2020 is hard to capture on the page. Some coped with COVID-19 by outright denial. Others processed it by obsessively watching the news. Still others kept themselves calm by maniacally washing everything from doorknobs to groceries to letters and packages. None, however, could simply ignore what the eerie quiet of their formerly car-filled streets, customer-filled restaurants, and plane-filled skies were telling them: people were vulnerable, under serious threat like at no other time in collective memory, even in wartime. Why? Because despite the extraordinary progress humankind had made, people's vulnerability had come down to the permeability of their very own cells.

It was terrifying. But far more deadly for the nation was Americans' inability to accept that this virus did not care *whose* body those cells were in. And, thus, as 2020 wore on, this country's way of dealing with COVID became intensely individualistic, highly classed and racist, and catastrophic. In short, those with means and power were able to cope with this new contagion by spending the remainder of 2020 hunkering down, protecting their own, taking a needed break from the rat race of life. They worked out, rebonded with teenage kids, reconnected with spouses, and dragged out dusty games of Scrabble and aged bottles of rye. These were people with access to large houses (for easy social distancing), the best physicians and hospitals to care for them should they still get sick, enough money so their children would not fall behind during at-home online school, and the sort of jobs where they could still get paid to work from home.

Meanwhile, however, the virus was attacking the cells of everyone else in America with a vengeance—those without means and power, without spacious homes to ride out the worst of the pandemic, without investments or uninterrupted incomes, without health insurance, and without a trace of Pfizer or Moderna coursing through their veins. Some had damn good historical reasons to fear vaccines; some believed the president when he said that vaccines were poisonous. Others would not have the chance to get vaccinated because the rest of the nation decided they didn't deserve to be protected from COVID, or even death.

Remarkably few Americans were concerned that this group included nearly 1.8 million human beings living inside of this nation's thousands of prisons and jails.

These institutions housed very ordinary Americans—people's mothers, fathers, sisters, brothers, and children—some who had committed significant harm, but so many were there for nonviolent "crimes." Virtually everyone had endured a great suffering in life before ending up incarcerated. But this nation's reflexive passion for punishment ensured that these people would additionally suffer in almost unimaginable ways throughout the pandemic.

And yet, what few stopped to consider is this: ultimately, this nation could suffer the most excruciating trauma and pay the very highest price there is to pay—and lose the protracted war it has been fighting to vanquish the deadly coronavirus—if it continues to let its passion for punishment blind it to what this pandemic has revealed in the starkest, most glaring, painful, and beautiful terms. COVID has laid bare the fundamental truths that serving time does not diminish humanity. What we do to people behind bars, we do to ourselves. Thus, our nation's prison system is a clear and present danger to the entire country.

* * *

By the time this country was a year and a half into the pandemic, one in three people in its prisons had contracted COVID.[1] Worse, the death rates for incarcerated Americans were staggering: 199.6 deaths per 100,000 compared to an already unfathomable 80.9 per 100,000.[2]

The American jail and prison system was already a perilous place for health. This was true despite constitutional protections such as *Estelle v. Gamble* (which established the standard of what a prisoner must plead to claim a violation of their Eighth Amendment rights), the ostensible availability of correctional nurses and doctors, and the sad reality that for many incarcerated people the inside of a prison was the first time they ever received basic medical care. Nevertheless, they dreaded falling ill. Too many inside know people who have unnecessarily lost their lives, limbs, or organs because they needed medicine, treatment, or surgeries that they could not get while incarcerated. They know well that their most serious symptoms are too often dismissed, and they know their providers are too often undertrained and overburdened and have even been hired despite having lost their licenses to practice.

When it comes to protecting the incarcerated from communicable diseases, America's track record is grim. From its handling of hepatitis and tuberculosis to HIV/AIDS and the flu, corrections officials have repeatedly ignored the advice of health officials, the pleas of family members, and even their health-care staff. This neglect had often led to public relations and public health disasters, like in the late 1980s and early 1990s, when the tuberculosis epidemic inside of New York's prison system began spilling out into the public, deeply alarming everyone, incarcerated or free.[3]

But for the imprisoned, whether they were merely awaiting trials, could not afford bail, or were serving a sentence, cavalier officials and a wholly inadequate medical apparatus (sometimes one nurse and no medicines for thousands of people in a facility) was downright terrifying as word of COVID's death toll began to circulate. Everyone knew that there was no way to successfully social distance in these already severely overcrowded human warehouses. They were never going to get the PPE they needed to avoid getting sick. And there was no way in the world that if they got sick, they would have anyone with the skills needed to take care of them.

And so, those behind bars braced themselves for already inhumane conditions to get even worse.

Ultimately, overcrowding in America's penal facilities was the thing that unnerved incarcerated people the most because they knew that there was no way, short of letting thousands of people go home, that this problem could be solved. As one man in a rural prison in Oklahoma explained to a local newspaper, "There was no separation whatsoever. . . . There never was the whole time I was in there. . . . They'd stick you in the lunchroom with a couple hundred people at a time."[4] And so many of the people in jails, prisons, hospitals, and nursing homes could have been quickly sent home. Some governors recognized that reducing prison numbers was an essential strategy in the fight against COVID. The overwhelming majority did not. Although jail numbers did drop quite dramatically across the country, with some states eliminating cash bail to keep people out of overcrowded facilities, when it came to prisons, parole boards were granting fewer releases at the height of the pandemic than the year before.[5]

The barbaric practice of solitary confinement in America's prisons and jails had already been under fire prior to COVID, roundly condemned on moral, psychological, humanitarian, and ethical grounds. Unfortunately, solitary confinement became the first-line response of correctional authorities who quarantined anyone who seemed sick.[6]

As COVID raged through the Michigan prison system, the sheer number of those infected meant that people were being quarantined almost anywhere the facility found space, "in gyms, warehouses, [or] field houses." But the preferred and most dreaded quarantine was "in segregation." The horrors of solitary confinement, in turn, meant that "some [chose] to hide their symptoms and expose more people as a result."[7] By the end of September 2020, more than 80 percent of the men inside one rural prison had contracted the virus. Robert Lavern, who ended up in a sweltering solitary cell, locked down twenty-three hours a day, concluded that many "people would rather take a chance at dying than be sent in there."[8]

But as little choice as incarcerated adults had concerning their health care, the country's almost fifty thousand imprisoned children had even less. Juvenile detention centers had efar fewer resources, and children usually did not know their rights. Even in states where the practice of placing children in solitary confinement is banned, the COVID crisis has, in effect, brought back its use. As some of the kids in a New Orleans detention facility heartbreakingly explained to a lawyer, "they feel they have disappeared, and asked a school staff member to tell their parents they love them."[9]

Whether in solitary or not, being sick was frightening because there was no hope of receiving proper medical care. When Shelah Taurienen started to have intense chest pain in Michigan's only prison for women in late March of 2020, she was not given a COVID test because she didn't have a fever. Officers threw her in a segregation cell overnight, with no blankets or toilet paper. They moved her to a COVID ward the next day after finally testing her. It was a warehouse of incredibly sick people, with the heat so high the women could barely breathe. When they asked to have it turned down a bit, the corrections officers (COs) turned the system completely off. It then became so cold that the sick and feverish women could see their ragged breath in the air.

As Shelah, who managed to survive the virus, later reported, "There was just so little medical attention and medical care. We could have died from this, there have been inmates that have died from this. . . . We have messed up. But it just seems like it doesn't matter if we die because we're inmates."[10] It was a miracle that Shelah survived. As the American Friends Service Committee explained, "The entirety of the medical care she received was occasional Tylenol. The pain of the disease and the inhumanity of the treatment coalesced to feel like torture in that warehouse."[11]

As the pandemic raged through mid-2020, climate change fueled one of the hottest summers on record. Throughout America's thousands of jails and prisons, COs shut off ventilation and fan systems to avoid spreading COVID through the air. Even in a typical summer, many of Michigan's older prisons lack sufficient ventilation and cooling capabilities. The heat wave, combined with COVID fears, led to severe violations of prisoners' fundamental Eighth Amendment rights to be protected from cruel and unusual punishment. Turning off air conditioning systems in such extreme heat was tantamount to torture. According to Lamar Etter, the summer was hell, literally like living inside of an oven. "Everything in here is made of steel and concrete," he said, "and by nine in the morning everything is wet. Your clothes, paper you're trying to write on, even the walls are wet."[12]

Although it may have seemed like things could not get any worse for incarcerated people in 2020, they began suffering a new level of isolation during COVID that made imprisonment unbearable. As soon as the pandemic hit, jails and prisons cut off all prisoners' contact with the outside world, from regular access to mail to family visitations.

For the incarcerated, receiving letters, cards, and photographs is an essential lifeline. It is a way to endure harsh conditions and endless sentences. As the pandemic grew worse, those behind bars were soon getting their mail less frequently, and sometimes not at all.[13] There was fear the mail itself possibly carried the virus. But even after that fear had been scientifically discredited, many departments of correction did not resume regular mail service. Regardless of why this happened, the already too-isolated men, women, and children on the inside were now even more cut off from the outside world. Meanwhile, due to new COVID safety protocols imposed on them, weekly phone calls home had been suspended in many facilities, as had any ability to use the email system offered by private vendors.[14]

Not communicating with loved ones was burdening, but the most severe blow was the suspension of all family visitations. Like with the mail service, even when it was possible to resume visitations safely, its suspension long outlived any rationale. According to the Marshall Project, twelve states have continued to suspend all visitation, twenty-seven only allow the incarcerated to receive visits by their lawyers, and thirteen others allow family visits only on a minimal schedule. Louisiana began resuming visitations, but made it clear they would "prioritize family visits over in-person attorney visits—which were going to remain off limits."[15]

So much of the incarcerated's fear and isolation might have been mitigated had prisoner programming continued. But then that was taken away.

In Michigan, one of the most critical programming resources for adults and children alike has been weekly workshops offered by the Prison Creative Arts Program (at the University of Michigan). The relationships forged within these programs are profound, lifelong, and often end up being the very thing that helps someone find their way forward when they return home. All of these in-person workshops shut down and remain shut today.[16]

As programming in prisons and jails continued to be canceled across the country, this also meant an end to essential counseling services, substance abuse programs, anger management programs, parenting classes, and more. One twenty-year-old former participant explained sadly, "We're not doing GOGI [Getting Out by Going In]. We're not doing the step-up program. We're not doing my DBTs [Dialectical Behavioral Therapy]."[17]

Unlike other institutions, prisons and jails lacked the technological infrastructure to move to online learning, which meant that without a true eradication of the virus, the likelihood of many of these programs ever coming back looked grim. The impact of this lack of programming was not just psychologically devastating but also had other material consequences. "For many students," one study found, "this has resulted in the loss of a year or more of progress toward a certificate or degree. It might also have affected the ability of incarcerated students to earn good-time credits during this period, in states where time off is rewarded for college participation."[18]

As with the deleterious impacts of the carceral system more broadly, this collateral damage done by correction officials' response to the pandemic has been felt even more acutely by children. In New Orleans, not only did kids lose the ability to see their families, they also lost access to teachers. Their "classes have been temporarily replaced with packets the kids complete on their own," NBC News found. "Social workers and religious staff are not able to visit. Orleans Parish Juvenile Court has closed until April . . . delaying a chance for the children's lawyers to argue that they should be allowed to go home."[19]

* * *

That the American public was largely untroubled by any of this during the earliest days of the pandemic is not altogether surprising. Everyone on the outside was initially so fearful for their own lives, they couldn't think beyond that. Everything that goes on behind bars is hard to learn about; it takes a while for this kind of information to come to light. In time, though, the COVID death rate of people in America's jails was so staggering that it should have triggered public outrage. Many who perished in jails had never even been convicted of a crime. They were simply too poor to post cash bail.[20]

The fact that so few Americans have argued for health-care rights for the incarcerated is stunning. It speaks to the true extent to which the punitive ideologies of the carceral state have taken hold in this country, and the degree to which they have obscured the fact that it has left the social and economic fabric of countless communities in tatters. Yet the abysmal health-care system that exists for the incarcerated now poses a direct threat to the public health of all Americans, because America's jails and prison cells are as permeable as the cells of human beings.

Still, another public health issue of the carceral state was the flow of civilian staff in and out these facilities, the majority of whom lived in the nation's rural areas where prisons are, and in the urban center's densest communities of color where city jails are located. And, thus, while the incarcerated were unable to protect themselves with PPE, or to seek medical care if they should become ill, every single day they were being exposed to correction officers, cooks, janitors, and other state and city employees who were contracting COVID outside of work, and bringing it inside where it then spread like wildfire.

Notably, the CDC did not even bother to aggregate statistics regarding COVID deaths in prisons and jails.[21] But new studies suggest that nearly every decision made in these facilities caused both needless spreading of the virus and, thus, needless suffering and death. Gregory Hooks and Wendy Sawyer showed that "nationally, this impact reached a tragic scale: Mass incarceration added more than a half-million cases in just three months."[22]

As several news outlets have reported, "in a given week more than 200,000 people are booked into jails across the USA, and the same number leave each week."[23] As one justice advocate explained, "A recent paper reported that close to 16% of all COVID-19 cases in Chicago and in the state of Illinois early in the epidemic were associated with population cycling through the Cook County Jail."[24] By December of 2020, seven hundred people in the El Paso, Texas, jail had COVID-19, with several shifts of employees returning home to their families, spreading countless cases throughout the entire community.[25]

As the Prison Policy Initiative put it, "Mass incarceration and the failure to reduce prison and jail populations quickly led directly to an increase in COVID-19 cases, not just inside correctional facilities, but in the communities and counties that surround them."[26] Even employees of the penal system lacked sufficient PPE (if they had any at all).[27] As one of the leaders of the SEIU union who represents prison technicians noted bluntly, COVID-19 "works its way through the system until it has no more individuals to infect."[28]

By the spring of 2021, when the vaccine was approved, it would make logical sense for the incarcerated to be among the first groups to receive shots. As bioethics professor Arthur Caplan put it, "If they're at risk and they're older or sicker, they should just get vaccinated. If they're in conditions that don't allow them to isolate, they should get vaccinated. I see no reason to distinguish."[29] Countless justice advocacy and prisoner rights organizations pushed to vaccinate prisoners, too. According to a board member of the American Medical Association (AMA), "Being incarcerated or detained should not be synonymous with being left totally vulnerable to COVID-19." Still, the organization was loath to insist that correctional facilities should be the first or even a main priority of states considering vaccine allotment.[30]

Initially, vaccine scarcity meant making hard choices about who would be eligible. But the hostility with which so many Americans, and more importantly, elected officials, greeted the idea that prisoners be included did not bode well for the hundreds of thousands of people locked in penal facilities across this country. As the governor of Colorado said, "there's no way [the vaccine] is going to go to prisoners before it goes to the people who haven't committed any crime. That's obvious."[31] Alabama's governor took things a step farther, vowing to use COVID-relief funds to build more prisons.[32] Even the Democratic governor Andrew Cuomo was clear that prisoners were not going to be among the first people vaccinated.[33]

The departments of corrections in most states prioritized corrections staff over the incarcerated for the vaccine. By December 2020, only forty of forty-nine departments had made their intention to vaccinate the incarcerated clear.[34] States such as Oregon (where one in four prisoners had been infected) refused to vaccinate its prisoners at all and only began doing so when forced by a federal judge, who wrote in disgust: "Our constitutional rights are not suspended during a crisis. . . . On the contrary, during difficult times, we must remain the most vigilant to protect the constitutional rights of the powerless. Even when faced with limited resources, the state must fulfill its duty of protecting those in custody."[35]

To be sure, the only way those behind bars received any type of health-care during the pandemic is because they refused to remain silent, they filed lawsuits, and they even took over their own facilities.

Incarcerated people were getting sick at such a rapid pace that there were eruptions of fear and frustration. After two people tested positive for the virus at the Neuse Correctional Institution in Goldsboro, North Carolina, on April 2, 2020, something just snapped. As correction officials explained it, "prisoners from different dorms came outside and refused orders from staff and the warden to return to their cells." They were engaging in what "can be best characterized as an organized offender protest."[36] That same month protests broke out at the St. Louis County Jail because COVID rates were rampant, and by the summer prisoners in California were on a hunger strike, hoping to call the nation's attention to how serious the pandemic was inside San Quentin.[37] The next April more prisons and jails had joined in the protests, including the St. Louis Jail for a second time.[38]

The desperation to bring attention to the crisis inside of America's detention facilities during the pandemic was not confined to adults.[39] Children, too, felt helpless, hopeless, and, thus, they too erupted. So terrible were the conditions for confined kids in Louisiana during the pandemic that they staged a massive group rebellion, with some of them trying to escape.[40]

★ ★ ★

As more and more Americans get the vaccine and return to their regular, prepandemic routines, COVID-19 is hardly forgotten within America's prisons and jails. And major fears remain about the nation's inability to vanquish the virus fully thanks to the damage done by the antivaxxers—and more generally, by right-wing extremists. But this is only part of what stands between us and the ability finally to return to a world where we do not have to live in fear of new COVID mutations.

As long as this country treats incarcerated persons as less than human, the carceral state will be an existential threat to us all. This is true on many levels—does not simply undermine our moral, spiritual, and ethical well-being but is also a threat to our physical health on the most basic level. Given the vulnerability, trauma, loss, and death suffered by the incarcerated, if COVID-19 should have taught Americans nothing else, it is this devastating but fundamental and inescapable truth: the walls that separate those we deem criminal have never been anything other than porous; those who live behind bars are human beings just like we are; and, ultimately, what we do or do not do on their behalf, we are doing—or not doing—to ourselves.

NINETEEN

DREAMS OF MY GREAT-GRANDFATHER

Yohuru Williams

I sat uncomfortably poised in front of my laptop on the afternoon of June 4, 2020, a small lamp pointed directly at my face, partly obscuring the view of the monitor before me. I quickly adjusted my seat as I watched the well-dressed mix of predominately Black dignitaries and celebrities—including the Reverend Al Sharpton—file into the auditorium centered on my screen. They came to a memorial service for George Floyd, a Black man suffocated to death under the knee of the Minneapolis police officer Derek Chauvin on May 25, 2020.[1]

I had been asked by the Canadian Television Network (CTV) to watch and comment on the proceedings. It was something I had done many times from a studio but never from my home office, the same office where I spent countless hours working after Minnesota Governor Tim Waltz issued stay-at-home orders on March 27, 2020, in an effort to combat the spread of COVID-19. It was also the same space where I provided commentary on the long history of police brutality against African Americans in the United States after cell phone footage of Floyd's brutal murder became public. It was same place where I glimpsed (or more accurately, smelled) the first fumes of noxious smoke arising from the widespread arson and rioting that broke out after days of peaceful protests in response to Floyd's killing.

All these thoughts raced through my head as I adjusted my audio to chat with the producer, who asked me to raise my camera a bit. I absentmindedly went through the motions of repositioning my laptop, a common chore associated with the new reality of online pandemic life. Fumbling through my desk for something to give the camera a little lift, I pulled out a fraying manilla folder marked "family history" and jostled it under my computer and sat back to listen.

I jotted down a few notes as three of Floyd's family members and attorney Benjamin Crump spoke movingly of Floyd's life and the need for justice. Then I leaned in as the civil rights activist, media personality, and minister Al Sharpton was introduced. Impeccably dressed in a navy suit, accented by a pair of black gloves, Sharpton wasted no time in connecting George Floyd's murder to the general failures of the criminal justice system: he described Floyd's death as a "common American criminal justice malfunction."[2] I hurriedly scribbled down these words on the edge of my family history folder, hoping that I would be able to emphasize this point in my explanation of the long history of American police brutality against Black and Brown people, and the trauma left in its wake.

I assumed that Sharpton would continue along these lines and was caught off guard when he pivoted a few minutes later to a discussion of Black history. Using the metaphor of the knee as a symbol of racial terror, white power, and racial oppression, Sharpton's invocation of that history framed much more than the murder of yet another unarmed Black man; it framed the collective struggle of a people. "George Floyd's story," he thundered from the podium, "has been the story of Black folks." "Because ever since 401 years ago, the reason we could never be who we wanted and dreamed of being is you kept your knee on our neck. We were smarter than the underfunded schools you put us in, but you had your knee on our neck. We could run corporations, and not hustle in the street, but you had your knee on our neck."[3]

Although regarded as a polarizing figure in some circles, Sharpton's spellbinding oratory captivated the audience. "What happened to Floyd," he continued, "happens every day in this country, in education, in health services, and in every area of American life, it's time for us to stand up in George's name and say get your knee off our necks."[4]

Toward the end of this rhetorical flourish, I looked down to see my family history folder peeking out from underneath my laptop. For a moment I lost focus, connecting Sharpton's words and Floyd's murder with a traumatic piece of my own family history and the long history of "criminal justice malfunctions" that punctuate "the story of Black folks" in America.

* * *

Like many others at the very start of the pandemic, I had decided to resume a few projects I relegated to the back burner before the shelter-in-place order afforded us all more time to occupy ourselves with such pursuits. I began by finishing an article I had been working on about the 1861 lynching of a free Delaware field hand named Jacob Hamilton.

I was motivated to complete that work by a seventeen-year-old activist named Savannah Shepherd, who was working with Bryan Stevenson's Equal Justice Initiative. Shepherd had taken my research on another Delaware lynching, the public burning of George White in 1903, and compelled state officials to erect a historical marker documenting the incident. Soon after the marker went up in June of 2019, it was stolen. Residents rallied to help pay for a replacement a few months later, only to be unveiled during a political controversy President Donald Trump caused on Twitter, as he classified the impeachment proceedings against him as a "lynching." Trump's tweet provoked an immediate response from Illinois congressman and former Black Panther Party member

Bobby Rush: "Do you know how many people who look like me have been lynched, since the inception of this country, by people who look like you?"[5]

In 1956, Mitford Mathews, editor of *A Dictionary of Americanisms on Historical Principles*, broadly defined lynch law as "the practice or custom by which persons are punished for real or alleged crimes without due process of law."[6] While this definition eschewed the racial implications of the crime, it was useful in encompassing a wide range of killing, like the murder of George Floyd that involved summary punishment without due process. It was, in some sense, this element of Sharpton's observations that stuck with me: "Now is the time for dealing with accountability in policing." I could not help but think of what activists have been saying for decades—centuries!—about the criminal injustice system. The metric for determining whether an injustice has occurred, as Khalil Muhammad has argued, is not the guilt or innocence of the party so aggrieved but punishment without due process.[7]

This consistent denial of due process, of "simple justice," in a very real sense has been "the story of Black folks" when it comes to "common malfunctions" of the criminal justice system. It is a story that touches every Black person not only viscerally but often directly and traumatically through their own family histories. This story has informed the more familiar themes of migration and activism that make up the African American experience.

In recent years, psychiatrists and neuroscientists have debated the concept of epigenetics. In essence, the question is whether the impact of historical traumas, such as wars, pogroms, and other atrocities, as well as natural disasters suffered by a particular person or community, could be passed down through DNA and expressed in human behaviors. In this way, the past is never just past; the bleakest moments in history continue to reverberate in our contemporary moment.[8]

African American history studies many such traumatic events, including enslavement, migration, and the struggle for civil rights, all punctuated by the spectacular savagery of spectacle lynching, racial violence, and mass death. African American history courses pivot around such moments, from the horrors of the Middle Passage and the brutality of American chattel slavery to the Tulsa race riot of 1921 and the murder of Emmett Till. They are often critical touchstones that anchor accounts of the struggle for Black equality against the backdrop of violence and mass death. As with Indigenous peoples, these injuries have left deep scars that continue to impact us—individually and collectively.

Those wounds are reflected in the stories we share. When Barack Obama began to lead the polls in February of 2008, for instance, older African Americans truly feared for his safety.[9] Tempered by the assassinations of Martin Luther King Jr., Malcolm X, and Medgar Evers, and by the long trail of political violence against African Americans, their concerns not only triggered a dialogue but also exposed deeply felt anxieties with equally deep roots in history.

As a Black child of the 1970s, I knew these anxieties well. Although there were examples of Black leaders in my hometown of Bridgeport, Connecticut, as a young person it bothered me that martyrdom and murder seemed to be both the price and inevitable outcome of a certain type of charismatic Black leadership.

And yet somehow, I had never directly confronted this element of Black history within my own family history. I did so partly, I later surmised, out of a desire to shield myself from the wound.

My parents raised me with a profound sense of history. My father, who worked as a music and arts instructor at a local community arts center, infused African and African American history into his lessons. He, along with my mother (who worked for a time as an educator), filled our home with books, from Lerone Bennett Jr.'s *Before the Mayflower* and Alex Haley's *The Autobiography of Malcolm X* to Frantz Fanon's *The Wretched of the Earth* and the poetry of Audre Lorde. Like many African American families in the 1970s, we were also obsessed with Alex Haley's *Roots*.

As for my own family history, that remained largely a mystery. Unraveling it not only exposed the wound but connected it in a powerful way to Al Sharpton's oratory.

★ ★ ★

For a long time, my brother and I were the only male cousins in the family. My mother, the oldest of four children, had two sisters and one brother; and when we were growing up, all had daughters—seven in total. Along with my father and occasionally my uncle Richard, we were often the only male presence at family gatherings. As a young child, I found this absence of men on my mother's side perplexing. It was revealed in a little jingle we wrote as kids to document our history matrilineally: "Rose had Grandma. Grandma had Nana. Nana had my momma. And my momma had me."

When I was about ten years old, I asked my great-grandmother Ottie Corrine Echols Waller how my great-grandfather died. She told me that he was murdered. Those words always stuck with me. They resonated even more so when I uttered them for the first time while completing a genetic profile in advance of the birth of my first child, a son, in 1998. I swore that afternoon that I would uncover the circumstances of my great-grandfather's death. A few days later, I called my great-grandmother Ottie's daughter Rebecca, whom we called Nana, and inquired about him. She could not remember much. She was just nine or ten years old when he died, she told me. She recalled visiting him in the hospital and nursing him shortly before he succumbed to his injuries, but she couldn't recall much else. The event had been very traumatic for her. In fact, it changed the course of her life.

When my grandmother, Nana, passed away in 2019, I resolved to return to working on that history, but life got in the way. While revisiting the lynching research, I reactivated my dormant Ancestry.com account. Late one evening while tracking down some census data, I turned my attention back to my own family history.

I needed to uncover the truth behind what happened to my great-grandfather, connecting it to the larger African American experience.

I knew parts of that story. Like many of the Black women chronicled in the works of scholars Elizabeth Clark-Lewis and Tera Hunter, my great-grandmother left Virginia after my great-grandfather's death and found work as a domestic in the town of Chester, Pennsylvania, where she settled. She worked for two prominent college professors, a pioneering professor of economics at the University of Pennsylvania and his equally successful partner, a professor of child psychology at Bryn Mawr.

When I was applying to college, I recall my great-grandma offering to ask one of them to write a letter on my behalf. I declined. Even then, with my meager knowledge of African American history, but fresh off reading Ralph Ellison's *Invisible Man*, I couldn't stomach the thought. I couldn't reconcile this act of kindness with the pain I imagined she endured in working for them, although she never spoke critically of them. Her pain was inextricably etched in other aspects of her life, including the clean but modest home she maintained in a small public housing complex across from the Commodore Barry Bridge—and her dependency on state aid despite working diligently all her life.

Ironically, my great-grandmother never talked about racism directly. But she often shared stories that were chilling in their disregard for her personhood. Nana was more up-front about her experiences. She once worked for a family, for instance, that had a parakeet they trained to say, "N----- stealing!" For the first few days of her employment, Nana dreaded the bird that repeated those horrific words incessantly. It wasn't until her employer told her to pay no attention to the fowl that she was able to relax. I could not fathom how she was able to work under those conditions. I could not imagine how she endured.

The wound I felt for my great-grandmother ran much deeper. She worked for the professors most of her life. Her devotion to the family and attentiveness to their needs often left her own grand-children feeling neglected, as my mother once revealed. As she explained, "We thought she loved their children more than us." Her loyalty was rewarded not with a pension or health benefits but "kindness" when they "assisted" with her medical bills after she suffered a serious heart attack. A deeply religious woman, my great-grandmother was grateful. But I remember bristling with anger when I first heard this as a teenager.

The professors had also promised to take care of her when she retired. They provided her with a stipend of one hundred dollars a month. My mother explained how they told my great-grand-mother that the reason they were not giving her more was to keep her from squandering it. I suppose they presumed it was a lesson in financial stewardship for an eighty-plus-year-old woman. It was the only time my mother recalled her grandmother expressing hurt and disappointment. I imagine the professors supposed that my great-grandmother would be thankful for their benevolence. I couldn't imagine how a world-class economist could even begin to think that one hundred dollars a month would be sufficient to meet the needs of a woman her age. The racist plantation pater-nalism of it all deeply disturbed me.

But it also reawakened the desire to know what happened to my great-grandfather. What were the circumstances of his death that had left my great-grandmother and my family so economi-cally vulnerable?

★ ★ ★

William McKinley Echols, my great-grandfather, was born in Dan-ville, Virginia, in 1908, the oldest of four children, including three boys all named for US presidents: William McKinley, Woodrow Wilson, and Taft Dewey. What other paltry details I gathered about his life come filtered through questionable census data, my mother's childhood memories, decades-old conversations with my grand-mother and great-grandmother, and scant news accounts. From the last, I learned that he was no saint, and the work of recovering his story, like his life itself, would be both difficult and complicated.

My great-grandfather was just twenty-nine at the time of his death, still living and working in Danville, where he was employed in a tobacco factory. My great-grandmother rarely spoke of her dead husband. I don't recall any pictures of him. Nana remembered her father as a handsome man with a big personality and a somewhat cruel sense of humor. She further intimated that he might have been cheating on my great-grandmother at the time of his death; this may have even been the motive behind his murder. This, like so many other elements of his life, I proved unable to confirm.

Danville, which white residents proudly referred to as "the last capital of the Confederacy" down to the 1960s, was thoroughly segregated. My great-grandparents lived in a home in Danville's Black district, known as Brucetown, situated off West Main Street near Stewart Street.[10]

Work in the tobacco factories, which shut down every year from May to September, made life for African Americans especially difficult. Many turned to the informal economy and petty crime as a means of survival. Law enforcement, for its part, kept a tight rein on the Black community, fostering numerous complaints of police harassment and brutality. The portrait that emerges of the Danville police is a familiar one. The police blotter was full of African Americans charged with minor infractions, peppered by countless accusations of police misconduct. In 1941, the celebrated civil rights activist Ella Baker identified police brutality as one of the primary challenges to Black people in the region. Her assessment certainly squared with what I learned about my relatives.[11]

My grandmothers never spoke of my great-grandfather's run-ins with the police. News accounts from the last year of his life, however, paint the portrait of a family (especially his younger brother Woodrow Wilson) who were acutely under the gaze of local law enforcement.

In February 1937, Woodrow was charged, along with three other people, with felonious assault in connection to a cutting fray at a local dance that left several people injured.[12] Although the investigating officer, Lieutenant O. S. Mayberry, told the *Danville Bee* that "it would take a Philadelphia lawyer to unscramble the facts in this case," the four suspects were nevertheless charged. Their cases were dropped a week later after the injured wrote letters saying their wounds were not serious. Woodrow and the other men, however, were still required to pay court costs.[13]

Four months later, in June, Woodrow was arrested again for allegedly cursing out the same police officer, Lieutenant Mayberry, over the telephone. Curiously, Mayberry acknowledged that the call was part of some type of sting operation directed against my great-uncle that backfired. The police, nevertheless, succeeded in their purpose: "the original count against Echols" on a liquor case, "did not materialize . . . [and] he was arrested on the profanity count." The fine of $24.45, the equivalent of about $449.74 in 2021 dollars, was characteristic of the policing of Danville's Black community.[14]

African Americans could expect stiff penalties for relatively minor offenses and little justice for crimes committed against them regardless of the perpetrator. James R. Wilson, the Black man who shot my great-grandfather, received an eight-year sentence for his murder. He first told authorities that he shot my great-grandfather simply because he "nagged" him, but at trial he changed his story to one of self-defense: he allegedly saw him reaching for a weapon. Despite his testimony, the local newspaper reported that "It was in evidence that Echols was shot in the back[;] the bullet ranging through the stomach with fatal effect."[15] In exchange for Wilson changing his plea to guilty, the presiding judge imposed the minimum sentence.

After his brother's murder, Woodrow assumed responsibility for taking care of the entire family, including his brother's widow and daughter. Woodrow ran a small grocery right in the heart of Brucetown with his nineteen-year-old brother-in-law Charles

Fitzgerald. Woodrow was also reputed to be a bootlegger, and Charles his wheelman. In the two years prior to my great-grandfather's murder, the men had been involved in several incidents with the police, including a serious traffic accident after Charles led officers on a high-speed chase in a vehicle allegedly carrying illegal spirits.[16]

Life inside the family home was not much calmer. Woodrow and his wife Janie frequently quarreled. In October of 1937, Woodrow was hospitalized after Janie allegedly shot him in the leg during a domestic dispute. Although Janie faced arrest, Woodrow refused to press charges against his wife, and the case was eventually dropped.[17]

Whatever fragile peace that followed dissipated late on the afternoon of February 28, 1938, when Woodrow and his business partner—Janie's brother—Charles got into an argument. Woodrow accused Charles of embezzling funds from a joint bank account the pair maintained to run the grocery. While Charles later claimed to have used the money to purchase Christmas gifts the previous December, this was money that Woodrow needed to support his family, including his brother's widow and child. During the quarrel, both men were said to have drawn weapons, but Charles fired first—fatally wounding my great-uncle.[18]

Questioned by police in the same hospital where his brother died just eight months earlier, Woodrow made a dying declaration absolving his brother-in-law of guilt. With the earlier loss of his brother and his own impending death, his motivation may have been to spare the family the loss of yet another male family member and offer some financial protection for his wife and children, not to mention his brother's family. Less than two weeks later, based on the testimony of the officers who interviewed Woodrow, Magistrate Charles Carter dismissed the murder charge against Charles, and he was released.[19]

If Woodrow's act was meant to offer some security for the family, it proved to be in vain. Less than a month after the charges were dismissed, Charles was driving an automobile with his friend Joe Pass when they were spotted by police officers Joseph W. Wilson and J. D. Davis. The officers, who had also been a part of the high-speed chase with Charles in 1936, initially claimed that they attempted to stop the car because they knew Charles had outstanding traffic violations. Local Black residents claimed that the police had a habit of harassing African Americans with little to no provocation. The officers later changed their story, claiming "to have seen a liquor can in the car and gave pursuit."

During the ensuing chase, Officer Davis shot out the tires of the automobile just before it (allegedly) crossed the state line into North Carolina. Riding with one rim, the vehicle careened out of control and smashed into a tractor being operated by two white farmers, J. Y. Chandler and J. W. Dabbs. All four men were killed in the ensuing wreck. The local newspaper described the scene of carnage: "Both negroes were dying, and the white men were seen to be in a desperate condition . . . [and] ambulances took the white men in. A negro concern was sent for to bring in the negroes. One was already dead, and Pass died on the way to Providence Hospital."[20]

At least initially, the Virginia officers' account of the accident was not challenged. But as bitterness over the killing of the white farmers grew, local officials convened a special commission to investigate. The wanton brutality of the officer's actions led one commissioner to question the necessity of such chases, considering the petty nature of the offense. The commission even debated issuing a policy statement "putting an end to the practice of deflating tires of automobiles in flight with the accompanying danger and menace to innocent users of the highways."[21]

In the meantime, Wilson and Davis, who remained on active duty in Virginia while awaiting trial, appeared to face no real legal jeopardy. During the proceedings, the defense argued that the primary cause of the accident was not the shooting out of the tire as much as "the determination of the negroes to continue to drive their crippled car when they knew that with one flat tire it could not be properly controlled."[22]

In stark contrast to the officers' account, a Black witness named Charles Campbell testified that police fired as many as four or five shots at the vehicle. A white farmer named E. A. Rimmer, who was driving the vehicle in which Campbell was a passenger, confirmed his testimony. Stopping at the scene and seeing the condition of Fitzgerald and Pass, Rimmer testified that he told the officers, "We must do something. They are dying." Officer Davis, he recalled, merely laughed and replied, "Let 'em die."[23]

Despite this testimony and the clear evidence of negligence in shooting out the tire, after only four hours of deliberation the jury acquitted the officers of the charge of manslaughter. They found them guilty instead of the lesser charge of assault with a deadly weapon. Neither man served any jail time. Any fines possibly imposed were not disclosed in court documents. A subsequent civil suit filed by the father of Joe Pass was dismissed the following year. The officers went on to enjoy long careers with the Danville police.

In the grand tradition of Alex Haley's *Roots*, I sometimes wish my grandfather's and great-granduncle's stories belonged to a nobler legacy. The reality is that the basic human dignity they and my great-grandmother, and countless other African Americans were denied, is what the Civil Rights Movement and the Black Power Movement fought for.

★ ★ ★

These observations weighed heavily on me just a week before the verdict in the Derek Chauvin trail was expected. While all of Minneapolis—and all of America—waited on that verdict, on April 11, 2021, in Brooklyn Center, Minnesota, twenty-year-old Daunte Wright was fatally shot by police officer Kimberly Potter. His killing occurred during a routine traffic stop that turned into an attempted arrest for an outstanding arrest warrant. After a brief struggle with officers, Wright was shot at close range. Potter claimed to have mistaken her gun for her nonlethal Taser. After the homicide, critics questioned why the stop was even necessary on such a minor violation. While Potter was charged in the case, details of Wright's lengthy criminal past were also used by the media to mitigate her guilt.[24]

Predictably some Americans began discussing the victims of police murder as ill-chosen symbols: why mourn George Floyd and Daunte Wright? Why so much hand-wringing over "thugs" and "criminals?"

Floyd and Wright were both fathers with loving families. Each, in his own way, was eking out a means of survival in a nation where, despite the myth of abundance, opportunities for African Americans remain appallingly limited. And their stories, like my great-grandfather's and my great-granduncle's, and so many countless others, have been a significant part of the "story of Black folks" in America. Their deaths stand as examples of what Martin Luther King Jr. called the triple evils of poverty, racism, and militarism.[25]

It is not only the increasingly more visible stories of those killed by police that should occupy our attention—we should also listen to the testimony of their survivors. In the aftermath of her father's death, George Floyd's seven-year-old daughter Gianna proclaimed, "My Daddy changed the world."[26] For this to be true, we must go beyond the "accountability in policing" called for by Reverend Sharpton. It would mean dismantling a system of white supremacy and the violence that has upheld it.

Police killings obscure the more insidious, debilitating death that comes from deliberate policies, practices, and procedures that feed unemployment and underemployment, foster housing and food insecurity, and fuel the social determinants of health. These things leave hard working Americans at the end of life with no health care and no safety net. The testament to George Floyd's legacy won't be found solely in police reforms but in Gianna Floyd's future, and the future of her children and her children's children. For the most insidious wound of all may be the markers of racial injustice and violence left due to epigenetic harm, passed down from generation to generation, inscribed in the scores of nameless, faceless people, so many of them dismissed by society as drug dealers, rumrunners, and petty criminals. But they were ultimately survivors—of both the burdens of American history and centuries of racial injustice.

STRESS TEST AND SAVING THE SOUL OF AMERICA

Keri Leigh Merritt and Yohuru Williams

"These are revolutionary times. . . . We are now faced with the fact, my friends, that tomorrow is today. We are confronted with the fierce urgency of now. . . . If we will make the right choice, we will be able to transform the jangling discords of our world into a beautiful symphony of brotherhood. If we will but make the right choice, we will be able to speed up the day, all over America and all over the world, when justice will roll down like waters, and righteousness like a mighty stream."

—Martin Luther King Jr., "Beyond Vietnam—
A Time to Break Silence"

The long shadow of death in 2020 raises important questions about how Americans historically have dealt with the isolation, despair, and mourning that accompany periods of mass death. No facet of American life has been spared over the past few years. Given the profound changes to our society, Americans are now reinterpreting everything we thought we knew, including well-worn cultural practices, and we are deriving new meanings from politics, literature, music, film, art, and even our nation's own history.

The early 2020s are unquestionably those kinds of years: years that will change lives— define lives—forever. For most people, this precious timing only occurs once in a lifetime, if at all. Some never get to experience it. It is not just the chance to replace the establishment—our nation's decaying political, economic, and social structure. It is also the chance to rebuild a better world.

Perhaps more than anything, the 2020s turned the concept of American exceptionalism upside down. The deadly, highly contagious virus and no universal health care, coupled with the racial reckoning growing out of the murder of George Floyd, exposed significant problems within our nation.

Adding fuel to the fire, Trump emboldened and encouraged white supremacists; he reversed decades, even centuries, of international relationships and diplomacy; he turned the federal government into a mob organization of grift, greed, and fraud; and he flagrantly attempted to undermine the democratic process, contributing significantly to a loss of faith in government.

The deep issues exposed in 2020 had firm roots in the half century lead-up to Trump's election, in the slow backlash against the various civil rights movements of the 1960s. From Richard Nixon and the so-called silent majority to the war on drugs and the rise of the Tea Party, white rage has long been simmering in America, waiting for just the right temperature to boil.[1]

As the federal government attempted to dismantle every social safety net program (the "welfare state"), they simultaneously increased policing and mass incarceration.[2]

Keeanga-Yamahtta Taylor has written that by the early 1970s, Black unemployment was on the rise, leading "to a palpable desire in Black communities for more to be done—as the affluence of the sixties turned into recession and stagnation in the seventies, the politics of racial resentment gained new traction." In the thirty years following the late 1970s, spending on state and local police skyrocketed, increasing from $42 to $115 billion.[3]

With a powerful police state, Trump's penchant for white supremacy became tied to "law and order": in 1989, he paid for a full-page ad in the *New York Times* appealing to lawmakers to reinstate the death penalty for the Central Park Five, a group of young Black boys wrongfully convicted of sexually assaulting a jogger in New York's Central Park. "Bring Back the Death Penalty," Trump's odious ad read, "Bring Back Our Police."[4]

But the full extent of Trump's bigotry would be revealed only after the election of the nation's first Black president, Barack Obama, in 2008. Along with his wife Melania, Trump gained media attention arguing that Obama was not American—that he had been born in Kenya. As Carol Anderson has observed, one of the main triggers for "white rage" is "Black advancement." Obama's election provided a very effective rallying tool for Trump. Whenever Trump found himself in trouble, Anderson noted, "he would throw another kilo of white supremacy down on the table."[5] It was effective—like it always had been throughout American history.

But racism didn't just take the form of rhetoric and invective. It translated into law and policy. Soon after Obama's election, twenty states adopted new restrictions on voting, aimed at keeping people of color disenfranchised. Republican state officials across the nation began closing polling places in Black and Latino communities and purging voters from registration lists.[6] Finally, in 2013, in *Shelby County v. Holder*, the Supreme Court gutted the crown jewel of the Civil Rights Movement, the Voting Rights Act of 1965. There were no longer legal protections against denying citizens the right to vote based on race. Democracy was in peril.

THE 2020 ELECTION AND DISPUTE

Despite Russian interference and a concerted campaign of disinformation on behalf of Trump, the Democrat Joe Biden won the 2020 election. Amid the country's dystopian pain, grief, and strife, in many ways the story of 2020 is embodied in the story of Biden, our mourner in chief who lost a wife and two children to premature death. In this third attempt at becoming president, Biden won by the largest margin of popular votes for a president ever.[7] With 306 to 232 votes in the Electoral College, Biden became the oldest person to take office, and former senator Kamala Harris became the first woman, Black person, and person of South Asian descent to assume the vice presidency.

When Biden first announced his candidacy, he argued that America was at war, citing the deadly 2017 Unite the Right rally in Charlottesville, Virginia. "If it wasn't clear before," he explained, "it's clear now: We are living through a battle for the soul of this nation."[8]

Asked about Biden's comments, the US poet laureate Joy Harjo (of the Muscogee Nation) said, "When I think of the soul of the nation, I think of the process of becoming, and what it is we want to become." Even when everything seems "broken," she explained, "We are at a point of great wounding, where everyone is standing and looking within themselves and each other." The only question left for Americans to ponder as they were locked away in quarantine, in mourning, in the voting booths, or in the streets protesting was: "What do [you] want to become?"[9]

The election, however, would not deter Trump from trying to remain in power. Even before the election happened, Trump spent months riling his base with claims of widespread voter fraud. As early as April 2020, he declared that if his reelection campaign failed it was due to tampering by the Democrats, making the baseless allegations more than seventy times over the following half a year. On election night, the hashtag #StoptheSteal began trending on Twitter after several doctored videos "documenting" voter fraud went viral.[10]

When it was clear that he would not be victorious, Trump immediately demanded a recount of votes in Wisconsin and Michigan, challenging the integrity of the hundreds of thousands of ballots yet to be counted. He further sought to contest the outcome of the vote in Arizona. His maneuvering set the stage for legal challenges in other states, further eroding public confidence, in American democracy.[11]

Subverting justice in a way no president had done before, Trump personally called election officials, tampering with election results. On January 2, 2021, a desperate Trump instructed Georgia's secretary of state Brad Raffensperger (Republican) to "just find 11,780 votes" so he could win the state, which had gone Democratic for the first time since the Georgian Jimmy Carter ran.[12]

Trump also made two separate attempts to contact Arizona's election supervisor Clint Hickman (Republican), presumably to explore similar options for flipping that state in his favor.[13] Still, despite losing in more than sixty cases, including in the Supreme Court, Trump refused to back down, ramping up his rhetoric to remain in office by claiming the election had been "rigged" and "stolen."[14]

THREE WEDNESDAYS IN JANUARY: INSURRECTION, IMPEACHMENT, AND INAUGURATION

The culmination of Trump's violent, provocative speech reached a peak on January 6, when he held a rally in Washington, DC, to "stop the steal" just an hour before Congress began the process of confirming Biden's win in the Electoral College. Trump called on Vice President Pence not to surrender. "We will never give up, we will never concede," Trump crowed.[15]

The angry mob of white supremacists became irate throughout Trump's speech. As soon as the rally ended, the insurrectionists stormed the US Capitol over his claims of a rigged election. As the rioters scaled the Capitol's walls, planted pipe bombs, and dangled from its railings, the pictures and videos were both stunning and revolting.

The bright reds of the Confederate and Nazi flags and matching MAGA hats simmered against a sea of Trump flags, a noose, a raised wooden cross reminiscent of Ku Klux Klan lynchings, and a sweater reading "Camp Auschwitz." Just like their Confederate forebears, the coup members angrily rejected legitimate election results, vowing vengeance and committing murder.[16]

The terror unleashed on that day cannot be overstated. They killed five innocent people, and one of the victims was a police officer. Two other police officers would later commit suicide. Black officers testified they were called racial slurs while taunted by the crowd. Others were made national heroes that day. Officer Eugene Goodman likely saved scores of lives when he bravely diverted the mob by running away from the chambers where the nation's leadership was evacuating, as hundreds chased him through the halls of the Capitol.

Systematically, the Capitol police had been ineffective against the insurrection, whether purposefully or not. The *Washington Post* found that police negligence began days before January 6, "when law enforcement agencies across Washington failed to prepare for an assault on the Capitol—even as Trump supporters openly plotted one online. They were compounded by the slow response on the day of the siege." Worse, the *Post* concluded, the police "did not head off a mass of Trump supporters who descended on the Capitol, egged on by the president himself, and command within the complex broke down."[17]

As John Grant wrote, the world watched in disbelief "as Washington DC was transformed into a fenced-in armed camp with thousands of National Guard troops marching around and sleeping on the marble floor of the Capitol building."[18]

Given the nature of insurrection, comparisons to the Civil War abounded. As several historians argued, the Confederacy may have lost the war itself, but it won the long-term battle over memory and memorial. The investigation quickly revealed the depth of a new "Lost Cause" narrative that positioned the insurrectionists as freedom fighters who had answered the call of their leader. They had shown up patriotically to "stop the steal," and thus protect "their" country.[19]

The Lost Cause, also known as the Lost Cause of the Confederacy, was an ahistorical theory advocating the erroneous belief that all white Southerners valiantly fought for the Confederacy to save true "American" (read: white supremacist) values. It centers on the incorrect delusion that slavery was often benign and even welcomed by the enslaved.[20]

Trump's efforts to "stop the steal" brought together a broad range of groups united in their false claims about the outcome of the election, including the neofascist Proud Boys and the Three Percenters, QAnon, and the loosely organized Boogaloo Bois, known for their calls for a second Civil War. The White House chief of staff Mark Meadows and Republican representatives Paul Gosar (Arizona), Lauren Boebert (Colorado), Louie Gohmert (Texas), and Marjorie Taylor Greene (Georgia), among others, were also found to have been involved in preplanning the event.[21]

The investigation's initial findings left Americans to ponder just how close the nation came to another type of loss—the loss of our ideal of democracy. The lingering threat is real and reveals the deep and lasting connections between the Civil War and our present struggle for human and civil rights.

On the second Wednesday in January, the thirteenth, the House of Representatives voted 232 to 197 to impeach Trump a second time, making him the first president in history with that dubious distinction—this time for incitement of insurrection.[22] Even Republican Representative Liz Cheney was unapologetic about her impeachment vote. "The President of the United States," she proclaimed, "summoned this mob, assembled the mob, and lit the flame of this attack. Everything that followed was his doing."[23] The Senate ultimately would acquit Trump in February 2021—and it remains to be seen if there will ever be justice for his actions.[24]

Finally, during the third Wednesday in January—Inauguration Day—Joe Biden embraced the role of comforter in chief as he led a national mourning ceremony to honor the victims of COVID-19. With the specter of January 6 still fresh, four hundred lights, in honor of the over 400,000 dead Americans, surrounded the reflecting pool at the Lincoln Memorial, as Biden and Harris soberly addressed the nation.

The day, however, belonged to twenty-two-year-old poet Amanda Gorman, whose stirring poem, "The Hill We Climb," sought to inspire hope, a fitting charge to a nation grappling with both a global pandemic and the scourge of racism:

> This is the era of just redemption.
> We feared it in its inception.
> We did not feel prepared to be the heirs of such a terrifying hour, but within it, we found the power to author a new chapter.

To offer hope and laughter to ourselves.[25]

★ ★ ★

What does it do to the soul of a nation to withstand so much needless suffering? At times like this, it is best to remember Abraham Lincoln's warning that "if destruction be our lot, we must ourselves be its author and finisher." We have the ability, as well as the power, to help drag America firmly into the twenty-first century.[26]

The 2020s, thus far, has been a time of great uncertainty and great anxiety. But it is also an exhilarating time—a time of deep contemplation, of historical reckoning, and psychological healing. It is a time when many people are willing to think and feel beyond themselves—beyond the interests of the individual, and instead, focus on what's best for the collective, the community. It is a time that often only occurs once in a human being's life: a time where great, important changes are, for a brief moment, possible.

Today, America is at a crossroads. As wealth inequality deepens due to a prolonged pandemic, so too does political disenfranchisement—partly through voter suppression and partly as increasing numbers of people no longer see the point in participating in a political process that never serves their needs.

With growing inequities, with the excesses and absurdities of the insatiable carceral system, with unwieldy and extremely expensive foreign policy, and with a federal government either incapacitated or careening out of control, the time is now— undoubtedly and unequivocally—to become vocal dissidents. The time is now to reassess the nation's staggering wealth gap and the Thirteenth Amendment loophole, allowing slavery as punishment for a crime. The time is now to act upon centuries of injustice, upon centuries of inequity, and upon the continuing legacies of slavery.

Indeed, we must ask ourselves: Why do we let the worst parts of our history continue to dictate the future? We have a solemn and morally righteous task ahead: to help lead the charge against the sins of the present, as they are intimately bound to the past.

In one of Martin Luther King Jr.'s final speeches, "Remaining Awake for a Great Revolution," delivered just days before his death, he passionately called for an intensified and racially unified movement to advance the rights of poor and working-class Americans. In a country filled with such opulence, King wanted to continue the fight against poverty. "Ultimately, a great nation is a compassionate nation," he preached, yet "America has not met its obligations and its responsibilities to the poor."[27]

It's time once again—at this precipitous historic moment to usher in a Third Reconstruction. We all must act, no matter how small or seemingly insignificant. As King continued, "There is nothing new about poverty. What is new is that we now have the techniques and the resources to get rid of poverty." "The real question," he asked, "is whether we have the will."[28]

These points, made so eloquently half a century ago, are essential to understanding the tragedies afflicting America today. Indeed, rampant, systemic racism, the persistence of poverty, and a deep division between poor and working-class people of different races have made us one of the most unequal societies in the industrialized world.

To effect any kind of real change, to get politicians to support reparations and a Third Reconstruction, we need a massive inter-racial grassroots social movement—a movement of the people—the likes of which no one from even *our* generation has ever seen. But to create this movement, we need leaders. We need revolutionary change agents. We need doers. And we need knowledge keepers—the activists, the intellectuals, the academics, the teachers—to light the path and lead the way.

This kind of revolutionary change will be the only way we finally get money out of politics, establish *real* social safety nets, provide a decent education to all citizens, or abolish the carceral state. It is the only way to ensure that we are constantly striving for equity and justice, and that in one of the richest countries in the world, no child goes hungry.

It's time—in fact, it's past time—to turn our outrage, anger, and deep, disheartening sadness into action. We've now been on the defense—in resistance—for years. It's time to step back and · rethink strategy.

In that same speech, King clearly explained why Americans could no longer wait on the government to act. Time "can be used either constructively or destructively. And I am sorry to say . . . that I am absolutely convinced that the forces of ill will in our nation, the extreme rightists of our nation—the people on the wrong side—have used time much more effectively than the forces of goodwill," he concluded. "And it may well be that we will have to repent in this generation. Not merely for the vitriolic words and the violent actions of the bad people, but for the appalling silence and indifference of the good people who sit around and say, 'Wait on time.'"[29]

In closing, don't wait on time any longer. Time is not on our side here. Instead, spend that time turning your anger into power, your mourning into passion. Outrage, it turns out, can be generative.

Our call to action in these borrowed years—in this *after life*—is quite clear: the path forward is one of uplift and radical hope.

Stop being paralyzed by fear and anxiety; start being motivated by hope and passion.

Stop feeling all alone within the current crisis; start connecting and organizing.

Stop allowing other people and events to dictate a reaction; start being the action itself.

Stop resisting; start creating.

We have been given the incredible gift of life; we have survived one of the deadliest pandemics in history, and in so doing, we have realized the vast importance of every single moment we have on this earth.

We have been given an after life. Use that after life to create the present you desire, and the future of your American dreams.

A BRIEF HISTORY OF PUBLIC HEALTH IN AMERICA

Rhae Lynn Barnes and Keri Leigh Merritt

The health of the people should be the supreme law.

—*Cicero, De Legibus*

The ever-presence of death, loss, and grief has been a universal constant throughout human history. Americans born into the twenty-first century had been fortunate to largely evade the persistent specter of mass death or the perpetual fear of succumbing to an untreatable viral illness.

The health of a nation is dependent on the health of its citizens and inhabitants. Illness accounted for about 90 percent of deaths during the American Revolutionary era. After the Continental Army was devastated by smallpox, George Washington ordered the first mass military inoculation. He insisted all his troops be protected from the mottling virus, and smallpox particles (generally from pus) were placed directly into small incisions in the soldiers' skin. On January 6, 1777, Washington ordered the inoculation of all soldiers marching through Philadelphia, lamenting that America had "more to dread" from smallpox "than from the Sword of the Enemy."[1]

One hundred and seventy years after America declared its independence, the Centers for Disease Control (CDC) was founded. The CDC defines public health as "the science of protecting and improving the health of people and their communities." The CDC committed itself to "promoting healthy lifestyles, researching disease and injury prevention, and detecting, preventing and responding to infectious diseases" for the safety of people not only in the United States but throughout the world.[2]

Public health crises have shaped modern American life: they helped create contemporary architecture and domestic spaces, mandated proper ventilation and sanitation practices, and contributed to the modern welfare state. Even President Herbert Hoover, a staunch conservative, said in 1929 that "public health service should be as fully organized and as universally incorporated into our governmental system as is public education." As a believer in limiting federal intervention, Hoover still astutely recognized that an effective system of public health ultimately led to less governmental interference and lower costs over the long term: "The returns are a thousand fold in economic benefits," he proclaimed, "and infinitely more in reduction of suffering and promotion of human happiness."[3]

It may seem counterintuitive in the era of COVID-19, but public health systems developed and evolved over centuries; they were pivotal to the development of modern state formation itself.[4] And while Americans have not always agreed on cures or procedures, we have dealt with tragedies like COVID-19 before. Historians have petitioned politicians to learn from the past, but to little avail.[5]

Yet as you can see in the pages that follow, while American history details what *not* to do during public health crises, it also provides multiple models on handling disasters efficiently and effectively we can learn from. As technological innovations have made travel more accessible over time, germs—and thus, public health emergencies—have spread more rapidly worldwide. Globalized war, migration, trade, and slave-based capitalism transmitted illness and disease with continually increasing momentum, at times leading to genocides—aided by germs. These public health disasters all served to entrench and deepen inequality in the United States, a pattern we still see today as we remain the only wealthy nation with no system of universal health care. American exceptionalism can be deadly.

Contagious Contact: Native America and European Colonization

Indigenous Americans did not live in a paradise free of sickness or death before white colonial settlers arrived. Pre-Columbian urbanization led to the rapid spread of diseases in cities like Tenochtitlan, the capital of the Aztec Empire.[6] In 1528, a hurricane derailed seafaring Spanish explorer Álvar Núñez Cabeza de Vaca and three others in Florida. Crossing the Gulf to Texas, the men survived enslavement under Native tribes on their way to Mexico's Pacific coast. The explorers acted as mystical healers of common ills among tribes, applying alternative understandings of medicine and science that impressed their captors.

European colonization of North and South America was world shattering for Native Americans. It is estimated that 90 percent—about 54.5 out of 70 million Indigenous people— were killed in what came to be known as the Great Dying. Alfred Crosby called these ravaging diseases "virgin soil epidemics." Colonizers introduced smallpox, measles, malaria, yellow fever, influenza, and tuberculosis into Indigenous communities, populations with no previous contact with these diseases. Native Americans were immunologically defenseless. European diseases disproportionately killed Native Americans in the primes of their lives, between twenty and forty years old. These were the caretakers for both the elderly and the young; they were responsible for securing food, lodging, and defense.[7] The loss of the caretakers affected their larger societies as this wave of mass death set up intergenerational disasters that replayed with each exposure to new or mutated diseases. The only appropriate word to describe what happened is apocalyptic. There were 20,000 Massachusett people before the 1631 smallpox outbreak.[8] By 1633, only 750 remained; in two years, 95 percent of the village inhabitants had died.[9]

Recent studies argued that as epidemic waves hit, violent European colonialism, enslavement, and land theft upended Indigenous communities (even those with some immunities) by depleting their natural resources and forcing expulsions, leading to starvation. Malnutrition, in turn, made fighting diseases cumbersome and natural reproduction harder.[10] Joyce Chaplin has argued that the Great Dying gave European colonists a deceptive veneer of scientific and biological superiority.[11]

Empire building and warfare led to a circular problem: because of the scarcity of goods in times of devastation, epidemics led to warfare and warfare led to epidemics as empires expanded. Mourning wars—or sweeping raids on rival Indigenous nations—became a critical component of Iroquoian warfare, especially after they allied with European imperial forces between the 1670s and 1760s. "Plunder in the form of pelts and trade goods" helped replenish their plummeting population and expand political power. The Iroquoian story of disease, death, and warfare would repeat throughout Indigenous American history.[12]

Health and the Pursuit of Life and (White) Liberty: Colonial America and the Early Republic

On a November day in 1721, a small bomb was hurled through the window of a Boston Puritan minister named Cotton Mather. Attached to the explosive, which fortunately did not detonate, was the message: "Cotton Mather, you dog, dam you! I'll inoculate you with this; with a pox to you." The violent attack was not due to Mather's fervent religious convictions but his embrace of science:

he promoted smallpox inoculation after losing most of his family to the horrific virus.

The Boston smallpox epidemic of 1721, one of the deadliest epidemics of colonial America, would ultimately become the catalyst for the first wave of preventive inoculations in the Western hemisphere. Highly contentious public debate swirled around the issue, especially given the average colonists' medical knowledge at the time, but the success of these inoculations facilitated the creation of the vaccine in the early 1800s by Edward Jenner.[13]

By 1775, just one year before the Declaration of Independence, true horror was unleashed across North America. The historian Elizabeth Fenn argued that the smallpox epidemic that struck North America between 1775 and 1782 killed more people than the concurrent American Revolutionary War, reaching Indigenous populations on the Pacific coast.[14]

For the Enlightenment-era founders, health was central to a new future. They endured the revolution, but they also survived one of the most devastating epidemics in our country's history. Once vaccines were deemed safe, Thomas Jefferson would champion their national adoption.[15] The Vaccine Act of 1813, intended to combat smallpox, "encouraged," not mandated, vaccination, but it was still the first time the federal government endorsed any medical practice and the regulation of pharmaceuticals. It also appointed an agent to maintain and distribute the vaccine.[16]

Wealth protected elite white families from many things, but it could not wholly shield them from disease. Many notorious tragedies bedeviled the Kennedy political dynasty in the twentieth century, but colonial Americans made the Kennedy family seem lucky. Colonial Americans—both colonized and colonizer—knew tremendous loss. Before becoming president, Thomas Jefferson lost four of his six children to illness; some of Jefferson's grandchildren died in their infancy. In 1787, Jefferson wrote his wife, Martha, "Experience learns us to be always anxious about the health of those whom we love." Soon after his letter, Martha would be gone, too,

likely from childbirth complications. Commiserating with his bereaved daughter, Jefferson wrote, "I shall not say—nor attempt consolation when I know that time and silence are the only medicines"
for such devastating loss. Later in life, Jefferson would also lose one
of his remaining two adult daughters to infection following childbirth, infections that today's simple antibiotics would cure.[17]

The sequential loss of women in Jefferson's life must have
seemed never ending. He ended up with only one surviving child
of his six white, legally recognized children, and was constantly
anxious that the last "chord of parental affection" would break.
This was a knowing bond shared with other founders. John and
Abigail Adams lost four of their six children.[18] Martha Washington and Dolley Madison lost entire families in their first marriages.
Had the founders' children not been a generation wiped out by
disease, the concentration of American political power and wealth
might have looked chillingly different during the antebellum era.[19]

Regardless of race, colonial women, not just midwives, were
expected to learn medicinal practices and cultivate medicinal
herbs. Almanacs and family recipe books told how to make meals
and medicines, tonics, potions, and cures. Medicine and food were
interchangeable, especially as most early Americans continued to
understand health to be a delicate balance between humors like
blood and bile. Spices, herbs, and alcohol were of significant value
not just to season bland food but as curatives, and their commercial exchange helped spur expansion and slavery. Cures could also
include blistering, bleeding, or purging the infirm and were carried out in patients' homes.[20]

Part of why women needed to know medicine was the constant sickness and staggering loss of children. Some grieving parents lost offspring in childbirth, others in infancy. It was such a
common experience throughout early America that it left indelible
imprints on the larger culture. Women also had to care for each
other, also by creating abortifacients that would eliminate un-
wanted pregnancies. Martha Ballard, an exceptionally successful

midwife in Massachusetts and Maine, lost three of her six children in ten days during a hot summer, all while seven months pregnant. Her aunt Mary buried eight of her eleven children; their tiny head-stones lined in a neat row. As Laurel Thatcher Ulrich argued, Ballard's so-called natural sympathy as a midwife was not just a result' of her gendered ability to labor through childbirth herself—it was also a product of grief.[21]

Disease and Death During the Middle Passage, Slavery, and the Civil War

The self-emancipated abolitionist and public intellectual Frederick Douglass was a founding father for Black America. Despite being one of the most well-connected individuals in the Western hemisphere (Douglass was, for instance, the most photographed American of the nineteenth century), he was still unable to ward off the dogged claws of death. During his life he lost his ten-year-old daughter Annie, his first wife, and twelve of his grandchildren.[22]

Until 1820, five times more Africans crossed the Atlantic than Europeans. The Middle Passage was the greatest forced migration of modern history. It represented the part of the triangular trade between Europe, Africa, and the "New World" that transported Black men, women, and children to the Americas for enslavement, the bulwark of eighteenth-century capitalism and colonial expansion. The Portuguese, Dutch, Spanish, French, and British stole roughly twelve million Africans as enslaved captives from West Africa, often through corporations like England's Royal African Company.

Death was synonymous with the slave trade. Nearly two million Africans died en route to the African coast from the interior. Another two million died somewhere on the Middle Passage. Death was so common that sharks followed slave ships, waiting for corpses to be thrown overboard. Still another million enslaved Africans died in what was euphemistically called the "seasoning period," where they were acclimated to the new environment. Out of the twelve million enslaved people transported, only nine million survived. Each one of those people had families, friends, and dreams, all collapsed into a two-foot space in a ship's hull, surrounded by human excrement, filth, bacteria, and disease.[23] Racist white scientific beliefs that Africans and Native Americans could not feel pain in the same way as people of northern European descent was used to justify brutal torture on the ships. The primary issue on the slave ships was overcrowding: to maximize capital gains, enslavers also expedited the spread of illnesses.

Despite the incredible linguistic, geographic, and ethnic diversity of the people aboard slave ships, they all had one thing in common: they were exposed to an extraordinary rate of disease and death. Doctors would find passengers shackled to dead bodies. Captives were unable to perform mortuary rituals. The unrelenting death without grieving mired the Middle Passage and "produced a crisis of enormous proportions," Stephanie Smallwood has written, "as Africans labored under the cumulative weight of these deaths that remained unresolved."[24]

Slave traders starved captives, feeding them cheap, empty-calorie foods that (unlike the yams, maize, bananas, goat, chicken, fish, and pork they were accustomed to) did not "sustain life," as Smallwood has maintained, "but attempted only to systematically control its depletion." This starvation weakened their ability to fight captors and disease.[25]

Death was an inescapably powerful force during the colonial period. Vincent Brown has theorized that slavery created a type of "mortuary politics" in which people invoked or manipulated the dead to shape the actions of the living. For white enslavers, this might entail postmortem mutilation, humiliation, and the public display of Black corpses—all done to terrify, intimidate, and control the living.[26]

Geography, weather, and production practices created their own hazards for the enslaved. The only original colony with a Black majority, South Carolina, was known for unrelenting disease all along the coastal Lowcountry. Stagnant water and floodgating used in rice and indigo cultivation bred mosquitos, and thus, illness and death in the form of either "fever and ague" or the "seasonal fever," malaria. As early as 1717, locals realized a connection between water and disease: "the Wett Summer" led to "Sickly Fall."[27]

By the early nineteenth century, nearly one million African Americans were sold internally within the United States, generally from the Upper South to places in the Deep South and Southwest. Within this "internal slavetrade," New Orleans became a global hub for the cotton economy. At the auction block, African Americans were physically manhandled ("examined for disease") by potential enslavers. This process led to forms of sexual assault, as Black men, women, and even children were poked, prodded, and examined in front of crowds.[28]

The internal slave trade led to another morbid side business during the age of "King Cotton": slave insurance. Insurance companies took calculated risks to insure the lives and health of the enslaved. All settlements, of course, benefited the enslavers.[29] This coverage was only to protect the purchasers; the enslaved themselves rarely received medical attention, resulting in chronic disability from dental neglect, severed limbs, branding, blindness, deafness, and more. In the case of Harriet Tubman, a fractured skull left her with lifelong seizures along with the unrelenting traumas of life in slavery.

As Deborah Gray White has argued, slavery and resistance against it was gendered. Black enslaved women had to reproduce the labor force, making childbirth central to their lives. Men and women resisted enslavement differently. Unattached young men could run away, talk back, or break tools, while young Black women who were pregnant, nursing, birthing, or child-rearing feigned illness. These women used their health as a limited power source,[30] but pregnancy did not give them safety. Lizzie Williams remembered watching as a pregnant enslaved woman was pushed face down to the ground with her belly in a dirt hole while she was whipped.[31]

Enslaved women's power was rare and fleeting.[32] As Deirdre Cooper Owens has shown, "the father of modern gynecology," Dr. James Marion Sims, gained medical knowledge by operating—often without anesthetics—on enslaved women in Alabama. His experiments on Black women like Anarcha, Lucy, and Betsy were primitive, crude, and violent. While the enslaved women he tortured never received compensation (worse, their owners were paid for their "lease"), Sims gained accolades, serving as president of both the American Medical Association (1875) and the American Gynecological Society (1879).[33] As Harriet Washington so aptly concluded, "much of what we now think of as public health emerged from the slave system."[34]

Disability among the enslaved often meant being sold from their families and communities, abandoned in woods to fend for themselves, or even loaned or sold for medical experiments or so-called freak shows. In the urban North, entertainers like P. T. Barnum merged hucksterism, medical curiosities, disease, and slavery to create modern American entertainment. He showcased international sensations such as the first so-called Siamese twins, conjoined at the chest, Chang and Eng Bunker, and Joice Heth, a Black woman Barnum claimed was the 161-year-old wet nurse of George Washington. Heth was blind, emaciated, and toothless. After her death, he drummed up fanfare for a live autopsy. Over a thousand white Americans watched, rapt, as a formerly enslaved Black woman was dissected for spectacle.[35]

Anti-immigrant sentiments applied to Irish immigrants were conflated with uncleanliness, urban overcrowding, and disease. In print and on stage, the "Famine Irish" (arriving between 1845–1852) were portrayed in demeaning caricatures as overpopulating Catholics who birthed witless club-wielding brutes, red-haired, freckled wild apes riddled with alcoholism, poverty, and criminality. Their working-class status was depicted in tattered ragtag hand-me-down clothes crawling with flies, fleas, and filth in an era when uncleanliness meant disease.[36] Hidetaka Hirota has shown that these nativist reactions were instrumental to developing (what eventually became) a restrictive federal immigration regime by the end of the nineteenth century.[37]

* * *

The American Civil War was the most unprecedented medical crisis of white and Black mass death in our country prior to COVID. At the 1862 Battle of Williamsburg, one minister encountered "hundreds of dead strewn in every direction, trampled on, mangled, half-buried in mud," while the wounded lay "beckoning with the hand and pleading with piteous moans for help; hundreds of dead and dying horses lay scattered through the field" along with mangled carriages, guns, and cannons. As a result, the Civil War also became a moment of rapid medical and technological advancement out of necessity. Drew Gilpin Faust has averred that the Civil War's mass death led to the refrigeration of train cars to transport bodies, advancements in embalming (allowing Abraham Lincoln's body to be on view for days), and the creation of modern photography, as artists like Mathew Brady photographed and popularized the scenes of carnage.[38]

Entire industries cropped up surrounding the materiality of the dead that allowed the bereaved to immerse themselves in a sensory world of grief. Mourning ritual books gave step-by-step accounts of properly observing death in the home and society. Mourning fashion was retailed with elaborate etiquette rules, stereotypes to commemorate funerals were exchanged, memorial quilts were sewn of the dead's clothing, sheet music was played in home parlors, and locks of hair were fashioned into jewelry so the dead could adorn the living. Of course, the most macabre was the unholy black market of body snatching that funneled cadavers, mainly unknown soldiers who could not be returned to their families, to the related explosion of American medical universities.

Public Health in the Late Nineteenth Century: From Reconstruction to Wounded Knee

The Civil War affected soldiers' and veterans' public health, but as medical historian Jim Downs discovered, a smallpox epidemic among Black freedmen and women raged: "By late March 1863, hundreds had died in Alexandria, Virginia. The mortality rate had almost doubled in just one night and quadrupled in other parts of the country." Between 1865 and 1867, official records showed that 49,000 people died of smallpox. But the rapid, unchecked explosion of the virus occurred "not because of a lack of protocols or knowledge—a vaccine even existed—but because political leaders simply didn't care about the group that was getting sick," Downs concluded.[39]

Reconstruction was one of the bloodiest times in the nation's history. During slavery, white plantation owners had an economic incentive to keep the enslaved alive. Following emancipation, that incentive, however vile, was gone. Instead of torture and whippings, Black Americans could lose their lives for the slightest transgressions, typically for being too economically successful. As disease cycled through new communities of Black Americans, they also confronted another deadly threat: lynching. The Equal Justice Initiative has officially confirmed the lynching of at least 4,400 Black Americans between 1877 and 1950, but the real numbers of death are higher.[40]

The American Civil War also meant large swaths of the West now fell under US control. Indian Wars, especially in the Great Plains, led to more loss. By the Wounded Knee massacre in December 1890, the federal government had pushed most Indigenous people onto reservations in remote lands, with limited natural resources. This mass incarceration of America's tribes damned them to intergenerational poverty and inequality in health care while solidifying the erroneous cultural stereotype that historians call the "trope of the vanishing Indian," which allowed white Americans to perpetually marginalize Indians as a disappearing people who were lodged in primitive ways and outside the confines of modern America and technology.[41] By the early twentieth century, children were stolen from reservations and enrolled in boarding schools in an attempt to "civilize" Native Americans. These boarding schools tended to be genocidal and left thousands of young children dead. And one of their justifications was that Indigenous people were supposedly civically unfit and needed to learn hygiene. "Dirty," "Filthy," and "Lice" litter school intake forms.[42]

Perhaps the one epidemic that *did* rapidly disrupt capitalism and the supply chain in American life—from wheat to alcohol to cotton to coal—was not an epidemic transmitted between humans but the 1872 equine influenza that took down one of nineteenth-century America's greatest power sources: horses. Millions of horses died, coughing and dropping in urban streets, leaving rotting carcasses all over cobbled cities like Boston and pushing America into the throes of a recession. The mail slowed. Interstate travel crawled. The vast modern cityscape designed around horse-drawn carriages and trolleys forced passengers to become pedestrians.[43]

The Language of Disease during Asian and Latinx Immigration

Asian immigration to North America began in earnest in the mid-nineteenth century, peaking during the California gold rush of 1848–1855, when approximately 35,000 Chinese immigrants came to San Francisco, the "Gold Mountain," to secure jobs in agriculture and mining. The federal government forbade slavery in California during the Compromise of 1850, and Chinese immigrants filled the state's call for cheap, exploitable labor. These workers would ultimately help build our national infrastructure on the West Coast, creating transcontinental railroads that connected thousands of cities and towns into a matrix of commercial markets.[44]

Despite their invaluable contributions, Chinese Americans were not assimilated as US citizens. In 1882, in response to a white supremacist backlash against Chinese laborers, the United States passed the Chinese Exclusion Act, banning the immigration of anyone from China for ten years. White workers perceived Chinese men as labor competition, but nearly all stated reasons for exclusion were couched in the language of disease, whether literally or figuratively. The Chinese Exclusion Act was the only American Act to exclude immigrants based on national origin. Renewed and made a permanent law in 1902, it remained in place for forty-one years until the Magnuson Act in 1943.[45]

"Irrational fear, hatred, and hostility toward immigrants has been a defining feature of our nation from the colonial era to the Trump era," the historian Erika Lee wrote. The story of nonwhite immigration to America—primarily from Asia and Latin America—perfectly illustrates her point. Ever since Asian immigration to America began, white Americans demonized Asians as "medical menaces," even blaming them for the 1876 smallpox epidemic in San Francisco. As Nayan Shah has written, "Public health authorities depicted Chinese immigrants as filthy and diseased, as the carriers of such incurable afflictions as smallpox, syphilis, and bubonic plague."[46]

About a generation later, another epidemic in San Francisco, the bubonic plague, rekindled old tropes. Asian Americans and immigrants alike were targeted by white supremacists, spurred on by an incendiary, racist press. Approximately 35,000 residents of Chinatown were quarantined in a roped-off, police-patrolled lockdown. Meanwhile, white residents were encouraged to leave by the San Francisco Board of Health.[47]

Off the coast of San Francisco sits Angel Island Immigration Station, often called the Ellis Island of the West. Between 1910 and 1940, at least 300,000 Asian immigrants (including 100,000 Chinese and 85,000 Japanese) were "processed" and quarantined there. They were subjected to extended interrogations, sometimes lasting months, and medical inspections for communicable and parasitic diseases. The walls of the two-story wooden barrack contain hundreds of poems the incarcerated etched, documenting their experiences. One detainee, Mr. Quan, wrote about the unsanitary conditions: "A hundred symptoms of sickness developed; it is difficult to put our misery into words."[48]

Santa Ana, California, torched its Chinatown in May 1906 after one man, Wong Woh Ye, was alleged to have leprosy. A thousand white citizens screamed cheers as Chinese American homes were set ablaze.[49] These barbaric stereotypes, classifying Asian Americans as "unclean" perpetual "foreigners," justifying unrelenting violence, persisted into the 2020s. Yet Asian Americans are not alone in being discriminated against; immigrants from Latin America also share their pain, all victims of white supremacy that deems them "illegal" invaders—despite many of them being Indigenous Americans.[50]

The historian Mae Ngai found that the "legal regime of restriction that commenced in the 1920s—its statutory architecture, judicial genealogies, administrative enforcement, differential treatment of Filipinos, Mexicans, Japanese, and Chinese" eventually led to the term "illegal alien." This nomenclature represented "a new legal and political subject whose inclusion in the nation was a social reality but a legal impossibility—a subject without rights and excluded from citizenship."[51]

Natalia Molina came to similar conclusions, writing that the tests, physical examinations, and humiliations that took place among Asian and Latinx immigrants were all part of a process determining whether they were "fit to be citizens." Using resilient concerns over illness and disease to "demean, diminish, discipline, and ultimately define racial groups," public health ultimately led to the racialization of these immigrants, particularly Mexican Americans. "Scientific discourses and public health practices played a key role in assigning negative racial characteristics to the group," Molina concluded.[52]

For Mexican immigrants, being "illegal" brought myriad other problems, even when they were in America as migrant workers. According to Ngai, the Depression-era policy of expelling Mexican nationals was overturned in 1942 when the state-sponsored, contracted-labor *bracero* program (translating to "helping arms") brought four million temporary workers from Mexico to the United States. Simultaneously, the Immigration and Naturalization Service (INS), created during the Great Depression in 1933, worked with the Mexican government to create "Operation Wetback," an attempt to control the flow of these temporary migrant laborers.

After World War II, returning white soldiers began complaining about competing with Mexican laborers for jobs, much as they had done several generations earlier with Chinese immigrants. Operation Wetback established immigration quotas and limits on time spent in the United States, sending countless laborers (many of whom were in the US legally) back to Mexico. As the program revealed, nonwhite immigrants have always been associated with illness, accused of carrying diseases, and being inherently "dirty," especially during labor crises. However, learning the long history of these epithets shows that epidemics were not white America's primary concern. Instead, they were much more worried about maintaining white supremacy and solidifying the status quo of wealth and power.[53]

As Roxanne Dunbar-Ortiz has argued, white Americans have never truly comprised a "nation of immigrants," and that the United States was never a "land of opportunity." The ruling class actually created these "ideas" in the 1960s as a way to mute demands for "decolonialization, justice, reparations, and social equality." The reality is a long history of genocide, slavery, and settler colonialism, and we are still dealing with the inequities from that history today. Dunbar-Ortiz concludes that "this feel good—but inaccurate—story promotes a benign narrative of progress, obscuring that the country was founded in violence as a settler state, and imperialist since its inception."[54]

Health-Care Advocacy in the Progressive Era

The iconic and pioneering photographs of overcrowded grimy tenements shot by photojournalist Jacob Riis during the late nineteenth century led to a profound change in American living and health-care advocacy in what became known as the Progressive Era. His images immortalized in his book *How the Other Half Lives* (1890) illuminated the darkest corners of New York City's suffering. Shoeless children slept on street grates for warmth; immigrants lived underneath dumps and piers and in airless basements; and rag-picking women tended to babies in dodgy alleys, worked in sweatshops, and slept on the floor in squalid, overcrowded tenements.[55] Some of the results were immediate, like the New York State Tenement House Act of 1901 that radically rethought health, disease, overcrowding in multifamily housing, and urban space in America's largest city. It required apartments to have outward-facing windows (light and fresh air ventilation), water, indoor plumbing, and fire escapes.[56]

The publication of Riis's photography in many ways signaled the beginning of the Progressive Era (late 1890s to 1920s) that sought to use advocacy, urban committees, charities, and federal policies to rid America of "pestilence." It made remarkable headway in controlling and containing the diseases that ravaged nineteenth-century America.[57] Women used their sphere of influence as mothers of society to clean house. Much of their systematic organizing to fight disease, crime, and reform helped in their mass organization for the right to vote that came on the heels of World War I and the 1918 influenza pandemic. During both crises, women stepped up to serve America through organizations like the Red Cross.

In World War I, the death toll of trench warfare was eclipsed by another calamity that terrorized soldiers and civilians alike. The influenza pandemic of 1918, commonly (and erroneously) referred to as the "Spanish flu," infected between 20 and 30 percent of the world's population. Much like the diseases that ravaged Native

Americans post-Columbian contact, this pandemic similarly struck and killed Americans in the primes of their lives. In places like Philadelphia, 1918 seemed to have turned back the hands of time centuries as wagons went up and down the streets calling for the shuttered to bring out their dead.[58]

Luckily, by this time, many major cities had established health boards to help with sanitation and the collection of records about the sick and diseased. According to John Fabian Witt, New York's board, established in 1866, had the authority to "disinfect infected properties, and even go door to door to wipe out unsanitary practices. Diseases like cholera were essentially eradicated."[59] Following public outrage over Upton Sinclair's *The Jungle* (1906), in which the unsanitary conditions of Chicago stockyards are described, the federal government became more active in promoting public health as well. In 1906, it passed the Pure Food and Drugs Act, creating the modern Food and Drug Administration (FDA).[60] Federal regulation of public health was not always in the people's best interests, of course. It had long been an excuse for the federal government to regulate sexuality, particularly for women and nonheterosexuals. As Margot Canaday found, in 1909, the US Bureau of Immigration began screening people for a new threat: "undesirable immigrants" who engaged in same-sex relations. They labeled them "perverts," "pederasts," and "sodomites," connecting homosexuality with psychological and physiological deviancy that could be read in the physical body.[61]

Local governments similarly policed women sex workers in the post–Civil War era. When poor and working-class women in New York City resorted to crime and prostitution, Christine Stansell has written, "genteel bourgeois women" became the era's social reformers, creating settlement houses and programs to alleviate grave poverty among women.[62]

In Chicago, Jane Addams's Hull House became a "shining example of how intervention in the poorest slums could have remarkable results for the families concerned." By 1922, there were over five hundred settlement houses—many of them imitations of the Hull House stressing white American values—across the United States.[63]

Public Health from World War II to the AIDS Epidemic

Of course, the obstacles that poor and working-class white women faced were not comparable to the horrors that women of color—particularly Black women—continued to deal with throughout the twentieth century. Medical history for Black women is not just a story of racism but also misogyny. Fannie Lou Hamer, who gave brave testimony about her terrifying experiences with police brutality, voter intimidation, and her life as a civil rights activist, boldly declared with undying urgency on live television, "I am sick and tired of being sick and tired!" For Hamer, and the women she descended from (like her mother who had twenty children), bodily autonomy was central to freedom. "A Black woman's body was never hers alone," she said. Like Hamer, untold numbers of Black, Brown, and poor white women endured "Mississippi appendectomies," or forced sterilization, a widespread practice throughout the Deep South and in Puerto Rico.[64]

Born in Roanoke, Virginia, in 1920, Henrietta Lacks was a poor Black woman who worked as a farm laborer. In her early thirties, she found a lump on her cervix while taking a bath and had a biopsy at Johns Hopkins Hospital in 1951. Although she died from cancer just a few months after the biopsy, Lacks's cells became the first "immortal" human cells grown in culture, having today "been bought and sold by the billions." Taken without her knowledge, Henrietta Lacks's cells became "one of the most important tools in medicine," according to her biographer Rebecca Skloot. Her cells were essential in developing the polio vaccine; they helped in cloning, gene mapping, and even in vitro fertilization, leading to advances in cancer and viral research.[65] Her family was never compensated.

When we consider the skepticism of some older African Americans to the new COVID-19 vaccines, we must remember the context. Black men suffered from racist medical studies, sometimes at the federal government's hands. An egregious case of racist medical practices in modern America was the USPHS Syphilis Study at Tuskegee, conducted by the US Public Health Service from 1932 to 1972. Initially involving six hundred Black men (399 with syphilis, 201 without), participants were not notified that they had the venereal disease. Told they were being treated for "bad blood," the patients received free meals, medical exams, and, unironically, burial insurance. Even when penicillin became the "treatment of choice" for syphilis in the early 1940s, the men in the Tuskegee Study were not given the medicine needed to save their lives. All of this was conducted under the watch of the US surgeon general. The argument made by many of the nation's white supremacist doctors that African Americans deserved this type of treatment "because of their prodigal behavior and lack of hygiene" was embodied in this inhumane treatment of the Tuskegee men.[66]

Medicine and public health in Jim Crow America were segregated and inherently unequal. Dr. Martin Luther King Jr. called segregation a "social leprosy," recasting the legal construct into medical terms of biblical proportions. The horrific way Black men were treated under the Tuskegee Study stands in stark contrast with the similarly timed fight against polio. Polio (infantile paralysis) had broken out in the northeastern United States in 1916, infecting over 27,000 people, causing over 2,500 deaths in New York City alone. At the time of the outbreak, it was incorrectly believed that Black children were less prone to polio, when in fact, their lower numbers were the result of urban and rural segregation.[67]

The mid-twentieth century saw multiple instances of mass vaccination under government leadership. In 1947 a man traveled via bus from Mexico to New York City. He fell ill and rapidly died. It was quickly discovered that he had smallpox and it was spreading.

Israel Weinstein, who served as the New York City Health Commissioner, declared 7.8 million New Yorkers needed to receive a smallpox booster if they had not had one since childhood. They mobilized private doctors, the fire department, police, health departments, hospitals, and mobile clinics to administer the vaccine along with private laboratories and later the army and navy. Their slogan was "Be sure, be safe, get vaccinated!" and it worked. Six hundred thousand New Yorkers rolled up their sleeves in the first week alone for a shot. Ultimately, millions would receive the vaccination.[68]

Polio had a wealthy, well-connected white "savior" in President Franklin Delano Roosevelt, who was personally afflicted with the disease in 1921 when thirty-nine years old. His health problems very likely influenced his attempts at passing universal health care, social security, and support for those with disabilities. Roosevelt devoted the rest of his life to raising as much money as possible for the cause. More pointedly, though, Roosevelt founded and worked closely with the National Foundation for Infantile Paralysis in Warm Springs, Georgia, a segregated national center for polio research, education, treatments, and fundraising. The March of Dimes (its fundraising wing) raised millions of dollars throughout the 1940s. FDR came to be known as a "driving force" behind the March of Dimes, which brought together celebrities, print media, television, and local goodwill campaigns to help fund the creation of the polio vaccine by Jonas Salk. Because there was an initial fear that the polio vaccine would be dangerous, celebrities like Elvis Presley allowed their vaccinations to be photographed. On the tenth anniversary of Roosevelt's death in April 1955, the March of Dimes declared the vaccine "safe, effective, and potent," and there has not been a case of polio of United States origin since 1979.[69]

As successful as America's fight against polio had been, the rise of HIV/AIDS in the early 1980s showed the other end of the spectrum: the government's disregard of a dire health crisis due to racism, homophobia, and the moralization of sexuality and drug use. "Government inaction or delay—due to racial discrimination, homophobia, stigma, and apathy—have shaped the course of many epidemics in our country," Jim Downs wrote.[70]

The legacies of Presidents Ronald Reagan and George H. W. Bush are marred by their inaction during the AIDS crisis. When the activist Mark Fisher died in 1992 from the disease, friends carried out his last wishes by taking his body to the New York City reelection headquarters for George Bush. The group carried a banner honoring Fisher, plainly stating that he "died of aids / [was] murdered by George Bush." Fisher had hoped this provocative move would shock people into paying attention. "We Americans are terrified of death," he wrote. "Death takes place behind closed doors and is removed from reality, from the living. I want to show the reality of my death, to display my body in public; I want the public to bear witness."[71]

When Americans could not visualize the staggering scale of the loss, the NAMES Project created the AIDS Memorial Quilt in 1987. The quilt became a physical space to memorialize lost lives and the grief of families who had struggled to find adequate memorial spaces or burial sites for their loved ones. Every square represented a lost life. One of the more famous panels, created by twenty-two-year-old Duane Kearns Puryear, says, "I made this panel myself. If you are reading it, I am dead."[72]

Thirty years after Mark Fisher's death, AIDS is still an ongoing pandemic, but Americans largely ignore it because of who and what it impacts. The virus has not shut down the economy, nor has it ravaged the rich and powerful. It disproportionately affects poor Black, Brown, and Native Americans, and many gay or bisexual men. People living with HIV are increasingly concentrated in the American South, leaving the federal government with little economic incentive to try and solve the problem. As of 2019, more than 1.2 million Americans were living with HIV, with an average of 35,000 new cases every year. Experts estimate that

700,000 people have died from HIV/AIDS in the United States over the last forty years.[73]

Where Public Health Care Stands

On September 11, 2001, one year into the twenty-first century, 2,996 Americans were killed in terrorist attacks at the World Trade Center in New York City, the Pentagon in Virginia, and on United Airlines Flight 93 in Pennsylvania. In the decades since, first responders, contractors, rescuers, and people who lived and worked near Ground Zero have contracted a panoply of illnesses from respiratory issues to cancers. Deaths from 9/11 illnesses now outnumber the deaths during the actual terrorist attack, with tens of thousands sick.[74]

Largely due to the lack of universal coverage, the American health care system remains roiled by racism and classism, leading to significant disparities in mortality rates. The consequences of these failures are real, measured in the deaths of human beings. At the turn of the twenty-first century, there was still a 10 percent difference in mortality between Black and white Americans attributable to infectious disease alone.[75]

Historically, even without universal health care, pandemics and epidemics have increased the role of government regulation. The American public has responded in a relatively well-coordinated way, with citizens, researchers, medical charities, medical experts, and institutions working alongside the government for the greater good. But pandemics and epidemics have also increased xenophobia and racism, emboldening white supremacists and restricting the flow of immigration.

Even during Trump's early campaign days, historians recognized his efforts to stoke historically based racism against immigrants. In January 2018, in a discussion about a new bill protecting immigrants from Haiti, El Salvador, and African countries, Trump reportedly asked a group of senators, "Why are we having all these people from shithole countries come here?" Instead, he recommended courting immigrants from "great European countries," such as Norway, "and also from Asian countries, since they could help America economically."[76]

A few years later, as COVID-19 spread to America in early 2020, hate crimes against Asian Americans skyrocketed by 150 percent. Because the first documented case occurred in Wuhan, China, racist white Americans, led by Trump, began calling COVID the "China virus" and "kung flu." Verbal abuse, arson, vandalism, and even deadly assaults against Asian Americans spiked, with more than 2,800 documented hate incidents reported. Despite their ethnic and national diversity, all Asian Americans became possible targets of anti-Chinese hatred.[77]

When we explore the roots of all these problems, from epidemics to immigration, one fact becomes clear: while germs and disease may have killed millions of Americans, white supremacy is our nation's real illness.

In the twenty-first century, many of us naively believed that our nation would never have to deal with an extremely contagious, deadly virus like COVID-19. As of early spring 2022, the official death toll approached one million. Tragically, this number could have been lower had white supremacy not reemerged—emboldened and explosive—under Trump's encouragement. The number of COVID-19 deaths could have been lower with humane immigration policies, a universal health care system, faith in science and facts, and policy leadership. As we stare down the rest of the decade, and the century, nothing short of direct action will save us. The time has come.

BLACK LIVES MATTER AND THE BEGINNINGS OF THE THIRD RECONSTRUCTION

Yohuru Williams

Instead of birthing a new era of freedom, the "afterlives" of other frustrated attempts at racial reckoning and American renewal like Reconstruction and the Civil Rights Movement live on in what Saidiya Hartman has described as the "skewed life chances, limited access to health and education, premature death, incarceration, and impoverishment" endemic to the African American community. For Hartman, this also includes the continuing presence of slavery's racialized violence. That violence was evident for all the world to see in the horrendous murder of George Floyd under the knee of Minneapolis police officer Derek Chauvin on May 25, 2020.[1]

Rather than being the starting point, Floyd's murder will likely be remembered as a grim but significant milestone in what may be called America's Third Reconstruction. The first Reconstruction refers to the period following the Civil War, as the freedoms that Black Americans fought so hard for were enshrined in our Constitution, with the Thirteenth, Fourteenth, and Fifteenth Amendments ending slavery, establishing birthright citizenship and equal protection under the laws, and ensuring that suffrage rights cannot be based upon race respectively.[2] Most Americans are less familiar with what historians and activists refer to as the Second Reconstruction, the title given to the Civil Rights Movement of the 1950s and 1960s. The Second Reconstruction accomplished much politically, including, at the federal level, the passage of the Civil Rights Act of 1964 and the Voting Rights Act of 1965.[3]

It is impossible to talk about the beginnings of the Third Reconstruction—the movement we are in today—without addressing the battles that proceeded it. Like the Second Reconstruction, these battles were not fought by armies in the field but by mass-protest efforts aimed at establishing equality before the law. And just like in the mid-twentieth century, no sector of American society—from politics to sports to entertainment—has been out of the reach of activists and freedom fighters.

While no single issue was solely responsible for the ruptures, there are turning points, like the Fugitive Slave Act of 1850, the Dred Scott decision (1856), *Brown v. Board of Education* (1954), the murder of Emmett Till (1955), and, in our contemporary moment, the killing of Trayvon Martin (2012) and the Supreme Court's gutting of the Voting Rights Act of 1965 in *Shelby County v. Holder* (2013). These moments illustrate the underlying tensions that ultimately forced the nation to confront the malignant issue of racial inequality head-on.

The historian C. Vann Woodward described these underlying tensions in the 1850s as a part of a much larger "psychic crisis" that ultimately led to civil war. As Woodward conceptualized the problem, in "the course of the crisis each antagonist, according to the immemorial pattern had become convinced of the depravity and evilness of the other. Each believed itself persecuted, menaced . . . [and] paranoia continued to induce counter paranoia, each antagonist infecting the other reciprocally, until the vicious spiral ended in war."[4] Notwithstanding the "immemorial pattern," the two sides in that crisis still influence subsequent reckonings over racial justice, with one committed to the fulfillment of the promise of American democracy and the other firmly committed to the maintenance of white supremacy.

The "vicious spiral" toward the culture war in our contemporary moment followed the election of the nation's first Black president, Barack Obama, in 2008. The ripples from Obama's historic win set off seismic reverberations resulting in new political formations in the guise of the Tea Party, efforts to curtail or roll back Black voting rights, and outright appeals to white supremacy in the form of "birtherism," a conspiracy theory falsely asserting that Obama was born in Africa.[5]

Furthermore, between 2009 and 2020, the unpunished murders of unarmed Black people by police and vigilantes came to powerfully represent the most visible element of that conflict—the wanton disregard for Black life. The disproportionate impact of COVID-19 among Black and Brown people, and the failure of the larger society to address these disparities, reinforced this, all before a ruthless murder in Minneapolis centered attention on both issues.

George Floyd and the Rebirth of Black Lives Matter

At 8:00 p.m. on the evening of Monday, May 25, 2020, the then seventeen-year-old Darnella Frazier used her iPhone to record the brutal strangulation of George Floyd by the police officer Derek Chauvin outside the convenience store Cup Foods, at the intersection of Thirty-Eighth Street and Chicago Avenue in Minneapolis. An employee at the convenience store called the police on Floyd for supposedly passing a counterfeit twenty-dollar bill to purchase cigarettes.[6]

Officers arrived, and, after handcuffing Floyd, they attempted to place the forty-six-year-old man in a waiting squad car, which he resisted. Floyd told officers he was claustrophobic and that he could not breathe. The struggle ended with Floyd facedown on the concrete as Chauvin brutally "restrained" him with a knee to Floyd's neck.

As a small group of onlookers gathered to plead with Chauvin to remove his knee and summon medical attention for Floyd, Frazier began recording the exchange, documenting the agonizing nine minutes and twenty-nine seconds it took for Chauvin to render Floyd unconscious and unresponsive. Floyd was later declared dead at the hospital. Police initially reported his death as the consequence of Floyd's resisting arrest.[7]

Around midnight, Darnella Frazier decided to post her video to Facebook, a tool that helped her reach the masses in hours (but also made profits for a corporation infamously invested in surveillance and disinformation). It is estimated that by June 5, 2020, the video of Floyd's public lynching by police was watched a mind-blowing 1.4 billion times. Once the footage began to circulate, a chorus of protests erupted not only in South Minneapolis but around the nation. With most of the country still in lockdown from the pandemic, reaction to the video encapsulated the feelings shared by millions regarding the rampant killing of Black people by an increasingly militarized police force.[8]

On Tuesday, May 26, 2020, protesters began to gather in Minneapolis, Minnesota, bearing signs that read, "Say his name" and "I can't breathe"—grim social media hashtags that had become rallying cries of the national Black Lives Matter movement. The movement began some eight years earlier, following the murder of the Florida teen Trayvon Martin in 2012 by a self-appointed neighborhood watch captain named George Zimmerman. Zimmerman's initial release and later acquittal on murder charges (under Florida's controversial Stand Your Ground law, which authorized individuals to use deadly force against perceived threats) ignited a national debate over racial profiling and the policing of Black and Brown citizens in public spaces. It also sparked a wave of peaceful protests throughout the country.[9]

Black Lives Matter also had its own social media hashtag, digitally linking anyone in the world who clicked on the hyperlinked posts tagged #BlackLivesMatter (or #BLM). It grew into a national organizing body after three Black women activists—Alicia Garza, Patrisse Cullors, and Ayọ Tometi—worked to establish a Black-focused mass organizing and mobilization movement. BLM's mission was to "eradicate white supremacy and build local power to intervene in violence inflicted on Black communities by the state and vigilantes."[10]

The movement gained even more exposure in 2014, after the brutal police killings of Eric Garner in New York and Michael Brown in Ferguson, Missouri. By the time of George Floyd's murder in May 2020, Black Lives Matter had grown into a global phenomenon, challenging systemic inequality and protesting police brutality.

These issues took center stage most prominently in the National Football League (NFL) after several players, including twenty-nine-year-old San Francisco 49ers quarterback Colin Kaepernick, refused to stand during the national anthem. Kaepernick's protest was first noticed in August of 2016. When reporters asked him to explain, Kaepernick responded, "I am not going to stand up to show pride in a flag for a country that oppresses Black people and people of color. . . . To me," he concluded, "this is bigger than football and it would be selfish on my part to look the other way. There are bodies in the street and people getting paid leave and getting away with murder."[11]

Kaepernick, who eventually changed his method of protest (from sitting to kneeling on one knee out of respect for veterans), became the focus of a national debate on Black Lives Matter that intensified in September of 2016. Then-presidential candidate Donald Trump said the protesters had "a great lack of respect and appreciation for our country," inviting Kaepernick and others to "try another country, see if they like it better." A year later, with Kaepernick effectively banished from the league, Trump cackled to an adoring crowd, "Get that son of a bitch off the field right now!"[12]

Kaepernick's example inspired additional demonstrations, leading to a wave of protests by a multitude of athletes, dubbed by sportswriter Dave Zirin as "the Kaepernick Effect." For Zirin, Kaepernick and his followers became "the canary in the coal mine, signaling the coming struggle and also laying the groundwork for what we saw in 2020." The Kaepernick Effect was "crystallized in the juxtaposition of two images," Zirin wrote: Kaepernick bravely kneeling during the national anthem and Minneapolis officer Derek Chauvin murderously kneeling on the neck of George Floyd.[13]

While the battle raging within the NFL occupied massive media attention, it was only one manifestation of the culture war raging across the nation. Activists were demanding the removal of Confederate monuments and statues of enslavers and even colonizers—tying history to current issues of police brutality and the murder of Black people.

The Confederate monuments removal movement came to a head in Charlottesville, Virginia, on August 12, 2017, during the Unite the Right rally organized by white supremacists. They were counterprotesting racially progressive groups like BLM who were calling for the removal of a massive, prominent statue of the Confederate general Robert E. Lee. During the rally, white supremacist sympathizer James Alex Fields Jr. murderously plowed his car into a crowd of peaceful counterprotesters, killing the thirty-two-year-old antiracist activist Heather Heyer and injuring thirty-five others.[14]

Police Murders and Protests

In a notable departure from other police killings of unarmed Black people, on May 26, 2020, the Minneapolis Police Chief Madeira Arradondo fired the officers involved in George Floyd's murder. He also called for an FBI investigation into Floyd's death. The chief's actions were not enough, however, to stem the growing tide of anger and frustration across the Twin Cities. Prompted not only by the murder of George Floyd but also by several other high-profile killings of Black people (including the murder of Ahmaud Arbery by a pair of would-be vigilantes in Georgia and the killing of Breonna Taylor by police in Louisville, Kentucky), demonstrations quickly spread beyond Minneapolis to other cities. The protests were often marked by peaceful nonviolent demonstrations by day, sometimes followed by episodes of arson, looting, and sporadic violence by night.[15]

After protests in Minneapolis turned violent on May 27, 2020, with looting, rioting, and the burning down of the city's third police precinct building the following evening, the Minneapolis mayor Jacob Frey requested that the governor send in the National Guard to assist in maintaining order.[16]

Characteristically incendiary, President Trump further inflamed the situation, stoking the flames of racism with a tweet that recalled the violent treatment of protesters from the 1960s: "These THUGS are dishonoring the memory of George Floyd, and I won't let that happen. Just spoke to Governor Tim Walz and told him that the Military is with him all the way. Any difficulty and we will assume control but, when the looting starts, the shooting starts. Thank you!"[17]

The Black Lives Matter protests blossomed during the long, hot summer of 2020—and they were absolutely surreal. It was the first time most Americans had been in a crowd in three months. For many, it was the first time they left their homes at all since mid-March. To some, it was terrifying: going to a protest was possibly putting your life on the line. Not only did protesters have to worry about police violence, but they also had to fear COVID-19. But the cause was more pressing than the risk. Despite all the unknowns about the pandemic, Americans poured out of their homes and into the streets in hundreds of cities.

The *New York Times* described these protests as the largest movement in the country's history. While the precise number of demonstrators remains contested, estimates greatly exceed the numbers of other protests, such as the Women's March of 2017. But the uprisings during the summer of 2020 were not only significant in terms of volume but also in scale. One report documented more than 4,700 demonstrations—an average of 140 per day—across the country, with turnout ranging from dozens to tens of thousands, in about 2,500 cities and towns across the United States.[18]

Initially, activists and scholars expressed optimism. In Washington, DC, the battle over how to address issues of police violence toward African Americans found expression in the drafting of the George Floyd Justice in Policing Act, which passed in the House of Representatives by a vote of 236 to 181 on June 25. The bill sought to encourage accountability and transparency in policing by establishing new requirements for training and best practices. It also outlawed certain police practices and issued new guidelines for data collection.[19] A newfound awareness and sensitivity around issues of racial justice, branded "wokeism" by critics, spurred countless corporate responsibility statements and expressions of solidarity by previously silent or indifferent people and organizations.[20]

In his eulogy for George Floyd, the Reverend Al Sharpton also called out the number of white protesters supporting Black Lives Matter as a source of hope.[21] "I'm more hopeful today than ever," he noted. "When I looked this time and saw marches where, in some cases, young whites outnumbered the blacks marching. I know it's a different time and a different season."[22]

The Backlash: White Rage

Despite initial optimism, support for BLM protests began to wane after some encounters turned violent, and when elements within the coalition attempted to pursue more radical agendas. In many cities, activists focused their attention on inflated police budgets, maintaining that prior efforts at reform had failed to halt misconduct. In Seattle, defunding the police by 50 percent quickly became a top demand at demonstrations. Calls to "defund the police" (which became a new hashtag) proved frightening to more moderate supporters who were frustrated with police brutality but unprepared to take such a radical step.[23]

Cities like Seattle, Washington, and Portland, Oregon, became touchstones in those debates—as protesters refused to yield the streets and, in some cases, declared autonomous, police-free zones. Portland saw massive crowds gathering on a nightly basis accompanied by escalating violence between police, protesters, and emboldened members of armed alt-right and white supremacist organizations such as Patriot Prayer and the Three Percenters.[24]

After police in Seattle abandoned a precinct in the wake of demonstrations to minimize the threat of further violence following eight straight days of clashes with protesters, activists took over the structure and declared the Capitol Hill Occupied Protest (CHOP), an eclectic police-free zone centered around the abandoned police station. Protesters used the opportunity to create a sustained occupation-style protest in the area, working with city officials to block off street traffic in a six-block radius around the precinct.[25]

Pointing to the sustained action associated with what began in many cases as spontaneous demonstrations, it was only disbanded on July 1, 2020, after four deadly shootings and reports of other crimes and sexual assaults led the city to act. A similar police-free zone that emerged in Minneapolis (where Floyd was killed) was demolished by the city shortly after Chauvin was convicted of murder. Both areas borrowed from the model of the Occupy Wall Street movement of the early 2010s.[26]

Anti-Black Lives Matter protests developed in some areas, leading to confrontations between armed white nationalists and protesters. The most significant of these took place in August 2020, after the nonfatal shooting of Jacob Blake by police in Kenosha, Wisconsin.[27] Authorities acted quickly to announce an investigation, placing the officers on leave, and the following day the state's governor deployed the National Guard to Kenosha, where an emergency curfew was imposed.[28] Despite the quick response, incidents of vandalism, arson, and looting accompanied curfew violations. Reports that Blake survived the shooting would be tempered by the news delivered by his father that as a result of the "eight holes" in Blake's body, his son was permanently paralyzed. In anticipation of another night of potentially violent protests, city officials extended the curfew yet again.[29]

Rather than encouraging peace, President Trump once again took to Twitter to call for law and order, encouraging far-right extremists to engage in acts of violence. The seventeen-year-old Illinoisian Kyle Rittenhouse was one of the people Trump emboldened. Rittenhouse traveled to Kenosha as one of numerous armed antiprotesters, seeking to assist law enforcement. Early on the morning of August 26, 2020, Rittenhouse shot and killed two people, leaving a third seriously injured. Rather than condemning the murders, Trump again stoked the flames of discord when he expressed sympathy for Rittenhouse.[30]

Conclusion: The Beginnings of the Third Reconstruction

The president's response to the Kenosha shootings were in some ways a fitting epitaph for his presidency regarding race relations. Looking back on the last several years, Trump's lasting legacy of authoritarian rule, centered on a cult of personality—was premised on one thing, and one thing alone: white supremacy. After years of being a laughable figure on the fringes of tabloids, irrelevant outside of reality TV (where he secured a national audience by coldly firing Americans in an era of intense inequality), Trump had reignited his fame by accusing America's first Black president, Barack Obama, of not being born in America and of thus being ineligible for the presidency. Deeming nonwhite American-born citizens as "foreign" would soon become a deadly theme of Trump's rule.[31]

Riding the coattails of hate straight to the Oval Office, Trump was ultimately elected by racists, fearful of their own loss of status in a rapidly changing nation. Within another generation or two, white Americans will no longer comprise the majority, and Trump successfully cultivated their anger and fear into a violent white backlash, creating the most racially fraught year in America since the end of the Civil Rights Movement.

By sowing all the hatred he possibly could, Trump also inadvertently ushered in the beginnings of America's Third Reconstruction, the first real Civil Rights Movement of the twenty-first century.

Fortunately, in spite of the violence and racial terror that fueled it, the hopefulness that characterized early struggles for racial justice remains. In his final letter published posthumously in the *New York Times*, "Together, You Can Redeem the Soul of Our Nation," Congressman John Lewis, a lion of the Civil Rights Movement, argued that historical empathy is our most powerful tool to gain insight during moments of national crisis. Using his last hours of energy, Lewis surveyed the newly christened Black Lives Matter Plaza outside the White House in Washington, DC.

From the first two words of the letter's title alone, Lewis argued that ordinary individuals have an extraordinary capacity to enact change when working together—with the guiding light of history. "Humanity has been involved in this soul-wrenching, existential struggle for a very long time," he wrote, fully understanding that America was inching toward the ledge of a moral precipice. "People on every continent have stood in your shoes, through decades and centuries before you. The truth does not change, and that is why the answers worked out long ago can help you find solutions to the challenges of our time." It was time for a new generation to take to the streets and get to the voting box. It was time for a new generation to get into what John Lewis so famously called "good trouble"—to fight for the soul of a new and better America.[32]

ACKNOWLEDGMENTS

The editors would like to sincerely thank the wonderful team at Haymarket Books, Alexandra Alves, Blaire Rodenbiker, Brynn Kimel, Daniel Lazar, David M. Henkin, Debbie Gershinowitz, Elizabeth Hohl, Geri Thomas, Glenda Goodman, Henry Louis Gates Jr., Henry Perlowski, Jenni Ostwinkle Silva, Jessica Parr, Joan Brookbank, Joseph Malcomson, Leah Lagrone, Lisa Munro, Marissa Nicosia, Naomi Rendina, Nils Gilman, Rob Bowman, Robert Tsai, Roland Greene, the Stanford Humanities Center, Virginia Summey, and Will Holub-Moorman for their support.

NOTES

Preface: American Culture after Life

1   Will Stone, "COVID-19 Deaths Draw Comparisons to Other Tragic Death Tolls," *NPR*, January 26, 2021.

2   Madeline Holcolme, "1 in Every 500 US Residents Have Died of Covid-19," *CNN*, September 15, 2021.

3   Becky Sullivan, "New Study Estimates More Than 900,000 People Have Died Of COVID-19 in U.S.," *NPR*, May 6, 2021.

4   "The Pandemic's True Death Toll: Our Daily Estimate of Excess Deaths around The World," *Economist*, updated October 4, 2021.

5   Robert Lea, "How Many Americans Died from Spanish Flu and How Did the Pandemic End?" *Newsweek*, September 21, 2021; Sandra Opdycke, *The Flu Epidemic of 1918: America's Experience in the Global Health Crisis* (New York: Taylor & Francis, 2014).

6   Historians estimate that between 620,000 and 750,000 people died in the Civil War. See Guy Gugliotta, "New Estimate Raises Civil War Death Toll," *New York Times*, April 2, 2012.

7   Crista E. Johnson-Agbakwu et al., "Racism, COVID-19, and Health Inequity in the USA: A Call to Action," *Journal of Racial and Ethnic Health Disparities*, November 16, 2020, 1–7, Drew Faust, *This Republic of Suffering: Death and the American Civil War* (New York: Random House, 2008).

8   Max Bayer, "About 1 in 515 U.S. Kids Has Lost a Caregiver Due to COVID: Study," *CBS News*, October 7, 2021.

9   Rhitu Chatterjee and Carmel Roth, "COVID Deaths Leave Thousands of U.S. Kids Grieving Parents or Primary Caregivers," *NPR*, October 7, 2021.

10 Amiri Baraka, "Understanding Readiness," in *The LeRoi Jones/Amiri Baraka Reader* (New York: Basic Books, 1999).

11 Franklin Delano Roosevelt, "Franklin Roosevelt's Re-Nomination Acceptance Speech," July 27, 1936, https://www.americanyawp.com/reader/23-the-great-depression/franklin-roosevelts-re-nomination-acceptance-speech-1936/.

12 Leon F. Litwack, *How Free Is Free? The Long Death of Jim Crow* (Cambridge: Harvard University Press, 2009).

13 *I Am Not Your Negro*, directed by Raoul Peck (Velvet Film, Artemis Productions, and Close Up Films, 2016).

Introduction: The Present Crisis

1 Laurel Morales, "A Navajo Translator in Hospitals During COVID Is Now Pursuing Her Nursing Dreams," *NPR*, August 25, 2021.

2 "Intelligence Report Warned of Coronavirus Crisis as Early as November: Sources," *ABC News*, April 9, 2020.

3 "WHO Director-General's Remarks at the Media Briefing on 2019-nCoV on 11 February 2020," World Health Organization, February 11, 2020, https://www.who.int/director-general/speeches/detail/who-director-general-s-remarks-at-the-media-briefing-on-2019-ncov-on-11-february-2020.

4 Myah Ward, "15 Times Trump Praised China as Coronavirus Was Spreading across the Globe," *Politico*, April 15, 2020.

5 "Transcript for the CDC Telebriefing Update on COVID-19," CDC, February 26, 2020, https://www.cdc.gov/media/releases/2020/t0225-cdc-telebriefing-covid-19.html.

6 "Transcript for the CDC Telebriefing Update on COVID-19."

7 "Notice on the Continuation of the National Emergency Concerning the Coronavirus Disease 2019 (COVID-19) Pandemic," White House Briefing Room, February 24, 2021, https://www.whitehouse.gov/briefing-room/presidential-actions/2021/02/24/notice-on-the-continuation-of-the-national-emergency-concerning-the-coronavirus-disease-2019-covid-19-pandemic/.

8 Liz Frazier, "The Coronavirus Crash of 2020, and the Investing Lesson It Taught Us," *Forbes*, February 11, 2021.

9 Donald J. Trump, "Presidential Address on the Coronavirus Outbreak," transcript, *C-SPAN*, March 11, 2020, https://www.c-span.org/video/?470284-1/president-trump-travel-europe-us-suspended-30-days-uk.

10 Sarah Evanega et al., "Coronavirus Misinformation: Quantifying Sources and Themes in the COVID-19 'Infodemic,'" *JMIR Preprints*, submitted October 19, 2020 (Ithaca: Cornell University, The Cornell Alliance for Science, Department of Global Development, July 23, 2020), 1.

11 Joyce Lupiani, "List of Unproven Cures, Treatments for COVID-19," *CBS 46 News*, September 24, 2021.

12 "Coronavirus Disease (COVID-19): Hydroxychloroquine," World Health Organization, April 30, 2021, https://www.who.int/news-room/q-a-detail/coronavirus-disease-(covid-19)-hydroxychloroquine; Libby Cathey et al., "Trump Says He's Taking Hydroxychloroquine, Unproven Drug He's Touted for COVID-19," *ABC News*, May 19, 2020; Ashton Pittman, "Person Hospitalized after Taking Livestock Ivermectin from Feed Store to Treat COVID-19," *Mississippi Free Press*, August 20, 2021.

13 Peter Wade, "2012 Rand Paul Pushed to Make Illegal What 2020 Rand Paul Did," *Rolling Stone*, August 12, 2021.

14 Nathan Robinson, "US Senators Accused of Coronavirus Insider Trading Are a Symbol of Moral Bankruptcy," *Guardian*, March 21, 2020.

15 Dan Milmo and David Pegg, "Facebook Admits Site Appears Hardwired for Misinformation, Memo Reveals," *Guardian*, October 25, 2021.

16 Maegan Vasquez et al., "Donald Trump's Presidency by the Numbers," *CNN*, December 18, 2020.

17 "Shock, Rage Flare Over Trump's 'Reckless' Tweet Downplaying COVID Danger," *Kaiser Health News*, October 6, 2020; Donie O'Sullivan, "Facebook Removes Trump Post Falsely Saying Flu is More Lethal Than Covid," *CNN*, October 6, 2020.

18 Steven Nelson, "Trump Suspends Travel from Europe over Coronavirus Fears," *New York Post*, March 11, 2020.

19 Juliana Kaplan, "14 Countries that are Paying Their Workers During Quarantine—And How They Compare to America's $1,200 Stimulus Checks," *Business Insider*, May 8, 2020.

20 Sheri Fink, "Maker of Popular Covid Test Told Factory to Destroy Inventory," *New York Times*, August 20, 2021.

21 David Leonhardt, "Where Are the Tests?" *New York Times*, September 21, 2021.

22 The Morning News with Dave Lee, "Dr. Michael Osterholm Warns That Coronavirus is Airborne and Easily Spreadable," *WCCO News/Talk 830*, April 29, 2020; Erika Edwards, "CDC Reverses Again, Now Says Covid-19 is 'Sometimes Airborne,'" *NBC News*, October 5, 2020.

23 J. V. Chamary, "WHO Finally Admits Coronavirus Is Airborne. It's Too Late," *Forbes*, May 4, 2021; Roni Caryn Rabin and Emily Anthes, "The Virus is an Airborne Threat, the C.D.C. Acknowledges," *New York Times*, May 7, 2021.

24 Elizabeth Cohen and John Bonifield, "People Vaccinated against Covid-19 Can Go without Masks Indoors and Outdoors, CDC Says," *CNN*, May 13, 2021; Kaitlin Collins et al., "CDC Changes Mask Guidance in Response to Threat of Delta Variant of Covid-19," *CNN*, July 27, 2021.

25 Chris Hamby and Sheryl Gay Stolberg, "How One Firm Put an 'Extraordinary Burden' on the U.S.'s Troubled Stockpile," *New York Times*, March 6, 2021.

26 "Herman Cain, Ex-Presidential Candidate Who Refused to Wear Mask, Dies after COVID-19 Diagnosis," Reuters, July 30, 2020.

27 "A Timeline of Trump's Battle with Covid-19," *CNN*, updated October 12, 2020.

28 Brian Resnick, "Was the White House Reception for Amy Coney Barrett a Superspreading Event?" *Vox*, October 3, 2020.

29 Anthony Wallace, "'We Are Not Guinea Pigs': Trust Issues and a COVID-19 Vaccine Trial in the Navajo Nation," *WHYY NPR*, November 11, 2020.

30   "Navajo Nurse Marquerita Donald Saves Her Own Life," August 3, 2021,
     in *2 Lives*, produced by Laurel Morales, podcast, https://www.2lives.org/
     listen/marquerita-donald1.

31   "Navajo Nation: Where COVID-19 Claims Whole Families," *ABC News*,
     May 21, 2020.

32   "Coronavirus Disease 2019 (COVID-19) Situation Report 51," World
     Health Organization, March 11, 2020, https://www.who.int/docs/
     default-source/coronaviruse/situation-reports/20200311-sitrep-51-
     covid-19.pdf.

33   "Public Health Emergency Order No. 2020-005," Navajo Department
     of Health, April 5, 2020, https://www.navajo-nsn.gov/News%20
     Releases/NNDOH/2020/Apr/NDOH%20Public%20Health%20
     Emergency%20Order%202020-005%20Dikos%20Ntsaaigii-19.pdf;
     "Public Health Emergency Order No. 2020-003," Navajo Department
     of Health, March 20, 2020, https://www.navajo-nsn.gov/News%20
     Releases/NNDOH/2020/March/NDOH%20Public%20Health%20
     Emergency%20Order%202020-003%20Dikos%20Ntsaaigii-19.pdf.

34   "Navajo Nation Dikos Ntsaaígíí-19 (COVID-19)," Navajo Department
     of Health, last updated October 9, 2021, https://www.ndoh.navajo-nsn.
     gov/COVID-19/Data; Philip Deloria, "The Invention of Thanksgiving:
     Massacres, Myths and the Making of the Great November Holiday," *New
     Yorker*, November 18, 2019.

35   "Strategies to Mitigate Healthcare Personnel Staffing Shortages," CDC,
     updated March 10, 2021, https://www.cdc.gov/coronavirus/2019-ncov/
     hcp/mitigating-staff-shortages.html.

36   "Strategies for Optimizing the Supply of Disposable Medical
     Gloves," CDC, updated December 23, 2020, https://www.cdc.gov/
     coronavirus/2019-ncov/hcp/ppe-strategy/gloves.html.

37   Sara Berg, "Half of Health Workers Report Burnout amid
     COVID-19," American Medical Association, July 20, 2021, https://
     www.ama-assn.org/practice-management/physician-health/
     half-health-workers-report-burnout-amid-covid-19.

38   Ian Thomas, "How McDonald's, Wendy's and Other Fast Food Brands
     are Dealing with Labor Shortages," *MSNBC*, November 11, 2021.

39   Christina Pazzanese, "Labor Economist Lawrence Katz Looks at 'Great
     Resignation' and Where it Might Lead," *Harvard Gazette*, October 20, 2021.

40   W. E. B. Du Bois, *Black Reconstruction in America, 1860–1880* (1935; repr.,
     New York: Free Press, 1998).

41   Carmen Reinecke, "Unemployment Surged to 14.7% in April as the US
     Lost a Record 20.5 Million Jobs," *Business Insider*, May 8, 2020.

42   Steve Almasy, "Detroit Bus Driver Dies from Coronavirus Days after
     Making Angry Video about Coughing Passenger," *CNN*, updated April 3,
     2020.

43   Adam Blacker, "Instacart and Grocery Delivery Apps Set Consecutive
     Days of Record Downloads," *apptopia* (blog), March 16, 2020,

https://blog.apptopia.com/instacart-and-grocery-delivery-apps-set-consecutive-days-of-record-downloads; Steve Markenson, "COVID-19's Impact on Grocery Shopping in Just Five Weeks," *FMI* (blog), April 24, 2020, https://www.fmi.org/blog/view/fmi-blog/2020/04/24/covid-19-s-impact-on-grocery-shopping-in-just-five-weeks.

44 Olivia Paschal, "COVID-19 Pounded Arkansas Poultry Workers as Government and Industry Looked On," *Facing South*, August 20, 2020; Olivia Paschal, "Emails Show Tyson's Sway over Arkansas Mayor during COVID Surge in Plants," *Facing South*, February 5, 2021.

45 Alice Driver, "Arkansas Poultry Workers: 'We're Not Essential, We're Expendable,'" *NPR-UALR*, May 12, 2020.

46 Annelise Orleck, "And the Virus Rages On: 'Contingent' and 'Essential' Workers in the Time of COVID-19," *International Labor and Working-Class History* 99 (2021): 1–14.

47 "Largest Single-State Worksite Enforcement Action in Nation's History Conducted by ICE and DOJ at Various Sites Across Mississippi," US Attorney's Office, Department of Justice, August 7, 2019, https://www.justice.gov/usao-sdms/pr/largest-single-state-worksite-enforcement-action-nation-s-history-conducted-ice-and-doj.

48 Ashuka Mukpo, "Bloody Masks and Fevers on Shift: Immigrant Workers Face Abuse in Nebraska Meatpacking Plant," ACLU, November 23, 2020, https://www.aclu.org/news/immigrants-rights/bloody-masks-and-fevers-on-shift-immigrant-workers-face-abuse-in-nebraska-meatpacking-plant/.

49 Jeff Platsky et al., "COVID-19 Ravaged these New York Factories· This is How it Happened," *Utica Observer Dispatch*, July 23, 2020.

50 Orleck, "And the Virus Rages On."

51 Althea Legaspi, "Arizona Workers Blast 'Live and Let Die' While Maskless Trump Tours Factory," *Rolling Stone*, May 5, 2020.

52 Clifford Colby, "How Much was the First Stimulus Check? Your Tax Return May Need that Total," *MSN*, April 11, 2021.

53 Orleck, "And the Virus Rages On."

54 Greg Rosalsky, "How 'Chaos' in The Shipping Industry Is Choking the Economy," *NPR*, June 15, 2021.

55 David J. Lynch, "Inside America's Broken Supply Chain," *Washington Post*, updated October 2, 2021.

56 Ann Koh, "One Stuck Box of Fertilizer Shows the Global Supply Chain Crisis," *Bloomberg*, August 28, 2021.

57 Tiffany Hudson, "Port of Los Angeles Terminal Shut Down Due to Labor Strike," *News Nation*, April 14, 2021.

58 Nathaniel Meyersohn, "Grocery Store Shelves Aren't Going Back to Normal This Year," *CNN*, October 9, 2021.

59 Abay Asfaw, "Cost of Lost Work Hours Associated with the COVID-19 Pandemic—United States, March 2020 through February 2021," *American Journal of Industrial Medicine* (Nov. 2021).

60 Catie Edmondson, "5 Key Things in the $2 Trillion Coronavirus
    Stimulus Package," *New York Times*, March 25, 2020; Tara Siegel Bernard
    and Ron Lieber, "F.A.Q. on Stimulus Checks, Unemployment and the
    Coronavirus Plan," *New York Times*, June 2, 2021.

61 Eric B. Elbogen et al., "Suicidal Ideation and Thoughts of Self-Harm
    during the COVID-19 Pandemic: The Role of COVID-19-Related Stress,
    Social Isolation, and Financial Strain," *Anxiety and Depression Association of
    America* 38 (2021): 739–48.

62 Anne Case and Angus Deaton, "The Great Divide: Education, Despair,
    and Death," *NBER Working Paper* 29241, September 2021.

63 Jeff Asher, "Murder Rose by Almost 30% in 2020: It's Rising at a Slower
    Rate in 2021," *New York Times*, September 23, 2021.

64 Anneken Tappe, "America's Women Are Still on the Sidelines, Even as the
    Jobs Recovery Picks up Steam," *CNN*, November 8, 2021.

65 See, for instance, Judy Stone, "Covid-19 Vaccination Rates Are Poor
    among Healthcare Workers: How Can We Do Better?" *Forbes*, June 28,
    2021; and Nathaniel Weixel, "Low Vaccination Rates among Nursing
    Home Staff Imperil Elderly," *The Hill*, July 25, 2021.

66 Megan Brenan, "Women Still Handle Main Household Tasks in U.S.,"
    Gallup, January 29, 2020; Terry Gross, "Pandemic Makes Evident
    'Grotesque' Gender Inequality In Household Work," *NPR*, May 21, 2020.

67 Dylan Stableford, "Chauvin Trial Opens With 9-Minute Video of Former
    Officer Kneeling on George Floyd's Neck," *Yahoo News*, March 29, 2021.

68 Gerald Horne, *Fire This Time: The Watts Uprising and the 1960s*
    (Charlottesville: University Press of Virginia, 1995); Josh Sides, *L.A. City
    Limits: African American Los Angeles from the Great Depression to the Present*
    (Berkeley: University of California Press, 2003); Governor's Commission
    on the Los Angeles Riots, *Violence in the City—an End or a Beginning?* (Los
    Angeles, 1965).

69 See Colin Kaepernick, *Abolition for the People: The Movement for a Future
    without Policing and Prisons* (New York: Kaepernick, 2021).

70 Stella Chan and David Williams, "Man Who Filmed Rodney King's 1991
    Beating by Police Dies of Covid-19, Friend Says," *CNN*, September 21,
    2021.

71 Richard Fausset, "What We Know About the Shooting Death of Ahmaud
    Arbery," *New York Times*, October 16, 2021.

72 Richard A. Oppel Jr., Derrick Bryson Taylor, and Nicholas Bogel-
    Burroughs, "What to Know About Breonna Taylor's Death," *New York
    Times*, April 26, 2021.

73 Savannah Smith, Jiachuan Wu, and Joe Murphy, "Map: George Floyd
    Protests around the World," *NBC News*, June 9, 2020.

74 Simone Perez and Paola Ramos, "Coronavirus is Devastating Navajo
    Nation," *Vice News*, July 20, 2020.

75 Perez and Ramos, "Coronavirus is Devastating Navajo Nation."

76 Perez and Ramos, "Coronavirus is Devastating Navajo Nation."

77 "Navajo Nation Funeral COVID-19 Guidelines," Navajo Department of Health, accessed March 30, 2022, https://www.ndoh.navajo-nsn.gov/Portals/0/COVID-19/News/NN%20Funeral%20Guidelines-ONLINE.pdf?ver=IyX-nYi0S_pTIYqnUgqyLg%3d%3d.

78 "Navajo Nation Surpasses New York State as Highest Covid-19 Infection Rate in US," *CNN*, May 18, 2020.

79 Amanda Gold and Jessica Shakesprere, "Four Ways to Improve Water Access in Navajo Nation during COVID-19," *Urban Wire* (the blog of the Urban Institute), September 29, 2020, https://www.urban.org/urban-wire/four-ways-improve-water-access-navajo-nation-during-covid-19.

80 Julia A. Wolfson and Cindy W. Leung, "Food Insecurity during COVID-19: An Acute Crisis with Long-Term Health Implications," *American Journal of Public Health* 110, no. 12 (2020): 1763–65.

81 Eliza W. Kinsey et al., "School Closures during COVID-19: Opportunities for Innovation in Meal Service." *American Journal of Public Health* 110, no. 11 (2020): 1635–43.

82 Chelsea Curtis, "St. Mary's Gives Food to 2,000 Navajo Nation Families in its Largest Mobile Distribution Ever," *Arizona Republic*, April 14, 2020; Josh Sanders, "Tuba City Lines Up for Massive Food Distribution," *12News*, April 14, 2020.

83 Mariame Kaba, "Mariame Kaba: Everything Worthwhile Is Done With Other People," interview by Eve L. Ewing, *ADI Magazine*, Fall 2019; also see Mariame Kaba, *We Do This 'Til We Free Us: Abolitionist Organizing and Transforming Justice* (Chicago: Haymarket Books, 2021).

84 "A Navajo Translator in Hospitals During COVID Is Now Pursuing Her Nursing Dreams."

85 On the Navajo Code Talkers see Alison R. Bernstein, *American Indians and World War II: Toward a New Era in Indian Affairs* (Norman: University of Oklahoma Press, 1991); Davis Goode Jr., "Proud Tradition of the Marines' Navajo Code Talkers: They Fought with Words—Words No Japanese Could Fathom," *Marine Corps League* 46, no. 1 (Spring 1990): 16–26.

86 Linda Moon Stumpff, "The Navajo Horse Policy Dilemma: Too Many Horses? T'ooahayoo Nihilii?" The Evergreen State College, 2014, https://nativecases.evergreen.edu/sites/nativecases.evergreen.edu/files/case-studies/navajo-horse-policy-case-study.pdf.

87 "A Navajo Translator in Hospitals During COVID Is Now Pursuing Her Nursing Dreams."

88 Spero M. Manson and Dedra Buchwald, "Bringing Light to the Darkness: COVID-19 and Survivance of American Indians and Alaska Natives," *Health Equity* 5, no. 1 (2021): 59–63.

89 Sanora Babb, *Whose Names Are Unknown: A Novel* (1939; repr., University of Oklahoma Press, 2012), author's note.

90 Kurtis Alexander, "Wildfire Smoke Linked to Thousands of COVID-19 Cases," *San Francisco Chronicle*, August 13, 2021.

Chapter 1: El Paso in Mourning

1   Simon Romero and Nicholas Bogel-Burroughs, "El Paso Shooting: Massacre That Killed 20 Being Investigated as Domestic Terrorism," *New York Times*, August 4, 2019; Manny Fernandez and Sarah Murvosh, "Soccer Coach in El Paso Shooting Dies 9 Months Later," *New York Times*, April 27, 2020.

2   Maria Cortez Gonzalez, "El Paso, New Mexico Florists Create Tribute to Walmart Mass Shooting Victims," *El Paso Times*, July 31, 2020.

3   For more on this long history of medical officials criminalizing and pathologizing ethnic Mexicans and border residents, see John McKiernan Gonzalez, *Fevered Measures: Public Health and Race at the Texas-Mexico Border, 1848–1942* (Durham: Duke University Press, 2012). While some claim the El Paso massacre was the deadliest single-shooter attack against Latinxs in modern US history, the Pulse nightclub shooting in Orlando in 2016, although targeted at the LGBTQ community, likely resulted in more Latinxs deaths.

4   Fernandez and Murvosh, "Soccer Coach in El Paso Shooting Dies 9 Months Later."

5   Gregory Korte and Alan Gomez, "Trump Ramps Up Rhetoric on Undocumented Immigrants: 'These Aren't People. These Are Animals,'" *USA Today*, May 16, 2018; "Family Separation under the Trump Administration—a Timeline," Southern Poverty Law Center, June 17, 2020, https://www.splcenter.org/news/2020/06/17/family-separation-under-trump-administration-timeline.

6   Alex Samuels, "People Want to Donate Diapers and Toys to Children at Border Patrol Facilities in Texas: They're Being Turned Away," *Texas Tribune*, June 24, 2019; Claudia Tristán, "'It Was Fueled by Hate and Bigotry': One Year on from the El Paso Shooting," *Guardian*, August 3, 2020.

7   Suzanne Gamboa, "'Hellish': Covid Deaths Have Struck Younger Latinos: Here's the Economic, Social Fallout," *NBC News*, December 28, 2020.

8   Michael Balsamo, "Hate Crimes in US Reach Highest Level in More Than a Decade, according to an FBI Report: 'Reminder That We Have Much Work to Do,'" *Chicago Tribune*, November 16, 2020.

9   Tristán, "'It Was Fueled by Hate and Bigotry'"; KTSM Report, "Operation H.O.P.E. Will Continue Assisting with COVID-19 Funeral Arrangements," *KTSM.com*, January 4, 2021; Katharine Q. Seelye, "Harrison Johnson, Pastor at Funeral in Mass Shooting, Dies at 65," *New York Times*, October 23, 2020.

10   Suzanne Gamboa and the Associated Press, "Rise in Reports of Hate Crimes against Latinos Pushes Overall Number To 11-Year High," *NBC News*, November 16, 2020; Michelle Ye Hee Lee, "Donald Trump's False Comments Connecting Mexican Immigrants and Crime," *Washington Post*, July 8, 2015.

11   Adam Serwer, "Jeff Session's Unqualified Praise for a 1924 Immigration Law," *Atlantic*, January 10, 2017.

12   The following history is detailed in my book: Monica Muñoz Martinez, *The Injustice Never Leaves You: Anti-Mexican Violence in Texas* (Cambridge: Harvard University Press, 2018).

13   Martinez, *The Injustice Never Leaves You*, 209.

14   Martinez, *The Injustice Never Leaves You*, 19.

15   Martinez, *The Injustice Never Leaves You*, 87–88; Monica Muñoz Martinez, testimony, US House Committee on the Judiciary Subcommittee on Immigration and Citizenship, "Oversight of the Trump Administration Border Policies and the Relationship Between Anti-Immigrant Rhetoric and Domestic Terrorism," September 6, 2019, https://www.congress.gov/116/meeting/house/109889/witnesses/HHRG-116-JU01-Wstate-MunozMartinezM-20190906.pdf.

16   Martinez, *The Injustice Never Leaves You*, 155.

17   Martinez, *The Injustice Never Leaves You*, 17–18.

18   Martinez, *The Injustice Never Leaves You*, 17–18; "Refugees Start Trek to Marfa," *El Paso Herald*, January 14, 1914, 1; "Prisoners Are Due at Daylight—Hog Tight Stockade to Surround Camp," *El Paso Herald*, January 19, 1914, 1.

19   "Mexican Refugees Won't Be Sent Back," *New York Times*, January 13, 1914; "2,000 Prisoners Leave El Paso," *El Paso Herald*, May 4, 1914, 1.

20   Unnamed, February 1914, certificate number 254/3195, Bureau of Vital Statistics, State Registrar Office, Austin; Unnamed child of Francisco Palomino, April 1914, certificate number 554, Bureau of Vital Statistics, State Registrar Office, Austin; Anacleto Esquibel, May 1914, certificate number 626, Bureau of Vital Statistics, State Registrar Office, Austin; Unnamed, February 1914, certificate number 246/3201, Bureau of Vital Statistics, State Registrar Office, Austin; "Vanguard of Refugees is in Marfa Ready to Board Trains for Fort Bliss," *El Paso Herald*, January 19, 1914, 1.

21   David Dorado Romo, *Ringside Seat to a Revolution: An Underground Cultural History of El Paso and Juarez, 1893–1923* (El Paso: Cinco Puntos Press, 2005); Andrea Grajeda, "El Paso Border Practices Influence the Holocaust," The Texas Story Project, Bullock Texas State History Museum, April 06, 2018, https://www.thestoryoftexas.com/discover/texas-story-project/el-paso-holocaust-influence; Maclovio Perez Jr., "El Paso Bath House Riots (1917)," *Handbook of Texas Online*, Texas State Historical Association, July 30, 2016, https://www.tshaonline.org/handbook/entries/el-paso-bath-house-riots-1917.

22   "16 Dead; 19 Injured in City Jail Fire," *El Paso Herald*, March 7, 1916; "Grand Jury Probing Jail Fire, One More Victim is Identified," *El Paso Herald*, March 8, 1916; Stern, Alexandra Minna, "Buildings, Boundaries, and Blood: Medicalization and Nation-Building on the U.S.-Mexico Border, 1910–1930," *Hispanic American Historical Review* 79, no. 1 (Feb. 1999), 61–63.

23   Stern, "Buildings, Boundaries, and Blood," 41–81; Romo, *Ringside Seat to a Revolution*; Grajeda, "El Paso Border Practices Influence the Holocaust."

24   "Neglect and Abuse of Unaccompanied Immigrant Children by U.S. Customs and Border Protection," International Human Rights Clinic, May 2018, https://chicagounbound.uchicago.edu/cgi/viewcontent. cgi?article=1001&context=ihrc; Government Accountability Project, "Second Protected Whistleblower Disclosures of Gross Mismanagement by the Department of Health and Human Services at Fort Bliss," July 28, 2021, https://whistleblower.org/wp-content/uploads/2021/07/072821-2nd-Fort-Bliss-Whistleblower-Disclosure-FINAL.pdf; "Migrant Children in US Tent Camp Faced Depression and Filthy Conditions, Whistleblowers say," CBS News, July 28, 2021; "Third Complaint Filed against Unaccompanied Migrant Center at Fort Bliss," KFOX 14, September 14, 2021.

25   Dianne Solis and Allie Morris, "Are Migrants Fueling the COVID-19 Surge? 'No, This is the Pandemic of the Unvaccinated,'" Dallas Morning News, August 9, 2021.

26   Raul A. Reyes, "Greg Abbott's Outrageous Covid Order to Scapegoat Immigrants in Texas," CNN, July 30, 2021; Solis and Morris, "Are Migrants Fueling the COVID-19 Surge?"

27   Jill Ament and Caroline Covington, "'We Believe in the Good That the Vaccines Can Do': A 70% Vaccination Rate Is Helping El Paso Keep Hospitalizations at Bay," Texas Standard KUT, August 20, 2021; "COVID-19 Vaccinations: County and State Tracker," New York Times, updated October 27, 2021.

Chapter 2: 2020

1   McGirt v. Oklahoma, 140 S. Ct. 2452, 2459 (2020) (emphasis added).

2   Jonodev O. Chaudhuri, "Opinion: Our Muscogee People Suffered for Generations in the Hope of a Better Tomorrow: It's Finally Here," Washington Post, July 14, 2020.

3   Joy Harjo, "After a Trail of Tears, Justice for 'Indian Country,'" New York Times, July 14, 2020.

4   Anna Lee et al., "Jo Ellen Darcy: Stop the Dakota Access Pipeline," petition, Change.org, April 2016, https://www.change.org/p/jo-ellen-darcy-stop-the-dakota-access-pipeline.

5   Saul Elbein, "The Youth Group That Launched a Movement at Standing Rock," New York Times Magazine, January 31, 2017.

6   "Supplemental Declaration of Tim Mentz, Sr. in Support of Motion For Preliminary Injunction at 1," Standing Rock Sioux Tribe v. U.S. Army Corps of Engineers, 205 F. Supp. 3d 4 (D.D.C. 2016) (No. 1:16-cv-01534-JEB); Sam Levin, "Guards for North Dakota Pipeline Could Be Charged for Using Dogs on Activists," Guardian, October 26, 2016.

7   Brown v. Board of Education, 347 U.S. 483 (1954); Plessy v. Ferguson, 163 U.S. 537 (1896); McGirt v. Oklahoma.

8   Strate v. A-1 Contractors, 520 U.S. 438 (1997).

9   Dollar General Corp. v. Mississippi Band of Choctaw Indians, 579 U.S. 545 (2016).

Chapter 4: Somewhere, USA

1   This essay is drawn from the author's personal memories and research, though the names of certain people and places have been changed for privacy reasons and to suggest a certain universality of experience.

2   Peter Simpson, ed., *City of Dreams: A Guide to Port Townsend* (Port Townsend, WA: Bay Press, 1986); *With Pride in Heritage: History of Jefferson County* (Port Townsend, WA, 1966).

3   Tristan Baurick, "Climate Change May be Turning Gulls into Cannibals," *Kitsap Sun*, July 23, 2016.

4   Sol H. Lewis, "A History of the Railroads in Washington," *Washington Historical Quarterly* 3, no. 3 (July 1912): 186–97.

5   Beth Lew-Williams, *The Chinese Must Go: Violence, Exclusion, and the Making of the Alien in America* (Cambridge: Harvard University Press, 2018); Jean Pfaelzer, *Driven Out: The Forgotten War Against Chinese Americans* (New York: Random House, 2007); Erika Lee, *At America's Gates: Chinese Immigration During the Exclusion Era, 1882–1943* (Chapel Hill: University of North Carolina Press, 2003); Robert L. Tsai, "Racial Purges," *Michigan Law Review* 118 (2020): 1127–56.

6   Michael Sandel, *The Tyranny of Merit: What's Become of the Common Good?* (New York: Farrar, Straus and Giroux, 2020); Daniel Markovits, *The Meritocracy Trap: How America's Foundational Myth Feeds Inequality, Dismantles the Middle Class, and Devours the Elite* (New York: Penguin Press, 2019).

Chapter 5: Confederates Take the Capitol

1   W. E. B. Du Bois, *The Souls of Black Folk. Essays and Sketches* (Chicago. A.C. McClurg, 1903); and *Black Reconstruction: A History of the Part Which Black Folk Played in the Attempt to Reconstruct Democracy in America, 1860–1880* (New York: Harcourt Brace, 1935).

2   See Beverly Daniel Tatum, *Why Are All the Black Kids Sitting Together in the Cafeteria? And Other Conversations About Race* (New York: Basic Books, 1997).

3   Annie Dillard, "Living Like Weasels," in *Teaching a Stone to Talk: Expeditions and Encounters* (Edinburgh. Canongate Books, 1982).

4   John Caldwell Calhoun, *Speeches of John C. Calhoun* (New York: Harper & Brothers, 1843), 225; John C. Calhoun, *Speech on the Reception of Abolition Petitions: Revised Report*, February 6, 1837.

5   Charles Sumner, "Are We a Nation? Address of Hon. Charles Sumner before the New York Young Men's Republican Union, at the Cooper Institute, Tuesday evening, Nov. 19, 1867," New York Young Men's Republican Union.

6   Joe Kukura, "Feds Charge Capitol Insurrection Rioter," *SFist*, May 19, 2021.

7   Benjamin Franklin Cooling, *Jubal Early's Raid on Washington* (Tuscaloosa: University of Alabama Press, 2008).

8   "Trump Told Top U.S. Generals to 'Just Shoot' Racism Protestors, Book Claims," *Guardian*, June 25, 2021.

9   Brian Naylor, "Read Trump's Jan. 6 Speech," *NPR*, February 10, 2021.

10   See Stephen Berry and James Hill Welborn III, "The Cane of His Existence: Depression, Damage, and the Brooks-Sumner Affair," *Southern Cultures* 20, no. 4 (Summer 2014); Mary Boykin Chesnut, *A Diary from Dixie* (New York: D. Appleton, 1905), 74.

11   Heather McGhee, *The Sum of Us: What Racism Costs Everyone and How We Can Prosper Together* (New York: One World, 2021); Thomas Frank, *What's the Matter with Kansas: How Conservatives Won the Heart of America* (New York: Picador, 2005).

12   "No Gradual Emancipation," *New York Times*, February 25, 1864.

13   Gordon Fraser, "Conspiracy, Pornography, Democracy: The Recurrent Aesthetics of the American Illuminati," *Journal of American Studies* 54, no. 2 (May 2020): 273–94.

14   Gregory Krieg, "'I Didn't Think That I Was Just Going to be Killed': Ocasio-Cortez on Her Fears on January 6," *CNN*, August 9, 2021; Maeve Reston, "'I Will Never Forget': Christine Blasey Ford Recounts Her Trauma in Raw Testimony," *CNN*, September 27, 2018.

15   Abraham Lincoln, "The Perpetuation of Our Political Institutions: Address Before the Young Men's Lyceum of Springfield, Illinois," January 27, 1838, in *The Collected Works of Abraham Lincoln*, ed. Roy P. Basler, vol. 1 (New Brunswick: Rutgers University Press, 1953).

16   Lincoln, "The Perpetuation of Our Political Institutions."

17   Lincoln, "The Perpetuation of Our Political Institutions."

18   Abraham Lincoln to William H. Seward, June 28, 1862, in *The Collected Works of Abraham Lincoln*, ed. Roy P. Basler, vol. 5 (New Brunswick: Rutgers University Press, 1953).

19   Lloyd Lewis, *Sherman, Fighting Prophet* (New York: Harcourt, Brace, 1932).

Chapter 6: Two Catastrophes and Ten Parallels

I thank Dr. Erlanger A. Turner, my copanelist at "Mental Health in Times of Crisis," Cabinet Conversations: Conversations on Creativity, History and Leadership, Ford's Theatre, Washington, DC, livestreamed, October 2020, who helped spark some of the ideas here.

1   Deidre McPhillips, "US Reports More Than 900,000 Total Covid-19 Deaths," *CNN*, February 4, 2022.

2   J. David Hacker, "A Census-Based Count of the Civil War Dead," *Civil War History* 57 (2011), 307–48.

3   Edwin Greble, Sr. to Susan Greble, Baltimore, MD, April 16, 1865, Greble Papers, Manuscript Division, Library of Congress, Washington, DC (hereafter LC); "Nannie" to Charles E. Snyder, n.p., April 16, 1865, Miscellaneous Documents Relating to Abraham Lincoln, MS Am 2605, box 1, Houghton Library, Harvard University, Cambridge, MA (hereafter HLH); John G. Nicolay to Therena Bates, Steamer Santiago de Cuba, Chesapeake

Bay, April 17, 1865, box 3, Nicolay Papers, LC; on "to realize," see Drew Gilpin Faust, *This Republic of Suffering: Death and the American Civil War* (New York: Alfred A. Knopf, 2008), 169; Levi S. Graybill diary, April 17, 1865, Graybill Papers, Huntington Library, San Marino, CA. (hereafter HL).

4   Freeman Bradford to Charles Harris, Auburn, ME, April 15, 1865, box 1, Emerson Family Papers, Beineke Library, Yale University, New Haven, CT (question mark added for clarity); Rachel Bowman Cormany diary, April 15, 1865, in James C. Mohr and Richard E. Winslow, eds., *The Cormany Diaries: A Northern Family in the Civil War* (Pittsburgh: University of Pittsburgh Press, 1982), 543; Mary Mellish to George H. Mellish, Woodstock, VT, April 16, 1865, Mellish Papers, HL.

5   Margaret B. Howell diary, April 17, 1865, Historical Society of Pennsylvania, Philadelphia; Holiday Ames to wife, Decatur, AL, April 23, 1865, in Louis Filler, ed., "Waiting for the War's End: The Letter of an Ohio Soldier in Alabama," *Ohio History* 74 (1965), 56; Susannah A. Milner-Gibson to Jane Poultney Bigelow, Folkestone, England, April 28, 1865, Bigelow Family Papers, Manuscripts and Archives Division, New York Public Library, New York, NY; Horace O. Gilmore to Lucy Gilmore, Petersburg, VA, April [15], 1865, Gilmore Papers, Manuscripts and Special Collections, New York State Library, Albany (hereafter NYSL); Edward Everett Hale diary, April 24, 1865, box 54, Hale Papers, NYSL.

6   Henry Baker, "An Expression by the Colored People of New Orleans," in *Louisiana's Tribute to the Memory of Abraham Lincoln: Public Demonstration in the City of New Orleans, April 22, 1865* (New Orleans: Picayune, 1881), 37; Joseph A. Prime, "Sermon Preached in the Liberty Street Presbyterian Church (Colored)," in *A Tribute of Respect by the Citizens of Troy to the Memory of Abraham Lincoln* (Troy, NY: Young and Benson, 1865), 155; Jacob Thomas, "Sermon Preached in the African Methodist Episcopal Zion Church," in *Tribute of Respect*, 44; "From Baltimore," *New York Anglo-African*, May 6, 1865; "From the Regiments," letter from Richard H. Black, 3rd USCT, Fernandina, FL, *New York Anglo-African*, May 27, 1865; Frederick Douglass, "Our Martyred President: An Address Delivered in Rochester, New York, on 15 April 1865," in *The Frederick Douglass Papers*, eds. John W. Blassingame and John R. McKivigan (New Haven: Yale University Press, 1979–92), ser. 1, 4:76; Theodore L. Cuyler, "Sermon IX," in *Our Martyr President, Abraham Lincoln: Voices from the Pulpit of New York and Brooklyn. Oration by Hon. Geo. Bancroft, Oration at the Burial, by Bishop Simpson* (New York: Tibbals and Whiting, 1865), 170; S. H. Fowler to "Mr. Whiting," Headley, MA, April 21, 1865, #57688, reel 91, American Missionary Association Archives, Amistad Research Center, Tulane University, microfilm (hereafter AMA).

7   Photographs of signs in New York, NY, and Swarthmore, PA, by the author, Spring 2020.

8   Charles A. Sanford to Edward Payson Goodrich, Washington, DC, April 18, 1865, in "Two Letters on the Event of April 14, 1865," *Bulletin of the*

William L. Clements Library of American History 47 (February 12, 1946), facsimile, n.p.; Julia Adelaide Shepard to father, near Washington, DC, April 16, 1865, in "Lincoln's Assassination Told by an Eye-Witness," *Century Magazine* 77 (1909), 918; Anonymous Diary, McLellan Lincoln Collection, John Hay Library, Brown University, Providence, RI (hereafter JHL), reproduced with annotations in Ted Widmer, "New York's Lincoln Memorial," Op-Archive: Lincoln Memorial Diary, *New York Times*, April 17, 2009, http://documents.nytimes.com/lincoln-assassination-new-york-memorial-diary (spelling corrected for clarity).

9   Mary Peck to Henry J. Peck, Jonesville, NY, April 16, 1865, Peck Correspondence, NYSL; Thomas Francis Johnson diary, April 15, 1865, box 42, Johnson Family Papers, H. Furlong Baldwin Library, Maryland Historical Society, Baltimore.

10   Emma F. LeConte diary, April 20 and "Friday" [April 21], 1865, reel 22, Southern Historical Collection, University of North Carolina, Chapel Hill, American Women's Diaries: Southern Women, Readex Newsbank, microfilm; H. B. Greely to George Whipple, Saint Augustine, FL, April 29, 1865 (misdated 1864), #18655, reel 28, AMA; Thomas Outten, file MM 2544, RG 153, Court-Martial Case Files, entry 15, Records of the Office of the Judge Advocate General (Army), National Archives and Records Administration, Washington, DC (hereafter NARA); Max Puhan, file OO 1277, RG 153-NARA. NB: The original text uses the racial slur in its entirety.

11   John Worthington to Mary Worthington, Cooperstown, NY, April 15, 1865, Autograph File, HLH; "Em" to Lewis J. Nettleton, part of Henry Cornwall to Lewis J. Nettleton, Milford, CT, April 16, 1865, Nettleton-Baldwin Family Papers, David M. Rubenstein Rare Book and Manuscript Library, Duke University, Durham, NC (hereafter Duke); Anonymous Diary, JHL, reproduced with annotations in Ted Widmer, "New York's Lincoln Memorial," Op-Archive: Lincoln Memorial Diary, *New York Times*, April 17, 2009, http://documents.nytimes.com/lincoln-assassination-new-york-memorial-diary.

12   "Funeral Oration by Bishop Simpson," in B. F. Morris, *Memorial Record of the Nation's Tribute to Abraham Lincoln* (Washington, DC: W.H. and O.H. Morrison, 1865), 229; Edward Everett Hale to Charles Hale, Boston, MA, May 2, 1865, box 6, Hale Papers, NYSL.

13   F. C. Chambers diary, April 20, 1865, Chambers Family Diaries, Rare Books and Special Collections, Princeton University, Princeton, NJ; Caroline Dall journal, April 22, 1865, vol. J27, Dall Papers, Massachusetts Historical Society, (hereafter MHS); Ebenezer Paul diary, April 14, 19, 1865, vol. 2, Henry F. Howe Collection II, MHS; Bayard Taylor to George Palmer Putnam, Kennett Square, Pa., April 28, 1865, HM14640, HL.

14   Edgar Dinsmore to Carrie Drayton, St. Andrews Parish, SC, May 29, 1865, Dinsmore Papers, Duke.

15 Levi S. Graybill diary, April 17, 1865, Graybill Papers, HL; Thomas, "Sermon Preached in the African Methodist Episcopal Zion Church," in *Tribute of Respect*, 46; Abigail Williams May to Eleanor Goddard May, Boston, April 16, 1865, May and Goddard Family Papers, Schlesinger Library on the History of Women in America, Radcliffe Institute for Advanced Study, Harvard University, Cambridge, MA.

16 Mary Ann Starkey to "My dear Friend," New Bern, NC, April 20, 1865, Edward W. Kinsley Papers, Duke; Anna M. Ferris diary, April 16, 1865, Ferris Family Papers, Friends Historical Library, Swarthmore College, Swarthmore, PA; Minute Book, April 18, 1865, in "Mourning Observance for Abraham Lincoln by the B'nai B'rith Lodge of Marysville, California," *Western States Jewish Historical Quarterly* 1 (1967), 172.

17 Abby Goodnough, "Fauci Expects Americans Could Still Need to Wear Face Masks in 2022," *New York Times*, February 21, 2021. For a sampling of preserved COVID-19 experiences, see: "History Now: The Pandemic Diaries Project," New York Public Library, accessed March 30, 2022, https://www.nypl.org/pandemic-diaries; COVID University New York (CVNY), podcast, mp3 audio, accessed March 30, 2022, https://www.gothamcenter.org/covid-university-new-york; "Tell Your Story—California In the Time of COVID-19," California Historical Society, San Francisco, accessed March 30, 2022, https://californiahistoricalsociety.org/initiatives/tell-your-story-california-during-the-time-of-covid-19/; The Coronavirus Days: Archive Your Story, Indiana University-Bloomington, August 24, 2020, https://libraries.indiana.edu/coronavirus-days-archive-story accessed March 30, 2022; "Witness to History: What Are Your COVID-19 Experiences?" Massachusetts Historical Society, Boston, accessed March 30, 2022, https://www.masshist.org/projects/covid/index.php; "A Journal of the Plague Year," accessed March 30, 2022, https://covid-19archive.org/s/archive/page/welcome; Covid Collections Project, Initiative for Critical Disaster Studies, NYU Gallatin School of Individualized Study, accessed March 30, 2022, https://wp.nyu.edu/disasters/covid-collections-project/; The Zip Code Memory Project, accessed March 30, 2022, https://zcmp.org/.

18 George White diaries and account books, April 16, 1865, vol. 32, Historical and Special Collection, Harvard Law School Library, Harvard University, Cambridge, MA; Elizabeth Blackwell to Barbara Bodichon, New York, NY, May 23, 1865, box 1, Blackwell Letters, Rare Book and Manuscript Library, Columbia University, New York, NY; Stephen Greenleaf Bulfinch diary, April 16, 1865, vol. 2, Bulfinch Family Papers, MHS.

19 "Assassination and Funeral of President Lincoln," scrapbook arranged by Candace Crawford Carrington for her son Edward Carrington Jr., finished February 10, 1871, in Charles Woodberry McLellan Collection of Lincolniana, JHL. And see Ellen Gruber Garvey, *Writing with Scissors: American Scrapbooks from the Civil War to the Harlem Renaissance* (New York: Oxford University Press, 2013), 87–130; and Ellen Gruber Garvey,

"Scrapbooking the Civil War," *New York Times*, Opinionator (blog), November 13, 2012.

20 On Mary Lincoln, see Catherine Clinton, *Mrs. Lincoln: A Life* (New York: Harper Collins, 2009), 248–70; Jean H. Baker, *Mary Todd Lincoln: A Biography* (New York: Norton, 1987), 244–54; on Henry Rathbone, see Mark E. Neely Jr., *The Abraham Lincoln Encyclopedia* (New York: McGraw Hill, 1982), 256–57; R. Gerald McMurtry, "Major Rathbone and Miss Harris: Guests of the Lincolns in the Ford's Theatre Box," *Lincoln Lore* 1602 (August 1971), 1–3; Martha Thomas, "Synopsis of Record," case #3245, entry 66, July 16, 1872, box 11, stack area 12 W 2 A, RG 418, Records of Saint Elizabeths Hospital, NARA (I thank Ashley Bowen-Murphy for transcribing and sharing this document).

21 George P. Rawick, ed., *The American Slave: A Composite Autobiography*, 18 vols.; supplement ser. 1, 12 vols.; supplement ser. 2, 10 vols. (Westport, CT: Greenwood, 1972–79), suppl. 2, vol. 4, part 3: 1271; suppl. 1, vol. 1: 257; vol. 16, part 4: 72.

22 Henry B. James diary, April 15, 20, May 9, 13, 1865, James Papers, MHS; James Thomas Ward diary, May 1, 1865, Ward Papers, LC.

23 Abial H. Edwards to Anna L. Conant, Darlington, SC., September 15, 1865, and Abial H. Edwards to Anna L. Conant, Darlington, SC, October 18, 1865, in Beverly Hayes Kallgren and James L. Crouthamel, eds., *"Dear Friend Anna": The Civil War Letters of a Common Soldier from Maine* (Orono: University of Maine Press, 1992), 137, 138.

Chapter 7: COVID-19

1 Lazaro Gamio, "The Workers Who Face the Greatest Coronavirus Risk," *New York Times*, March 15, 2020; Richard A. Oppel Jr. et al., "The Fullest Look Yet at the Racial Inequity of Coronavirus," *New York Times*, July 5, 2020.

2 Tera W. Hunter, *To 'Joy My Freedom: Southern Black Women's Lives and Labors After the Civil War* (Cambridge: Harvard University Press, 1997), 50.

3 Stuart Galishoff, "Germs Know No Color Line: Black Health and Public Policy in Atlanta, 1900–1918," *Journal of the History of Medicine and Allied Sciences* 40, no. 1 (January 1985), 22–41.

4 "Coronavirus," Indian Health Service, accessed October 25, 2021, https://www.ihs.gov/coronavirus/.

5 Miriam Jordan and Caitlin Dickerson, "Poultry Worker's Death Highlights Spread of Coronavirus in Meat Plants," *New York Times*, April 9, 2020.

6 Sarah Westwood and Sunlen Serfaty, "HHS Secretary Tells Lawmakers Lifestyles of Meat-Processing Plant Employees Worsened Covid-19 Outbreak," *CNN*, May 7, 2020; Michelle A. Waltenburg et al., "Update: COVID-19 among Workers in Meat and Poultry Processing Facilities— United States, April–May 2020," Morbidity and Mortality Weekly

Report (MMWR) 69, no. 27, 887–92, July 10, 2020, https://www.cdc.gov/mmwr/volumes/69/wr/mm6927e2.htm.

7   Kelly M. Hoffman et al., "Racial Bias in Pain Assessment and Treatment Recommendations, and False Beliefs about Biological Differences between Blacks And Whites," *Proceedings of the National Academy of Sciences of the United States of America* 113, no. 16 (2016): 4296–301.

Chapter 8: From the Colfax Massacre to the 2020 Election

1   Tom Dreisbach and Meg Anderson, "Nearly 1 In 5 Defendants in Capitol Riot Cases Served in the Military," *NPR*, January 21, 2021.

2   Gwendolyn Midlo Hall, *Haunted by Slavery: A Southern White Woman in the Freedom Struggle* (New York: Haymarket, 2020).

3   LeeAnna Keith, *The Colfax Massacre: The Untold Story of Black Power, White Terror, and the Death of Reconstruction* (Oxford: Oxford University Press, 2008); also see W. E. B. Du Bois, *Black Reconstruction in America, 1860–1880* (1935; repr., New York: Free Press, 1991); United States v. Cruikshank et al., 92 U.S. 542 (1876).

4   Eric Foner, *Reconstruction: America's Unfinished Revolution, 1863–1877* (New York: Harper and Row, 1988), 437; also see Donna A. Barnes and Catherine Connolly, "Repression, the Judicial System, and Political Opportunities for Civil Rights Advocacy during Reconstruction," *The Sociological Quarterly* 40, no. 2 (1999): 327–45; James K. Hogue, "The 1873 Battle of Colfax: Paramilitarism and Counterrevolution in Louisiana," paper presented at the Southern Historical Association, November 6, 1997; Joel M. Sipress, "From the Barrel of a Gun: The Politics of Murder in Grant Parish," *Louisiana History: The Journal of the Louisiana Historical Association* 42, no. 3 (2001): 303–21; Ivory A. Toldson, "Black History is the First Weapon against White Supremacy," *Journal of Negro Education* 88, no. 4 (2019): 125–26.

5   Enrico Dal Lago, *Civil War and Agrarian Unrest: The Confederate South and Southern Italy* (New York: Cambridge University Press, 2018), 375.

6   G. P. Whittington, "Concerning the Loyalty of Slaves in North Louisiana in 1863: Letters from John H. Ransdell to Gov. Thomas O. Moore dated 1863," *Louisiana Historical Quarterly* 14, no. 4 (October 1931): 487–502.

7   Alan W. Trelease, *White Terror: The Ku Klux Klan Conspiracy and Southern Reconstruction*, (1979; repr., Baton Rouge: Louisiana State University Press, 1995), 103–9; also see Joe Gray Taylor, *Louisiana Reconstructed, 1863–1877* (Baton Rouge: Louisiana State University Press, 1974), 63, 138–39.

8   Mark L. Bradley, *The Army and Reconstruction, 1865–1877* (Washington, DC: The Center for Military History, 2015), 14; David Vergun, "150 Years Ago: Army Takes on Peacekeeping Duties In Post-Civil War South," Army.mil, August 4, 2015, https://www.army.mil/article/153230/150_years_ago_army_takes_on_peacekeeping_duties_in_post_civil_war_south.

9   Taylor, *Louisiana Reconstructed*, 10, 11, 67, 68, 254–91.

10 Trelease, *White Terror*, 93.

11   Report of Special Committee to Investigate Conditions in the South, 2/23/1875, 43rd Congress, 2nd Session, Report No. 261, 10.

12   Taylor, *Louisiana Reconstructed*, 168; Trelease, *White Terror*, xliii; Taylor, 92, 94, 421.

13   "'Unite the Right' Rally Could Be Largest White Supremacist Gathering in a Decade," Anti-Defamation League, August 7, 2017, https://www. adl.org/blog/unite-the-right-rally-could-be-largest-white-supremacist-gathering-in-a-decade.

14   Simon Ostrovsky, "Extremism in the Ranks: Some at the January 6 Capitol Riot Were Police, Active Military," *PBS News Hour*, March 13, 2021; and Michael Biesecker, Jake Bleiberg, and James LaPorta, "Capitol Rioters Included Highly Trained Ex-Military and Cops," Associated Press, January 15, 2021; also see Kathleen Belew, *Bring the War Home: The White Power Movement and Paramilitary America* (Cambridge: Harvard University Press, 2018).

15   LeeAnna Keith, *The Colfax Massacre; Foner, Reconstruction; James K. Hogue, Uncivil War: Five New Orleans Street Battle and the Rise and Fall of Radical Reconstruction* (Baton Rouge: Louisiana State University Press, 2006); Charles Lane, *The Day Freedom Died: The Colfax Massacre, the Supreme Court, and the Betrayal of Reconstruction* (New York: Henry Holt, 2008); also see Steven Hahn, *A Nation Under Our Feet: Black Political Struggles in the Rural South from Slavery to the Great Migration* (Cambridge: Harvard University Press, 2003), 292–96.

16   "Scalawag" was a derogatory term for white southern Republicans who banded together with Blacks during Reconstruction.

17   Sipress, "From the Barrel of a Gun," 308–11.

18   Lane, *The Day Freedom Died*, 13; Barnes and Connolly, "Repression, the Judicial System, and Political Opportunities," 331–33.

19   Keith, *The Colfax Massacre*; Hogue, *Uncivil War*, 2.

20   Hogue, *Uncivil War*, 2.

21   Hogue, "The 1873 Battle of Colfax"; Sipress, "From the Barrel of a Gun," 303–4.

22   Barnes and Connolly, "Repression, the Judicial System, and Political Opportunities," 331–33; Sipress, "From the Barrel of a Gun," 304.

23   Ella Lena Boyd Grant Lieux et al., *Descendants of Richard Grant of Louisiana, 1818–1885* (Madison: University of Wisconsin Press, 1993).

24   *Louisiana Historical Quarterly*, vol. 13 (New Orleans: Louisiana Historical Society, 1930), 407.

25   W. E. B. Du Bois, "Behold the Land," closing address to the Southern Youth Legislature in Columbia, South Carolina, on October 20, 1946, https://www.blackpast.org/african-american-history/1946-w-e-b-dubois-behold-land/.

Chapter 9: Man of Means by No Means

This essay is drawn from the author's personal letters and diary during the pandemic; the names of certain people and places have been changed for privacy reasons. This essay is dedicated to EWL, my pandemic pen pal, who asked me to keep writing.

1   Kevin Quealy, "The Richest Neighborhoods Emptied Out Most As Coronavirus Hit New York City," *New York Times*, May 15, 2020; Hannah Kanik, "More People Moved out of New Jersey Than Any Other State in 2020," *Philly Voice*, January 9, 2021.

2   Joan Didion, "Goodbye To All That," in *Slouching Towards Bethlehem* (New York: Farrar, Straus and Giroux, 1968).

3   Clayton Guse, "MTA Reported First COVID Death a Year Ago—and at Least 156 Transit Workers Have Died since as Disease Ravaged Agency," *New York Daily News*, March 26, 2021.

4   Donald Trump (@realDonaldTrump), "LIBERATE VIRGINIA, and save your great 2nd Amendment. It is under siege!" Twitter, April 17, 2020, https://twitter.com/realDonaldTrump/status/1251169987110330372; Aaron Rupar, "Trump's Dangerous "LIBERATE" Tweets Represent the Views of a Small Minority—Don't Let Fox News and the President Fool You," *Vox*, April 17, 2020; Lauren Egan, "Trump Says Some State Orders Are 'Too Tough', Stands By 'LIBERATE' Tweets Encouraging Anti-Lockdown Groups," *NBC News*, April 17, 2020; Charlie Sykes, "Did Trump and Kushner Ignore Blue State COVID-19 Testing as Deaths Spiked?" *NBC News*, August 4, 2020.

5   Arielle Mitropoulos and Mariya Moseley, "Beloved Brooklyn Teacher, 30, Dies of Coronavirus after She Was Twice Denied a COVID-19 Test," *ABC News*, April 28, 2020.

6   "Driver Charged in Biscayne Blvd Hit & Run," *4CBS Miami*, July 26, 2012.

7   Richard Wightman Fox, *Lincoln's Body: A Cultural History* (New York: Norton, 2015).

8   David K. Nartonis, "The Rise of 19th-Century American Spiritualism, 1854–1873," *Journal for the Scientific Study of Religion* (2010): 361.

9   Kimberly N. Kutz, "Chief of a Nation of Ghosts: Images of Abraham Lincoln's Spirit in the Immediate Post-Civil War Period," *Journal of American Culture* 36, no. 2 (2013): 112; Jean H. Baker, "Only a Slight Veil Separates Us: Mary Lincoln's Solace in Spiritualism," *Ford's Theatre* (blog), January 15, 2015, https://www.fords.org/blog/post/only-a-slight-veil-separates-us-mary-lincoln-s-solace-in-spiritualism/.

10   Jean H. Baker, *Mary Todd Lincoln: A Biography* (New York: Norton, 1987), 220; Fox, *Lincoln's Body: A Cultural History*.

11   Ann Braude, "Radical Spirits: Spiritualism and Women's Rights in Nineteenth-Century America," *Nova Religio: The Journal of Alternative and Emergent Religions* 8, no. 3 (2005): 132–33.

12   Amy DeFalco Lippert, *Consuming Identities: Visual Culture in Nineteenth-
      Century San Francisco* (New York: Oxford University Press, 2018); David
      M. Henkin, *The Postal Age: The Emergence of Modern Communications in
      Nineteenth-Century America* (Chicago: University of Chicago Press, 2007).
13   Simone Natale, *Supernatural Entertainments: Victorian Spiritualism and the
      Rise of Modern Media Culture* (University Park, PA: Penn State University
      Press, 2016).
14   Joel Porte, ed., *Emerson in His Journals* (Cambridge, MA: Belknap Press,
      1982).

Chapter 10: The Afterlife of Black Political Radicalism

1   W. E. B. Du Bois, *The Souls of Black Folk* (Chicago: A. C. McClurg, 1903).
2   Graham Rapier, "How a Small Georgia City Far from New York Became
      One of the Worst Coronavirus Hotspots in the Country," *Business Insider*,
      April 7, 2020; Nicole Chavez, Angela Barajas and Dianne Gallagher,
      "Updated: 'It Was Like A Domino Effect': How Two Funerals Helped Turn
      Albany Into A Hotspot For Coronavirus," *CBS Atlanta*, April 3, 2020.
3   "How George Floyd Died, And What Happened Next" *New York Times*,
      May 25, 2021.
4   Ryan W. Miller, "Charges Dismissed against Amy Cooper, White Woman
      Who Called 911 on Black Bird-Watcher," *USA Today*, February 16, 2021.
      See also Stephanie E. Jones-Rogers, *They Were Her Property: White Women
      as Slave Owners in the American South* (New Haven: Yale University Press,
      2019); Frank B. Wilderson III offers a fascinating discussion of white
      women and racial slavery through an analysis of the film *Twelve Years a
      Slave* in *Afropessimism* (New York: Liveright, 2020).
5   Peniel E. Joseph, *Waiting 'Til the Midnight Hour: A Narrative History of Black
      Power in America* (New York: Henry Holt, 2006); Joshua Bloom and Waldo
      E. Martin Jr., *Black Against Empire: The History and Politics of the Black Panther
      Party* (Oakland: University of California Press, 2013); Jama Lazerow and
      Yohuru Williams, eds., *In Search of the Black Panther Party: New Perspectives on
      a Revolutionary Movement* (Durham: Duke University Press, 2006); Peniel E.
      Joseph, "Black Liberation Without Apology: Rethinking the Black Power
      Movement," *Black Scholar* 31, nos. 3–4, (2001): 2–17.
6   Joseph, *Waiting 'Til the Midnight Hour*; Peniel E. Joseph, ed., *The Black
      Power Movement: Rethinking the Civil Rights-Black Power Era* (New York:
      Routledge, 2006); Peniel E. Joseph, ed., *Neighborhood Rebels: Black
      Power at the Local Level* (New York: Palgrave Macmillan, 2010); Peniel E.
      Joseph, "The Black Power Movement: A State of the Field," *The Journal of
      American History* 96 (2009): 751–76; Peniel E. Joseph, "The Black Power
      Movement, Democracy, and America in the King Years," *The American
      Historical Review* 114 (2009): 1001–16; Peniel E. Joseph, "Rethinking the
      Black Power Era," *The Journal of Urban History* 75 (2009): 707–16; Peniel
      E. Joseph, ed., "Reinterpreting the Black Power Movement," *Magazine of
      History* 22 (July 2008).

7   Tera W. Hunter, *Bound in Wedlock: Slave and Free Black Marriage in the Nineteenth Century* (Cambridge, MA: Belknap Press, 2017); Carol Anderson, *White Rage: The Unspoken Truth of Our Racial Divide* (New York: Bloomsbury, 2016).

8   W. E. B. Du Bois, *Black Reconstruction: An Essay Toward a History of the Part Which Black Folk Played in the Attempt to Reconstruct Democracy in America, 1860–1880* (New York: Harcourt, Brace and Company, 1935); Jelani M. Favors, *Shelter in A Time of Storm: How Black Colleges Fostered Generations of Leadership and Activism* (Chapel Hill: University of North Carolina Press, 2019); David Zucchino, *Wilmington's Lie: The Murderous Coup of 1898 and the Rise of White Supremacy* (New York: Grove Press, 2020).

9   John Dittmer, *Local People: The Struggle for Civil Rights in Mississippi* (Urbana: University of Illinois Press, 1994); Manning Marable, *Race, Reform, and Rebellion: The Second Reconstruction and Beyond in Black America, 1945–2006*, 3rd ed. (Jackson: University of Mississippi Press, 2007); Barbara Ransby, *Ella Baker and the Black Freedom Movement: A Radical Democratic Vision* (Chapel Hill: University of North Carolina Press, 2003); Rod Bush, *We are Not What We Seem: Black Nationalism and Class Struggle in the American Century* (New York: New York University Press, 1999); Adam Fairclough, *To Redeem the Soul of America: The Southern Christian Leadership Conference and Martin Luther King, Jr.* (Athens: University of Georgia Press, 1987); Taylor Branch, *Parting the Waters: America in the King Years, 1954–1963* (New York: Simon and Schuster, 1988); Tommie Shelby and Brandon M. Terry, eds., *To Shape a New World: Essays on the Political Philosophy of Martin Luther King, Jr.* (Cambridge, MA: Belknap Press, 2018).

10 Peniel E. Joseph, *The Sword and the Shield: The Revolutionary Lives of Malcolm X and Martin Luther King Jr.* (New York: Basic Books, 2020).

11 Joseph, *The Sword and the Shield*.

12 See the Movement for Black Lives, https://m4bl.org. See also Beth E. Richie, *Arrested Justice: Black Women, Violence, and America's Prison Nation* (New York: New York University Press, 2012); Joy James, ed., *Warfare in the American Homeland: Policing and Prison in a Penal Democracy* (Durham: Duke University Press, 2007); Angela J. Davis, ed., *Policing the Black Man* (New York: Pantheon Books, 2017); Sarah Haley, *No Mercy Here: Gender, Punishment, and the Making of Jim Crow Modernity* (Chapel Hill: University of North Carolina Press, 2016); Talitha L. LeFlouria, *Chained in Silence: Black Women and Convict Labor in the New South* (Chapel Hill: University of North Carolina Press, 2015).

13 See Black Lives Matter, accessed March 30, 2022, https://blacklivesmatter.com/herstory/; Christopher J. Lebron, *The Making of Black Lives Matter: A Brief History of an Idea* (New York: Oxford University Press, 2017); See also Cedric Robinson, *Black Marxism: The Making of the Black Radical Tradition* (Chapel Hill: University of North Carolina Press, 2000); Derrick Bell, *Faces at the Bottom of the Well: The Permanence of Racism* (New York: Basic Books, 1992).

14   Ta-Nehisi Coates, "The Life Breonna Taylor Lived, in the Words of Her Mother," *Vanity Fair*, August 24, 2020.

15   Manning Marable, *How Capitalism Underdeveloped Black America* (Boston: South End Press, 1983); Dayo F. Gore, Jeanne Theoharis, and Komozi Woodard, eds., *Want To Start a Revolution?: Radical Women in the Black Freedom Struggle* (New York: New York University Press, 2009); Robin D. G. Kelley, *Hammer and Hoe: Alabama Communists During the Great Depression* (Chapel Hill: University of North Carolina Press, 1990); Michael O. West, William G. Martin, and Fanon Che Wilkins, eds., *From Toussaint to Tupac: The Black International since the Age of Revolution* (Chapel Hill: University of North Carolina Press, 2009); Dayo Gore, *Radicalism at the Crossroads: African American Women Activists in the Cold War* (New York: New York University Press, 2011); Michael C. Dawson, *Black Visions: The Roots of Contemporary African-American Political Thought* (Chicago: The University of Chicago Press, 2001); Rhonda Y. Williams, *Concrete Demands: The Search for Black Power in the 20th Century* (New York: Routledge, 2015); Cornel West, *Democracy Matters: Winning the Fight Against Imperialism* (New York: The Penguin Press, 2004) Vincent Brown, *Tacky's Revolt: The Story of An Atlantic Slave War* (Cambridge: Harvard University Press, 2020); Imani Perry, *Looking for Lorraine: The Radiant and Radical Life of Lorraine Hansberry* (Boston: Beacon Press, 2018); Eddie S. Glaude Jr., *Begin Again: James Baldwin's America and Its Urgent Lessons for Our Own* (New York: Crown, 2020); Michael Eric Dyson, *Long Time Coming: Reckoning with Race in America* (New York: St. Martin's Press, 2020); Daphne A. Brooks, *Liner Notes for the Revolution: The Intellectual Life of Black Feminist Sound* (Cambridge: Harvard University Press, 2021).

16   Kimberlé Williams Crenshaw, "Mapping the Margins: Intersectionality, Identity Politics, and Violence Against Women of Color," in *The Public Nature of Private Violence: The Discovery of Domestic Abuse*, eds. Martha Albertson Fineman and Roxanne Mykitiuk (New York: Routledge, 1994), and Kimberlé Williams Crenshaw, Luke Charles Harris, Daniel Martinez HoSang and George Lipsitz, eds., *Seeing Race Again: Countering Colorblindness across the Disciplines* (Oakland: The University of California Press, 2019).

17   Mariame Kaba, *We Do This Till We Free Us: Abolitionist Organizing and Transforming Justice* (Chicago: Haymarket Books, 2021); Alicia Garza, *The Purpose of Power: How We Come Together When We Fall Apart* (New York: One World, 2020); Angela Y. Davis, *The Meaning of Freedom and Other Difficult Dialogues* (San Francisco: City Lights Books, 2012); Williams J. Barber II with Jonathan Wilson-Hartgrove, *The Third Reconstruction: How A Moral Movement is Overcoming the Politics of Division and Fear* (Boston: Beacon Press, 2016); Sandra E. Weissinger, Dwayne A. Mack, and Elwood Watson, eds., *Violence Against Black Bodies: An Intersectional Analysis of How Black Lives Continue to Matter* (New York: Routledge, 2017); George Yancy, *On Race: Thirty-Four Conversations in a Time of Crisis* (New York: Oxford

University Press, 2017); Adam Serwer, *The Cruelty is the Point: The Past, Present, and Future of Trump's America* (New York: One World, 2021).

18 Angela Y. Davis, *Are Prisons Obsolete?* (New York: Seven Stories Press, 2003); Du Bois, *Black Reconstruction*. See also Clint Smith, *How the Word is Passed: A Reckoning with the History of Slavery Across America* (New York: Little Brown and Company, 2021) and Ana Lucia Araujo, *Slavery in the Age of Memory: Engaging the Past* (London: Bloomsbury, 2021).

19 Larry Buchanan, Quoctrung Bui and Jugal K. Patel, "Black Lives Matter May Be The Largest Movement in U.S. History," *New York Times*, July 3, 2020; Peniel E. Joseph, "How Black Lives Matter Transformed the Fourth of July," *CNN*, July 2, 2020; and "What Black Children Will Learn from Floyd's Death," *CNN*, June 2, 2020.

20 Maya King, "How Stacey Abrams and Her Band of Believers Turned Georgia Blue," *Politico*, November 8, 2020; Reid J. Epstein and Astead W. Herndon, "The 10-Year Stacey Abrams Project to Flip Georgia Has Come to Fruition," *New York Times*, January 6, 2021.

21 Chandler Davidson and Bernard Grofman, eds., *Quiet Revolution in the South: The Impact of the Voting Rights Act, 1965–1990* (Princeton: Princeton University Press, 1994); Laughlin McDonald, "An Aristocracy of Voters: The Disfranchisement of Blacks in South Carolina," *South Carolina Law Review* 37, no. 4, (1986); Jones, *Vanguard*; Paula Giddings, *When and Where I Enter: The Impact of Black Women on Race and Sex in America* (New York: Bantam, 1984); Deborah Gray White, *Too Heavy a Load: Black Women in Defense of Themselves, 1894–1994* (New York: Norton, 1999); Bevery Guy-Sheftall, ed., *Words of Fire: An Anthology of African-American Feminist Thought* (New York: The New Press, 1995); Ashley D. Farmer, *Remaking Black Power: How Black Women Transformed an Era* (Chapel Hill: University of North Carolina Press, 2017); Keisha N. Blaine, *Set the World on Fire. Black Nationalist Women and the Global Struggle for Freedom* (Philadelphia: University of Pennsylvania Press, 2018); Mia Bay, Farah J. Griffin, Martha S. Jones, and Barbara D. Savage, eds., *Toward an Intellectual History of Black Women* (Chapel Hill: The University of North Carolina Press, 2015); Diana Ramey Berry and Kali Nicole Gross, *A Black Woman's History of the United States* (Boston: Beacon Press, 2020).

22 Ta-Nehisi Coates, *We Were Eight Years in Power: An American Tragedy* (New York: One World, 2017).

23 Conor Friedersdorf, "When Kamala Was a Top Cop," *Atlantic*, August 25, 2019.

24 Rhae Lynn Barnes and Keri Leigh Merritt, "A Confederate Flag at the Capitol Summons America's Demons," *CNN*, January 7, 2021.

25 "The 1619 Project," *New York Times Magazine*, August 14, 2019. See also Ibram X. Kendi and Keisha N. Blain, eds., *Four Hundred Souls: A Community History of African America, 1619–2019* (New York: One World, 2021); Isabel Wilkerson, *Caste: The Origins of Our Discontents* (New York: Random House, 2020).

26 Joseph, *The Sword and the Shield.*

27 Ray Sanchez and Eric Levenson, "Derek Chauvin Sentenced to 22.5 Years in Death of George Floyd," *CNN*, June 25, 2021.

28 C. L. R. James, *The Black Jacobins: Toussaint L'Ouverture and the San Domingo Revolution* (New York: Vintage Books, 1963). See also Michel-Rolph Trouillot, *Silencing the Past: Power and the Production of History* (Boston: Beacon Press, 2015); Laurent Dubois, *Haiti: The Aftershocks of History* (New York: Metropolitan Books, 2012); Sudhir Hazareesingh, *Black Spartacus: The Epic Life of Toussaint Louverture* (New York: Farrar, Straus and Giroux, 2020).

29 Anushka Patil, "How a March for Black Trans Lives Became a Huge Event," *New York Times*, June 15, 2020.

Chapter 11: The Grief That Came before the Grief

I am grateful to Lisa Levenstein, Nancy MacLean, Della Pollock, my sister Jeanne Grimm, and the editors of this volume for their comments and encouragement.

1 Margaret Renkl, "The Bomb That Struck the Heart of Nashville," *New York Times*, December 30, 2020.

2 Jacquelyn Dowd Hall, "Last Words," *Journal of American History* 89 (June 2002): 30–36; and "The Good Fight," in *Mothers and Strangers: Essays on Motherhood from the New South*, eds. Samia Serageldin and Lee Smith (Chapel Hill: University of North Carolina Press, 2019), 120–26.

3 That loan was made possible by the National Defense Education Act of 1958, a Cold War response to the space race with the Soviet Union. I, of course, had no idea that the same global assertion of American power that benefited me helped to set off a Red Scare that ruined lives and distorted domestic political culture.

4 Virginia Mae (Jinx) Dowd to Jacquelyn Jan Dowd, Feb. 26, [1963], author's personal papers.

5 Virginia Mae (Jinx) Dowd to Jacquelyn Jan Dowd, [1964], author's personal papers.

6 Mary Oliver, "The Summer Day," *New and Selected Poems* (Boston: Beacon Press, 1992).

Chapter 12: An Uncountable Casualty

I am grateful to Deborah Dinner and Jacqueline Wernimont for helpful comments on this essay, and to the editors of this volume, whose vision enabled me to write it.

1 "Coronavirus in the U.S.: Latest Map and Case Count," *New York Times*, March 14, 2021. "Coronavirus World Map: Tracking the Global Outbreak," *New York Times*, March 14, 2021.

2 On the management of self-presentation, see Irving Goffman, *The Presentation of Self in Everyday Life* (New York: Doubleday, 1959). Extensive treatment of numbers and social life appears in Gary Urton, *The Social*

Life of Numbers: A Quechua Ontology of Numbers and Philosophy of Arithmetic (with Primitivo Nina Llanos) (Austin: University of Texas Press, 2010).

3   Charles Dickens, *A Christmas Carol* (London: Chapman and Hall, 1843).

4   Jacqueline Wernimont, *Numbered Lives: Life and Death in Quantum Media* (Cambridge: MIT Press, 2018), 39–40.

5   Marilyn B. Young, "Counting the Bodies in Vietnam," in *Making the Forever War: Marilyn B. Young on the Culture and Politics of American Militarism*, Mark Bradley and Mary L. Dudziak, eds. (Amherst: University of Massachusetts Press, 2021), 108–19.

6   David Zucchino, "U.S. Conducts Drone Strike in Kabul and Winds Down Airlift as Deadline Nears," *New York Times*, August 29, 2021. On the concept of "collateral damage," see Helen M. Kinsella, *The Image before the Weapon: A Critical History of the Distinction between Combatant and Civilian* (Ithaca: Cornell University Press, 2011).

7   Matthieu Aikins and Alissa J. Rubin, "First Tied to ISIS, Then to U.S.: Family in Drone Strike Is Tarnished Twice," *New York Times*, September 21, 2021.

8   Mary L. Dudziak, "Foreword: How 9/11 Made 'History,'" *OAH Magazine of History* 25, no. 3 (2011): 5–7.

9   Marilyn B. Young, "Ground Zero: Enduring War," in *September 11 in History: A Watershed Moment?* ed. Mary L. Dudziak (Durham: Duke University Press, 2003), 10–34.

10 Thomas W. Laqueur, *The Work of the Dead: A Cultural History of Mortal Remains* (Princeton: Princeton University Press, 2015).

11 Brenda Gayle Plummer, "Civil Rights Has Always Been a Global Movement: How Allies Abroad Help the Fight Against Racism at Home," *Foreign Affairs*, June 19, 2020.

12 Christian Paz, "All the President's Lies About the Coronavirus," *Atlantic*, November 2, 2020.

13 Jada Yuan, "Burials on Hart Island, where New York's Unclaimed Lie in Mass Graves, Have Risen Fivefold," *Washington Post*, April 16, 2020; Christopher Robbins, "NYPD Seizes Drone of Photojournalist Documenting Mass Burials on Hart Island," *Gothamist*, April 17, 2020.

14 George H. Roeder Jr., *The Censored War: American Visual Experience During World War Two* (New Haven: Yale University Press, 1995).

15 "Update: COVID-19 among Workers in Meat and Poultry Processing Facilities—United States, April–May 2020," Morbidity and Mortality Weekly Report, Centers for Disease Control, July 10, 2020, https://www.cdc.gov/mmwr/volumes/69/wr/mm6927e2.htm.

16 Covid's Hidden Toll, *Frontline PBS*, July 21, 2020.

17 Timothy Pachirat, *Every Twelve Seconds: Industrialized Slaughter and the Politics of Sight* (New Haven: Yale University Press, 2011), 251.

18 This goes beyond food production, and includes manufacture of textiles, electronics, and other goods the privileged rely on every day. See, for example, Chelsey Sanchez, "A Century Later, Garment Workers Still Face

the Unfair Labor Conditions That Sparked International Women's Day," *Harper's Bazaar*, March 8, 2021; Richard Bilton, "Apple 'Failing to Protect Chinese Factory Workers,'" *BBC News*, December 14, 2018.

19　Timothy B. Tyson, *The Blood of Emmett Till* (New York: Simon and Schuster, 2017).

Chapter 13: Sometimes I Feel Like a Motherless Child

1　"Sometimes I Feel Like a Motherless Child" is a traditional Black spiritual dating back to the days of slavery. It was commonly sung at marches during the Civil Rights Movement of the 1950s and 1960s and was even performed at Woodstock. The "sometimes" qualifier offers a note of lingering hope during a time of immense pain.

2　Claude Brown, *Man Child in the Promised Land* (New York: Touchstone, 1965); Malcolm X with Alex Haley, *The Autobiography of Malcolm X* (New York: Grove Press, 1965); John Howard Griffin, *Black Like Me* (New York: Houghton-Mifflin, 1961); Martin Luther King Jr., *Stride Toward Freedom: The Montgomery Story* (New York: Harper & Brothers, 1958).

Chapter 14: Losing My Starbucks Table

1　Ula Y. Taylor, "The Death of Dry Tears," in *Telling Histories: Black Women Historians in the Ivory Tower*, ed. Deborah Gray White (Chapel Hill: University of North Carolina Press, 2008), 172–81.

2　See "Number of Starbucks Worldwide 2022/2023: Facts, Statistics, and Trends," Finances Online, accessed March 30, 2022, https://financesonline.com/number-of-starbucks-worldwide/.

3　See "Starbucks Net Worth 2006–2021/SBUX," Macrotrends, accessed March 30, 2022, https://www.macrotrends.net/stocks/charts/SBUX/starbucks/net-worth.

4　Mona Holmes, "Magic Johnson Starbucks Closes After Two Decades in Ladera Heights," *Eater Los Angeles*, October 23, 2018.

5　Kemberley Williams, "Covid-19 Has Had a Disproportionate Financial Impact on Black Small Business," *Forbes Advisor*, June 3, 2021.

6　Catherine Ho, "Five Bay Area Counties to Enact Strict Stay-At-Home Order ahead of State Edict, Starting Sunday," *Stamford Advocate*, December 4, 2020.

7　Misty L. Heggeness, Jason Fields, Yazmin A. Garcia Trejo, and Anthony Schulzetenberg, "Moms, Work, and the Pandemic: Tracking Job Losses for Mothers of School-Age Children During a Health Crisis," United States Census Bureau, March 3, 2021, https://www.census.gov/library/stories/2021/03/moms-work-and-the-pandemic.html.

8　Monica Hesse, "The Pandemic Didn't Create Working Moms' Struggle: But It Made It Impossible to Ignore," *Washington Post*, July 8, 2021.

9　Korin Miller, "'Schedules Are out the Window': How Frontline Mom's Have Coped with Parenting During a Pandemic," *Yahoo! Life*, March 26, 2021.

10 Public Health Ontario, "Synopsis: COVID-19 What We Know So Far
    About . . . Asymptomatic Infection and Asymptomatic Transmission,"
    May 22, 2020, https://www.publichealthontario.ca/-/media/documents/
    ncov/what-we-know-jan-30-2020.pdf?la=en.

11 Melissa Jenco, "Study: COVID-19 Pandemic Exacerbated Hardships for
    Low-Income, Minority Families," *American Academy of Pediatrics*, June 3,
    2020.

12 Kelly Glass, "Black Families Were Hit Hard by the Pandemic. The Effects
    on Children May Be Lasting," *New York Times*, June 29, 2020.

13 Alexis Sobel Fitts, "The Psychology of Living in Small Spaces,"
    Undark, May 31, 2016, https://undark.org/2016/05/31/
    psychology-living-small-spaces/.

14 Molly M. McLay, "When 'Shelter-in-Place' Isn't Shelter That's Safe: A
    Rapid Analysis of Domestic Violence Cases during Covid-19 Pandemic
    and Stay-at-Home Orders," *Journal of Family Violence* (2021): 1–10.
    Amalesh Sharma and Sourav Bikash Borah, "Covid-19 and Domestic
    Violence: An Indirect Path to Social and Economic Crisis," *Journal of
    Family Violence* (2020): 1–7.

15 Congressman Don Beyer, United States Government Joint
    Economic Committee, October 14, 2020, https://www.
    jec.senate.gov/public/index.cfm/democrats/2020/10/
    covid-19-economic-pressure-and-americans-mental-health.

16 During the COVID-19 pandemic I have watched a lot of Netflix shows,
    including *Buried by the Bernards*. Office Manager Debbie Bernard is my
    favorite "reality show" subject: in the season one (2021) episode "Daddy
    Daughter Day," she said, "If gossip was a sport, we would go pro."

17 Tatiana Sanchez, "Coronavirus Cases and Deaths Soared in Nursing
    Homes Across California. Here's Why," *San Francisco Chronicle*, November
    30, 2020.

Chapter 15: Buried History

1 "Rev. Donald S. Kelley, August 9, 1937–February 29, 2020," obituary,
   accessed March 30, 2022, https://www.lopesfuneralhome.com/obituary/
   RevDonald-Kelley.

2 Joe Hernandez, "Read this Powerful Statement from Darnella Frazier,
   Who Filmed George Floyd's Murder," *NPR*, May 26, 2021.

3 These events have been well documented. See, for example,
   CampaignJustice.org, *Say Their Names: 101 Black Unarmed Women, Men
   and Children Killed by Law Enforcement* (Campaign Justice, 2020), 11–15,
   143–48, 459–70; Derecka Purnell, *Becoming Abolitionists: Police, Protests,
   and the Pursuit of Freedom* (New York: Astra House, 2021).

4 US Census Bureau, Sixteenth Census of the United States, 1940,
   Winston-Salem, Forsyth County, North Carolina; page 14A, Enumeration
   District 34–58.

5   US Census Bureau, Sixteenth Census of the United States, 1940; US Census Bureau, Fifteenth Census of the United States, 1930, Winston-Salem, Forsyth County, North Carolina, page 5B, Enumeration District, 34–49; Rafe D. Kelley, WWII Draft Registration Card, Serial No. 2566, Order No., 1463 (October 16, 1940). On the history of Black workers at R. J. Reynolds, see Robert R. Korstad, *Civil Rights Unionism: Tobacco Workers and the Struggle for Democracy in the Mid-Twentieth Century South* (Chapel Hill: University of North Carolina Press, 2003).

6   "African Americans and Tobacco Use," Centers for Disease Control and Prevention, November 16, 2020, https://www.cdc.gov/tobacco/disparities/african-americans/index.htm.

7   She may have died in South Carolina before the family moved to Winston-Salem, but I'm not sure. I could not find any record of her death, and the stories I've heard are conflicting.

8   US Census Bureau, Fifteenth Census of the United States, 1930, Winston-Salem, Forsyth County, North Carolina, page 5B, Enumeration District 34–49.

9   Lottie Mae Hodges, Social Security Application, *U.S., Social Security Applications and Claims Index, 1936–2007* (database online). In addition, the 1920 Census recorded her age as one and a half years old in April of 1920. US Census Bureau, Fourteenth Census of the United States, 1920, Clyde, Darlington County, South Carolina, page 17B, Enumeration District 12.

10 Certificate of Live Birth, Donald Sheralton Kelley, State of North Carolina, filed February 8, 1938, in author's possession.

11 Tera W. Hunter, *Bound in Wedlock: Slave and Free Marriage in the Nineteenth Century* (Cambridge: Harvard University Press, 2017), 376.

12 *Reverend Rafe David Kelley, October 4, 1906–April 7, 1996* (Funeral Program, n.d.), in author's possession; "Our Founder: Rev. Rafe D. Kelley," St. Johns' Missionary Baptist Church, accessed March 30, 2022, https://www.sjmb-bos.org/new-page; The Colored Methodist Episcopal Church changed its name to the Christian Methodist Episcopal Church in 1954. See Othal Hawthorne Lakey, *The History of the CME Church*, rev. ed. (Memphis: CME Publishing House, 1997); Raymond R. Sommerville, Jr., *An Ex-Colored Church: Social Activism in the CME Church, 1870–1970* (Macon, GA: Mercer University Press, 2004).

13 *Boston City Directory* (1947), 2441; *Boston City Directory* (1948), 2758; *Boston City Directory* (1952), 1688; "Fire Rips Roxbury Baptist Church," *Boston Globe*, August 27, 1963; Bertha Peppeard, "Mothers' Day to Be Noted from Pulpits," *Boston Globe*, May 13, 1950; "Roxbury," *Jewish Advocate*, June 25, 1909. In 1980, St. John's moved to a newly constructed million-dollar building at 230 Warren St., where it currently stands. Gayle Pollard, "Joy in a Roxbury Church," *Boston Globe*, March 10, 1980; Cheryl Devall, "A Firm Rock in Turbulent Seas: Roxbury Baptist Church Quiet Haven for Faithful," *Boston Globe*, September 5, 1981.

14   "Passengers Departed," *Daily Gleaner,* December 29, 1949. Typical of
     many Jamaican migrants, my mother entered the US in Miami and then
     continued to New York. The figures for Caribbean migrants do not
     include Puerto Ricans since they were counted as US citizens. See Kyle
     D. Crowder and Lucky M. Tedrow, "West Indians and the Residential
     Landscape of New York," in *Islands in the City: West Indian Migration to*
     New York, ed. Nancy Foner (Berkeley: University of California Press,
     2001), 81–114.
15   "Obituary: Florence B.," *Boston Globe,* July 12, 1966.
16   Lyn Shepard, "Recruiting of Blacks Stepped Up: Jobs and Bias Market
     Target sighted 'Negroes' Harvard' Search for Engineers Emphasis on
     Basic Courses Starting Salaries," *Christian Science Monitor,* July 29, 1969;
     "Boeing Opens Runway of Opportunity," *Philadelphia Tribune,* April 20,
     1968; Herbert Northrup, "The Negro in Aerospace Work," *California*
     Management Review 11, no. 4 (Summer 1969), 11–27.

Chapter 16: Suicide and Survival

1   COVID changed the ways many people dreamed. See, for example, Tore
     Nielsen, "The COVID-19 Pandemic Is Changing Our Dreams," *Scientific*
     American, October 1, 2020, and "COVID-19 Spurs Anxious, Upsetting
     Dreams," *American Psychological Association,* September 25, 2020.
2   "Borderline Personality Disorder," National Institute of Mental Health,
     last revised December 2017, https://www.nimh.nih.gov/health/topics/
     borderline-personality-disorder.
3   Standard Certificate of Death, State of South Carolina, for Samuel Neely
     Miller Jr., May 30, 1933, Ancestry.com.
4   John Egerton, *Speak Now Against the Day: The Generation Before the Civil*
     Rights Movement in the South (Chapel Hill: University of North Carolina
     Press, 1995), 15.
5   US Census Bureau, 1940, Easley, Pickens County, South Carolina,
     39–20, Ancestry.com.
6   For more stories about the misery—including starvation—of Americans
     during the Great Depression, see the works of Sanora Babb, including
     Whose Names are Unknown (1939, repr., Norman: University of Oklahoma
     Press, 2006), and *On the Dirty Plate Trail: Remembering the Dust Bowl*
     Refugee Camps (1939; repr., Austin: University of Texas Press, 2007).
7   Certificate of Death, Clarence Joseph Constance Sr., State of South
     Carolina, January 20, 1964, Ancestry.com.
8   Many people have asked me how I came to write about poor whites in
     Masterless Men: Poor Whites and Slavery in the Antebellum South (New York:
     Cambridge University Press, 2017). I generally say I write about poor
     whites because I come from them. My mother's abuse—her epithets for
     us—were the real reasons.
9   Anne Case and Angus Deaton, *Deaths of Despair and the Future of Capitalism*
     (Princeton: Princeton University Press, 2020).

10   Elyse R Grossman et al., "Alcohol Consumption during the COVID-19 Pandemic: A Cross-Sectional Survey of US Adults," *International Journal of Environmental Research and Public Health* 17, no. 24 (Dec. 2020); see also "Study Shows Uptick in U.S. Alcohol Beverage Sales During COVID-19 Pandemic," Columbia, Mailman School of Public Health, August 20, 2021, https://www.publichealth.columbia.edu/public-health-now/news/study-shows-uptick-us-alcohol-beverage-sales-during-covid-19-pandemic.

11   Anne Case and Angus Deaton, "The Great Divide: Education, Despair, and Death," *NBER* Working Paper 29241, September 2021.

12   Case and Deaton, "The Great Divide"; also see Anne Case and Angus Deaton, "Trump's Pet Theory about the Fatal Dangers of Quarantine Is Very Wrong," *Washington Post*, June 1, 2020.

Chapteer 17: "How Do We Live?"

1   Robert O'Hara, "Insurrection: Holding History," in *The Fire This Time: African American Plays for the 21st Century*, eds. Harry J. Elam Jr. and Robert Alexander (New York: Theatre Communications Group, 2004).

2   Scott Poulson-Bryant, "The Noise You Make Should Be Your Own," *Sounding Out* (blog), August 30, 2010, https://soundstudiesblog.com/2010/08/30/the-noise-you-make-should-be-your-own/.

Chapter 18: The Permeability of Cells

1   "Prison Policy Initiative COVID-19 Resources," Prison Policy Initiative, October 26, 2021, https://www.prisonpolicy.org/virus/.

2   Neal Marquez et al., "COVID-19 Incidence and Mortality in Federal and State Prisons Compared with the US Population, April 5, 2020, to April 3, 2021," *JAMA*, October 6, 2021.

3   Heather Ann Thompson, "The Policy Mistakes from the 1990s That Have Made Covid-19 Worse," *Washington Post*, May 4, 2020.

4   Keaton Ross, "'It Was Hell': Inside an Oklahoma Prison Coronavirus Outbreak," *Oklahoma Watch*, November 19, 2020.

5   "Criminal Justice Responses to the Coronavirus Pandemic," Prison Policy Initiative, October 12, 2021, https://www.prisonpolicy.org/virus/virusresponse.html; Tiana Herring, "Parole Boards Approved Fewer Releases in 2020 than in 2019, despite the Raging Pandemic," Prison Policy Initiative, February 3, 2021, https://www.prisonpolicy.org/blog/2021/02/03/parolegrants/.

6   Katja Ridderbusch, "COVID Precautions Put More Prisoners in Isolation. It Can Mean Long-Term Health Woes," *NPR*, October 4, 2021.

7   Natalie Holbrook et al., "'I Don't Want To Die in Prison': Prison Conditions, Decarceration, and Mutual Aid in the Age of COVID-19," Michigan Criminal Justice Program and Carceral State Project, July 2021, https://sites.lsa.umich.edu/dcc-project/wp-content/uploads/sites/789/2020/08/AFSC-CSP-COVID-19-White-Paper.pdf.

8   Ross, "'It Was Hell.'"

9   Eli Hager, "Solitary, Brawls, No Teachers: Coronavirus Makes Juvenile
    Jails Look Like Adult Prisons," The Marshall Project, May 12, 2020,
    https://www.themarshallproject.org/2020/05/12/solitary-brawls-no-
    teachers-coronavirus-makes-juvenile-jails-look-like-adult-prisons.

10 Holbrook et al., "'I Don't Want to Die in Prison.'"

11 Holbrook et al.

12 Holbrook et al.

13 James David Dickson, "New MDOC Mail Policy: Inmates to Receive
    Photocopies, Not Originals," *Detroit News*, October 16, 2020.

14 Clare Hymes, "No Phone or Email for Nearly 4,000 Inmates at Three
    Federal Prisons in Effort to Fight Virus," *CBS News*, May 1, 2020.

15 Julie O'Donoghue, "Louisiana Prisons Hastily Pull Plug on Resuming
    Family Visits during COVID-19," *Louisiana Illuminator*, November 19, 2020.

16 Holbrook et al., "'I Don't Want to Die in Prison.'"

17 David C. Pyrooz et al., "Views on COVID-19 from Inside Prison:
    Perspectives of High-Security Prisoners," *Justice Evaluation Journal* 3, no. 2
    (July 2020): 294–306.

18 Caisa E. Royer et al., "COVID-19 and Higher Education in Prison
    Programs," Alliance for Higher Education in Prison, 2021, https://www.
    higheredinprison.org/publications/covid-19.

19 Tyler Kingkade, "Coronavirus in Juvenile Detention Is a 'Nightmare
    Scenario,' Doctors and Advocates Say," *NBC News*, March 27, 2020.

20 Jerusalem Demsas, "80 Percent of Those Who Died of Covid-19 in Texas
    County Jails Were Never Convicted of a Crime," *Vox*, November 12,
    2020.

21 Homer Venters, "Covid-19 and the Struggle for Health
    Behind Bars," Brennan Center for Justice, June 14, 2021,
    https://www.brennancenter.org/our-work/analysis-opinion/
    covid-19-and-struggle-health-behind-bars.

22 Gregory Hooks and Wendy Sawyer, "Mass Incarceration, COVID-19, and
    Community Spread," Prison Policy Initiative, December 2020, https://
    www.prisonpolicy.org/reports/covidspread.html.

23 Nayanah Siva, "Experts Call to Include Prisons in COVID-19 Vaccine
    Plans," *Lancet* 396, no. 10266 (December 2020): 1870.

24 Siva, "Experts Call to Include Prisons in COVID-19 Vaccine Plans."

25 Lance Benzel, "El Paso County Jail Sets State Record for Largest
    COVID-19 Outbreak among Inmates, with 690 Sickened," *Gazette*,
    November 3, 2020.

26 Hooks and Sawyer, "Mass Incarceration, COVID-19, and Community
    Spread."

27 Rodrigo Torrejon, "Family of Correctional Officer Who Died from
    COVID-19 Plans to Sue N.J. County for Not Providing PPE," *NJ.com*,
    November 11, 2020.

28 Ken Kolker, "COVID-19 behind Bars: A Death Sentence," *WOODTV.com*,
    May 8, 2020.

29   Sam Meredith, "Prison Experts Have Been Excluded from Covid Vacinne Plans and Health Experts are Sounding the Alarm," *CBS*, December 16, 2020.

30   Siva, "Experts Call to Include Prisons in COVID-19 Vaccine Plans."

31   Alex Burness, "Gov. Polis Says Colorado Prisoners Shouldn't Get COVID-19 Vaccine before Free People," *Denver Post*, December 1, 2020.

32   Adela Suliman, "Alabama Governor Defends Plan to Use Covid Relief Funds to Build New Prisons," *Washington Post*, September 29, 2021.

33   Eric Lach, "Andrew Cuomo's Refusal to Vaccinate Inmates Is Indefensible," *New Yorker*, February 13, 2021.

34   Katie Rose Quandt, "Incarcerated People and Corrections Staff Should Be Prioritized in COVID-19 Vaccination Plans," Prison Policy Initiative, December 8, 2020, https://www.prisonpolicy.org/blog/2020/12/08/covid-vaccination-plans/.

35   Maura Turcotte, Rachel Sherman, and Derek M. Norman, "In a First, a Federal Judge Orders Oregon State Prisons to Vaccinate Inmates," *New York Times*, February 3, 2021.

36   "COVID-19 List of Prisoner Actions," *Perilous Chronicle*, October 26, 2021.

37   Michael Bott, "Hunger Strike: San Quentin Prisoners With COVID-19 Protest 'Dismal' Conditions," *NBC Bay Area*, July 1, 2020.

38   Kiara Alfonseca, "St. Louis Inmates Protest Again over Long Trial Wait Times, COVID-19 Fears," *ABC News*, April 6, 2021.

39   Hager, "Solitary, Brawls, No Teachers."

40   Matt Sledge, "Coronavirus Outbreak, Riot and Mass Escape Add Fuel to Debate over Louisiana Youth Prison Releases," *Nola*, April 21, 2020.

Chapter 19: Dreams of My Great-Grandfather

1   Evan Hill et al., "Video: How George Floyd Was Killed in Police Custody," *New York Times*, June 1, 2020.

2   "'Get Your Knee off Our Necks,' Activist Sharpton Tells George Floyd Memorial," Reuters, June 4, 2020.

3   Rachel Olding and Justin Glawe, "'Get Your Knee Off Our Necks': Family Bids Farewell to 'Big Floyd' in Fiery Memorial Service," *Daily Beast*, June 4, 2020.

4   "After the Original Was Stolen, Marker in Memory of Only Documented Lynching in Delaware Replaced," *News Journal*; Wm. Shawn Weigel, "George White Marker Replaced after August Theft," *Dover Post*; on the lynching of George White, see Yohuru Williams, "A Tragedy with a Happy Ending? The Lynching of George White in History and Memory," *Pennsylvania History* 72, no. 3 (2005): 292–304.

5   Yohuru Williams, "Political 'Lynching': Misusing a Scourge of History." Progressive.Org, October 23, 2019; For Congressman Bobby Rush's tweet see Bobby Rush (@RepBobbyRush), Twitter, October 22, 2019, https://twitter.com/RepBobbyRush/status/1186613817704366081.

6   Mitford Mathews, ed., *A Dictionary of Americanisms on Historical Principles*
     (Chicago: University of Chicago Press, 1951), 1010.
7   Khalil Gibran Muhammad, *The Condemnation of Blackness: Race, Crime, and
     the Making of Modern Urban America* (Cambridge: Harvard University Press,
     2010).
8   Rachel Yehuda and Amy Lehrner, "Intergenerational Transmission
     of Trauma Effects: Putative Role of Epigenetic Mechanisms," *World
     Psychiatry* 17, no. 3 (2018): 243–57.
9   Jeff Zeleny, "In Memories of a Painful Past, Hushed Worry About
     Obama," *New York Times*, February 25, 2008; Matthew Jaffe, "Obama
     Security Challenge as Popularity Grows," *ABC News*, February 28, 2008.
10   "Danville," Virginia Museum of History & Culture, accessed March 30,
     2022, https://virginiahistory.org/learn/historical-book/chapter/danville;
     Gordon Brooks Powell Jr., "Black Cloud over Danville: The Negro
     Movement in Danville, Virginia in 1963" (master's thesis, University of
     Richmond, 1968).
11   Barbra Ransby, *Ella Baker and the Black Freedom Movement: A Radical
     Democratic Vision*, (Chapel Hill: University of North Carolina Press,
     2003), 117; Samantha Bryant, "Black Lives, Policing, and Historical
     Memory," AAIHS (blog), May 2, 2018, https://www.aaihs.org/
     black-lives-policing-and-historical-memory/.
12   "Red Color Scheme Marks Brucetown's Saturday Dance," *Danville Bee*,
     February 15, 1937.
13   "Injured Relent and Cutting Bee Cases Are Dropped," *Danville Bee*,
     February 17, 1937.
14   "Cussin' Out Cop on Phone Brings Him $24.45 Fine," *Danville Bee*, June
     14, 1937; "Danville Negro Fined for Cussing on Phone" *Times Dispatch*,
     June 16, 1937.
15   "Negro Gives Himself Up on Shooting Charge," *Danville Bee*, July 9, 1937,
     1; "Wounded Negro In Grave Plight," *Danville Bee*, July 6, 1937; "James
     R, Wilson Draws 8 Years," *Danville Bee*, September 17, 1937, 1; "William
     Echols Succumbs to Wound," *Danville Bee*, July 26, 1937, 1; "Wilson Goes
     On Trial For Echols Death," *Danville Bee*, September 16, 1937.
16   "Negro Arrested After Wild Chase of Liquor Car," *Danville Bee*, March 23,
     1936.
17   "Shot in the Leg," *Danville Bee*, Danville, Virginia, October 18, 1937.
18   "Quarrel Over Santa Claus Proves Fatal," *Danville Bee*, March 1, 1938.
19   "Fitzgerald Wins Exoneration in Killing Charge," *Danville Bee*, March 11,
     1938.
20   "Police Probe Certain of Four Deaths," *Danville Bee*, April 11, 1938.
21   "Police Probe Certain of Four Deaths."
22   "Davis-Wilson Case Goes to Jury Following Final Pleas; No Defense
     Evidence Given," *Danville Bee*, August 16, 1938.
23   "Davis-Wilson Case Goes to Jury Following Final Pleas; No Defense
     Evidence Given."

24 "What to Know About the Death of Daunte Wright," *New York Times*, April 23, 2021.

25 Martin Luther King Jr., *Where Do We Go from Here: Chaos or Community?* (Boston: Beacon Press, 1967).

26 "CNN Heroes: Gianna Floyd: 'Daddy Changed the World,'" *CNN*, November 17, 2020.

Conclusion: Stress Test and Saving the Soul of America

1 Rick Perlstein, *Nixonland: The Rise of a President and the Fracturing of America* (New York: Scribner, 2008); Rick Perlstein, *Reaganland: America's Right Turn, 1976–1980* (New York: Simon and Schuster, 2020).

2 Elizabeth Hinton, *From the War on Poverty to the War on Crime: The Making of Mass Incarceration in America* (Cambridge: Harvard University Press, 2016). Also see Elizabeth Hinton, *America on Fire: The Untold History of Police Violence and Black Rebellion Since the 1960s* (New York: Liveright, 2021).

3 Keeanga-Yamahtta Taylor, "We Should Still Defund the Police," *New Yorker*, August 14, 2020 (adjusted for inflation).

4 Oliver Laughland, "Donald Trump and the Central Park Five: The Racially Charged Rise of a Demagogue," *Guardian*, February 17, 2016.

5 Carol Anderson, *White Rage* (New York: Bloomsbury, 2017); Jonathan Capehart, "From 'White Fragility' to 'White Rage': The Broken Promise of America," *Washington Post*, June 18, 2020.

6 Vann R. Newkirk II, "How a Pivotal Voting Rights Act Case Broke America," *The Atlantic*, July 10, 2018.

7 "Presidential Election Results: Biden Wins," *New York Times*, November 3, 2020.

8 Joe Biden, "We Are Living Through a Battle for the Soul of This Nation," *The Atlantic*, August 27, 2017.

9 Elizabeth Diaz, "Biden and Trump Say They're Fighting for America's 'Soul.' What Does That Mean?" *New York Times*, October 17, 2020.

10 Marianna Spring, "'Stop the Steal': The Deep Roots of Trump's 'Voter Fraud' Strategy," *BBC*, November 23, 2020.

11 Nancy Cook and Gabby Orr, "Trump's Post-Election Marching Orders: Dispute Ballots, Contest Results," *Politico*, November 11, 2020.

12 Peter Stone, "Criminal Inquiry into Trump's Georgia Election Interference Gathers Steam," *Guardian*, October 5, 2021.

13 Yvonne Winget Sanchez, "Did Trump and His Allies Interfere with the Maricopa County Election? Secretary of State Katie Hobbs Wants an Inquiry," *AZ Central*, July 7, 2021.

14 Ann Gerhart, "Election Results under Attack: Here Are the Facts," *Washington Post*, updated March 11, 2021.

15 Dan Mangan, "Trump Lies about Election Results at Rally Challenging Biden Win," *CNBC*, January 6, 2021.

16 Rhae Lynn Barnes and Keri Leigh Merritt, "A Confederate Flag at the Capitol Summons America's Demons," *CNN*, January 7, 2021.

17   Peter Hermann et. al., "How the U.S. Capitol Police Were Overrun in a 'Monumental' Security Failure," *Washington Post*, January 8, 2021.

18   John Grant, "Three Wednesdays in January," *Counterpunch*, January 26, 2021.

19   Dan Barry, Mike McIntire, and Matthew Rosenberg, "'Our President Wants Us Here': The Mob That Stormed the Capitol," *New York Times*, January 9, 2021.

20   For articles comparing Trumpism to the Lost Cause, see David Blight, "How Trumpism May Endure: The Confederacy Built a Lasting Myth of Victory Out of Defeat: Trump and His Followers May Also Too," *New York Times*, January 9, 2021; Karen L. Cox, "What Trump Shares With the 'Lost Cause' of the Confederacy," *New York Times*, January 8, 2021; Caroline E. Janney, "The Next Lost Cause?: The South's Mythology Glamorized a Noble Defeat: Trump Backers May Do the Same," *Washington Post*, July 31, 2020; Angie Maxwell, "Donald Trump and the Lost Cause," *VQR*, March 30, 2016.

21   Hunter Walker, "Jan. 6 Protest Organizers Say They Participated in 'Dozens' of Planning Meetings With Members of Congress and White House Staff," *Rolling Stone*, October 24, 2021; Ray Sanchez, "America's Trio of Unforgettable Wednesdays," *CNN*, January 22, 2021.

22   Jacob Pramuk, "Trump Becomes First President to Be Impeached Twice, as Bipartisan Majority Charges Him with Inciting Capitol Riot," *CNBC*, January 13, 2021.

23   "Read Liz Cheney's Full Statement in Support of Trump's Impeachment," *Politico*, January 12, 2021; Ledyard King, "Read the Statement from GOP Rep. Liz Cheney, Chair of the House GOP Conference, on Why She'll Vote to Impeach Donald Trump," *USA Today*, January 13, 2021.

24   Domenico Montenaro, "Senate Acquits Trump In Impeachment Trial—Again," *NPR*, February 13, 2021.

25   Jean-Philippe McKenzie, "Read 22-Year-Old Amanda Gorman's Breathtaking Inauguration Poem," *Oprah Daily*, January 20, 2021.

26   Abraham Lincoln, "The Perpetuation of Our Political Institutions: Address Before the Young Men's Lyceum of Springfield, Illinois," January 27, 1838, in Roy P. Basler, ed., *The Collected Works of Abraham Lincoln* (New Brunswick: Rutgers University Press, 1953–1955); Thomas F. Schwartz, "The Springfield Lyceums and Lincoln's 1838 Speech," *Illinois Historical Journal* 83, no. 1 (1990): 45–49.

27   Martin Luther King Jr., "Remaining Awake for a Great Revolution," delivered at the National Cathedral, Washington, DC, March 31, 1968, Congressional Record, April 9, 1968.

28   King, "Remaining Awake for a Great Revolution."

29   King, "Remaining Awake for a Great Revolution."

APPENDIX I

1   Elizabeth A. Fenn, *Pox Americana: The Great Smallpox Epidemic of 1775–82* (New York: Hill and Wang, 2001), 69, 131.

2   "What is Public Health?" CDC, accessed March 30, 2022, https://www.cdcfoundation.org/what-public-health.

3   Herbert Hoover, "Inaugural Address," American Presidency Project, March 4, 1929, https://www.presidency.ucsb.edu/documents/inaugural-address-9.

4   William J. Novak, *The People's Welfare: Law and Regulation in Nineteenth-Century America* (Chapel Hill; University of North Carolina, 2020), 191.

5   See, for example, Monica Muñoz Martinez, "To Fix Our Abusive Border Policies, First We Must Face Our History," *Houston Chronicle*, October 17, 2021.

6   Richard H. Steckel and Jerome C. Rose, eds., *The Backbone of History: Health and Nutrition in the Western Hemisphere* (Cambridge: Cambridge University Press, 2002).

7   Alfred W. Crosby, "Virgin Soil Epidemics as a Factor in the Aboriginal Depopulation in America," *William and Mary Quarterly* 33, no. 2 (April 1976): 289–99.

8   A Native American tribe that lived in the present-day Greater Boston region in Massachusetts.

9   David M. Henkin and Rebecca M. McLennan, *Becoming America: A History for the 21st Century*, 2nd ed. (New York: McGraw-Hill, 2021), 48.

10   Jeffrey Ostler, *Surviving Genocide: Native Nations and the United States from the American Revolution to Bleeding Kansas* (New Haven: Yale University Press, 2019).

11   Joyce E. Chaplin, *Subject Matter: Technology, the Body, and Science on the Anglo-American Frontier, 1500–1676* (Cambridge: Harvard University Press, 2003).

12   Jon Parmenter, "After the Mourning Wars: The Iroquois as Allies in Colonial North American Campaigns, 1676–1760," *William and Mary Quarterly* 64, no. 1 (2007): 39–76.

13   Matthew Niederhuber, "The Fight Over Inoculation During the 1721 Boston Smallpox Epidemic," Harvard University Medical School, December 31, 2014, https://sitn.hms.harvard.edu/flash/special-edition-on-infectious-disease/2014/the-fight-over-inoculation-during-the-1721-boston-smallpox-epidemic/.

14   Fenn, *Pox Americana.*

15   Richard Gabriel and Karen Metz, *A History of Military Medicine*, vol. 2 (New York: Greenwood Press, 1992), 107; S. Riedel, "Edward Jenner and the History of Smallpox and Vaccination," *Baylor University Medical Center Proceedings* 18, no. 1 (2005): 21–25.

16   Tess Lanzarotta and Marco A. Ramos, "Mistrust in Medicine: The Rise and Fall of America's First Vaccine Institute," *American Journal of Public Health* (June 2018).

17   Annette Gordon-Reed, *The Hemingses of Monticello: An American Family* (New York: Norton, 2008); Jeanne E. Abrams, *Revolutionary Medicine: The*

Founding Fathers and Mothers in Sickness and in Health (New York: New York University Press, 2013).

18 Jeanne E. Abrams, *Revolutionary Medicine*, introduction.

19 Abrams, *Revolutionary Medicine*.

20 Holly Dugan, Marissa Nicosia, and Lisa Smith, "Smelling Contagion: The Sensory Experience of Plague in Seventeenth-Century London and the Covid-19 Pandemic," *Working Papers in Critical Disaster Studies*, series 1, *Historical Approaches to COVID-19* 8 (2021): 1–24; Marissa Nicosia, "Cinamon Watter," *Cooking in the Archives* (blog), October 27, 2021, https://rarecooking.com/2021/10/27/cinamon-watter/; Nicosia, "To Make India Curry," *Cooking in the Archives* (blog), October 14, 2019, https://rarecooking.com/2019/10/14/to-make-india-curry/.

21 Laurel Thatcher Ulrich, *A Midwife's Tale: The Life of Martha Ballard, Based on Her Diary, 1785–1812* (New York: Vintage, 1991), 12.

22 David W. Blight, *Frederick Douglass: Prophet of Freedom* (New York: Simon and Schuster, 2018).

23 Stephanie Smallwood, *Saltwater Slavery: A Middle Passage from Africa to American Diaspora* (Cambridge: Harvard University Press, 2007).

24 Smallwood, *Saltwater Slavery*, 152.

25 Smallwood, *Saltwater Slavery*, 51.

26 Vincent Brown, *The Reaper's Garden: Death and Power in the World of Atlantic Slavery* (Cambridge: Harvard University Press, 2010), 1.

27 Peter H. Wood, *Black Majority: Negroes in Colonial South Carolina from 1670 through the Stono Rebellion* (New York: Random House, 1974), 75.

28 Walter Johnson, *Soul by Soul: Life Inside the Antebellum Slave Market* (Cambridge: Harvard University Press, 2000).

29 Sarah Ann Murphy, *Investing in Life: Insurance in Antebellum America* (Baltimore: Johns Hopkins University Press, 2010); Dea H. Boster, "'Unfit for Ordinary Purposes': Disability, Slaves, and Decision Making in the Antebellum American South," in *Disability Histories*, eds. Susan Burch and Michael Rembis (University of Illinois Press, 2014), 201–17.

30 Deborah Gray White, *Ain't I a Woman? Female Slaves in the Plantation South* (New York: Norton, 1985).

31 Dorothy Roberts, *Killing the Black Body: Race, Reproduction, and the Meaning of Liberty* (New York: Pantheon, 1997), 40.

32 Also see Sharla M. Fett, *Working Cures: Healing, Health, and Power on Southern Slave Plantations* (Chapel Hill: University of North Carolina Press, 2002); and Sean Morey Smith and Christopher Willoughby, eds., *Medicine and Healing in the Age of Slavery* (Baton Rouge: University of Louisiana Press, 2021).

33 Deidre Cooper Owens, *Medical Bondage: Race, Gender, and the Origins of American Gynecology* (Athens, GA: University of Georgia Press, 2017).

34 Harriet A. Washington, *Medical Apartheid: The Dark History of Medical Experimentation on Black Americans from Colonial Times to the Present* (New York: Doubleday, 2007).

35   James W. Cook, *The Arts of Deception: Playing with Fraud in the Age of Barnum* (Cambridge, MA: Harvard University Press, 2001); "The What Is It Exhibit," The Lost Museum Archive, accessed March 30, 2022, https://lostmuseum.cuny.edu/archive/exhibit/what/; Holly E. Martin, "Chang and Eng Bunker, 'The Original Siamese Twins': Living, Dying, and Continuing under the Spectator's Gaze," *Journal of American Culture* 34, no. 4 (December 2011): 372–88.

36   Gregory B. Lee, "Dirty, Diseased and Demented: The Irish, the Chinese, and Racist Representation," *Journal of Global Cultural Stories* (December 2017).

37   Hidetaka Hirota, *Expelling the Poor: Atlantic Seaboard States and the Nineteenth-Century Origins of American Immigration Policy* (New York: Oxford University Press, 2019). Also see Noel Ignatiev, *How the Irish Became White* (New York: Routledge, 1995).

38   Drew Gilpin Faust, *This Republic of Suffering: Death and the American Civil War* (New York: Random House, 2009).

39   Jim Downs, "The Epidemics America Got Wrong," *Atlantic*, March 22, 2020; also see Jim Downs, *Maladies of Empire: How Colonialism, Slavery, and War Transformed Medicine* (Cambridge, MA: Belknap Press, 2021), and Jim Downs, *Sick from Freedom: African-American Illness and Suffering during the Civil War and Reconstruction* (New York: Oxford University Press, 2012).

40   Statistics quoted in Gillian Brockell, "More Than 4,000 People Have Been Lynched in the U.S. Trump Isn't One of Them," *Washington Post*, October 22, 2019.

41   Philip J. Deloria, *Indians in Unexpected Places* (Topeka: University Press of Kansas, 2004).

42   Kassidy Vavra, "'Great Dying' of Indigenous Peoples during Colonization of America Caused Earth's Climate to Change," *New York Daily News*, January 31, 2019.

43   Mary Ellen Gabriel, "Learning from Epidemics," University of Wisconsin-Madison, March 17, 2020, https://ls.wisc.edu/news/lessons-from-past-epidemics.

44   Jack Hang-Tat Leong, "The Hong Kong Connection for the Chinese Railroad Workers in North America," Stanford University Chinese Railroad Workers of North America Project, 2019, https://web.stanford.edu/group/chineserailroad/cgi-bin/website/the-hong-kong-connection-for-the-chinese-railroad-workers-in-north-america/.

45   "Chinese Exclusion Act: Primary Documents in American History," Library of Congress, updated June 1, 2020, https://guides.loc.gov/chinese-exclusion-act.

46   Nayan Shah, *Contagious Divides: Epidemics and Race in San Francisco's Chinatown* (University of California Press, 2001).

47   Katie Dowd, "San Francisco's Bubonic Plague Epidemic Has Eerie Parallels to Modern," *SF Gate*, April 10, 2020.

48 "Imprisonment in the Wooden Building," in *Island: Poetry and History of Chinese Immigrants on Angel Island, 1910–1940*, eds. Him Mark Lai, Genny Lim, and Judy Yung (Seattle: University of Washington Press, 1991), 130–39.

49 Gustavo Arellano, "A Racist Mob Burned Santa Ana's Chinatown to the Ground: It Still Serves as a Lesson," *LA Times*, updated March 18, 2021.

50 Xiao Wang, "Asian Americans Now See Why We Need to Fight Back against Racism, Not Ignore It," *NBC News*, March 5, 2021.

51 Mae M. Ngai, *Impossible Subjects: Illegal Aliens and the Making of Modern America* (Princeton: Princeton University Press, 2003).

52 Natalia Molina, *Fit to Be Citizens? Public Health and Race in Los Angeles, 1879–1939* (Oakland: University of California Press, 2006).

53 Ngai, *Impossible Subjects*.

54 Roxanne Dunbar-Ortiz, *Not "A Nation of Immigrants": Settler Colonialism, White Supremacy, and a History of Erasure and Exclusion* (New York: Beacon, 2021).

55 Jacob Riis, *How the Other Half Lives: Studies Among the Tenements of New York* (1957; repr., New York: Martino Fine Books, 2015).

56 William J. Fryer, ed., *The Tenement House Law of the City of New York* (New York: The Record and Guide, 1901).

57 Ted Brackemeyer, "Immigrants, Cities, and Disease: Immigration and Health Concerns in Late Nineteenth Century America," U.S. History Scene, accessed March 30, 2022, https://ushistoryscene.com/article/immigrants-cities-disease/.

58 John M. Barry, *The Great Influenza: The Story of the Deadliest Pandemic in History* (New York: Paw Prints, 2008), 5.

59 John Fabian Witt, "The Law of Salus Populi: Epidemics and the Law," *Yale Review*, March 30, 2020.

60 "When and Why was FDA Formed?" U.S. Food and Drug Administration, updated March 28, 2018, https://www.fda.gov/about-fda/fda-basics/when-and-why-was-fda-formed.

61 Margot Canaday, *The Straight State: Sexuality and Citizenship in Twentieth-Century America* (Princeton: Princeton University Press, 2011), 19–23.

62 Christine Stansell, *City of Women: Sex and Class in New York, 1789–1860* (New York: Knopf, 1986).

63 Jane Addams, *Twenty Years at Hull House* (New York: Macmillan, 1910).

64 Molly Ladd-Taylor, *Fixing the Poor: Eugenic Sterilization and Child Welfare in the Twentieth Century* (Baltimore: Johns Hopkins University Press, 2017); Laura Briggs, *Reproducing Empire: Race, Sex, Science, and U.S. Imperialism in Puerto Rico* (Berkeley: University of California Press, 2003); Danielle L. McGuire, *At the Dark End of the Street* (New York: Knopf, 2010); Kate Clifford Lawson, *Walk with Me: A Biography of Fannie Lou Hamer* (New York: Oxford University Press, 2021).

65 Rebecca Skloot, *The Immortal Life of Henrietta Lacks* (New York: Crown, 2010).

66 "The U.S. Public Health Service Syphilis Study at Tuskegee," CDC, updated April 22, 2021, https://www.cdc.gov/tuskegee/timeline. htm; Jinbin Park, "Historical Origins of the Tuskegee Experiment: The Dilemma of Public Health in the United States," *Korean Journal of Medical History* 26, no. 3 (Dec. 2017): 545–78.

67 Michael E. Ruane, "A Century Ago, Polio Struck a Handsome Young Politician—And Forged One of the Country's Greatest Presidents," *Washington Post*, August 2, 2021.

68 Kent A. Sepkowitz, "The 1947 Smallpox Vaccination Campaign in New York City, Revisited," *Emerging Infectious Diseases* 10, no. 5 (2004): 960–61.

69 David Skinner, "Elvis Presley Gets His Polio Shot," *Humanities* 41, no. 3 (Summer 2020).

70 Downs, "The Epidemics America Got Wrong." Also see Peter L. Allen, *The Wages of Sin: Sex and Disease, Past and Present* (Chicago: University of Chicago Press, 2002).

71 Masha Gessen, "George H. W. Bush's Presidency Erased People with AIDS: So Did the Tributes to Him," *New Yorker*, December 7, 2018.

72 Rhae Lynn Barnes, "How to Read a Quilt," National AIDS Memorial, forthcoming, https://www.aidsmemorial.org/quilt-history.

73 "The HIV/AIDS Epidemic in the United States: The Basics," Kaiser Family Foundation, June 7, 2021, https://www.kff.org/hivaids/fact-sheet/ the-hivaids-epidemic-in-the-united-states-the-basics/; Randy Shilts, *And the Band Played On: Politics, People, and the AIDS Epidemic* (1987; repr., New York: St. Martin's Griffin Press, 2007); Jonathan Engel, *The Epidemic: A Global History of AIDS* (Washington, DC: Smithsonian Press, 2006).

74 Nancy Cutler, "Deaths From 9/11 Diseases Will Soon Outnumber Those Lost On That Fateful Day," *USA Today*, September 06, 2018.

75 Jan H. Richardus and Anton E. Kunst, "Black-White Differences in Infectious Disease Mortality in the United States," *American Journal of Public Health* 91, no. 8 (Aug. 2001): 1251–53.

76 Ibram X. Kendi, "The Day Shithole Entered the Presidential Lexicon," *Atlantic*, January 13. 2019.

77 Katie Rogers et al., "Trump Defends Using 'Chinese Virus' Label, Ignoring Growing Criticism," *New York Times*, updated March 18, 2021.

APPENDIX II

1 Saidiya Hartman, *Lose Your Mother: A Journey Along the Atlantic Slave Trade Route Terror* (New York: Farrar, Straus and Giroux, 2007), 6.

2 For the best discussion on how these amendments were adopted and implemented, see Eric Foner, *Reconstruction: America's Unfinished Revolution, 1863–1877* (New York: Harper Perennial, 1989); W. E. B. Du Bois, *Black Reconstruction in America* (1935; repr., New York: The Free Press, 1999); and Martha S. Jones, *Birthright Citizens: A History of Race and Rights in Antebellum America* (New York: Cambridge University Press, 2018).

3   William Barber II, *The Third Reconstruction: How a Moral Movement is Overcoming the Politics of Division and Fear* (New York: Beacon, 2016). On the Second Reconstruction see Manning Marable, *Race, Reform, and Rebellion: The Second Reconstruction and Beyond in Black America, 1945–2006*, 3rd ed. (Jackson: University Press of Mississippi, 2007); Robert Mann, *When Freedom Would Triumph: The Civil Rights Struggle in Congress, 1954–1968* (Baton Rouge: Louisiana State University Press, 2007); Hugh Davis Graham, *The Civil Rights Era: Origins and Development of National Policy, 1960–1972* (New York: Oxford University Press, 1990).

4   C. Vann Woodward, "John Brown's Private War," in *America in Crisis*, ed. Daniel Aaron (New York: Alfred A. Knopf, 1952).

5   Kate Zernike, *Boiling Mad: Inside Tea Party America* (New York: Times Books/Henry Holt and Co, 2010); Tim Wise, *Between Barack and a Hard Place: Racism and White Denial in the Age of Obama* (San Francisco: City Lights Books, 2009); Ta-Nehisi Coates, *We Were Eight Years in Power: An American Tragedy* (New York: One World, 2017); Melanie Buffington, "Contemporary Culture Wars: Challenging the Legacy of the Confederacy," *Journal of Cultural Research in Art Education* 34 (January 2017): 45–59.

6   Evan Hill et al., "Video: How George Floyd Was Killed in Police Custody," *New York Times*, June 1, 2020; "One Week That Shook the World: George Floyd's Death Ignited Protests Far beyond Minneapolis," *Star Tribune*, June 3, 2020; Amy Forliti, "Teen Who Recorded Floyd's Arrest, Death Wins Pulitzer Nod," AP News, June 11, 2021.

7   Andy Mannix, "Prosecutor: Ex-Officers Pinned George Floyd for 9½ Minutes, Including after They Couldn't Find Pulse," *Star Tribune*, October 14, 2020.

8   The documentation of extralegal and police killings of African Americans has long been facilitated by new technologies, from abolitionism when lithography, journalism, and later photography were used to capture lynching to camcorders in the late twentieth century (used in the police beating of Rodney King).

9   Lizette Alvarez and Cara Buckley, "Zimmerman Is Acquitted in Killing of Trayvon Martin," *New York Times*, July 14, 2013; "Federal Officials Close Investigation Into Death of Trayvon Martin," Department of Justice, February 24, 2015, https://www.justice.gov/opa/pr/federal-officials-close-investigation-death-trayvon-martin.

10   Isaac Chotiner, "A Black Lives Matter Co-Founder Explains Why This Time Is Different," *New Yorker*, June 3, 2020; Opal Tometi, "Why I Co-Founded Black Lives Matter," *BBC News*, October 24, 2020.

11   Cindy Boren, "A Timeline of Colin Kaepernick Kneeling in Protest against Police Brutality, Four Years after They Began," *Washington Post*, August 26, 2020; Katie Reilly, "Colin Kaepernick Protests National Anthem Over Treatment of Minorities: 'There Are Bodies in the Street,'" *Time Magazine*, August 27, 2016.

12 Dave Zirin, *The Kaepernick Effect: Taking a Knee, Changing the World* (New York: The New Press, 2021).

13 Dave Zirin, The *Kaepernick Effect*, 9.

14 Mitch Smith, "James Fields Sentenced to Life in Prison for Death of Heather Heyer in Charlottesville," *New York Times*, June 28, 2019.

15 Richard Fausset, "What We Know About the Shooting Death of Ahmaud Arbery," *New York Times*, October 16, 2021; Richard A. Oppel Jr., Derrick Bryson Taylor, and Nicholas Bogel-Burroughs, "What to Know About Breonna Taylor's Death," *New York Times*, April 26, 2021.

16 "Video Shows Moment Minneapolis Police Abandon Torched Precinct," *New York Post*, May 29, 2020.

17 "Trump Says Violent Minneapolis Protests Dishonor George Floyd's Memory, Twitter Labels 'Shooting' Tweet as 'Glorifying Violence," *USA Today*, May 28, 2020; Krishnadev Calamur, Ayesha Rascoe, and Alana Wise, "Trump Says He Spoke with Floyd's Family, Understands Hurt and Pain of Community," *NPR*, May 29, 2020.

18 Matthew Wright, "Black Lives Matter Protests May Be the Largest in U.S. History as More Than 26 MILLION Americans Have Been at the More Than 4,700 Demonstrations around the Country," *Daily Mail*, July 3, 2020.

19 George Floyd Justice in Policing Act of 2021, H.R. 1280, 117th Cong., 2021, https://www.congress.gov/bill/117th-congress/house-bill/1280; Sean Collins, "The George Floyd Justice in Policing Act, Explained," *Vox*, March 3, 2021.

20 Wilfred Reilly, "Wokeism as Religion after George Floyd," *American Spectator*, May 30, 2021.

21 Daniella Silva and David K. Li, "Loved Ones Say Goodbye to George Floyd at Memorial Service," *Today*, June 4, 2020.

22 Silva and Li, "Loved Ones Say Goodbye to George Floyd at Memorial Service."

23 Marcus Harrison Green, "What Really Happened in CHOP?" *Seattle Met*, June 8, 2021.

24 Chad Sokol, "Patriot Prayer, Three Percenters Leaders to Speak at WSU," Associated Press, April 16, 2019; Jane Coaston, "The Pro-Trump, Patriot Prayer Group, Explained," *Vox*, September 8, 2020.

25 Katelyn Burns, "The Violent End of the Capitol Hill Organized Protest, Explained," *Vox*, July 2, 2020.

26 Arun Gupta, "Occupy Wall Street Trained a Generation in Class War" *In These Times*, September 16, 2021; Heather Gautney, "What Is Occupy Wall Street? The History of Leaderless Movements," *Washington Post*, October 10, 2011.

27 Christina Morales, "What We Know About the Shooting of Jacob Blake," *New York Times*, March 26, 2021.

28 Governor Tony Evers (@GovEvers), "The ability to exercise first amendment rights is a critically important part of our democracy and

pursuit of justice. But there remains a line between peaceful assembly and what we saw last night that individuals, families, and businesses in danger," Twitter, August 26, 2020, https://twitter.com/GovEvers/status/1298324994343055360.

29   Clare Spaulding, "Jacob Blake's Father Says Son's Paralyzed from Waist down after Police Shooting in Kenosha," *Chicago Sun-Times*, August 25, 2020.

30   Christina Maxouris, Paul P. Murphy, and Nicole Chavez, "Kenosha Shooting Suspect Faces More Homicide Charges," *CNN*, August 27, 2020.

31   Adam Serwer, "Birtherism of a Nation," *Atlantic*, May 14, 2020.

32   John Lewis, "Together, You Can Redeem the Soul of Our Nation," *New York Times*, July 30, 2020.

ABOUT THE CONTRIBUTORS

Rhae Lynn Barnes is an assistant professor at Princeton University and the Sheila Biddle Ford Foundation Fellow at the Hutchins Center for African & African American Research at Harvard University. She was the 2020 President of the Andrew W. Mellon Society of Fellows in Critical Bibliography. Barnes is the author of the forthcoming book *Darkology: When the American Dream Wore Blackface.*

Stephen Berry is Gregory Professor of the Civil War Era at the University of Georgia and author or editor of eight books, including his most recent, *Count the Dead: Coroners, Quants, and the Birth of Death As We Know It* (UNC Press, 2022). Berry also maintains the award-winning website CSI:Dixie (csidixie.org), which argues that every society has to answer for its morgue.

Philip J. Deloria is the Leverett Saltonstall Professor of History at Harvard University, where he attends to the histories of American Indian peoples and the United States. Author of *Playing Indian, Indians in Unexpected Places,* and *Becoming Mary Sully: Toward an American Indian Abstract,* he is an elected member of the American Philosophical Society and the American Academy of Arts and Sciences.

Mary L. Dudziak is the Asa Griggs Candler Professor of Law at Emory University and a leading historian of American law and the United States and the world. Her previous books include *War Time: An Idea, Its History, Its Consequences and Cold War Civil Rights: Race and* *the Image of American Democracy*. She is currently writing about the culture of US war death and the decline of democratic restraints on US war powers.

Keith Ellison is the thirtieth Attorney General of the State of Minnesota. A father of four young adults, Ellison is married to Monica Hurtado, Policy director for a local nonprofit organization. Ellison spent twelve years in the US Congress, focusing on consumer justice and criminal justice. He led the progressive caucus for three terms, building it to over 100 members. He also served as deputy chair of the Democratic National Committee, where he promoted voter outreach, and communication. As Minnesota's Attorney General Ellison has pursued litigation on climate, consumer protection, wage theft and antitrust. Ellison is the lead prosecutor on the investigation and prosecution of matter of death of George Floyd, who was killed by four Minneapolis police officers.

Jacquelyn Dowd Hall is the Julia Cherry Spruill Professor of History Emeritus at the University of North Carolina at Chapel Hill. Her most recent book, *Sisters and Rebels: A Struggle for the Soul of America*, won, among other prizes, the PEN America/Jacqueline Bograd Weld Award for Biography and the Southern Historical Association's Sydnor Award for the best book in southern history. She received a National Humanities Medal in 1999.

Martha Hodes, Professor of History at New York University, is the author of *Mourning Lincoln, The Sea Captain's Wife: A True Story of Love, Race, and War in the Nineteenth Century,* and *White Women, Black Men: Illicit Sex in the Nineteenth-Century South.* She has recently received fellowships from the Guggenheim Foundation and the Cullman Center for Scholars and Writers at the New York Public Library.

Tera W. Hunter is the Edwards Professor of American History and Professor of African-American Studies at Princeton University. She is a scholar of labor, gender, race, and Southern history. She is the author of: *Bound in Wedlock: Slave and Free Black Marriage in the Nineteenth Century* (The Belknap Press of Harvard University Press, 2017) and *To Joy My Freedom: Southern Black Women's Lives and Labors After the Civil War* (Harvard University Press, 1997).

Peniel E. Joseph is the Barbara Jordan Chair in Ethics and Political Values and Founding Director of the Center for the Study of Race and Democracy and Associate Dean of Justice, Equity, Diversity, and Inclusion at the LBJ School of Public Affairs and Professor of History at the University of Texas at Austin. He hosts the Race & Democracy podcast, is a contributing opinion writer for CNN.com, and the author of award-winning books, most recently *The Third Reconstruction: America's Struggle for Racial Justice in the 21st Century.*

Robin D. G. Kelley is the Gary B. Nash Endowed Chair in US History at UCLA. His books include: *Thelonious Monk: The Life and Times of an American Original; Hammer and Hoe: Alabama Communists During the Great Depression;* and *Freedom Dreams: The Black Radical Imagination.* His essays have appeared in several publications, including *The Nation, New York Times, Counterpunch,* and *the Boston Review,* for which he also serves as contributing editor.

Keri Leigh Merritt is a historian, writer, and activist based in Atlanta, Georgia. She is the author of *Masterless Men: Poor Whites and Slavery in the Antebellum South,* and the coeditor of *Reconsidering Southern Labor History: Race, Class, and Power.*

Gwendolyn Midlo-Hall is Professor Emerita of Latin American and Caribbean History at Rutgers University. Born in 1929, Midlo-Hall has been a lifelong civil rights and Black Power essayist and activist, multi-award-winning historian, digital humanities pioneer, and outstanding public intellectual still writing pioneering works as she reaches her ninety-third year.

Dr. Monica Muñoz Martinez is Associate Professor of History at the University of Texas at Austin. Her first book *The Injustice Never Leaves You: Anti-Mexican Violence in Texas* received six book awards. She cofounded the educational nonprofit Refusing to Forget and helped to secure four state historical markers commemorating the history of anti-Mexican violence in Texas. Martinez is a 2021 MacArthur Foundation Fellow and a distinguished lecturer for the Organization of American Historians.

Mary Kathryn Nagle is an enrolled citizen of the Cherokee Nation. She is an attorney whose work focuses on the restoration of tribal sovereignty and the inherent right of Indian Nations to protect their women and children from domestic violence and sexual assault. From 2015 to 2019, she served as the first Executive Director of the Yale Indigenous Performing Arts Program. Nagle is an alum of the 2013 Public Theater Emerging Writers Program.

Scott Poulson-Bryant is an American journalist and author. One of the cofounding editors of *Vibe* magazine in 1992, Poulson-Bryant's journalism, profiles, reviews, and essays have appeared in such publications as *The New York Times, The Village Voice, Rolling Stone, Spin, Essence, Ebony,* and *The Source.*

Ula Y. Taylor is a professor in African American studies at the University of California, Berkeley. She is the author of *The Promise of Patriarchy: Women and the Nation of Islam* (University of North Carolina Press) and *The Veiled Garvey: The Life and Times of Amy Jacques Garvey* (University of North Carolina Press). Taylor is most proud of her brilliant former students who are transforming the interdisciplinary field of Black Studies.

Heather Ann Thompson is a historian and the Pulitzer Prize and Bancroft Prize–winning author of *Blood in the Water: The Attica Prison Uprising of 1971 and its Legacy*, as well as a public intellectual who writes for such publications as *The New York Times*, *The New Yorker*, *TIME*, and *The Nation*. Thompson has received research fellowships from such institutions as Harvard University, Art for Justice, Cambridge University, and the Guggenheim, and her justice advocacy work has also been recognized with a number of distinguished awards.

Robert L. Tsai is Professor of Law at Boston University. Tsai's scholarship spans constitutional theory, legal history, and law and literature. He is the author of several books, including *Practical Equality* (W.W. Norton 2019) and *America's Forgotten Constitutions* (Harvard 2014). His essays have appeared in the *New York Review of Books*, *Politico*, *The Washington Post*, *Los Angeles Review of Books*, *Slate*, and *Boston Review*.

Yohuru Williams is Distinguished University Chair, professor of history, and founding director of the Racial Justice Initiative at the University of St. Thomas in St. Paul. He is the author of *Black Politics/White Power: Civil Rights Black Power and Black Panthers in New Haven* and *Teaching Beyond the Textbook: Six Investigative Strategies*, and coauthor with Bryan Shih of *The Black Panthers: Portrait of an Unfinished Revolution*.

INDEX

ABOUT HAYMARKET BOOK'

Haymarket Books is a radical, independent, nonprofit book publisher based in Chicago.

Our mission is to publish books that contribute to struggles for social and economic justice. We strive to make our books a vibrant and organic part of social movements and the education and development of a critical, engaged, international left.

We take inspiration and courage from our namesakes, the Haymarket martyrs, who gave their lives fighting for a better world. Their 1886 struggle for the eight-hour day—which gave us May Day, the international workers' holiday—reminds workers around the world that ordinary people can organize and struggle for their own liberation. These struggles continue today across the globe—struggles against oppression, exploitation, poverty, and war.

Since our founding in 2001, Haymarket Books has published more than five hundred titles. Radically independent, we seek to drive a wedge into the risk-averse world of corporate book publishing. Our authors include Noam Chomsky, Arundhati Roy, Rebecca Solnit, Angela Y. Davis, Howard Zinn, Amy Goodman, Wallace Shawn, Mike Davis, Winona LaDuke, Ilan Pappé, Richard Wolff, Dave Zirin, Keeanga-Yamahtta Taylor, Nick Turse, Dahr Jamail, David Barsamian, Elizabeth Laird, Amira Hass, Mark Steel, Avi Lewis, Naomi Klein, and Neil Davidson. We are also the trade publishers of the acclaimed Historical Materialism Book Series and of Dispatch Books.